STUDIES ON HYSTERIA

JOSEF BREUER

and

SIGMUND FREUD

STUDIES

ON

HYSTERIA

Translated from the German and edited by
JAMES STRACHEY

In collaboration with
ANNA FREUD

Assisted by
ALIX STRACHEY *and* ALAN TYSON

BASIC BOOKS, INC., PUBLISHERS
59 FOURTH AVENUE, NEW YORK 3, N. Y.

B
‾
B

First Printing, 1957

Published in the United States
by Basic Books, Inc., by arrangement with
The Hogarth Press, Ltd.

CONTENTS

★

STUDIES ON HYSTERIA (1893–1895)

NOTE

This is a reprint of Volume II of the Standard Edition of the Complete Psychological Works of Sigmund Freud (Hogarth Press, 1955). The editors have to thank Dr. C. F. Rycroft and Mr. Alan Tyson for reading the volume in proof and Miss Angela Richards for help in tracing and verifying references. They are especially indebted to Miss Anna Freud for the exhaustive advice she has given at every stage in the work of translation.

EDITOR'S INTRODUCTION

(A) ÜBER DEN PSYCHISCHEN MECHANISMUS HYSTERISCHER PHÄNOMENE (VORLÄUFIGE MITTEILUNG)

(a) GERMAN EDITIONS:

1893   *Neurol. Centralbl.*, **12** (1), 4–10 (Sections I–II), and **12** (2), 43–7 (Sections III–V). (January 1 and 15.)

1893   *Wien. med. Blätter*, **16** (3), 33–5 (Sections I–II), and **16** (4), 49–51 (Sections III–V). (January 19 and 26.)

1895, etc. In *Studien über Hysterie*. (See below.)

1906   *S.K.S.N.*, I, 14–29. (1911, 2nd. ed.; 1920, 3rd. ed.; 1922, 4th. ed.)

(b) ENGLISH TRANSLATIONS:

'The Psychic Mechanism of Hysterical Phenomena (Preliminary Communication)'

1909   *S.P.H.*, 1–13. (Tr. A. A. Brill.) (1912, 2nd. ed.; 1920, 3rd. ed.)

1936   In *Studies in Hysteria*. (See below.)

'On the Psychical Mechanism of Hysterical Phenomena'

1924   *C.P.*, **1**, 24–41. (Tr. J. Rickman.)

(B) STUDIEN ÜBER HYSTERIE

(a) GERMAN EDITIONS:

1895   Leipzig and Vienna: Deuticke. Pp. v + 269.

1909   2nd. ed. Same publishers. (Unchanged, but with new preface.) Pp. vii + 269.

1916   3rd. ed. Same publishers. (Unchanged.) Pp. vii + 269.

1922   4th. ed. Same publishers. (Unchanged.) Pp. vii + 269.

1925   *G.S.*, **1**, 3–238. (Omitting Breuer's contributions; with extra footnotes by Freud.)

1952   *G.W.*, **1**, 77–312. (Reprint of 1925.)

(*b*) ENGLISH TRANSLATIONS:

Studies in Hysteria

1909 *S.P.H.*, 1–120. (1912, 2nd. ed.; 1920, 3rd. ed.; 1922,
4th. ed.) (Tr. A. A. Brill.) (In part only: omitting
the case histories of Fräulein Anna O., Frau Emmy
von N. and Katharina, as well as Breuer's theoretical chapter.)

1936 New York: Nervous and Mental Disease Publishing Co.
(Monograph Series No. 61.) Pp. ix + 241. (Tr. A. A.
Brill.) (Complete, except for omitting Freud's extra
footnotes of 1925.)

The present, entirely new and complete translation by
James and Alix Strachey includes Breuer's contributions, but
is otherwise based on the German edition of 1925, containing
Freud's extra footnotes. The omission of Breuer's contributions from the two German collected editions (*G.S.* and *G.W.*)
led to some necessary changes and additional footnotes in
them, where references had been made by Freud in the original
edition to the omitted portions. In these collected editions, too,
the numbering of the case histories was altered, owing to the
absence of that of Anna O. All these changes are disregarded
in the present translation.—Abstracts both of the 'Preliminary
Communication' and of the main volume were included in
Freud's early collection of abstracts of his own works (1897*b*,
Nos. XXIV and XXXI).

(1)

SOME HISTORICAL NOTES ON THE STUDIES

The history of the writing of this book is known to us in
some detail.

Breuer's treatment of Fräulein Anna O., on which the whole
work was founded, took place between 1880 and 1882. By that
time Josef Breuer (1842–1925) already had a high reputation
in Vienna both as a physician with a large practice and as a
man of scientific attainments, while Sigmund Freud (1856–
1939) was only just qualifying as a doctor.[1] The two men had,

[1] Much of the material in what follows is derived from Ernest Jones's
life of Freud (Vol. I, and especially Chapter XI).

however, already been friends for some years. The treatment
ended early in June, 1882, and in the following November
Breuer related the remarkable story to Freud, who (though
at that time his main interests were centred on the anatomy
of the nervous system) was greatly impressed by it. So much
so, indeed, that when, some three years later, he was studying
in Paris under Charcot, he reported the case to him. 'But the
great man showed no interest in my first outline of the subject,
so that I never returned to it and allowed it to pass from my
mind.' (*An Autobiographical Study*, 1925d, Chapter II.)

Freud's studies under Charcot had centred largely on hysteria, and when he was back in Vienna in 1886 and settled
down to establish a practice in nervous diseases, hysteria provided a large proportion of his clientèle. To begin with he
relied on such currently recommended methods of treatment
as hydrotherapy, electro-therapy, massage and the Weir
Mitchell rest-cure. But when these proved unsatisfactory his
thoughts turned elsewhere. 'During the last few weeks', he
writes to his friend Fliess on December 28, 1887, 'I have taken
up hypnosis and have had all sorts of small but remarkable
successes.' (Freud, 1950a, Letter 2.) And he has given us a
detailed account of one successful treatment of this kind
(1892-3b). But the case of Anna O. was still at the back of his
mind, and 'from the first', he tells us (1925d) 'I made use of
hypnosis in *another* manner, apart from hypnotic suggestion'.
This 'other manner' was the cathartic method, which is the
subject of the present volume.

The case of Frau Emmy von N. was the first one, as we
learn from Freud (pp. 48 and 284), which he treated by the
cathartic method.[1] In a footnote added to the book in 1925 he
qualifies this and says it was the first case in which he made use
of that method 'to a large extent' (p. 105); and it is true that
at this early date he was still constantly employing hypnosis in
the conventional manner—for giving direct therapeutic suggestions. At about this time, indeed, his interest in hypnotic
suggestion was strong enough to lead him to translate one of
Bernheim's books in 1888 and another in 1892, as well as to

[1] A remark on p. 103 almost seems to imply, on the other hand, that
the case of Frau Cäcilie M. (mentioned below) preceded that of Frau
Emmy. But this impression may perhaps be due to an ambiguity in the
phrasing of the sentence.

pay a visit of some weeks to the clinics of Liébeault and Bernheim at Nancy in the summer of 1889. The extent to which he
was using therapeutic suggestion in the case of Frau Emmy is
shown very clearly by his day-to-day report of the first two or
three weeks of the treatment, reproduced by him from 'the
notes which I made each evening' (p. 48). We cannot unluckily be certain when he began this case (see Appendix A.,
p. 307); it was in May either of 1888 or of 1889—that is,
either about four or about sixteen months after he had first
'taken up hypnotism'. The treatment ended a year later, in
the summer of 1889 or 1890. In either alternative, there is a
considerable gap before the date of the next case history (in
chronological order, though not in order of presentation). This
was the case of Fräulein Elisabeth von R., which began in the
autumn of 1892 (p. 135) and which Freud describes (p. 139)
as his 'first full-length analysis of a hysteria'. It was soon followed
by that of Miss Lucy R., which began at the end of the same
year (p. 106).[1] No date is assigned to the remaining case, that
of Katharina (p. 125). But in the interval between 1889 and
1892 Freud certainly had experience with other cases. In
particular there was that of Frau Cäcilie M., whom he 'got to
know far more thoroughly than any of the other patients
mentioned in these studies' (p. 69 n.) but whose case could not
be reported in detail owing to 'personal considerations'. She
is however frequently discussed by Freud, as well as by Breuer,
in the course of the volume, and we learn (p. 178) from Freud
that 'it was the study of this remarkable case, jointly with
Breuer, that led directly to the publication of our "Preliminary
Communication"'.[2]

[1] It is to be noted that neither of these last two analyses had been
more than started at the time of the publication of the 'Preliminary
Communication'.

[2] The question of when it was that Freud first began using the
cathartic method is complicated still further by a statement made by
him in 1916. The circumstances were these. At the International
Medical Congress held in London in 1913, Pierre Janet had distinguished himself by making an absurdly ignorant and unfair attack
on Freud and psycho-analysis. A reply was published by Ernest Jones
in the *Journal of Abnormal Psychology*, 9 (1915), 400; and a German translation of this appeared in the *Int. Z. Psychoanal.*, 4 (1916), 34. In the
course of his diatribe Janet had said that whatever was of the slightest
value in psycho-analysis was entirely derived from his own early writings,
and in traversing this assertion Jones had remarked that, though it was

The drafting of that epoch-making paper (which forms the first section of the present volume) had begun in June 1892. A letter to Fliess of June 28 (Freud, 1950a, Letter 9) announces that 'Breuer has agreed that the theory of abreaction and the other findings on hysteria which we have arrived at jointly shall also be brought out jointly in a detailed publication'. 'A part of it', he goes on, 'which I at first wanted to write alone, is finished.' This 'finished' part of the paper is evidently referred to again in a letter to Breuer written on the following day, June 29, 1892 (Freud, 1941a): 'The innocent satisfaction I felt when I handed you over those few pages of mine has given way to . . . uneasiness.' This letter goes on to give a very condensed summary of the proposed contents of the paper. Next we have a footnote added by Freud to his translation of a volume of Charcot's *Leçons du Mardi* (Freud, 1892–3a, 107), which gives, in three short paragraphs, a summary of the thesis of the 'Preliminary Communication' and refers to it as being 'begun'.[1] Besides this, two rather more elaborate drafts have survived.[2] The first (Freud, 1940d) of these (in Freud's handwriting, though stated to have been written jointly with

true that the actual publication of Breuer and Freud's findings was later than that of Janet's (which were published in 1889), the work on which their first paper was based preceded Janet's by several years. 'The co-operation of the two authors', he went on, 'antedated their first communication by as much as ten years, and it is expressly stated in the *Studien* that one of the cases there reported was treated by the cathartic method more than fourteen years before the date of the publication.' At this point in the German translation (ibid., 42) there is a footnote signed 'Freud', which runs as follows: 'I am obliged to correct Dr. Jones on a point which is inessential so far as his argument is concerned but which is of importance to me. All that he says on the priority and independence of what was later named psycho-analytic work remains accurate, but it applies only to *Breuer's* achievements. My own collaboration began only in 1891–2. What I took over I derived not from Janet but from Breuer, as has often been publicly affirmed.' The date given here by Freud is a puzzling one. 1891 is two or three years too late for the beginning of the case of Frau Emmy and a year too early for that of Fräulein Elisabeth.

[1] It is not possible to date this precisely; for though Freud's preface to his translation is dated 'June 1892', the work came out in parts, some of which were published quite late in 1893. The footnote in question, however, appears on a relatively early page of the book, and may therefore be dated with fair certainty to the summer or autumn of 1892.

[2] All of these drafts and summaries will be found in full in the first volume of the *Standard Edition*.

Breuer) is dated 'End of November 1892'. It deals with hysterical attacks and its contents were mostly included, though in different words, in Section IV of the 'Preliminary Communication' (p. 13 ff.). One important paragraph, however, concerned with the 'principle of constancy', was unaccountably omitted, and in this volume the topic is treated only by Breuer, in the later part of the work (p. 197 ff.). Lastly there is a memorandum (Freud, 1941*b*) bearing the title 'III'. This is undated. It discusses 'hypnoid states' and hysterical dissociation, and is closely related to Section III of the published paper (p. 11 ff.).

On December 18, 1892 Freud wrote to Fliess (1950*a*, Letter 11): 'I am delighted to be able to tell you that our theory of hysteria (reminiscence, abreaction, etc.) is going to appear in the *Neurologisches Centralblatt* on January 1, 1893, in the form of a detailed preliminary communication. It has meant a long battle with my partner.' The paper, bearing the date 'December 1892', was actually published in two issues of the periodical: the first two Sections on January 1 and the remaining three on January 15. The *Neurologisches Centralblatt* (which appeared fortnightly) was published in Berlin; and the 'Preliminary Communication' was almost immediately reprinted in full in Vienna in the *Wiener medizinische Blätter* (on January 19 and 26). On January 11, while the paper was only half published, Freud gave a lecture on its subject-matter at the Wiener medizinischer Club. A full shorthand report of the lecture, 'revised by the lecturer', appeared in the *Wiener medizinische Presse* on January 22 and 29 (**34**, 122–6 and 165–7). The lecture (Freud, 1893*h*) covered approximately the same ground as the paper, but dealt with the material quite differently and in a much less formal manner.

The appearance of the paper seems to have produced little manifest effect in Vienna or Germany. In France, on the other hand, as Freud reports to Fliess in a letter of July 10, 1893 (1950*a*, Letter 13), it was favourably noticed by Janet, whose resistance to Freud's ideas was only to develop later. Janet included a long and highly laudatory account of the 'Preliminary Communication' in a paper on 'Some Recent Definitions of Hysteria' published in the *Archives de Neurologie* in June and July 1893. He used this paper as the final chapter of his book, *L'état mental des hystériques*, published in 1894. More unexpected, perhaps, is the fact that in April 1893—only three months after the publication of the 'Preliminary Communication'—a fairly full account of it was given by F. W. H. Myers at a general meeting of the Society for Psychical Research in London and was printed in their *Proceedings* in the following June. The 'Preliminary Communication' was also fully abstracted and discussed by Michell Clarke in *Brain* (1894, 125). The most surprising and unexplained reaction, however, was the publication in February and March 1893, in the *Gaceta médica de Granada* (**11**, 105–11 and 129–35), of a complete translation of the 'Preliminary Communication', in Spanish.

The authors' next task was the preparation of the case material, and already on February 7, 1894, Freud spoke of the book as 'half-finished: what remains to be done is only a small minority of the case histories and two general chapters'. In an unpublished passage in the letter of May 21 he mentions that he is just writing the last case history, and on June 22 (1950*a*, Letter 19) he gives a list of what 'the book with Breuer' is to contain: 'five case histories, an essay by him, with which I have nothing at all to do, on the theories of hysteria (summarizing and critical), and one by me on therapy which I have not started yet'. After this there was evidently a hold-up, for it is not until March 4, 1895 (ibid., Letter 22) that he writes to say that he is 'hurriedly working at the essay on the therapy of hysteria', which was finished by March 13 (unpublished letter). In another unpublished letter, of April 10, he sends Fliess the second half of the proofs of the book, and next day tells him it will be out in three weeks.

The *Studies on Hysteria* seem to have been duly published in May 1895, though the exact date is not stated. The book was unfavourably received in German medical circles; it was, for instance, very critically reviewed by Adolf von Strümpell, the well-known neurologist (*Deutsch. Z. Nervenheilk.*, 1896, 159). On the other hand, a non-medical writer, Alfred von Berger, later director of the Vienna Burgtheater, wrote appreciatively of it in the *Neue Freie Presse* (February 2, 1896). In England it was given a long and favourable notice in *Brain* (1896, 401) by Michell Clarke, and once again Myers showed his interest in it in an address of considerable length, first given in March 1897, which was ultimately included in his *Human Personality* (1903).

It was more than ten years before there was a call for a second edition of the book, and by that time the paths of its two authors had diverged. In May 1906 Breuer wrote to Freud agreeing on a reprint, but there was some discussion about whether a new joint preface was desirable. Further delays followed, and in the end, as will be seen below, two separate prefaces were written. These bear the date of July 1908 though the second edition was not actually published till 1909. The text was unaltered in this and the later editions of the book. But in 1924 Freud wrote some additional footnotes for the volume of his collected works containing his share of the *Studies* (published in 1925) and made one or two small changes in the text.

(2)

THE BEARING OF THE STUDIES ON PSYCHO-ANALYSIS

The *Studies on Hysteria* are usually regarded as the starting-point of psycho-analysis. It is worth considering briefly whether and in what respects this is true. For the purposes of this discussion the question of the shares in the work attributable to the two authors will be left on one side for consideration below, and the book will be treated as a whole. An enquiry into the bearing of the *Studies* upon the subsequent development of psycho-analysis may be conveniently divided into two parts, though such a separation is necessarily an artificial one. To what extent and in what ways did the technical procedures described in the *Studies* and the clinical findings to which they led pave the way for the practice of psycho-analysis? To what extent were the theoretical views propounded here accepted into Freud's later doctrines?

The fact is seldom sufficiently appreciated that perhaps the most important of Freud's achievements was his invention of the first instrument for the scientific examination of the human mind. One of the chief fascinations of the present volume is that it enables us to trace the early steps of the development of that instrument. What it tells us is not simply the story of the overcoming of a succession of obstacles; it is the story of the *discovery* of a succession of obstacles that have to be overcome.

Breuer's patient Anna O. herself demonstrated and overcame the first of these obstacles—the amnesia characteristic of the hysterical patient. When the existence of this amnesia was brought to light, there at once followed a realization that the patient's manifest mind was not the whole of it, that there lay behind it an *unconscious* mind (p. 45 ff.). It was thus plain from the first that the problem was not merely the investigation of *conscious* mental processes, for which the ordinary methods of enquiry used in everyday life would suffice. If there were also *unconscious* mental processes, some special instrument was clearly required. The obvious instrument for this purpose was hypnotic suggestion—hypnotic suggestion used, not for directly therapeutic purposes, but to persuade the patient to produce material from the unconscious region of the mind. With Anna O. only slight use of this instrument seemed necessary. She produced streams of material from her 'unconscious', and all Breuer had to do was to sit by and listen to them without interrupting her. But this was not so easy as it sounds, and the case history of Frau Emmy shows at many points how difficult it was for Freud to adapt himself to this new use of hypnotic suggestion and to listen to all that the patient had to say without any attempt at interference or at making short cuts (e.g. pp. 60 *n.* and 62 *n.* 1). Not all hysterical patients, moreover, were so amenable as Anna O.; the deep hypnosis into which she fell, apparently of her own accord, was not so readily obtained with everyone. And here came a further obstacle: Freud tells us that he was far from being an adept at hypnotism. He gives us several accounts in this book (e.g. p. 107 ff.) of how he circumvented this difficulty, of how he gradually gave up his attempts at bringing about hypnosis and contented himself with putting his patients into a state of 'concentration' and with the occasional use of pressure on the forehead. But it was the abandonment of hypnotism that widened still further his insight into mental processes. It revealed the presence of yet another obstacle—the patients' 'resistance' to the treatment pp. 154 and 268 ff.), their unwillingness to co-operate in their own cure. How was this unwillingness to be dealt with? Was it to be shouted down or suggested away? Or was it, like other mental phenomena, simply to be investigated? Freud's choice of this second path led him directly into the uncharted world which he was to spend his whole life in exploring.

In the years immediately following the *Studies* Freud abandoned more and more of the machinery of deliberate suggestion [cf. p. 110 *n*.] and came to rely more and more on the patient's flow of 'free associations'. The way was opened up to the analysis of dreams. Dream-analysis enabled him, in the first place, to obtain an insight into the workings of the 'primary process' in the mind and the ways in which it influenced the products of our more accessible thoughts, and he was thus put in possession of a new technical device—that of 'interpretation'. But dream-analysis made possible, in the second place, his own self-analysis, and his consequent discoveries of infantile sexuality and the Oedipus complex. All these things, apart from some slight hints,[1] still lay ahead. But he had already, in the last pages of this volume, come up against one further obstacle in the investigator's path—the 'transference' (p. 301 ff.). He had already had a glimpse of its formidable nature and had even, perhaps, already begun to recognize that it was to prove not only an obstacle but also another major instrument of psycho-analytic technique.

The main theoretical position adopted by the authors of the 'Preliminary Communication' seems, on the surface, a simple one. They hold that, in the normal course of things, if an experience is accompanied by a large amount of 'affect', that affect is either 'discharged' in a variety of conscious reflex acts or becomes gradually worn away by association with other conscious mental material. In the case of hysterical patients, on the other hand (for reasons which we shall mention in a moment), neither of these things happens. The affect remains in a 'strangulated' state, and the memory of the experience to which it is attached is cut off from consciousness. The affective memory is thereafter manifested in hysterical symptoms, which may be regarded as 'mnemic symbols'—that is to say as symbols of the suppressed memory (p. 90). Two principal reasons are suggested to explain the occurrence of this pathological outcome. One is that the original experience took place while the subject was in a particular dissociated state of mind described as 'hypnoid'; the other is that the experience was one which the subject's 'ego' regarded as 'incompatible' with itself

[1] See, for instance, the remarks on dreams in a footnote on p. 69, and a hint at the notion of free association on p. 56.

and which had therefore to be 'fended off'. In either case the therapeutic effectiveness of the 'cathartic' procedure is explained on the same basis: if the original experience, along with its affect, can be brought into consciousness, the affect is by that very fact discharged or 'abreacted', the force that has maintained the symptom ceases to operate, and the symptom itself disappears.

This all seems quite straightforward, but a little reflection shows that much remains unexplained. Why should an affect need to be 'discharged'? And why are the consequences of its not being discharged so formidable? These underlying problems are not considered at all in the 'Preliminary Communication', though they had been alluded to briefly in two of the posthumously published drafts (1941a and 1940d) and a hypothesis to provide an explanation of them was already in existence. Oddly enough, this hypothesis was actually stated by Freud in his lecture of January 11, 1893 (see p. xiv), in spite of its omission from the 'Preliminary Communication' itself. He again alluded to it in the last two paragraphs of his first paper on 'The Neuro-Psychoses of Defence' (1894a), where he specifically states that it underlay the theory of abreaction in the 'Preliminary Communication' of a year earlier. But this basic hypothesis was first formally produced and given a name in 1895 in the second section of Breuer's contribution to the present volume (p. 192 ff.). It is curious that this, the most fundamental of Freud's theories, was first fully discussed by Breuer (attributed by him, it is true, to Freud), and that Freud himself, though he occasionally reverted to its subject-matter (as in the early pages of his paper on 'Instincts and their Vicissitudes', 1915c), did not mention it explicitly till he wrote *Beyond the Pleasure Principle* (1920g). He did, as we now know, refer to the hypothesis by name in a communication to Fliess of uncertain date, possibly 1894 (Draft D, 1950a), and he considered it fully, though under another name (see below, p. xxiv), in the 'Project for a Scientific Psychology' which he wrote a few months after the publication of the *Studies*. But it was not until fifty-five years later (1950a) that Draft D and the 'Project' saw the light of day.

The 'principle of constancy' (for this was the name given to the hypothesis) may be defined in the terms used by Freud himself in *Beyond the Pleasure Principle*: 'The mental apparatus endeavours to keep the quantity of excitation present in it as low as possible or at least to keep it constant.' (*Standard Ed.*, **18**, 9.) Breuer states it below (p. 197) in very similar terms, but with a neurological twist, as 'a tendency to keep intra-cerebral excitation constant'.[1] In his discussion on p. 201 ff., he argues that the affects owe their importance in the aetiology of hysteria to the fact that they are accompanied by the produc-tion of large quantities of excitation, and that these in turn call for discharge in accordance with the principle of constancy. Similarly, too, traumatic experiences owe their pathogenic force to the fact that they produce quantities of excitation too large to be dealt with in the normal way. Thus the essential theoretical position underlying the *Studies* is that the clinical necessity for abreacting affect and the pathogenic results of its becoming strangulated are explained by the much more general tendency (expressed in the principle of constancy) to keep the quantity of excitation constant.

It has often been thought that the authors of the *Studies* attributed the phenomena of hysteria only to traumas and to ineradicable memories of them, and that it was not until later that Freud, after shifting the emphasis from infantile traumas to infantile phantasies, arrived at his momentous 'dynamic' view of the processes of the mind. It will be seen, however, from what has just been said, that a dynamic hypothesis in the shape of the principle of constancy already underlay the theory of trauma and abreaction. And when the time came for widen-ing the horizon and for attributing a far greater importance to instinct as contrasted with experience, there was no need to modify the basic hypothesis. Already, indeed, Breuer points out the part played by 'the organism's major physiological needs and instincts' in causing increases in excitation which call for discharge (p. 199), and emphasizes the importance of the 'sexual instinct' as 'the most powerful source of persisting increases of excitation (and consequently of neuroses)' (p. 200). Moreover the whole notion of conflict and the repression of

---

[1] Freud's statement of the principle in the lecture of January 11, 1893, was as follows: 'If a person experiences a psychical impression, some-thing in his nervous system which we will for the moment call the "sum of excitation" is increased. Now in every individual there exists a tendency to diminish this sum of excitation once more, in order to preserve his health . . .' (Freud, 1893 *h*.).

incompatible ideas is explicitly based on the occurrence of unpleasurable increases of excitation. This leads to the further consideration that, as Freud points out in *Beyond the Pleasure Principle* (*Standard Ed.*, **18,** 7 ff.), the 'pleasure principle' itself is closely bound up with the principle of constancy. He even goes further and declares (ibid., 62) that the pleasure principle 'is a tendency operating in the service of a function whose business it is to free the mental apparatus entirely from excitation or to keep the amount of excitation in it constant or to keep it as low as possible.' The 'conservative' character which Freud attributes to the instincts in his later works, and the 'compulsion to repeat', are also seen in the same passage to be manifestations of the principle of constancy; and it becomes clear that the hypothesis on which these early *Studies on Hysteria* were based was still being regarded by Freud as fundamental in his very latest speculations.

(3)

The Divergences between the Two Authors

We are not concerned here with the personal relations between Breuer and Freud, which have been fully described in the first volume of Ernest Jones's biography; but it will be of interest to discuss briefly their *scientific* differences. The existence of such differences was openly mentioned in the preface to the first edition, and they were often enlarged upon in Freud's later publications. But in the book itself, oddly enough, they are far from prominent; and even though the 'Preliminary Communication' is the only part of it with an explicitly joint authorship, it is not easy to assign with certainty the responsibility for the origin of the various component elements of the work as a whole.

We can no doubt safely attribute to Freud the later technical developments, together with the vital theoretical concepts of resistance, defence and repression which arose from them. It is easy to see from the account given on p. 268 ff. how these concepts followed from the replacement of hypnosis by the pressure technique. Freud himself, in his 'History of the Psycho-Analytic Movement' (1914*d*), declares that 'the theory of repression is the foundation stone on which the structure of psycho-analysis rests', and gives the same account as he does here of the way in which it was arrived at. He also asserts his belief that he reached this theory independently, and the history of the discovery amply confirms that belief. He remarks in the same passage that a hint at the notion of repression is to be found in Schopenhauer (1844), whose works, however, he read only late in life; and it has recently been pointed out that the word '*Verdrängung*' ('repression') occurs in the writings of the early nineteenth century psychologist Herbart (1824) whose ideas carried great weight with many of those in Freud's environment, and particularly with his immediate teacher in psychiatry, Meynert. But no such suggestions detract in any significant degree from the originality of Freud's theory, with its empirical basis, which found its first expression in the 'Preliminary Communication' (p. 10).

As against this, there can be no question that Breuer originated the notion of 'hypnoid states', to which we shall return shortly, and it seems possible that he was responsible for the terms 'catharsis' and 'abreaction'.

But many of the theoretical conclusions in the *Studies* must have been the product of discussions between the two authors during their years of collaboration, and Breuer himself comments (pp. 185–6) on the difficulty of determining priority in such cases. Apart from the influence of Charcot, on which Freud never ceased insisting, it must be remembered, too, that both Breuer and Freud owed a fundamental allegiance to the school of Helmholz, of which their teacher, Ernst Brücke, was a prominent member. Much of the underlying theory in the *Studies on Hysteria* is derived from the doctrine of that school that all natural phenomena are ultimately explicable in terms of physical and chemical forces.[1]

We have already seen (p. xix) that, though Breuer was the first to mention the 'principle of constancy' by name, he attributes the hypothesis to Freud. He similarly attaches Freud's name to the term 'conversion', but (as is explained below,

---

[1] The various influences that may possibly have played a part in determining Freud's views are very fully discussed by Ernest Jones (1953, **1**, 44 ff. and 407 ff.). In addition to the names referred to in the text above, special mention should be made of the psycho-physicist Fechner, to whom Freud himself acknowledged his indebtedness in the fifth chapter of his *Autobiographical Study* (1925*d*).

p. 206 *n.*) Freud himself has declared that this applies only to the *word* and that the concept was arrived at jointly. On the other hand there are a number of highly important concepts which seem to be properly attributable to Breuer: the notion of hallucination being a 'retrogression' from imagery to perception (p. 189), the thesis that the functions of perception and memory cannot be performed by the same apparatus (pp. 188-9 *n.*), and finally, and most surprisingly, the distinction between bound (tonic) and unbound (mobile) psychical energy and the correlated distinction between primary and secondary psychical processes (p. 194 *n.*).

The use of the term *'Besetzung'* ('cathexis'), which makes its first appearance on p. 89 in the sense that was to become so familiar in psycho-analytic theory, is probably to be attributed to Freud. The idea of the whole or a part of the mental apparatus carrying a charge of energy is, of course, presupposed by the principle of constancy. And though the actual term that was to be the standard one first came into use in this volume, the idea had been expressed earlier by Freud in other forms. Thus we find him using such phrases as *'mit Energie ausgestattet'* ('supplied with energy') (1895*b*), *'mit einer Erregungssumme behaftet'* ('loaded with a sum of excitation') (1894*a*), *'munie d'une valeur affective'* ('provided with a quota of affect') (1893*c*), *'Verschiebungen von Erregungssummen'* ('displacements of sums of excitation') (1941*a* [1892]) and, as long ago as in his preface to his first translation of Bernheim (1888-9), *'Verschiebungen von Erregbarkeit im Nervensystem'* ('displacements of excitability in the nervous system').

But this last quotation is a reminder of something of great importance that may very easily be overlooked. There can be no doubt that at the time of the publication of the *Studies* Freud regarded the term 'cathexis' as a purely physiological one. This is proved by the definition of the term given by him in Part I, Section 2, of his 'Project for a Scientific Psychology' by which (as is shown in the Fliess letters) his mind was already occupied, and which was written only a few months later. There, after giving an account of the recently discovered neurological entity, the 'neurone', he goes on: 'If we combine this account of neurones with an approach on the lines of the quantity theory, we arrive at the idea of a "cathected" neurone, filled with a certain quantity, though at other times it may be empty.'

The neurological bias of Freud's theories at this period is further shown by the form in which the principle of constancy is stated in the same passage in the 'Project'. It is given the name of 'the principle of neuronic inertia' and is defined as asserting 'that neurones tend to divest themselves of quantity'. A remarkable paradox is thus revealed. Breuer, as will be seen (p. 185), declares his intention of treating the subject of hysteria on purely psychological lines: 'In what follows little mention will be made of the brain and none whatever of molecules. Psychical processes will be dealt with in the language of psychology.' But in fact his theoretical chapter is largely concerned with 'intracerebral excitations' and with parallels between the nervous system and electrical installations. On the other hand Freud was devoting all his energies to explaining mental phenomena in physiological and chemical terms. Nevertheless, as he himself somewhat ruefully confesses (p. 160), his case histories read like short stories and his analyses are psychological ones.

The truth is that in 1895 Freud was at a half-way stage in the process of moving from physiological to psychological explanations of psychopathological states. On the one hand he was proposing what was broadly speaking a chemical explanation of the 'actual' neuroses—neurasthenia and anxiety neurosis—(in his two papers on anxiety neurosis, 1895b and 1895f), and on the other hand he was proposing an essentially psychological explanation—in terms of 'defence' and 'repression'—of hysteria and obsessions (in his two papers on 'The Neuro-Psychoses of Defence', 1894a and 1896b). His earlier training and career as a neurologist led him to resist the acceptance of psychological explanations as ultimate; and he was engaged in devising a complicated structure of hypotheses intended to make it possible to describe mental events in purely neurological terms. This attempt culminated in the 'Project' and was not long afterwards abandoned. To the end of his life, however, Freud continued to adhere to the chemical aetiology of the 'actual' neuroses and to believe that a physical basis for all mental phenomena might ultimately be found. But in the meantime he gradually came round to the view expressed by Breuer that psychical processes can only be dealt with in the language of psychology. It was not until 1905 (in his book on jokes, Chapter V) that he first explicitly repudiated all intention of using the term 'cathexis' in any but a psychological sense and all attempts at equating nerve-tracts or neurones with paths of mental association.[1]

What, however, were the essential scientific differences between Breuer and Freud? In his *Autobiographical Study* (1925*d*) Freud says that the first of these related to the aetiology of hysteria and could be described as 'hypnoid states versus neuroses of defence'. But once again, in this volume itself the issue is less clear-cut. In the joint 'Preliminary Communication' both aetiologies are accepted (p. 10 f.). Breuer, in his theoretical chapter, evidently lays most emphasis on hypnoid states (p. 215 ff.), but he also stresses the importance of 'defence' (pp. 214 and 235–6), though a little half-heartedly. Freud seems to accept the notion of 'hypnoid states' in his 'Katharina' case history (p. 128) [2] and, less definitely, in that of Frau Elisabeth (p. 167 *n*.). It is only in his final chapter that his scepticism begins to be apparent (p. 286). In a paper on 'The Aetiology of Hysteria' published in the following year (1896*c*) this scepticism is still more openly expressed, and in a footnote to his 'Dora' case history (1905*e*) he declares that the term 'hypnoid states' is 'superfluous and misleading' and that the hypothesis 'sprang entirely from the initiative of Breuer' (*Standard Ed.*, 7, 27 *n*.).

But the chief difference of opinion between the two authors upon which Freud later insisted concerned the part played by sexual impulses in the causation of hysteria. Here too, however, the *expressed* difference will be found less clear than would be expected. Freud's belief in the sexual origin of hysteria can be inferred plainly enough from the discussion in his chapter on psychotherapy (p. 257 ff.), but he nowhere asserts, as he was later to do, that in cases of hysteria a sexual aetiology was

---

[1] The insecurity of the neurological position which Freud was still trying to maintain in 1895 is emphasized by the correction that he felt obliged to make thirty years later in the very last sentence of the book. In 1895 he used the word '*Nervensystem*' ('nervous system'); in 1925 he replaced it by '*Seelenleben*' ('mental life'). Yet what was ostensibly a momentous change did not in the least affect the meaning of the sentence. The old neurological vocabulary had already been no more than a husk at the time when Freud penned the words.

[2] As he already had in his first paper on 'The Neuro-Psychoses of Defence' (1894*a*) and in the memorandum 'III' (1941*b*), almost certainly written in 1892 (see above p. xiv).

invariably present.[1] On the other hand, Breuer speaks at several points in the strongest terms of the importance of the part played by sexuality in the neuroses, particularly in the long passage on pp. 245–7. He says, for instance (as has already been remarked, p. xx), that 'the sexual instinct is undoubtedly the most powerful source of persisting increases of excitation (and consequently of neuroses)' (p. 200), and declares (p. 246) that 'the great majority of severe neuroses in women have their origin in the marriage bed'.

It seems as though, in order to find a satisfactory explanation of the dissolution of this scientific partnership, we should have to look behind the printed words. Freud's letters to Fliess show Breuer as a man full of doubts and reservations, always insecure in his conclusions. There is an extreme instance of this in a letter of November 8, 1895 (1950a, Letter 35), about six months after the publication of the *Studies*: 'Not long ago Breuer made a big speech about me at the Doktorenkollegium, in which he announced his conversion to belief in the sexual aetiology [of the neuroses]. When I took him on one side to thank him for it, he destroyed my pleasure by saying: "All the same I don't believe it." Can you understand that? I can't.' Something of the kind can be read between the lines of Breuer's contributions to the *Studies*, and we have the picture of a man half-afraid of his own remarkable discoveries. It was inevitable that he should be even more disconcerted by the premonition of still more unsettling discoveries yet to come; and it was inevitable that Freud in turn should feel hampered and irritated by his yoke-fellow's uneasy hesitations.

It would be tedious to enumerate the many passages in Freud's later writings in which he refers to the *Studies on Hysteria* and to Breuer; but a few quotations will illustrate the varying emphasis in his attitude to them.

In the numerous short accounts of his therapeutic methods and psychological theories which he published during the years immediately succeeding the issue of the *Studies* he was at pains to bring out the differences between 'psycho-analysis' and the cathartic method—the technical innovations, the extension of

---

[1] Indeed, in the fourth of his *Five Lectures* (1910a), he categorically asserts that at the time of the publication of the *Studies* he did not yet believe that this was so.

his procedure to neuroses other than hysteria, the establishment of the motive of 'defence', the insistence on a sexual
aetiology and, as we have already seen, the final rejection of
'hypnoid states'. When we reach the first series of Freud's
major works—the volumes on dreams (1900a), on parapraxes
(1901b), on jokes (1905c) and on sexuality (1905d)—there is
naturally little or no retrospective material; and it is not until
the five lectures at Clark University (1910a) that we find any
extensive historical survey. In those lectures Freud appeared
anxious to establish the continuity between his work and
Breuer's. The whole of the first lecture and much of the second
are devoted to a summary of the *Studies*, and the impression
given was that not Freud but Breuer was the true founder of
psycho-analysis.

The next long retrospective survey, in the 'History of the
Psycho-Analytic Movement' (1914d), was in a very different
key. The whole paper, of course, was polemical in its intent
and it is not surprising that in sketching the early history
of psycho-analysis Freud stressed his differences from Breuer
rather than his debts to him, and that he explicitly retracted
his view of him as the originator of psycho-analysis. In this
paper, too, Freud dilated on Breuer's inability to face the
sexual transference and revealed the 'untoward event' which
ended the analysis of Anna O. (pp. 40–1 *n*.).

Next came what seems almost like an *amende*—it has already
been mentioned on p. xxiii—the unexpected attribution to
Breuer of the distinction between bound and unbound psychical
energy and between the primary and secondary processes.
There had been no hint of this attribution when these hypotheses were originally introduced by Freud (in *The Interpretation
of Dreams*); it was first made in a footnote to Section V of the
metapsychological paper on 'The Unconscious' (1915e) and
repeated in *Beyond the Pleasure Principle* (1920g; *Standard Ed.*, **18**,
26–7 and 31). Not long after the last of these there were some
appreciative sentences in an article contributed by Freud to
Marcuse's *Handwörterbuch* (1923a; *Standard Ed.*, **18**, 236): 'In a
theoretical section of the *Studies* Breuer brought forward some
speculative ideas about the processes of excitation in the mind.
These ideas determined the direction of future lines of thought
. . .' In somewhat the same vein Freud wrote a little later in a
contribution to an American publication (1924f): 'The cathartic

method was the immediate precursor of psycho-analysis, and, in spite of every extension of experience and of every modification of theory, is still contained within it as its nucleus.'

Freud's next long historical survey, *An Autobiographical Study* (1925*d*), seemed once more to withdraw from the joint work: 'If the account I have so far given', he wrote, 'has led the reader to expect that the *Studies on Hysteria* must, in all essentials of their material content, be the product of Breuer's mind, that is precisely what I myself have always maintained . . . As regards the *theory* put forward in the book, I was partly responsible, but to an extent which it is to-day no longer possible to determine. That theory was in any case unpretentious and hardly went beyond the direct description of the observations.' He added that 'it would have been difficult to guess from the *Studies on Hysteria* what an importance sexuality has in the aetiology of the neuroses', and went on once more to describe Breuer's unwillingness to recognize that factor.

It was soon after this that Breuer died, and it is perhaps appropriate to end this introduction to the joint work with a quotation from Freud's obituary of his collaborator (1925*g*). After remarking on Breuer's reluctance to publish the *Studies* and declaring that his own chief merit in connection with them lay in his having persuaded Breuer to agree to their appearance, he proceeded: 'At the time when he submitted to my influence and was preparing the *Studies* for publication, his judgement of their significance seemed to be confirmed. "I believe", he told me, "that this is the most important thing we two have to give the world." Besides the case history of his first patient Breuer contributed a theoretical paper to the *Studies*. It is very far from being out of date; on the contrary, it conceals thoughts and suggestions which have even now not been turned to sufficient account. Anyone immersing himself in this speculative essay will form a true impression of the mental build of this man, whose scientific interests were, alas, turned in the direction of our psychopathology during only one short episode of his long life.'

PREFACE TO THE FIRST EDITION

In 1893 we published a 'Preliminary Communication'[1] on a new method of examining and treating hysterical phenomena. To this we added as concisely as possible the theoretical conclusions at which we had arrived. We are here reprinting this 'Preliminary Communication' to serve as the thesis which it is our purpose to illustrate and prove.

We have appended to it a series of case histories, the selection of which could not unfortunately be determined on purely scientific grounds. Our experience is derived from private practice in an educated and literate social class, and the subject matter with which we deal often touches upon our patients' most intimate lives and histories. It would be a grave breach of confidence to publish material of this kind, with the risk of the patients being recognized and their acquaintances becoming informed of facts which were confided only to the physician. It has therefore been impossible for us to make use of some of the most instructive and convincing of our observations. This of course applies especially to all those cases in which sexual and marital relations play an important aetiological part. Thus it comes about that we are only able to produce very incomplete evidence in favour of our view that sexuality seems to play a principal part in the pathogenesis of hysteria as a source of psychical traumas and as a motive for 'defence'—that is, for repressing ideas from consciousness. It is precisely observations of a markedly sexual nature that we have been obliged to leave unpublished.

The case histories are followed by a number of theoretical reflections, and in a final chapter on therapeutics the technique of the 'cathartic method' is propounded, just as it has grown up under the hands of the neurologist.

If at some points divergent and indeed contradictory opinions are expressed, this is not to be regarded as evidence of any fluctuation in our views. It arises from the natural and justifiable differences between the opinions of two observers who

[1] 'On the Psychical Mechanism of Hysterical Phenomena', *Neurologisches Centralblatt*, 1893, Nos. 1 and 2.

are agreed upon the facts and their basic reading of them, but who are not invariably at one in their interpretations and conjectures.

J. Breuer, S. Freud

April 1895

PREFACE TO THE SECOND EDITION

THE interest which, to an ever-increasing degree, is being directed to psycho-analysis seems now to be extending to these *Studies on Hysteria*. The publisher desires to bring out a new edition of the book, which is at present out of print. It appears now in a reprint, without any alterations, though the opinions and methods which were put forward in the first edition have since undergone far-reaching and profound developments. So far as I personally am concerned, I have since that time had no active dealings with the subject; I have had no part in its important development and I could add nothing fresh to what was written in 1895. So I have been able to do no more than express a wish that my two contributions to the volume should be reprinted without alteration.

BREUER

As regards my share of the book, too, the only possible decision has been that the text of the first edition shall be reprinted without alteration. The developments and changes in my views during the course of thirteen years of work have been too far-reaching for it to be possible to attach them to my earlier exposition without entirely destroying its essential character. Nor have I any reason for wishing to eliminate this evidence of my initial views. Even to-day I regard them not as errors but as valuable first approximations to knowledge which could only be fully acquired after long and continuous efforts. The attentive reader will be able to detect in the present book the germs of all that has since been added to the theory of catharsis: for instance, the part played by psychosexual factors and infantilism, the importance of dreams and of unconscious symbolism. And I can give no better advice to any one interested in the development of catharsis into psycho-analysis than to begin with *Studies on Hysteria* and thus follow the path which I myself have trodden.

FREUD

VIENNA, *July* 1908

I

PRELIMINARY COMMUNICATION
(1893)

(BREUER AND FREUD)

I

ON THE PSYCHICAL MECHANISM OF HYSTERICAL PHENOMENA: PRELIMINARY COMMUNICATION (1893) [1]

(BREUER AND FREUD)

I

A CHANCE observation has led us, over a number of years, to investigate a great variety of different forms and symptoms of hysteria, with a view to discovering their precipitating cause —the event which provoked the first occurrence, often many years earlier, of the phenomenon in question. In the great majority of cases it is not possible to establish the point of origin by a simple interrogation of the patient, however thoroughly it may be carried out. This is in part because what is in question is often some experience which the patient dislikes discussing; but principally because he is genuinely unable to recollect it and often has no suspicion of the causal connection between the precipitating event and the pathological phenomenon. As a rule it is necessary to hypnotize the patient and to arouse his memories under hypnosis of the time at which the symptom made its first appearance; when this has been done, it becomes possible to demonstrate the connection in the clearest and most convincing fashion.

This method of examination has in a large number of cases produced results which seem to be of value alike from a theoretical and a practical point of view.

They are valuable theoretically because they have taught us

[1] [As explained above in the preface to the first edition, this first chapter had appeared originally as a separate paper in 1893. It was reprinted not only in the present book, but also in the first of Freud's collected volumes of his shorter works, *Sammlung kleiner Schriften zur Neurosenlehre* (1906). The following footnote was appended to this latter reprint: 'Also printed as an introduction to *Studies on Hysteria*, 1895, in which Josef Breuer and I further developed the views expressed here and illustrated them by case histories.']

that external events determine the pathology of hysteria to an extent far greater than is known and recognized. It is of course obvious that in cases of 'traumatic' hysteria what provokes the symptoms is the accident. The causal connection is equally evident in hysterical attacks when it is possible to gather from the patient's utterances that in each attack he is hallucinating the same event which provoked the first one. The situation is more obscure in the case of other phenomena.

Our experiences have shown us, however, that the most various symptoms, which are ostensibly spontaneous and, as one might say, idiopathic products of hysteria, are just as strictly related to the precipitating trauma as the phenomena to which we have just alluded and which exhibit the connection quite clearly. The symptoms which we have been able to trace back to precipitating factors of this sort include neuralgias and anaesthesias of very various kinds, many of which had persisted for years, contractures and paralyses, hysterical attacks and epileptoid convulsions, which every observer regarded as true epilepsy, *petit mal* and disorders in the nature of *tic*, chronic vomiting and anorexia, carried to the pitch of rejection of all nourishment, various forms of disturbance of vision, constantly recurrent visual hallucinations, etc. The disproportion between the many years' duration of the hysterical symptom and the single occurrence which provoked it is what we are accustomed invariably to find in traumatic neuroses. Quite frequently it is some event in childhood that sets up a more or less severe symptom which persists during the years that follow.

The connection is often so clear that it is quite evident how it was that the precipitating event produced this particular phenomenon rather than any other. In that case the symptom has quite obviously been determined by the precipitating cause. We may take as a very commonplace instance a painful emotion arising during a meal but suppressed at the time, and then producing nausea and vomiting which persists for months in the form of hysterical vomiting. A girl, watching beside a sick-bed in a torment of anxiety, fell into a twilight state and had a terrifying hallucination, while her right arm, which was hanging over the back of her chair, went to sleep; from this there developed a paresis of the same arm accompanied by contracture and anaesthesia. She tried to pray but could find no words; at length she succeeded in repeating a children's prayer in English. When subsequently a severe and highly complicated hysteria developed, she could only speak, write and understand English, while her native language remained unintelligible to her for eighteen months.[1]—The mother of a very sick child, which had at last fallen asleep, concentrated her whole will-power on keeping still so as not to waken it. Precisely on account of her intention she made a 'clacking' noise with her tongue. (An instance of 'hysterical counter-will'.) This noise was repeated on a subsequent occasion on which she wished to keep perfectly still; and from it there developed a *tic* which, in the form of a clacking with the tongue, occurred over a period of many years whenever she felt excited.[2]—A highly intelligent man was present while his brother had an ankylosed hip-joint extended under an anaesthetic. At the instant at which the joint gave way with a crack, he felt a violent pain in his own hip-joint, which persisted for nearly a year.—Further instances could be quoted.

In other cases the connection is not so simple. It consists only in what might be called a 'symbolic' relation between the precipitating cause and the pathological phenomenon—a relation such as healthy people form in dreams. For instance, a neuralgia may follow upon mental pain or vomiting upon a feeling of moral disgust. We have studied patients who used to make the most copious use of this sort of symbolization.[3] In still other cases it is not possible to understand at first sight how they can be determined in the manner we have suggested. It is precisely the typical hysterical symptoms which fall into this class, such as hemi-anaesthesia, contraction of the field of vision, epileptiform convulsions, and so on. An explanation of our views on this group must be reserved for a fuller discussion of the subject.

Observations such as these seem to us to establish an analogy between the pathogenesis of common hysteria and that of traumatic neuroses, and to justify an extension of the concept of traumatic hysteria. In traumatic neuroses the operative cause of the illness is not the trifling

[1] [This patient is the subject of the first case history; see below, p. 21 ff.]

[2] [This patient is the subject of the second case history; see below, p. 48 ff. These episodes are also treated at some length in 'A Case of Successful Treatment by Hypnotism' (Freud, 1892–3*b*), where the concept of 'hysterical counter-will' is also discussed.]

[3] [See the account of Frau Cäcilie M., p. 176 ff. below.]

physical injury but the affect of fright—the psychical trauma. In an analogous manner, our investigations reveal, for many, if not for most, hysterical symptoms, precipitating causes which can only be described as psychical traumas. Any experience which calls up distressing affects—such as those of fright, anxiety, shame or physical pain—may operate as a trauma of this kind; and whether it in fact does so depends naturally enough on the susceptibility of the person affected (as well as on another condition which will be mentioned later). In the case of common hysteria it not infrequently happens that, instead of a single, major trauma, we find a number of partial traumas forming a *group* of provoking causes. These have only been able to exercise a traumatic effect by summation and they belong together in so far as they are in part components of a single story of suffering. There are other cases in which an apparently trivial circumstance combines with the actually operative event or occurs at a time of peculiar susceptibility to stimulation and in this way attains the dignity of a trauma which it would not otherwise have possessed but which thenceforward persists.

But the causal relation between the determining psychical trauma and the hysterical phenomenon is not of a kind implying that the trauma merely acts like an *agent provocateur* in releasing the symptom, which thereafter leads an independent existence. We must presume rather that the psychical trauma —or more precisely the memory of the trauma—acts like a foreign body which long after its entry must continue to be regarded as an agent that is still at work; and we find the evidence for this in a highly remarkable phenomenon which at the same time lends an important *practical* interest to our findings.

For we found, to our great surprise at first, that *each individual hysterical symptom immediately and permanently disappeared when we had succeeded in bringing clearly to light the memory of the event by which it was provoked and in arousing its accompanying affect, and when the patient had described that event in the greatest possible detail and had put the affect into words.* Recollection without affect almost invariably produces no result. The psychical process which originally took place must be repeated as vividly as possible; it must be brought back to its *status nascendi* and then given verbal utterance. Where what we are dealing with are phenomena involving stimuli (spasms, neuralgias and hallucinations) these re-appear once again with the fullest intensity and then vanish for ever. Failures of function, such as paralyses and anaesthesias, vanish in the same way, though, of course, without the temporary intensification being discernible.[1]

It is plausible to suppose that it is a question here of unconscious suggestion: the patient expects to be relieved of his sufferings by this procedure, and it is this expectation, and not the verbal utterance, which is the operative factor. This, however, is not so. The first case of this kind that came under observation dates back to the year 1881, that is to say to the 'pre-suggestion' era. A highly complicated case of hysteria was analysed in this way, and the symptoms, which sprang from separate causes, were separately removed. This observation was made possible by spontaneous auto-hypnoses on the part of the patient, and came as a great surprise to the observer.[2]

We may reverse the dictum *'cessante causa cessat effectus'* ['when the cause ceases the effect ceases'] and conclude from these observations that the determining process continues to operate in some way or other for years—not indirectly, through a chain of intermediate causal links, but as a *directly* releasing cause—just as a psychical pain that is remembered in waking consciousness still provokes a lachrymal secretion long after the event. *Hysterics suffer mainly from reminiscences.*[3]

[1] The possibility of a therapeutic procedure of this kind has been clearly recognized by Delbœuf and Binet, as is shown by the following quotations: 'On s'expliquerait dès lors comment le magnétiseur aide à la guérison. Il remet le sujet dans l'état où le mal s'est manifesté et combat par la parole le même mal, mais renaissant.' ['We can now explain how the hypnotist promotes cure. He puts the subject back into the state in which his trouble first appeared and uses words to combat that trouble, as it now makes a fresh emergence.'] (Delbœuf, 1889.)—'. . . peut-être verra-t-on qu'en reportant le malade par un artifice mental au moment même où le symptôme a apparu pour la première fois, on rend ce malade plus docile à une suggestion curative.' ['. . . we shall perhaps find that by taking the patient back by means of a mental artifice to the very moment at which the symptom first appeared, we may make him more susceptible to a therapeutic suggestion.'] (Binet, 1892, 243.)—In Janet's interesting study on mental automatism (1889), there is an account of the cure of a hysterical girl by a method analogous to ours.

[2] [The first event of this kind is reported on p. 34.]

[3] In this preliminary communication it is not possible for us to distinguish what is new in it from what has been said by other authors

II

At first sight it seems extraordinary that events experienced so long ago should continue to operate so intensely—that their recollection should not be liable to the wearing away process to which, after all, we see all our memories succumb. The following considerations may perhaps make this a little more intelligible.

The fading of a memory or the losing of its affect depends on various factors. The most important of these is *whether there has been an energetic reaction to the event that provokes an affect.* By 'reaction' we here understand the whole class of voluntary and involuntary reflexes—from tears to acts of revenge—in which, as experience shows us, the affects are discharged. If this reaction takes place to a sufficient amount a large part of the affect disappears as a result. Linguistic usage bears witness to this fact of daily observation by such phrases as 'to cry oneself out' ['*sich ausweinen*'], and to 'blow off steam' ['*sich austoben*', literally 'to rage oneself out']. If the reaction is suppressed, the affect remains attached to the memory. An injury that has been repaid, even if only in words, is recollected quite differently from one that has had to be accepted. Language recognizes this distinction, too, in its mental and physical consequences; it very characteristically describes an injury that has been suffered in silence as 'a mortification' ['*Kränkung*', lit. 'making ill'].—The injured person's reaction to the trauma only exercises a completely 'cathartic' effect if it is an *adequate* reaction—as, for instance, revenge. But language serves as a substitute for action; by its help, an affect can be 'abreacted' almost as effectively.[1] In other cases speaking is itself the adequate reflex, when, for instance, it is a lamentation or giving utterance to a tormenting secret, e.g. a confession. If there is no such reaction, whether in deeds or words, or in the mildest cases in tears, any recollection of the event retains its affective tone to begin with.

such as Moebius and Strümpell who have held similar views on hysteria to ours. We have found the nearest approach to what we have to say on the theoretical and therapeutic sides of the question in some remarks, published from time to time, by Benedikt. These we shall deal with elsewhere. [See below, p. 210 *n.*]

[1] ['Catharsis' and 'abreaction' made their first published appearance in this passage. Freud had used the term 'abreaction' previously (June 28, 1892), in a letter to Fliess referring to the present paper (Freud, 1950*a*, Letter 9).]

'Abreaction', however, is not the only method of dealing with the situation that is open to a normal person who has experienced a psychical trauma. A memory of such a trauma, even if it has not been abreacted, enters the great complex of associations, it comes alongside other experiences, which may contradict it, and is subjected to rectification by other ideas. After an accident, for instance, the memory of the danger and the (mitigated) repetition of the fright becomes associated with the memory of what happened afterwards—rescue and the consciousness of present safety. Again, a person's memory of a humiliation is corrected by his putting the facts right, by considering his own worth, etc. In this way a normal person is able to bring about the disappearance of the accompanying affect through the process of association.

To this we must add the general effacement of impressions, the fading of memories which we name 'forgetting' and which wears away those ideas in particular that are no longer affectively operative.

Our observations have shown, on the other hand, that the memories which have become the determinants of hysterical phenomena persist for a long time with astonishing freshness and with the whole of their affective colouring. We must, however, mention another remarkable fact, which we shall later be able to turn to account, namely, that these memories, unlike other memories of their past lives, are not at the patients' disposal. On the contrary, *these experiences are completely absent from the patients' memory when they are in a normal psychical state, or are only present in a highly summary form.* Not until they have been questioned under hypnosis do these memories emerge with the undiminished vividness of a recent event.

Thus, for six whole months, one of our patients reproduced under hypnosis with hallucinatory vividness everything that had excited her on the same day of the previous year (during an attack of acute hysteria). A diary kept by her mother without her knowledge proved the completeness of the reproduction [p. 33]. Another patient, partly under hypnosis and partly during spontaneous attacks, re-lived with hallucinatory clarity all the events of a hysterical psychosis which she had passed through ten years earlier and which she had for the most part forgotten till the moment at which it re-emerged. Moreover, certain memories of aetiological importance which dated back from fifteen to twenty-five years were found to be astonishingly intact and to possess remarkable sensory force, and when they returned they acted with all the affective strength of new experiences [pp. 178–80].

This can only be explained on the view that these memories constitute an exception in their relation to all the wearing-away processes which we have discussed above. *It appears, that is to say, that these memories correspond to traumas that have not been sufficiently abreacted*; and if we enter more closely into the reasons which have prevented this, we find at least two sets of conditions under which the reaction to the trauma fails to occur.

In the first group are those cases in which the patients have not reacted to a psychical trauma because the nature of the trauma excluded a reaction, as in the case of the apparently irreparable loss of a loved person or because social circumstances made a reaction impossible or because it was a question of things which the patient wished to forget, and therefore intentionally repressed [1] from his conscious thought and inhibited and suppressed. It is precisely distressing things of this kind

---

[1] [This is the first appearance of the term 'repressed' ('*verdrängt*') in what was to be its psycho-analytic sense. The concept, though not the term, had already been used by Breuer and Freud in the joint, post-humously published draft (1940*d*), which was written in November, 1892, only about a month before the present paper. Freud's own first published use of the word was in the second section of his first paper on anxiety neurosis (1895*b*); and it occurs several times in his later contributions to the present volume (e.g. on p. 116). At this period 'repression' was used as an equivalent to 'defence' ('*Abwehr*'), as is shown, for instance, in the joint Preface to the First Edition (p. xxix, above). The word 'defence' does not occur in the 'Preliminary Communication', however. It first appeared in Section I of Freud's first paper on 'The Neuro-Psychoses of Defence' (1894*a*), and, like 'repression' is freely used by him in the later parts of the *Studies* (e.g. on p. 147). Breuer uses both terms in his theoretical chapter (e.g. on pp. 214 and 245).—On some of its earlier appearances the term 'repressed' is accompanied (as here) by the adverb 'intentionally' ('*absichtlich*') or by 'deliberately' ('*willkürlich*'). This is expanded by Freud in one place (1894*a*), where he states that the act of repression is 'introduced by an effort of will, for which the motive can be assigned'. Thus the word 'intentionally' merely indicates the existence of a motive and carries no implication of *conscious* intention. Indeed, a little later, at the beginning of his second paper on 'The Neuro-Psychoses of Defence' (1896*b*), Freud explicitly describes the psychical mechanism of defence as 'unconscious'.—Some remarks on the origin of the concept of repression will be found in the Editor's Introduction, p. xxii.]

that, under hypnosis, we find are the basis of hysterical pheno-mena (e.g. hysterical deliria in saints and nuns, continent women and well-brought-up children).

The second group of conditions are determined, not by the content of the memories but by the psychical states in which the patient received the experiences in question. For we find, under hypnosis, among the causes of hysterical symptoms ideas which are not in themselves significant, but whose persistence is due to the fact that they originated during the prevalence of severely paralysing affects, such as fright, or during positively abnormal psychical states, such as the semi-hypnotic twilight state of day-dreaming, auto-hypnoses, and so on. In such cases it is the nature of the states which makes a reaction to the event impossible.

Both kinds of conditions may, of course, be simultaneously present, and this, in fact, often occurs. It is so when a trauma which is operative in itself takes place while a severely paralys-ing affect prevails or during a modified state of consciousness. But it also seems to be true that in many people a psychical trauma *produces* one of these abnormal states, which, in turn, makes reaction impossible.

Both of these groups of conditions, however, have in common the fact that the psychical traumas which have not been dis-posed of by reaction cannot be disposed of either by being worked over by means of association. In the first group the patient is determined to forget the distressing experiences and accordingly excludes them so far as possible from association; while in the second group the associative working-over fails to occur because there is no extensive associative connection between the normal state of consciousness and the pathological ones in which the ideas made their appearance. We shall have occasion immediately to enter further into this matter.

It may therefore be said that the ideas which have become pathological have persisted with such freshness and affective strength because they have been denied the normal wearing-away processes by means of abre-action and reproduction in states of uninhibited association.

III

We have stated the conditions which, as our experience shows, are responsible for the development of hysterical phenomena from psychical traumas. In so doing, we have already been obliged to speak of abnormal states of consciousness in which these pathogenic ideas arise, and to emphasize the fact that the recollection of the operative psychical trauma is not to be found in the patient's normal memory but in his memory when he is hypnotized. The longer we have been occupied with these phenomena the more we have become convinced that *the splitting of consciousness which is so striking in the well-known classical cases under the form of* 'double conscience'[1] *is present to a rudimentary degree in every hysteria, and that a tendency to such a dissociation, and with it the emergence of abnormal states of consciousness (which we shall bring together under the term 'hypnoid') is the basic phenomenon of this neurosis.* In these views we concur with Binet and the two Janets,[2] though we have had no experience of the remarkable findings they have made on anaesthetic patients.

We should like to balance the familiar thesis that hypnosis is an artificial hysteria by another—the basis and *sine qua non* of hysteria is the existence of hypnoid states. These hypnoid states share with one another and with hypnosis, however much they may differ in other respects, one common feature: the ideas which emerge in them are very intense but are cut off from associative communication with the rest of the content of consciousness. Associations may take place between these hypnoid states, and their ideational content can in this way reach a more or less high degree of psychical organization. Moreover, the nature of these states and the extent to which they are cut off from the remaining conscious processes must be supposed to vary just as happens in hypnosis, which ranges from a light drowsiness to somnambulism, from complete recollection to total amnesia.

If hypnoid states of this kind are already present before the onset of the manifest illness, they provide the soil in which the affect plants the pathogenic memory with its consequent somatic phenomena. This corresponds to *dispositional* hysteria. We have found, however, that a severe trauma (such as occurs in a traumatic neurosis) or a laborious suppression (as of a sexual affect, for instance) can bring about a splitting-off of groups of ideas even in people who are in other respects unaffected; and this would be the mechanism of *psychically acquired*

[1] [The French term ('dual consciousness').]
[2] [Pierre and Jules.]

hysteria. Between the extremes of these two forms we must assume the existence of a series of cases within which the liability to dissociation in the subject and the affective magnitude of the trauma vary inversely.

We have nothing new to say on the question of the origin of these dispositional hypnoid states. They often, it would seem, grow out of the day-dreams which are so common even in healthy people and to which needlework and similar occupations render women especially prone. Why it is that the 'pathological associations' brought about in these states are so stable and why they have so much more influence on somatic processes than ideas are usually found to do—these questions coincide with the general problem of the effectiveness of hypnotic suggestions. Our observations contribute nothing fresh on this subject. But they throw a light on the contradiction between the dictum 'hysteria is a psychosis' and the fact that among hysterics may be found people of the clearest intellect, strongest will, greatest character and highest critical power. This characterization holds good of their waking thoughts; but in their hypnoid states they are insane, as we all are in dreams. Whereas, however, our dream-psychoses have no effect upon our waking state, the products of hypnoid states intrude into waking life in the form of hysterical symptoms.[1]

IV

What we have asserted of chronic hysterical symptoms can be applied almost completely to hysterical *attacks*. Charcot, as is well known, has given us a schematic description of the 'major' hysterical attack, according to which four phases can be distinguished in a complete attack: (1) the epileptoid phase, (2) the phase of large movements, (3) the phase of *attitudes passionnelles* (the hallucinatory phase), and (4) the phase of terminal delirium. Charcot derives all those forms of hysterical attack which are in practice met with more often than the complete *grande attaque*, from the abbreviation, absence or isolation of these four distinct phases.[2]

---

[1] [A preliminary sketch of this section of the paper has survived in a posthumously published memorandum (Freud, 1941*b* [1892]), which is headed 'III'.]

[2] [Cf. Charcot, 1887, 261.]

Our attempted explanation takes its start from the third of these phases, that of the '*attitudes passionnelles*'. Where this is present in a well-marked form, it exhibits the hallucinatory reproduction of a memory which was of importance in bringing about the onset of the hysteria—the memory either of a single major trauma (which we find *par excellence* in what is called traumatic hysteria) or of a series of interconnected part-traumas (such as underlie common hysteria). Or, lastly, the attack may revive the events which have become emphasized owing to their *coinciding* with a moment of special disposition to trauma.

There are also attacks, however, which appear to consist exclusively of motor phenomena and in which the phase of *attitudes passionnelles* is absent. If one can succeed in getting into *rapport* with the patient during an attack such as this of generalized clonic spasms or cataleptic rigidity, or during an *attaque de sommeil* [attack of sleep]—or if, better still, one can succeed in provoking the attack under hypnosis—one finds that here, too, there is an underlying memory of the psychical trauma or series of traumas, which usually comes to our notice in a hallucinatory phase.

Thus, a little girl suffered for years from attacks of general convulsions which could well be, and indeed were, regarded as epileptic. She was hypnotized with a view to a differential diagnosis, and promptly had one of her attacks. She was asked what she was seeing and replied 'The dog! the dog's coming!'; and in fact it turned out that she had had the first of her attacks after being chased by a savage dog. The success of the treatment confirmed the choice of diagnosis.

Again, an employee who had become a hysteric as a result of being ill-treated by his superior, suffered from attacks in which he collapsed and fell into a frenzy of rage, but without uttering a word or giving any sign of a hallucination. It was possible to provoke an attack under hypnosis, and the patient then revealed that he was living through the scene in which his employer had abused him in the street and hit him with a stick. A few days later the patient came back and complained of having had another attack of the same kind. On this occasion it turned out under hypnosis that he had been re-living the scene to which the actual onset of the illness was related: the scene in the law-court when he failed to obtain satisfaction for his maltreatment.

In all other respects, too, the memories which emerge, or can be aroused, in hysterical attacks correspond to the precipitating causes which we have found at the root of *chronic* hysterical symptoms. Like these latter causes, the memories underlying hysterical attacks relate to psychical traumas which have not been disposed of by abreaction or by associative thought-activity. Like them, they are, whether completely or in essential elements, out of reach of the memory of normal consciousness and are found to belong to the ideational content of hypnoid states of consciousness with restricted association. Finally, too, the therapeutic test can be applied to them. Our observations have often taught us that a memory of this kind which had hitherto provoked attacks, ceases to be able to do so after the process of reaction and associative correction have been applied to it under hypnosis.

The motor phenomena of hysterical attacks can be interpreted partly as universal forms of reaction appropriate to the affect accompanying the memory (such as kicking about and waving the arms and legs, which even young babies do), partly as a direct expression of these memories; but in part, like the hysterical stigmata[1] found among the chronic symptoms, they cannot be explained in this way.

Hysterical attacks, furthermore, appear in a specially interesting light if we bear in mind a theory that we have mentioned above, namely, that in hysteria groups of ideas originating in hypnoid states are present and that these are cut off from associative connection with the other ideas, but can be associated among themselves, and thus form the more or less highly organized rudiment of a second consciousness, a *condition seconde*. If this is so, a chronic hysterical symptom will correspond to the intrusion of this second state into the somatic innervation which is as a rule under the control of normal consciousness. A hysterical attack, on the other hand, is evidence of a higher organization of this second state. When the attack makes its first appearance, it indicates a moment at which this hypnoid consciousness has obtained control of the subject's whole existence—it points, that is, to an acute hysteria; when it occurs on subsequent occasions and contains a memory, it points to a return of that moment. Charcot has already

[1] ['The permanent symptoms of hysteria.' (Charcot, 1887, 255.) Stigmata are discussed by Breuer below, p. 244 f.]

suggested that hysterical attacks are a rudimentary form of a *condition seconde*. During the attack, control over the whole of the somatic innervation passes over to the hypnoid consciousness. Normal consciousness, as well-known observations show, is not always entirely repressed. It may even be aware of the motor phenomena of the attack, while the accompanying psychical events are outside its knowledge.

The typical course of a severe case of hysteria is, as we know, as follows. To begin with, an ideational content is formed during hypnoid states; when this has increased to a sufficient extent, it gains control, during a period of 'acute hysteria', of the somatic innervation and of the patient's whole existence, and creates chronic symptoms and attacks; after this it clears up, apart from certain residues. If the normal personality can regain control, what is left over from the hypnoid ideational content recurs in hysterical attacks and puts the subject back from time to time into similar states, which are themselves once more open to influence and susceptible to traumas. A state of equilibrium, as it were, may then be established between the two psychical groups which are combined in the same person: hysterical attacks and normal life proceed side by side without interfering with each other. An attack will occur spontaneously, just as memories do in normal people; it is, however, possible to provoke one, just as any memory can be aroused in accordance with the laws of association. It can be provoked either by stimulation of a hysterogenic zone[1] or by a new experience which sets it going owing to a similarity with the pathogenic experience. We hope to be able to show that these two kinds of determinant, though they appear to be so unlike, do not differ in essentials, but that in both a hyperaesthetic memory is touched on.

In other cases this equilibrium is very unstable. The attack makes its appearance as a manifestation of the residue of the hypnoid consciousness whenever the normal personality is exhausted and incapacitated. The possibility cannot be dismissed that here the attack may have been divested of its original meaning and may be recurring as a motor reaction without any content.

It must be left to further investigation to discover what it is

---

[1] [This is a term regularly used by Charcot, e.g. 1887, 85 ff.]

that determines whether a hysterical personality manifests itself in attacks, in chronic symptoms or in a mixture of the two.[1]

V

It will now be understood how it is that the psychotherapeutic procedure which we have described in these pages has a curative effect. *It brings to an end the operative force of the idea which was not abreacted in the first instance, by allowing its strangulated affect to find a way out through speech; and it subjects it to associative correction by introducing it into normal consciousness (under light hypnosis) or by removing it through the physician's suggestion, as is done in somnambulism accompanied by amnesia.*

In our opinion the therapeutic advantages of this procedure are considerable. It is of course true that we do not cure hysteria in so far as it is a matter of disposition. We can do nothing against the recurrence of hypnoid states. Moreover, during the productive stage of an acute hysteria our procedure cannot prevent the phenomena which have been so laboriously removed from being at once replaced by fresh ones. But once this acute stage is past, any residues which may be left in the form of chronic symptoms or attacks are often removed, and permanently so, by our method, because it is a radical one; in this respect it seems to us far superior in its efficacy to removal through direct suggestion, as it is practised to-day by psychotherapists.

If by uncovering the psychical mechanism of hysterical phenomena we have taken a step forward along the path first traced so successfully by Charcot with his explanation and artificial imitation of hystero-traumatic paralyses, we cannot conceal from ourselves that this has brought us nearer to an understanding only of the *mechanism* of hysterical symptoms and not of the internal causes of hysteria. We have done no more than touch upon the aetiology of hysteria and in fact have been able to throw light only on its acquired forms—on the bearing of accidental factors on the neurosis.

VIENNA, *December* 1892

---

[1] [A preliminary draft of this discussion on hysterical attacks, written in November, 1892, was published posthumously (Breuer and Freud, 1940). The subject was dealt with much later by Freud in a paper on hysterical attacks (1909*a*).]

II

CASE HISTORIES

(Breuer and Freud)

II

CASE HISTORIES

(Breuer and Freud)

CASE 1

Fräulein Anna O. (Breuer)

At the time of her falling ill (in 1880) Fräulein Anna O. was twenty-one years old. She may be regarded as having had a moderately severe neuropathic heredity, since some psychoses had occurred among her more distant relatives. Her parents were normal in this respect. She herself had hitherto been consistently healthy and had shown no signs of neurosis during her period of growth. She was markedly intelligent, with an astonishingly quick grasp of things and penetrating intuition. She possessed a powerful intellect which would have been capable of digesting solid mental pabulum and which stood in need of it—though without receiving it after she had left school. She had great poetic and imaginative gifts, which were under the control of a sharp and critical common sense. Owing to this latter quality she was *completely unsuggestible*; she was only influenced by arguments, never by mere assertions. Her will-power was energetic, tenacious and persistent; sometimes it reached the pitch of an obstinacy which only gave way out of kindness and regard for other people.

One of her essential character traits was sympathetic kindness. Even during her illness she herself was greatly assisted by being able to look after a number of poor, sick people, for she was thus able to satisfy a powerful instinct. Her states of feeling always tended to a slight exaggeration, alike of cheerfulness and gloom; hence she was sometimes subject to moods.[1] The element of sexuality was astonishingly undeveloped in her.[1] The patient, whose life became known to me to an extent to

[1] [Freud quoted this sentence (not quite verbatim) in a footnote to the first of his *Three Essays on the Theory of Sexuality* (1905*d*), *Standard Ed.*, **7**, 164 *n.*, and in Chapter II of his autobiography (1925 *d*).]

which one person's life is seldom known to another, had never been in love; and in all the enormous number of hallucinations which occurred during her illness that element of mental life never emerged.

This girl, who was bubbling over with intellectual vitality, led an extremely monotonous existence in her puritanically-minded family. She embellished her life in a manner which probably influenced her decisively in the direction of her illness, by indulging in systematic day-dreaming, which she described as her 'private theatre'. While everyone thought she was attending, she was living through fairy tales in her imagination; but she was always on the spot when she was spoken to, so that no one was aware of it. She pursued this activity almost continuously while she was engaged on her household duties, which she discharged unexceptionably. I shall presently have to describe the way in which this habitual day-dreaming while she was well passed over into illness without a break.

The course of the illness fell into several clearly separable phases:

(A) Latent incubation. From the middle of July, 1880, till about December 10. This phase of an illness is usually hidden from us; but in this case, owing to its peculiar character, it was completely accessible; and this in itself lends no small pathological interest to the history. I shall describe this phase presently.

(B) The manifest illness. A psychosis of a peculiar kind, paraphasia, a convergent squint, severe disturbances of vision, paralyses (in the form of contractures), complete in the right upper and both lower extremities, partial in the left upper extremity, paresis of the neck muscles. A gradual reduction of the contracture to the right-hand extremities. Some improvement, interrupted by a severe psychical trauma (the death of the patient's father) in April, after which there followed

(C) A period of persisting somnambulism, subsequently alternating with more normal states. A number of chronic symptoms persisted till December, 1881.

(D) Gradual cessation of the pathological states and symptoms up to June, 1882.

In July, 1880, the patient's father, of whom she was passionately fond, fell ill of a peripleuritic abscess which failed to clear up and to which he succumbed in April, 1881. During the first months of the illness Anna devoted her whole energy to nursing her father, and no one was much surprised when by degrees her own health greatly deteriorated. No one, perhaps not even the patient herself, knew what was happening to her; but eventually the state of weakness, anaemia and distaste for food became so bad that to her great sorrow she was no longer allowed to continue nursing the patient. The immediate cause of this was a very severe cough, on account of which I examined her for the first time. It was a typical *tussis nervosa*. She soon began to display a marked craving for rest during the afternoon, followed in the evening by a sleep-like state and afterwards a highly excited condition.

At the beginning of December a convergent squint appeared. An ophthalmic surgeon explained this (mistakenly) as being due to paresis of one abducens. On December 11 the patient took to her bed and remained there until April 1.

There developed in rapid succession a series of severe disturbances which were *apparently* quite new: left-sided occipital headache; convergent squint (diplopia), markedly increased by excitement; complaints that the walls of the room seemed to be falling over (affection of the obliquus); disturbances of vision which it was hard to analyse; paresis of the muscles of the front of the neck, so that finally the patient could only move her head by pressing it backwards between her raised shoulders and moving her whole back; contracture and anaesthesia of the right upper, and, after a time, of the right lower extremity. The latter was fully extended, adducted and rotated inwards. Later the same symptom appeared in the left lower extremity and finally in the left arm, of which, however, the fingers to some extent retained the power of movement. So, too, there was no complete rigidity in the shoulder-joints. The contracture reached its maximum in the muscles of the upper arms. In the same way, the region of the elbows turned out to be the most affected by anaesthesia when, at a later stage, it became possible to make a more careful test of this. At the beginning of the illness the anaesthesia could not be efficiently tested, owing to the patient's resistance arising from feelings of anxiety.

It was while the patient was in this condition that I undertook her treatment, and I at once recognized the seriousness of the psychical disturbance with which I had to deal. Two entirely distinct states of consciousness were present which alternated very frequently and without warning and which became more and more differentiated in the course of the illness. In one of these states she recognized her surroundings; she was melancholy and anxious, but relatively normal. In the other state she hallucinated and was 'naughty'—that is to say, she was abusive, used to throw the cushions at people, so far as the contractures at various times allowed, tore buttons off her bed-clothes and linen with those of her fingers which she could move, and so on. At this stage of her illness if something had been moved in the room or someone had entered or left it [during her other state of consciousness] she would complain of having 'lost' some time and would remark upon the gap in her train of conscious thoughts. Since those about her tried to deny this and to soothe her when she complained that she was going mad, she would, after throwing the pillows about, accuse people of doing things to her and leaving her in a muddle, etc.

These '*absences*' [1] had already been observed before she took to her bed; she used then to stop in the middle of a sentence, repeat her last words and after a short pause go on talking. These interruptions gradually increased till they reached the dimensions that have just been described; and during the climax of the illness, when the contractures had extended to the left side of her body, it was only for a short time during the day that she was to any degree normal. But the disturbances invaded even her moments of relatively clear consciousness. There were extremely rapid changes of mood leading to excessive but quite temporary high spirits, and at other times severe anxiety, stubborn opposition to every therapeutic effort and frightening hallucinations of black snakes, which was how she saw her hair, ribbons and similar things. At the same time she kept on telling herself not to be so silly: what she was seeing was really only her hair, etc. At moments when her mind was quite clear she would complain of the profound darkness in her head, of not being able to think, of becoming blind and deaf, of having two selves, a real one and an evil one which forced her to behave badly, and so on.

In the afternoons she would fall into a somnolent state which lasted till about an hour after sunset. She would then wake up

¹ [The French term.]

and complain that something was tormenting her—or rather, she would keep repeating in the impersonal form 'tormenting, tormenting'. For alongside of the development of the contractures there appeared a deep-going functional disorganization of her speech. It first became noticeable that she was at a loss to find words, and this difficulty gradually increased. Later she lost her command of grammar and syntax; she no longer conjugated verbs, and eventually she used only infinitives, for the most part incorrectly formed from weak past participles; and she omitted both the definite and indefinite article. In the process of time she became almost completely deprived of words. She put them together laboriously out of four or five languages and became almost unintelligible. When she tried to write (until her contractures entirely prevented her doing so) she employed the same jargon. For two weeks she became completely dumb and in spite of making great and continuous efforts to speak she was unable to say a syllable. And now for the first time the psychical mechanism of the disorder became clear. As I knew, she had felt very much offended over something and had determined not to speak about it. When I guessed this and obliged her to talk about it, the inhibition, which had made any other kind of utterance impossible as well, disappeared.

This change coincided with a return of the power of movement to the extremities of the left side of her body, in March, 1881. Her paraphasia receded; but thenceforward she spoke only in English—apparently, however, without knowing that she was doing so. She had disputes with her nurse who was, of course, unable to understand her. It was only some months later that I was able to convince her that she was talking English. Nevertheless, she herself could still understand the people about her who talked German. Only in moments of extreme anxiety did her power of speech desert her entirely, or else she would use a mixture of all sorts of languages. At times when she was at her very best and most free, she talked French and Italian. There was complete amnesia between these times and those at which she talked English. At this point, too, her squint began to diminish and made its appearance only at moments of great excitement. She was once again able to support her head. On the first of April she got up for the first time.

On the fifth of April her adored father died. During her

illness she had seen him very rarely and for short periods. This was the most severe psychical trauma that she could possibly have experienced. A violent outburst of excitement was succeeded by profound stupor which lasted about two days and from which she emerged in a greatly changed state. At first she was far quieter and her feelings of anxiety were much diminished. The contracture of her right arm and leg persisted as well as their anaesthesia, though this was not deep. There was a high degree of restriction of the field of vision: in a bunch of flowers which gave her much pleasure she could only see one flower at a time. She complained of not being able to recognize people. Normally, she said, she had been able to recognize faces without having to make any deliberate effort; now she was obliged to do laborious 'recognizing work' [1] and had to say to herself 'this person's nose is such-and-such, his hair is such-and-such, so he must be so-and-so'. All the people she saw seemed like wax figures without any connection with her. She found the presence of some of her close relatives very distressing and this negative attitude grew continually stronger. If someone whom she was ordinarily pleased to see came into the room, she would recognize him and would be aware of things for a short time, but would soon sink back into her own broodings and her visitor was blotted out. I was the only person whom she always recognized when I came in; so long as I was talking to her she was always in contact with things and lively, except for the sudden interruptions caused by one of her hallucinatory 'absences'.

She now spoke only English and could not understand what was said to her in German. Those about her were obliged to talk to her in English; even the nurse learned to make herself to some extent understood in this way. She was, however, able to read French and Italian. If she had to read one of these aloud, what she produced, with extraordinary fluency, was an admirable extempore English translation.

She began writing again, but in a peculiar fashion. She wrote with her left hand, the less stiff one, and she used Roman printed letters, copying the alphabet from her edition of Shakespeare.

She had eaten extremely little previously, but now she refused nourishment altogether. However, she allowed me to feed her,

[1] [In English in the original.]

so that she very soon began to take more food. But she never consented to eat bread. After her meal she invariably rinsed out her mouth and even did so if, for any reason, she had not eaten anything—which shows how absent-minded she was about such things.

Her somnolent states in the afternoon and her deep sleep after sunset persisted. If, after this, she had talked herself out (I shall have to explain what is meant by this later) she was clear in mind, calm and cheerful.

This comparatively tolerable state did not last long. Some ten days after her father's death a consultant was brought in, whom, like all strangers, she completely ignored while I demonstrated all her peculiarities to him. 'That's like an examination,' [1] she said, laughing, when I got her to read a French text aloud in English. The other physician intervened in the conversation and tried to attract her attention, but in vain. It was a genuine 'negative hallucination' of the kind which has since so often been produced experimentally. In the end he succeeded in breaking through it by blowing smoke in her face. She suddenly saw a stranger before her, rushed to the door to take away the key and fell unconscious to the ground. There followed a short fit of anger and then a severe attack of anxiety which I had great difficulty in calming down. Unluckily I had to leave Vienna that evening, and when I came back several days later I found the patient much worse. She had gone entirely without food the whole time, was full of anxiety and her hallucinatory *absences* were filled with terrifying figures, death's heads and skeletons. Since she acted these things through as though she was experiencing them and in part put them into words, the people around her became aware to a great extent of the content of these hallucinations.

The regular order of things was: the somnolent state in the afternoon, followed after sunset by the deep hypnosis for which she invented the technical name of 'clouds'. [2] If during this she was able to narrate the hallucinations she had had in the course of the day, she would wake up clear in mind, calm and cheerful. She would sit down to work and write or draw far into the night quite rationally. At about four she would go to bed. Next day the whole series of events would be repeated. It was a truly remarkable contrast: in the day-time the

<hr/>

¹ [In English in the original.]   ² [In English in the original.]

irresponsible patient pursued by hallucinations, and at night the girl with her mind completely clear.

In spite of her euphoria at night, her psychical condition deteriorated steadily. Strong suicidal impulses appeared which made it seem inadvisable for her to continue living on the third floor. Against her will, therefore, she was transferred to a country house in the neighbourhood of Vienna (on June 7, 1881). I had never threatened her with this removal from her home, which she regarded with horror, but she herself had, without saying so, expected and dreaded it. This event made it clear once more how much the affect of anxiety dominated her psychical disorder. Just as after her father's death a calmer condition had set in, so now, when what she feared had actually taken place, she once more became calmer. Nevertheless, the move was immediately followed by three days and nights completely without sleep or nourishment, by numerous attempts at suicide (though, so long as she was in a garden, these were not dangerous), by smashing windows and so on, and by hallucinations unaccompanied by *absences*—which she was able to distinguish easily from her other hallucinations. After this she grew quieter, let the nurse feed her and even took chloral at night.

Before continuing my account of the case, I must go back once more and describe one of its peculiarities which I have hitherto mentioned only in passing. I have already said that throughout the illness up to this point the patient fell into a somnolent state every afternoon and that after sunset this period passed into a deeper sleep—'clouds'. (It seems plausible to attribute this regular sequence of events merely to her experience while she was nursing her father, which she had had to do for several months. During the nights she had watched by the patient's bedside or had been awake anxiously listening till the morning; in the afternoons she had lain down for a short rest, as is the usual habit of nurses. This pattern of waking at night and sleeping in the afternoons seems to have been carried over into her own illness and to have persisted long after the sleep had been replaced by a hypnotic state.) After the deep sleep had lasted about an hour she grew restless, tossed to and fro and kept repeating 'tormenting, tormenting', with her eyes shut all the time. It was also noticed how, during her *absences* in day-time she was obviously creating some situation or episode

to which she gave a clue with a few muttered words. It happened then—to begin with accidentally but later intentionally
—that someone near her repeated one of these phrases of hers
while she was complaining about the 'tormenting'. She at once
joined in and began to paint some situation or tell some story,
hesitatingly at first and in her paraphasic jargon; but the longer
she went on the more fluent she became, till at last she was
speaking quite correct German. (This applies to the early period
before she began talking English only [p. 25].) The stories were
always sad and some of them very charming, in the style of
Hans Andersen's *Picture-book without Pictures*, and, indeed, they
were probably constructed on that model. As a rule their
starting-point or central situation was of a girl anxiously sitting
by a sick-bed. But she also built up her stories on quite other
topics.—A few moments after she had finished her narrative
she would wake up, obviously calmed down, or, as she called it,
'*gehäglich*'.[1] During the night she would again become restless,
and in the morning, after a couple of hours' sleep, she was
visibly involved in some other set of ideas.—If for any reason
she was unable to tell me the story during her evening hypnosis
she failed to calm down afterwards, and on the following day
she had to tell me *two* stories in order for this to happen.

The essential features of this phenomenon—the mounting
up and intensification of her *absences* into her auto-hypnosis in
the evening, the effect of the products of her imagination as
psychical stimuli and the easing and removal of her state of
stimulation when she gave utterance to them in her hypnosis
—remained constant throughout the whole eighteen months
during which she was under observation.

The stories naturally became still more tragic after her
father's death. It was not, however, until the deterioration of
her mental condition, which followed when her state of somnambulism was forcibly broken into in the way already described, that her evening narratives ceased to have the character
of more or less freely-created poetical compositions and changed
into a string of frightful and terrifying hallucinations. (It was
already possible to arrive at these from the patient's behaviour
during the day.) I have already [p. 27] described how completely her mind was relieved when, shaking with fear and

[1] [She used this made-up word instead of the regular German
'*behaglich*', meaning 'comfortable'.]

horror, she had reproduced these frightful images and given verbal utterance to them.

While she was in the country, when I was unable to pay her daily visits, the situation developed as follows. I used to visit her in the evening, when I knew I should find her in her hypnosis, and I then relieved her of the whole stock of imaginative products which she had accumulated since my last visit. It was essential that this should be effected completely if good results were to follow. When this was done she became perfectly calm, and next day she would be agreeable, easy to manage, industrious and even cheerful; but on the second day she would be increasingly moody, contrary and unpleasant, and this would become still more marked on the third day. When she was like this it was not always easy to get her to talk, even in her hypnosis. She aptly described this procedure, speaking seriously, as a 'talking cure', while she referred to it jokingly as 'chimney-sweeping'.[1] She knew that after she had given utterance to her hallucinations she would lose all her obstinacy and what she described as her 'energy'; and when, after some comparatively long interval, she was in a bad temper, she would refuse to talk, and I was obliged to overcome her unwillingness by urging and pleading and using devices such as repeating a formula with which she was in the habit of introducing her stories. But she would never begin to talk until she had satisfied herself of my identity by carefully feeling my hands. On those nights on which she had not been calmed by verbal utterance it was necessary to fall back upon chloral. I had tried it on a few earlier occasions, but I was obliged to give her 5 grammes, and sleep was preceded by a state of intoxication which lasted for some hours. When I was present this state was euphoric, but in my absence it was highly disagreeable and characterized by anxiety as well as excitement. (It may be remarked incidentally that this severe state of intoxication made no difference to her contractures.) I had been able to avoid the use of narcotics, since the verbal utterance of her hallucinations calmed her even though it might not induce sleep; but when she was in the country the nights on which she had not obtained hypnotic relief were so unbearable that in spite of everything it was necessary to have recourse

[1] [These two phrases are in English in the original.]

to chloral. But it became possible gradually to reduce the dose.

The persisting somnambulism did not return. But on the other hand the alternation between two states of consciousness persisted. She used to hallucinate in the middle of a conversation, run off, start climbing up a tree, etc. If one caught hold of her, she would very quickly take up her interrupted sentence without knowing anything about what had happened in the interval. All these hallucinations, however, came up and were reported on in her hypnosis.

Her condition improved on the whole. She took nourishment without difficulty and allowed the nurse to feed her; except that she asked for bread but rejected it the moment it touched her lips. The paralytic contracture of the leg diminished greatly. There was also an improvement in her power of judgement and she became much attached to my friend Dr. B., the physician who visited her. She derived much benefit from a Newfoundland dog which was given to her and of which she was passionately fond. On one occasion, though, her pet made an attack on a cat, and it was splendid to see the way in which the frail girl seized a whip in her left hand and beat off the huge beast with it to rescue his victim. Later, she looked after some poor, sick people, and this helped her greatly.

It was after I returned from a holiday trip which lasted several weeks that I received the most convincing evidence of the pathogenic and exciting effect brought about by the ideational complexes which were produced during her *absences*, or *condition seconde*, and of the fact that these complexes were disposed of by being given verbal expression during hypnosis. During this interval no 'talking cure' had been carried out, for it was impossible to persuade her to confide what she had to say to anyone but me—not even to Dr. B. to whom she had in other respects become devoted. I found her in a wretched moral state, inert, unamenable, ill-tempered, even malicious. It became plain from her evening stories that her imaginative and poetic vein was drying up. What she reported was more and more concerned with her hallucinations and, for instance, the things that had annoyed her during the past days. These were clothed in imaginative shape, but were merely formulated in stereotyped images rather than elaborated into poetic productions. But the situation only became tolerable after I had arranged for the patient to be brought back to Vienna for a week and evening after evening made her tell me three to five stories. When I had accomplished this, everything that had accumulated during the weeks of my absence had been worked off. It was only now that the former rhythm was re-established: on the day after her giving verbal utterance to her phantasies she was amiable and cheerful, on the second day she was more irritable and less agreeable and on the third positively 'nasty'. Her moral state was a function of the time that had elapsed since her last utterance. This was because every one of the spontaneous products of her imagination and every event which had been assimilated by the pathological part of her mind persisted as a psychical stimulus until it had been narrated in her hypnosis, after which it completely ceased to operate.

When, in the autumn, the patient returned to Vienna (though to a different house from the one in which she had fallen ill), her condition was bearable, both physically and mentally; for very few of her experiences—in fact only her more striking ones—were made into psychical stimuli in a pathological manner. I was hoping for a continuous and increasing improvement, provided that the permanent burdening of her mind with fresh stimuli could be prevented by her giving regular verbal expression to them. But to begin with I was disappointed. In December there was a marked deterioration of her psychical condition. She once more became excited, gloomy and irritable. She had no more 'really good days' even when it was impossible to detect anything that was remaining 'stuck' inside her. Towards the end of December, at Christmas time, she was particularly restless, and for a whole week in the evenings she told me nothing new but only the imaginative products which she had elaborated under the stress of great anxiety and emotion during the Christmas of 1880 [a year earlier]. When the scenes had been completed she was greatly relieved.

A year had now passed since she had been separated from her father and had taken to her bed, and from this time on her condition became clearer and was systematized in a very peculiar manner. Her alternating states of consciousness, which were characterized by the fact that, from morning onwards, her *absences* (that is to say, the emergence of her *condition seconde*) always became more frequent as the day advanced and took entire possession by the evening—these alternating states had differed from each other previously in that one (the first) was normal and the second alienated; now, however, they differed further in that in the first she lived, like the rest of us, in the winter of 1881–2, whereas in the second she lived in the winter of 1880–1, and had completely forgotten all the subsequent events. The one thing that nevertheless seemed to remain conscious most of the time was the fact that her father had died. She was carried back to the previous year with such intensity that in the new house she hallucinated her old room, so that when she wanted to go to the door she knocked up against the stove which stood in the same relation to the window as the door did in the old room. The change-over from one state to another occurred spontaneously but could also be very easily brought about by any sense-impression which vividly recalled the previous year. One had only to hold up an orange before her eyes (oranges were what she had chiefly lived on during the first part of her illness) in order to carry her over from the year 1882 to the year 1881. But this transfer into the past did not take place in a general or indefinite manner; she lived through the previous winter day by day. I should only have been able to *suspect* that this was happening, had it not been that every evening during the hypnosis she talked through whatever it was that had excited her on the same day in 1881, and had it not been that a private diary kept by her mother in 1881 confirmed beyond a doubt the occurrence of the under-lying events. This re-living of the previous year continued till the illness came to its final close in June, 1882.

It was interesting here, too, to observe the way in which these revived psychical stimuli belonging to her secondary state made their way over into her first, more normal one. It happened, for instance, that one morning the patient said to me laughingly that she had no idea what was the matter but she was angry with me. Thanks to the diary I knew what was happening; and, sure enough, this was gone through again in the evening hypnosis: I had annoyed the patient very much on the same evening in 1881. Or another time she told me there was some-thing the matter with her eyes; she was seeing colours wrong. She knew she was wearing a brown dress but she saw it as a blue one. We soon found that she could distinguish all the colours of the visual test-sheets correctly and clearly, and that the disturbance only related to the dress-material. The reason was that during the same period in 1881 she had been very busy with a dressing-gown for her father, which was made with the same material as her present dress, but was blue instead of brown. Incidentally, it was often to be seen that these emergent memories showed their effect in advance; the disturbance of her normal state would occur earlier on, and the memory would only gradually be awakened in her *condition seconde*.[1]

Her evening hypnosis was thus heavily burdened, for we had to talk off not only her contemporary imaginative products but also the events and 'vexations'[2] of 1881. (Fortunately I had already relieved her at the time of the imaginative products of that year.) But in addition to all this the work that had to be done by the patient and her physician was immensely increased by a third group of separate disturbances which had to be disposed of in the same manner. These were the psychical events involved in the period of incubation of the illness between July and December, 1880; it was they that had produced the whole of the hysterical phenomena, and when they were brought to verbal utterance the symptoms disappeared.

When this happened for the first time—when, as a result of an accidental and spontaneous utterance of this kind, during the evening hypnosis, a disturbance which had persisted for a considerable time vanished—I was greatly surprised. It was in the summer during a period of extreme heat, and the patient was suffering very badly from thirst; for, without being able to account for it in any way, she suddenly found it impossible to drink. She would take up the glass of water she longed for, but as soon as it touched her lips she would push it away like someone suffering from hydrophobia. As she did this, she was obviously in an *absence* for a couple of seconds. She lived only on fruit, such as melons, etc., so as to lessen her tormenting thirst. This had lasted for some six weeks, when one day during hypnosis she grumbled about her English lady-companion whom she did not care for, and went on to describe, with every sign of disgust, how she had once gone into that lady's room and how her little dog—horrid creature!—had drunk out of a glass there. The patient had said nothing, as she had wanted to be polite. After giving further energetic expression to the anger she had held back, she asked for something to

---

[1] [Cf. The similar phenomenon in the case of Frau Cäcilie, p. 70 *n*.]
[2] [In English in the original.]

drink, drank a large quantity of water without any difficulty and woke from her hypnosis with the glass at her lips; and thereupon the disturbance vanished, never to return. A number of extremely obstinate whims were similarly removed after she had described the experiences which had given rise to them. She took a great step forward when the first of her chronic symptoms disappeared in the same way—the contracture of her right leg, which, it is true, had already diminished a great deal. These findings—that in the case of this patient the hysterical phenomena disappeared as soon as the event which had given rise to them was reproduced in her hypnosis—made it possible to arrive at a therapeutic technical procedure which left nothing to be desired in its logical consistency and systematic application. Each individual symptom in this complicated case was taken separately in hand; all the occasions on which it had appeared were described in reverse order, starting before the time when the patient became bed-ridden and going back to the event which had led to its first appearance. When this had been described the symptom was permanently removed.

In this way her paralytic contractures and anaesthesias, disorders of vision and hearing of every sort, neuralgias, coughing, tremors, etc., and finally her disturbances of speech were 'talked away'. Amongst the disorders of vision, the following, for instance, were disposed of separately: the convergent squint with diplopia; deviation of both eyes to the right, so that when her hand reached out for something it always went to the left of the object; restriction of the visual field; central amblyopia; macropsia; seeing a death's head instead of her father; inability to read. Only a few scattered phenomena (such, for instance, as the extension of the paralytic contractures to the left side of her body) which had developed while she was confined to bed, were untouched by this process of analysis,[1] and it is probable, indeed, that they had in fact no immediate psychical cause [cf. below, pp. 44–5].

It turned out to be quite impracticable to shorten the work by trying to elicit in her memory straight away the first provoking cause of her symptoms. She was unable to find it, grew confused, and things proceeded even more slowly than if she was allowed quietly and steadily to follow back the thread of memories on which she had embarked. Since the latter method,

---

[1] [See footnote 2, p. 48.]

however, took too long in the evening hypnosis, owing to her being over-strained and distraught by 'talking out' the two other sets of experiences—and owing, too, to the reminiscences needing time before they could attain sufficient vividness—we evolved the following procedure. I used to visit her in the morning and hypnotize her. (Very simple methods of doing this were arrived at empirically.) I would next ask her to concentrate her thoughts on the symptom we were treating at the moment and to tell me the occasions on which it had appeared. The patient would proceed to describe in rapid succession and under brief headings the external events concerned and these I would jot down. During her subsequent evening hypnosis she would then, with the help of my notes, give me a fairly detailed account of these circumstances.

An example will show the exhaustive manner in which she accomplished this. It was our regular experience that the patient did not hear when she was spoken to. It was possible to differentiate this passing habit of not hearing as follows:

(*a*) Not hearing when someone came in, while her thoughts were abstracted. 108 separate detailed instances of this, mentioning the persons and circumstances, often with dates. First instance: not hearing her father come in.

(*b*) Not understanding when several people were talking. 27 instances. First instance: her father, once more, and an acquaintance.

(*c*) Not hearing when she was alone and directly addressed. 50 instances. Origin: her father having vainly asked her for some wine.

(*d*) Deafness brought on by being shaken (in a carriage, etc.). 15 instances. Origin: having been shaken angrily by her young brother when he caught her one night listening at the sick-room door.

(*e*) Deafness brought on by fright at a noise. 37 instances. Origin: a choking fit of her father's, caused by swallowing the wrong way.

(*f*) Deafness during deep *absence*. 12 instances.

(*g*) Deafness brought on by listening hard for a long time, so that when she was spoken to she failed to hear. 54 instances.

Of course all these episodes were to a great extent identical in so far as they could be traced back to states of abstraction or *absences* or to fright. But in the patient's memory they were so clearly differentiated, that if she happened to make a mistake in their sequence she would be obliged to correct herself and put them in the right order; if this was not done her report came to a standstill. The events she described were so lacking in interest and significance and were told in such detail that there could be no suspicion of their having been invented. Many of these incidents consisted of purely internal experiences and so could not be verified; others of them (or circumstances attending them) were within the recollection of people in her environment.

This example, too, exhibited a feature that was always observable when a symptom was being 'talked away': the particular symptom emerged with greater force while she was discussing it. Thus during the analysis of her not being able to hear she was so deaf that for part of the time I was obliged to communicate with her in writing.[1] The first provoking cause was habitually a fright of some kind, experienced while she was nursing her father—some oversight on her part, for instance.

The work of remembering was not always an easy matter and sometimes the patient had to make great efforts. On one occasion our whole progress was obstructed for some time because a recollection refused to emerge. It was a question of a particularly terrifying hallucination. While she was nursing her father she had seen him with a death's head. She and the people with her remembered that once, while she still appeared to be in good health, she had paid a visit to one of her relatives. She had opened the door and all at once fallen down unconscious. In order to get over the obstruction to our progress she visited the same place again and, on entering the room, again fell to the ground unconscious. During her subsequent evening hypnosis the obstacle was surmounted. As she came into the room, she had seen her pale face reflected in a mirror hanging opposite the door; but it was not herself that she saw but her father with a death's head.—We often noticed that her dread of a memory, as in the present instance, inhibited its emergence, and this had to be brought about forcibly by the patient or physician.

The following incident, among others, illustrates the high degree of logical consistency of her states. During this period,

---

[1] [This phenomenon is discussed at some length by Freud below (p. 296 f.), where he describes it as a symptom 'joining in the conversation'.]

as has already been explained, the patient was always in her *condition seconde*—that is, in the year 1881—at night. On one occasion she woke up during the night, declaring that she had been taken away from home once again, and became so seriously excited that the whole household was alarmed. The reason was simple. During the previous evening the talking cure had cleared up her disorder of vision, and this applied also to her *condition seconde*. Thus when she woke up in the night she found herself in a strange room, for her family had moved house in the spring of 1881. Disagreeable events of this kind were avoided by my always (at her request) shutting her eyes in the evening and giving her a suggestion that she would not be able to open them till I did so myself on the following morning. The disturbance was only repeated once, when the patient cried in a dream and opened her eyes on waking up from it.

Since this laborious analysis for her symptoms dealt with the summer months of 1880, which was the preparatory period of her illness, I obtained complete insight into the incubation and pathogenesis of this case of hysteria, and I will now describe them briefly.

In July, 1880, while he was in the country, her father fell seriously ill of a sub-pleural abscess. Anna shared the duties of nursing him with her mother. She once woke up during the night in great anxiety about the patient, who was in a high fever; and she was under the strain of expecting the arrival of a surgeon from Vienna who was to operate. Her mother had gone away for a short time and Anna was sitting at the bedside with her right arm over the back of her chair. She fell into a waking dream and saw a black snake coming towards the sick man from the wall to bite him. (It is most likely that there were in fact snakes in the field behind the house and that these had previously given the girl a fright; they would thus have provided the material for her hallucination.) She tried to keep the snake off, but it was as though she was paralysed. Her right arm, over the back of the chair, had gone to sleep and had become anaesthetic and paretic; and when she looked at it the fingers turned into little snakes with death's heads (the nails). (It seems probable that she had tried to use her paralysed right arm to drive off the snake and that its anaesthesia and paralysis had consequently become associated with the hallucination of the snake.) When the snake vanished, in her terror she tried to pray. But language failed her: she could find no tongue in which to speak, till at last she thought of some children's verses in English [1] and then found herself able to think and pray in that language. The whistle of the train that was bringing the doctor whom she expected broke the spell.

Next day, in the course of a game, she threw a quoit into some bushes; and when she went to pick it out, a bent branch revived her hallucination of the snake, and simultaneously her right arm became rigidly extended. Thenceforward the same thing invariably occurred whenever the hallucination was re-called by some object with a more or less snake-like appearance. This hallucination, however, as well as the contracture only appeared during the short *absences* which became more and more frequent from that night onwards. (The contracture did not become stabilized until December, when the patient broke down completely and took to her bed permanently.) As a result of some particular event which I cannot find recorded in my notes and which I no longer recall, the contracture of the right leg was added to that of the right arm.

Her tendency to auto-hypnotic *absences* was from now on established. On the morning after the night I have described, while she was waiting for the surgeon's arrival, she fell into such a fit of abstraction that he finally arrived in the room without her having heard his approach. Her persistent anxiety inter-fered with her eating and gradually led to intense feelings of nausea. Apart from this, indeed, each of her hysterical symp-toms arose during an affect. It is not quite certain whether in every case a momentary state of *absence* was involved, but this seems probable in view of the fact that in her waking state the patient was totally unaware of what had been going on.

Some of her symptoms, however, seem not to have emerged in her *absences* but merely in an affect during her waking life; but if so, they recurred in just the same way. Thus we were able to trace back all of her different disturbances of vision to different, more or less clearly determining causes. For in-stance, on one occasion, when she was sitting by her father's bedside with tears in her eyes, he suddenly asked her what time it was. She could not see clearly; she made a great effort, and brought her watch near to her eyes. The face of the watch now

[1] [In the 'Preliminary Communication' (pp. 4–5) what she thought of is described as a prayer. This, of course, involves no contradiction.]

seemed very big—thus accounting for her macropsia and con-vergent squint. Or again, she tried hard to suppress her tears so that the sick man should not see them.

A dispute, in the course of which she suppressed a rejoinder, caused a spasm of the glottis, and this was repeated on every similar occasion.

She lost the power of speech (*a*) as a result of fear, after her first hallucination at night, (*b*) after having suppressed a remark another time (by active inhibition), (*c*) after having been unjustly blamed for something and (*d*) on every analogous occasion (when she felt mortified). She began coughing for the first time when once, as she was sitting at her father's bedside, she heard the sound of dance music coming from a neighbour-ing house, felt a sudden wish to be there, and was overcome with self-reproaches. Thereafter, throughout the whole length of her illness she reacted to any markedly rhythmical music with a *tussis nervosa*.

I cannot feel much regret that the incompleteness of my notes makes it impossible for me to enumerate all the occasions on which her various hysterical symptoms appeared. She her-self told me them in every single case, with the one exception I have mentioned [p. 35, also below, pp. 44–5]; and, as I have already said, each symptom disappeared after she had described its first occurrence.

In this way, too, the whole illness was brought to a close. The patient herself had formed a strong determination that the whole treatment should be finished by the anniversary of the day on which she was moved into the country [June 7 (p. 28)]. At the beginning of June, accordingly, she entered into the 'talking cure' with the greatest energy. On the last day—by the help of re-arranging the room so as to resemble her father's sickroom—she reproduced the terrifying hallucination which I have described above and which constituted the root of her whole illness. During the original scene she had only been able to think and pray in English; but immediately after its repro-duction she was able to speak German. She was moreover free from the innumerable disturbances which she had previously exhibited.[1] After this she left Vienna and travelled for a while;

---

[1] [At this point (so Freud once told the present editor, with his finger on an open copy of the book) there is a hiatus in the text. What he had in mind and went on to describe was the occurrence which marked the

but it was a considerable time before she regained her mental balance entirely. Since then she has enjoyed complete health.

Although I have suppressed a large number of quite interesting details, this case history of Anna O. has grown bulkier than would seem to be required for a hysterical illness that was not in itself of an unusual character. It was, however, impossible to describe the case without entering into details, and its features seem to me of sufficient importance to excuse this extensive report. In just the same way, the eggs of the echinoderm are important in embryology, not because the sea-urchin is a particularly interesting animal but because the protoplasm of its eggs is transparent and because what we observe in them thus throws light on the probable course of events in eggs whose protoplasm is opaque.[1] The interest of the present case seems to me above all to reside in the extreme clarity and intelligibility of its pathogenesis.

There were two psychical characteristics present in the girl while she was still completely healthy which acted as predisposing causes for her subsequent hysterical illness:

(1) Her monotonous family life and the absence of adequate intellectual occupation left her with an unemployed surplus of mental liveliness and energy, and this found an outlet in the constant activity of her imagination.

(2) This led to a habit of day-dreaming (her 'private theatre'), which laid the foundations for a dissociation of her mental personality. Nevertheless a dissociation of this degree is still within the bounds of normality. Reveries and reflections

end of Anna O.'s treatment. He made short allusions to it at the beginning of his 'History of the Psycho-Analytic Movement' (1914*d*), where he spoke of it as, from Breuer's point of view, an 'untoward event', and in Chapter II of his *Autobiographical Study* (1925*d*). The whole story is told by Ernest Jones in his life of Freud (1953, **1**, 246 ff.), and it is enough to say here that, when the treatment had apparently reached a successful end, the patient suddenly made manifest to Breuer the presence of a strong unanalysed positive transference of an unmistakably sexual nature. It was this occurrence, Freud believed, that caused Breuer to hold back the publication of the case history for so many years and that led ultimately to his abandonment of all further collaboration in Freud's researches.]

[1] [This same analogy was similarly used by Freud many years later (Freud, 1913*h*, *Standard Ed.*, **13**, 193).]

during a more or less mechanical occupation do not in themselves imply a pathological splitting of consciousness, since if they are interrupted—if, for instance, the subject is spoken to—the normal unity of consciousness is restored; nor, presumably, is any amnesia present. In the case of Anna O., however, this habit prepared the ground upon which the affect of anxiety and dread was able to establish itself in the way I have described, when once that affect had transformed the patient's habitual day-dreaming into a hallucinatory *absence*. It is remarkable how completely the earliest manifestation of her illness in its beginnings already exhibited its main characteristics, which afterwards remained unchanged for almost two years. These comprised the existence of a second state of consciousness which first emerged as a temporary *absence* and later became organized into a '*double conscience*'; an inhibition of speech, determined by the affect of anxiety, which found a chance discharge in the English verses; later on, paraphasia and loss of her mother-tongue, which was replaced by excellent English; and lastly the accidental paralysis of her right arm, due to pressure, which later developed into a contractural paresis and anaesthesia on her right side. The mechanism by which this latter affection came into being agreed entirely with Charcot's theory of traumatic hysteria—a slight trauma occurring during a state of hypnosis.

But whereas the paralysis experimentally provoked by Charcot in his patients became stabilized immediately, and whereas the paralysis caused in sufferers from traumatic neuroses by a severe traumatic shock sets in at once, the nervous system of this girl put up a successful resistance for four months. Her contracture, as well as the other disturbances which accompanied it, set in only during the short *absences* in her *condition seconde* and left her during her normal state in full control of her body and possession of her senses; so that nothing was noticed either by herself or by those around her, though it is true that the attention of the latter was centred upon the patient's sick father and was consequently diverted from her.

Since, however, her *absences* with their total amnesia and accompanying hysterical phenomena grew more and more frequent from the time of her first hallucinatory auto-hypnosis, the opportunities multiplied for the formation of new symptoms of the same kind, and those that had already been formed became more strongly entrenched by frequent repetition. In addition to this, it gradually came about that any sudden distressing affect would have the same result as an *absence* (though, indeed, it is possible that such affects actually *caused* a temporary *absence* in every case); chance coincidences set up pathological associations and sensory or motor disturbances, which thenceforward appeared along with the affect. But hitherto this only occurred for fleeting moments. Before the patient took permanently to her bed she had already developed the whole assemblage of hysterical phenomena, without anyone knowing it. It was only after the patient had broken down completely owing to exhaustion brought about by lack of nourishment, insomnia and constant anxiety, and only after she had begun to pass more time in her *condition seconde* than in her normal state, that the hysterical phenomena extended to the latter as well and changed from intermittent acute symptoms into chronic ones.

The question now arises how far the patient's statements are to be trusted and whether the occasions and mode of origin of the phenomena were really as she represented them. So far as the more important and fundamental events are concerned, the trustworthiness of her account seems to me to be beyond question. As regards the symptoms disappearing after being 'talked away', I cannot use this as evidence; it may very well be explained by suggestion. But I always found the patient entirely truthful and trustworthy. The things she told me were intimately bound up with what was most sacred to her. Whatever could be checked by other people was fully confirmed. Even the most highly gifted girl would be incapable of concocting a tissue of data with such a degree of internal consistency as was exhibited in the history of this case. It cannot be disputed, however, that precisely her consistency may have led her (in perfectly good faith) to assign to some of her symptoms a precipitating cause which they did not in fact possess. But this suspicion, too, I consider unjustified. The very insignificance of so many of those causes, the irrational character of so many of the connections involved, argue in favour of their reality. The patient could not understand how it was that dance music made her cough; such a construction is too meaningless to have been deliberate. (It seemed very likely to me, incidentally, that each of her twinges of conscience brought on one of her regular spasms of the glottis and that the motor impulses which she felt—for she was very fond of dancing—transformed the spasm into a *tussis nervosa*.) Accordingly, in my view the patient's statements were entirely trustworthy and corresponded to the facts.

And now we must consider how far it is justifiable to suppose that hysteria is produced in an analogous way in other patients, and that the process is similar where no such clearly distinct *condition seconde* has become organized. I may advance in support of this view the fact that in the present case, too, the story of the development of the illness would have remained completely unknown alike to the patient and the physician if it had not been for her peculiarity of remembering things in hypnosis, as I have described, and of relating what she remembered. While she was in her waking state she knew nothing of all this. Thus it is impossible to arrive at what is happening in other cases from an examination of the patients while in a waking state, for with the best will in the world they can give one no information. And I have already pointed out how little those surrounding the present patient were able to observe of what was going on. Accordingly, it would only be possible to discover the state of affairs in other patients by means of some such procedure as was provided in the case of Anna O. by her auto-hypnoses. Provisionally we can only express the view that trains of events similar to those here described occur more commonly than our ignorance of the pathogenic mechanism concerned has led us to suppose.

When the patient had become confined to her bed, and her consciousness was constantly oscillating between her normal and her 'secondary' state, the whole host of hysterical symptoms, which had arisen separately and had hitherto been latent, became manifest, as we have already seen, as chronic symptoms. There was now added to these a new group of phenomena which seemed to have had a different origin: the paralytic contractures of her left extremities and the paresis of the muscles raising her head. I distinguish them from the other phenomena because when once they had disappeared they never returned, even in the briefest or mildest form or during the concluding and recuperative phase, when all the other symptoms became active again after having been in abeyance for some time. In the same way, they never came up in the hypnotic analyses and were not traced back to emotional or imaginative sources. I am therefore inclined to think that their appearance was not due to the same psychical process as was that of the other symptoms, but is to be attributed to a secondary extension of that unknown condition which constitutes the somatic foundation of hysterical phenomena.

Throughout the entire illness her two states of consciousness persisted side by side: the primary one in which she was quite normal psychically, and the secondary one which may well be likened to a dream in view of its wealth of imaginative products and hallucinations, its large gaps of memory and the lack of inhibition and control in its associations. In this secondary state the patient was in a condition of alienation. The fact that the patient's mental condition was entirely dependent on the intrusion of this secondary state into the normal one seems to throw considerable light on at least one class of hysterical psychosis. Every one of her hypnoses in the evening afforded evidence that the patient was entirely clear and well-ordered in her mind and normal as regards her feeling and volition so long as none of the products of her secondary state was acting as a stimulus 'in the unconscious'.[1] The extremely marked psychosis which appeared whenever there was any considerable interval in this unburdening process showed the degree to which those products influenced the psychical events of her 'normal' state. It is hard to avoid expressing the situation by saying that the patient was split into two personalities of which one was mentally normal and the other insane. The sharp division between the two states in the present patient only exhibits more clearly, in my opinion, what has given rise to a

---

[1] [This seems to be the first published occurrence of the term *'das Unbewusste'* ('the unconscious') in what was to be its psycho-analytic sense. It had, of course, often been used previously by other writers, particularly by philosophers (e.g. Hartmann, 1869). The fact that Breuer puts it in quotation marks may possibly indicate that he is attributing it to Freud. The term is used by Freud himself below, e.g. on p. 76 *n.* The adjectival form *'unbewusst'* ('unconscious') had been used some years earlier in an unpublished draft drawn up in November, 1892, jointly by Breuer and Freud (Freud, 1940*d*). Freud had used the term *'le sub-conscient'* in a French paper on motor paralyses (1893*c*) and uses *'unterbewusst'* ('subconscious') in the present work (p. 69 *n.*), as does Breuer very much more frequently (e.g. p. 222). Later, of course, Freud objected to the employment of this latter term. (Cf., for instance, the end of Section I of his paper on 'The Unconscious', 1915*e*.)]

number of unexplained problems in many other hysterical patients. It was especially noticeable in Anna O. how much the products of her 'bad self', as she herself called it, affected her moral habit of mind. If these products had not been continually disposed of, we should have been faced by a hysteric of the malicious type—refractory, lazy, disagreeable and ill-natured; but, as it was, after the removal of those stimuli her true character, which was the opposite of all these, always reappeared at once.

Nevertheless, though her two states were thus sharply separated, not only did the secondary state intrude into the first one, but—and this was at all events frequently true, and even when she was in a very bad condition—a clear-sighted and calm observer sat, as she put it, in a corner of her brain and looked on at all the mad business. This persistence of clear thinking while the psychosis was actually going on found expression in a very curious way. At a time when, after the hysterical phenomena had ceased, the patient was passing through a temporary depression, she brought up a number of childish fears and self-reproaches, and among them the idea that she had not been ill at all and that the whole business had been simulated. Similar observations, as we know, have frequently been made. When a disorder of this kind has cleared up and the two states of consciousness have once more become merged into one, the patients, looking back to the past, see themselves as the single undivided personality which was aware of all the nonsense; they think they could have prevented it if they had wanted to, and thus they feel as though they had done all the mischief deliberately.—It should be added that this normal thinking which persisted during the secondary state must have fluctuated enormously in its amount and must very often have been completely absent.

I have already described the astonishing fact that from beginning to end of the illness all the stimuli arising from the secondary state, together with their consequences, were permanently removed by being given verbal utterance in hypnosis, and I have only to add an assurance that this was not an invention of mine which I imposed on the patient by suggestion. It took me completely by surprise, and not until symptoms had been got rid of in this way in a whole series of instances did I develop a therapeutic technique out of it.

The final cure of the hysteria deserves a few more words. It was accompanied, as I have already said, by considerable disturbances and a deterioration in the patient's mental condition. I had a very strong impression that the numerous products of her secondary state which had been quiescent were now forcing their way into consciousness; and though in the first instance they were being remembered only in her secondary state, they were nevertheless burdening and disturbing her normal one. It remains to be seen whether it may not be that the same origin is to be traced in other cases in which a chronic hysteria terminates in a psychosis.[1]

[1] [A very full summary and discussion of this case history occupies the greater part of the first of Freud's *Five Lectures* (1910a).]

CASE 2

FRAU EMMY VON N., AGE 40, FROM LIVONIA (Freud)

ON May 1, 1889,[1] I took on the case of a lady of about forty
years of age, whose symptoms and personality interested me
so greatly that I devoted a large part of my time to her and
determined to do all I could for her recovery. She was a
hysteric and could be put into a state of somnambulism with
the greatest ease; and when I became aware of this I decided
that I would make use of Breuer's technique of investigation
under hypnosis, which I had come to know from the account he
had given me of the successful treatment of his first patient.
This was my first attempt at handling that therapeutic method
[pp. 105 *n.* and 284]. I was still far from having mastered it; in
fact I did not carry the analysis [2] of the symptoms far enough,
nor pursue it systematically enough. I shall perhaps be able
best to give a picture of the patient's condition and my medical
procedure by reproducing the notes which I made each evening
during the first three weeks of the treatment. Wherever later
experience has brought me a better understanding, I shall
embody it in footnotes and interpolated comments.

May 1, 1889.—This lady, when I first saw her, was lying on a
sofa with her head resting on a leather cushion. She still looked
young and had finely-cut features, full of character. Her face
bore a strained and painful expression, her eyelids were drawn
together and her eyes cast down; there was a heavy frown on
her forehead and the naso-labial folds were deep. She spoke in
a low voice as though with difficulty and her speech was

[1] [The chronology of this case history is self-contradictory as it stands
and there is a distinct possibility that the treatment began in 1888, not
in 1889. The dates which are given in all the German editions have
been retained in the present translation, but they are evidently in need
of correction. The question is fully discussed in Appendix A (p. 307).]

[2] [Freud had already used the term 'analysis' (as well as 'psychical
analysis', 'psychological analysis' and 'hypnotic analysis') in his first
paper on 'The Neuro-Psychoses of Defence' (1894*a*). He only later
introduced the word 'psycho-analysis' in a paper on the aetiology of
the neuroses, written in French (1896*a*).]

48

from time to time subject to spastic interruptions amounting to a stammer. She kept her fingers, which exhibited a ceaseless agitation resembling athetosis, tightly clasped together. There were frequent convulsive *tic*-like movements of her face and the muscles of her neck, during which some of them, especially the right sterno-cleido-mastoid, stood out prominently. Furthermore she frequently interrupted her remarks by producing a curious 'clacking' sound from her mouth which defies imitation.[1]

What she told me was perfectly coherent and revealed an unusual degree of education and intelligence. This made it seem all the more strange when every two or three minutes she suddenly broke off, contorted her face into an expression of horror and disgust, stretched out her hand towards me, spreading and crooking her fingers, and exclaimed, in a changed voice, charged with anxiety: 'Keep still!—Don't say anything! —Don't touch me!' She was probably under the influence of some recurrent hallucination of a horrifying kind and was keeping the intruding material at bay with this formula.[2] These interpolations came to an end with equal suddenness and the patient took up what she had been saying, without pursuing her momentary excitement any further, and without explaining or apologizing for her behaviour—probably, therefore, without herself having noticed the interpolation.[3]

I learned what follows of her circumstances. Her family came from Central Germany, but had been settled for two generations in the Baltic Provinces of Russia, where it possessed large estates. She was one of fourteen children, of which she herself is the thirteenth. Only four of them survive. She was brought up carefully, but under strict discipline by an over-energetic and severe mother. When she was twenty-three she

---

[1] This 'clacking' was made up of a number of sounds. Colleagues of mine with sporting experience told me, on hearing it, that its final notes resembled the call of a capercaillie—[according to Fisher (1955) 'a ticking ending with a pop and a hiss'].

[2] These words did in fact represent a protective formula, and this will be explained later on. Since then I have come across similar protective formulas in a melancholic woman who endeavoured by their means to control her tormenting thoughts—wishes that something bad might happen to her husband and her mother, blasphemies, etc.

[3] What we had here was a hysterical delirium which alternated with normal consciousness, just as a true *tic* intrudes into a voluntary movement without interfering with it and without being mixed up with it.

married an extremely gifted and able man who had made a high position for himself as an industrialist on a large scale, but was much older than she was. After a short marriage he died of a stroke. To this event, together with the task of bringing up her two daughters, now sixteen and fourteen years old, who were often ailing and suffered from nervous troubles, she attributed her own illness. Since her husband's death, fourteen years ago, she had been constantly ill with varying degrees of severity. Four years ago her condition was temporarily improved by a course of massage combined with electric baths. Apart from this, all her efforts to regain her health have been unsuccessful. She has travelled a great deal and has many lively interests. She lives at present in a country seat on the Baltic near a large town.[1] For several months she has once more been very ill, suffering from depression and insomnia, and tormented with pains; she went to Abbazia [2] in the vain hope of improvement, and for the last six weeks has been in Vienna, up till now in the care of a physician of outstanding merit.

I suggested that she should separate from the two girls, who had their governess, and go into a nursing home, where I could see her every day. This she agreed to without raising the slightest objection.

On the evening of *May 2* I visited her in the nursing home. I noticed that she started violently whenever the door opened unexpectedly. I therefore arranged that the nurses and the house physicians, when they visited her, should give a loud knock at her door and not enter till she had told them to come in. But even so, she still made a grimace and gave a jump every time anyone entered.

Her chief complaint to-day was of sensations of cold and pain in her left leg which proceeded from her back above the iliac crest. I ordered her to be given warm baths and I shall massage her whole body twice a day.

She is an excellent subject for hypnotism. I had only to hold up a finger in front of her and order her to go to sleep, and she sank back with a dazed and confused look. I suggested that she

---

[1] [This is referred to later on as 'D——'. There is reason to believe that, in order to disguise his patient's identity, Freud had transferred her home from quite another part of Europe.]

[2] [The at that time Austrian resort on the Adriatic.]

should sleep well, that all her symptoms should get better, and so on. She heard all this with closed eyes but with unmistakably concentrated attention; and her features gradually relaxed and took on a peaceful appearance. After this first hypnosis she retained a dim memory of my words; but already at the second there was complete somnambulism (with amnesia). I had warned her that I proposed to hypnotize her, to which she raised no difficulty. She has not previously been hypnotized, but it is safe to suppose that she has read about hypnotism, though I cannot tell what notions she may have about the hypnotic state.[1]

This treatment by warm baths, massage twice a day and hypnotic suggestion was continued for the next few days. She slept well, got visibly better, and passed most of the day lying quietly in bed. She was not forbidden to see her children, to read, or to deal with her correspondence.

May 8, morning.—She entertained me, in an apparently quite normal state, with gruesome stories about animals. She had read in the *Frankfurter Zeitung*, which lay on the table in front of her, a story of how an apprentice had tied up a boy and put a white mouse into his mouth. The boy had died of fright. Dr. K. had told her that he had sent a whole case of white rats to Tiflis. As she told me this she demonstrated every sign of horror. She clenched and unclenched her hand several times. 'Keep still!—Don't say anything!—Don't touch me!—Supposing a creature like that was in the bed!' (She shuddered.) 'Only think, when it's unpacked! There's a dead rat in among them— one that's been gn-aw-aw-ed at!'

During the hypnosis I tried to disperse these animal hallucinations. While she was asleep I picked up the *Frankfurter Zeitung*. I found the anecdote about the boy being maltreated,

[1] Every time she woke from hypnosis she looked about her for a moment in a confused way, let her eyes fall on me, seemed to have come to her senses, put on her glasses, which she took off before going to sleep, and then became quite lively and on the spot. Although in the course of the treatment (which lasted for seven weeks in this first year and eight in the second) we discussed every sort of subject, and although I put her to sleep twice almost every day, she never made any comment to me about the hypnosis or asked me a single question about it; and in her waking state she seemed, so far as possible, to ignore the fact that she was undergoing hypnotic treatment.

but without any reference to mice or rats. So she had introduced these from her delirium while she was reading. (I told her in the evening of our conversation about the white mice. She knew nothing of it, was very much astonished and laughed heartily.[1])

During the afternoon she had what she called a 'neck-cramp',[2] which, however, as she said, 'only lasted a short time—a couple of hours'.

Evening.—I requested her, under hypnosis, to talk, which, after some effort, she succeeded in doing. She spoke softly and reflected for a moment each time before answering. Her expression altered according to the subject of her remarks, and grew calm as soon as my suggestion had put an end to the impression made upon her by what she was saying. I asked her why it was that she was so easily frightened, and she answered: 'It has to do with memories of my earliest youth.' 'When?' 'First when I was five years old and my brothers and sisters often threw dead animals at me. That was when I had my first fainting fit and spasms. But my aunt said it was disgraceful and that I ought not to have attacks like that, and so they stopped. Then I was frightened again when I was seven and I unexpectedly saw my sister in her coffin; and again when I was eight and my brother terrified me so often by dressing up in sheets like a ghost; and again when I was nine and I saw my aunt in her coffin and her jaw suddenly dropped.'

This series of traumatic precipitating causes which she produced in answer to my question why she was so liable to fright was clearly ready to hand in her memory. She could not have collected these episodes from different periods of her childhood so quickly during the short interval which elapsed between

---

[1] A sudden interpolation like this of a delirium into a waking state was not uncommon with her and was often repeated later in my presence. She used to complain that in conversation she often gave the most absurd answers, so that people did not understand her. On the occasion when I first visited her I asked her how old she was and she answered quite seriously: 'I am a woman dating from last century.' Some weeks later she explained to me she had been thinking at the time in her delirium of a beautiful old cupboard which, as a connoisseur of old furniture, she had bought in the course of her travels. It was to this cupboard that her answer had referred when my question about her age raised the topic of dates.

[2] A species of migraine. [See p. 71 n.]

my question and her answer. At the end of each separate story she twitched all over and took on a look of fear and horror. At the end of the last one she opened her mouth wide and panted for breath. The words in which she described the terrifying subject-matter of her experience were pronounced with difficulty and between gasps. Afterwards her features became peaceful.

In reply to a question she told me that while she was describing these scenes she saw them before her, in a plastic form and in their natural colours. She said that in general she thought of these experiences very often and had done so in the last few days. Whenever this happened she saw these scenes with all the vividness of reality.[1] I now understand why she entertains me so often with animal scenes and pictures of corpses. My therapy consists in wiping away these pictures, so that she is no longer able to see them before her. To give support to my suggestion I stroked her several times over the eyes.

May 9, [morning].[2]—Without my having given her any further suggestion, she had slept well. But she had gastric pains in the morning. They came on yesterday in the garden where she stayed out too long with her children. She agreed to my limiting the children's visits to two and a half hours. A few days ago she had reproached herself for leaving the children by themselves. I found her in a somewhat excited state to-day; her forehead was lined, her speech was halting and she made her clacking noises. While she was being massaged she told me only that the children's governess had brought her an ethnological atlas and that some pictures in it of American Indians dressed up as animals had given her a great shock. 'Only think, if they came to life!' (She shuddered.)

Under hypnosis I asked why she had been so much frightened by these pictures, since she was no longer afraid of animals. She said they had reminded her of visions she had had (when she was nineteen) at the time of her brother's death. (I shall hold over enquiring into this memory until later.) I then asked

---

[1] Many other hysterical patients have reported to us that they have memories of this kind in vivid visual pictures and that this applied especially to their pathogenic memories.

[2] [All the German editions read 'evening', which in view of what follows seems certainly to be a mistake.]

her whether she had always spoken with a stammer and how long she had had her *tic* (the peculiar clacking sound).[1] Her stammering, she said, had come on while she was ill; she had had the *tic* for the last five years, ever since a time when she was sitting by the bedside of her younger daughter who was very ill, and had wanted to keep absolutely *quiet*. I tried to reduce the importance of this memory, by pointing out that after all nothing had happened to her daughter, and so on. The thing came on, she said, whenever she was apprehensive or frightened. I instructed her not to be frightened of the pictures of the Red Indians but to laugh heartily at them and even to draw my attention to them. And this did in fact happen after she had woken up: she looked at the book, asked whether I had seen it, opened it at the page and laughed out loud at the grotesque figures, without a trace of fear and without any strain in her features. Dr. Breuer came in suddenly with the house-physician to visit her. She was frightened and began to make her clacking noise, so that they soon left us. She explained that she was so much agitated because she was unpleasantly affected by the fact that the house-physician came in every time as well.

I had also got rid of her gastric pains during the hypnosis by stroking her, and I told her that though she would expect the pain to return after her midday meal it would not do so.

Evening.—For the first time she was cheerful and talkative and gave evidence of a sense of humour that I should not have expected in such a serious woman; and, among other things, in the strong feeling that she was better, she made fun of her treatment by my medical predecessor. She had long intended, she said, to give up that treatment but had not been able to find the right method of doing so till a chance remark made by Dr. Breuer, when he visited her once, showed her a way out. When I seemed to be surprised at this, she grew frightened and began to blame herself very severely for having been indiscreet. But I was able, it seemed, to re-assure her.—She had had no gastric pains, though she had expected them.

Under hypnosis I asked her to tell me further experiences which had given her a lasting fright. She produced a second series of this kind, dating from her later youth, with as much promptitude as the first series and she assured me once more

[1] I had already asked her this question about the *tic* during her waking state, and she had replied: 'I don't know; oh, a very long time.'

that all these scenes appeared before her often, vividly and in colours. One of them was of how she saw a female cousin taken off to an insane asylum (when she was fifteen). She tried to call for help but was unable to, and lost her power of speech till the evening of the same day. Since she talked so often about asylums in her waking state, I interrupted her and asked on what other occasions she had been concerned with insanity. She told me that her mother had herself been in an asylum for some time. They had once had a maid-servant one of whose previous mistresses had spent a long time in an asylum and who used to tell her horrifying stories of how the patients were tied to chairs, beaten, and so on. As she told me this she clenched her hands in horror; she saw all this before her eyes. I endeavoured to correct her ideas about insane asylums, and assured her that she would be able to hear about institutions of this kind without referring them to herself. At this, her features relaxed.

She continued her list of terrifying memories. One, at fifteen, of how she found her mother, who had had a stroke, lying on the floor (her mother lived for another four years); again, at nineteen, how she came home one day and found her mother dead, with a distorted face. I naturally had considerable difficulty in mitigating these memories. After a rather lengthy explanation, I assured her that this picture, too, would only appear to her again indistinctly and without strength.—Another memory was how, at nineteen, she lifted up a stone and found a toad under it, which made her lose her power of speech for hours afterwards.[1]

During this hypnosis I convinced myself that she knew everything that happened in the last hypnosis, whereas in waking life she knows nothing of it.

May 10, morning.—For the first time to-day she was given a bran bath instead of her usual warm bath. I found her looking cross and with a pinched face, with her hands wrapped in a shawl. She complained of cold and pains. When I asked her what was the matter, she told me that the bath had been uncomfortably short to sit in and had brought on pains. During the massage she started by saying that she still felt badly about having given Dr. Breuer away yesterday. I pacified her with a

[1] A special kind of symbolism must, no doubt, have lain behind the toad, but I unfortunately neglected to enquire into it.

white lie and said that I had known about it all along, where-upon her agitation (clacking, grimaces) ceased. So each time, even while I am massaging her, my influence has already begun to affect her; she grows quieter and clearer in the head, and even without questioning under hypnosis can discover the cause of her ill-humour on that day. Nor is her conversation during the massage so aimless as would appear. On the contrary, it contains a fairly complete reproduction of the memories and new impressions which have affected her since our last talk, and it often leads on, in a quite unexpected way, to pathogenic reminiscences of which she unburdens herself without being asked to. It is as though she had adopted my procedure and was making use of our conversation, apparently unconstrained and guided by chance, as a supplement to her hypnosis.[1] For instance, to-day she began talking about her family, and in a very roundabout way got on to the subject of a cousin. He was rather queer in the head and his parents had all his teeth pulled out at one sitting. She accompanied the story with horrified looks and kept repeating her protective formula ('Keep still!—Don't say anything!—Don't touch me!'). After this her face smoothed out and she became cheerful. Thus, her behaviour in waking life is directed by the experiences she has had during her somnambulism, in spite of her believing, while she is awake, that she knows nothing about them.

Under hypnosis I repeated my question as to what it was that had made her upset and I got the same answers but in the reverse order: (1) her indiscreet talk yesterday, and (2) her pains caused by her being so uncomfortable in the bath.—I asked her to-day the meaning of her phrase 'Keep still!', etc. She explained that when she had frightening thoughts she was afraid of their being interrupted in their course, because then everything would get confused and things would be even worse. The 'Keep still!' related to the fact that the animal shapes which appeared to her when she was in a bad state started moving and began to attack her if anyone made a movement in her presence. The final injunction 'Don't touch me!' was derived from the following experiences. She told me how, when her brother had been so ill from taking a lot of morphine—she was nineteen at the time—he used often to seize hold of her; and

---

[1] [This is perhaps the earliest appearance of what later became the method of free association.]

how, another time, an acquaintance had suddenly gone mad in the house and had caught her by the arm; (there was a third, similar instance, which she did not remember exactly;) and lastly, how, when she was twenty-eight and her daughter was very ill, the child had caught hold of her so forcibly in its delirium that she was almost choked. Though these four instances were so widely separated in time, she told me them in a single sentence and in such rapid succession that they might have been a single episode in four acts. Incidentally, all the accounts she gave of traumas arranged like these in groups began with a 'how', the component traumas being separated by an 'and'. Since I noticed that the protective formula was designed to safeguard her against a recurrence of such experiences, I removed this fear by suggestion, and in fact I never heard the formula from her again.

Evening.—I found her very cheerful. She told me, with a laugh, that she had been frightened by a small dog which barked at her in the garden. Her face was a little bit drawn, however, and there was some internal agitation which did not disappear until she had asked me whether I was annoyed by something she had said during the massage this morning and I had said 'no'. Her period began again to-day after an interval of scarcely a fortnight. I promised to regulate this by hypnotic suggestion and, under hypnosis, set the interval at 28 days.[1]

Under hypnosis, I also asked her whether she remembered the last thing she told me; in asking this what I had in mind was a task which had been left over from yesterday evening; but she began quite correctly with the 'don't touch me' from *this mornings* hypnosis. So I took her back to yesterday's topic. I had asked her the origin of her stammering and she had replied, 'I don't know'.[2] I had therefore requested her to remember it by the time of to-day's hypnosis. She accordingly answered me to-day without any further reflection but in great agitation and with spastic impediments to her speech: 'How

[1] A suggestion which was carried out.

[2] It is possible that this answer, 'I don't know', was correct; but it may quite as well have indicated reluctance to talk about the causes of the stammering. I have since observed in other patients that the greater the effort they have made to repress a thing from their consciousness the more difficulty they have in remembering it under hypnosis as well as in waking life.

the horses bolted once with the children in the carriage; and how another time I was driving through the forest with the children in a thunderstorm, and a tree just in front of the horses was struck by lightning and the horses shied and I thought: "You must keep quite still now, or your screaming will frighten the horses even more and the coachman won't be able to hold them in at all." It came on from that moment.' She was quite unusually excited as she told me this story. I further learnt from her that the stammer had begun immediately after the first of these two occasions, but had disappeared shortly afterwards and then came on for good after the second, similar occasion. I extinguished her plastic memory of these scenes, but asked her to imagine them once more. She appeared to try to do this and remained quiet as she did so; and from now on she spoke in the hypnosis without any spastic impediment.[1]

Finding her disposed to be communicative, I asked her what further events in her life had frightened her so much that they had left her with plastic memories. She replied by giving me a collection of such experiences:—[1] How a year after her mother's death, she was visiting a Frenchwoman who was a friend of hers, and had been sent into the next room with another girl to fetch a dictionary, and had then seen someone sit up in the bed who looked exactly like the woman she had just left behind in the other room. She went stiff all over and was rooted to the spot. She learnt afterwards that it was a specially arranged dummy. I said that what she saw had been a hallucination, and appealed to her good sense, and her face relaxed. [2] How she had nursed her sick brother and he had had such fearful attacks as a result of the morphine and had terrified her and seized hold of her. I remembered that she had already mentioned this experience this morning, and, as an experiment, I asked her on what other occasions this 'seizing hold' had happened. To my agreeable surprise she made a long pause this time before answering and then asked doubtfully 'My little girl?' She was quite unable to recall the other two occasions (see above [p. 57]). My prohibition—my expunging of her

---

[1] As we see from this, the patient's *tic*-like clacking and her spastic stammer were two symptoms which went back to similar precipitating causes and had an analogous mechanism. I have already commented on this mechanism in a short paper on hypnotic treatment (1892-3*b*), and I shall also return to it below. [See p. 91 ff.]

memories—had therefore been effective.—Further, [3] how, while she was nursing her brother, her aunt's pale face had suddenly appeared over the top of the screen. She had come to convert him to Catholicism.

I saw that I had come to the root of her constant fear of surprises, and I asked for further instances of this. She went on: How they had a friend staying at her home who liked slipping into the room very softly so that all of a sudden he was there; how she had been so ill after her mother's death and had gone to a health resort and a lunatic had walked into her room several times at night by mistake and come right up to her bed; and lastly, how, on the journey here from Abbazia a strange man had four times opened the door of her compartment suddenly and had fixed his eyes on her each time with a stare. She was so much terrified that she sent for the conductor.

I wiped out all these memories, woke her up and assured her she would sleep well to-night, having omitted to give her this suggestion in her hypnosis. The improvement of her general condition was shown by her remark that she had not done any reading to-day, she was living in such a happy dream—she, who always had to be doing something because of her inner unrest.

May 11, morning.—To-day she had an appointment with Dr. N., the gynaecologist, who is to examine her elder daughter about her menstrual troubles. I found Frau Emmy in a rather disturbed state, though this was expressed in slighter physical signs than formerly. She called out from time to time: 'I'm afraid, so afraid, I think I shall die.' I asked her what she was afraid of? Was it of Dr. N.? She did not know, she said; she was just afraid. Under hypnosis, which I induced before my colleague arrived, she declared that she was afraid she had offended me by something she had said during the massage yesterday which seemed to her to have been impolite. She was frightened of anything new, too, and consequently of the new doctor. I was able to soothe her, and though she started once or twice in the presence of Dr. N., she behaved very well apart from this and produced neither her clacking noises nor any inhibition of speech. After he had gone I put her under hypnosis once more, to remove any possible residue of the excitement caused by his visit. She herself was very much pleased with her behaviour and put great hopes in the treatment; and I tried to convince her from this example that there is no need to be afraid of what is new, since it also contains what is good.[1]

Evening.—She was very lively and unburdened herself of a number of doubts and scruples during our conversation before the hypnosis. Under hypnosis I asked her what event in her life had produced the most lasting effect on her and came up most often in her memory. Her husband's death, she said. I got her to describe this event to me in full detail, and this she did with every sign of deepest emotion but without any clacking or stammering:—How, she began, they had been at a place on the Riviera of which they were both very fond, and while they were crossing a bridge he had suddenly sunk to the ground and lain there lifeless for a few minutes but had then got up again and seemed quite well; how, a short time afterwards, as she was lying in bed after her second confinement, her husband, who had been sitting at breakfast at a small table beside her bed, reading a newspaper, had got up all at once, looked at her so strangely, taken a few paces forward and then fallen down dead; she had got out of bed, and the doctors who were called in had made efforts to revive him which she had heard from the next room; but it had been in vain. And, she then went on to say, how the baby, which was then a few weeks old, had been seized with a serious illness which had lasted for six months, during which she herself had been in bed with a high fever.— And there now followed in chronological order her grievances against this child, which she threw out rapidly with an angry look on her face, in the way one would speak of someone who had become a nuisance. This child, she said, had been very queer for a long time; it had screamed all the time and did not sleep, and it had developed a paralysis of the left leg which there had seemed very little hope of curing. When it was four it had had visions; it had been late in learning to walk and to talk, so that for a long time it had been believed to be imbecile. According to the doctors it had had encephalitis and inflammation of the spinal cord and she did not know what else besides. I interrupted her here and pointed out to her that this same

[1] Didactic suggestions of this kind always missed fire with Frau Emmy, as will be seen from what follows.

child was to-day a normal girl and in the bloom of health, and I made it impossible for her to see any of these melancholy things again, not only by wiping out her memories of them in their *plastic* form but by removing her whole recollection of them, as though they had never been present in her mind. I promised her that this would lead to her being freed from the expectation of misfortune which perpetually tormented her and from the pains all over her body, of which she had been complaining precisely during her narrative, after we had heard nothing of them for several days.[1]

To my surprise, after this suggestion of mine, she began without any transition speaking of Prince L., whose escape from an asylum was being talked about a great deal at the time. She brought out new fears about asylums—that people in them were treated with douches of ice-cold water on the head and put into an apparatus which turned them round and round till they were quiet. When, three days ago, she had first complained about her fear of asylums, I had interrupted her after her first story, that the patients were tied on to chairs. I now saw that I had gained nothing by this interruption and that I cannot evade listening to her stories in every detail to the very end. After these arrears had been made up, I took this fresh crop of fears from her as well. I appealed to her good sense and told her she really ought to believe me more than the silly girl from whom she had had the gruesome stories about the way in which asylums are run. As I noticed that she still stammered occasionally in telling me these further things, I asked her once more what the stammer came from. No reply. 'Don't you know?' 'No.' 'Why not?' 'Why not? Because I *mayn't*!' (She pronounced these words violently and angrily.) This declaration seemed to me to be evidence of the success of my suggestion, but she

---

[1] On this occasion my energy seems to have carried me too far. When, as much as eighteen months later, I saw Frau Emmy again in a relatively good state of health, she complained that there were a number of most important moments in her life of which she had only the vaguest memory [p. 84]. She regarded this as evidence of a weakening of her memory, and I had to be careful not to tell her the cause of this particular instance of amnesia.—The overwhelming success of the treatment in this respect was no doubt also due to the great detail in which I had got her to repeat these memories to me (in far greater detail than is shown in my notes), whereas with other memories I was too often satisfied with a mere mention.

expressed a desire for me to wake her up from her hypnosis, and I did so.[1]

May 12, [*morning*].—Contrary to my expectation, she had slept badly and only for a short time. I found her in a state of great anxiety, though, incidentally, without showing her usual physical signs of it. She would not say what the matter was, but only that she had had bad dreams and kept seeing the same things. 'How dreadful it would be,' she said, 'if they were to come to life.' During the massage she dealt with a few points in reply to questions. She then became cheerful; she told me about her social life at her dower house on the Baltic, of the important people whom she entertains from the neighbouring town, and so on.

Hypnosis.—She had had some fearful dreams. The legs and arms of the chairs were all turned into snakes; a monster with a vulture's beak was tearing and eating at her all over her body; other wild animals leapt upon her, etc. She then passed on to other animal-deliria, which, however, she qualified with the addition 'That was real' (not a dream): how (on an earlier occasion) she had been going to pick up a ball of wool, and it was a mouse and ran away; how she had been on a walk, and a big toad suddenly jumped out at her, and so on. I saw that my general prohibition had been ineffective and that I should have to take her frightening impressions away from her one by one.[2] I took an opportunity of asking her, too, why she had

---

[1] It was not until the next day that I understood this little scene. Her unruly nature, which rebelled, both in her waking state and in artificial sleep, against any constraint, had made her angry with me because I had assumed that her narrative was finished and had interrupted it by my concluding suggestion. I have come across many other proofs that she kept a critical eye upon my work in her hypnotic consciousness. She had probably wanted to reproach me with interrupting her story to-day just as I had previously interrupted her accounts of the horrors in the asylum; but she had not ventured to do so. Instead of this, she had produced these further stories [about asylums], apparently without any transition and without revealing the connecting thoughts. My blunder was made plain to me next day by a depreciatory comment on her part.

[2] I unfortunately failed to enquire into the significance of Frau Emmy's animal visions—to distinguish, for instance, what was symbolic in her fear of animals from what was primary horror, such as is characteristic of many neuropaths from youth onwards.

gastric pains and what they came from. (I believe that all her attacks of zoöpsia [animal hallucinations] are accompanied by gastric pains.) Her answer, which she gave rather grudgingly, was that she did not know. I requested her to remember by tomorrow. She then said in a definitely grumbling tone that I was not to keep on asking her where this and that came from, but to let her tell me what she had to say. I fell in with this, and she went on without preface: 'When they carried him out, I could not believe he was dead.' (So she was talking of her husband again, and I saw now that the cause of her ill-humour was that she had been suffering from the residues of this story which had been kept back.) After this, she said, she had hated her child for three years, because she always told herself that she might have been able to nurse her husband back to health if she had not been in bed on account of the child. And then after her husband's death there had been nothing but insults and agitations. His relatives, who had always been against the marriage and had then been angry because they had been so happy together, had spread a rumour that she had poisoned him, so that she had wanted to demand an enquiry. Her relatives had involved her in all kinds of legal proceedings with the help of a shady journalist. The wretch had sent round agents to stir people up against her. He got the local papers to print libellous articles about her, and then sent her the cuttings. This had been the origin of her unsociability and her hatred of all strangers. After I had spoken some calming words about what she had told me, she said she felt easier.

May 13, [morning].—Once again she had slept badly, owing to gastric pains. She had not eaten any supper. She also complained of pains in her right arm. But she was in a good mood; she was cheerful, and, since yesterday, has treated me with special distinction. She asked me my opinion about all sorts of things that seemed to her important, and became quite unreasonably agitated, for instance, when I had to look for the towels needed in massage, and so on. Her clacking and facial *tic* were frequent.

Hypnosis.—Yesterday evening it had suddenly occurred to her why the small animals she saw grew so enormous. It happened to her for the first time at D—— during a theatrical performance in which a huge lizard appeared on the stage.

This memory had tormented her a great deal yesterday as well.[1]

The reason for the re-appearance of the clacking was that yesterday she had abdominal pains and had tried not to show it by groaning. She knew nothing of the true precipitating cause of the clacking (see p. [54]). She remembered, too, that I had instructed her to discover the origin of her gastric pains. She did not know it, however, and asked me to help her. I asked whether, perhaps, on some occasion after a great excitement, she had forced herself to eat. She confirmed this. After her husband's death she had for a long time lost her appetite completely and had only eaten from a sense of duty; and her gastric pains had in fact begun at that time. I then removed her gastric pains by stroking her a few times across the epigastrium. She then began of her own accord to talk about the things that had most affected her. 'I have told you,' she said, 'that I was not fond of the child. But I ought to add that one could not have guessed it from my behaviour. I did everything that was necessary. Even now I reproach myself for being fonder of the elder one.'

May 14, [*morning*].—She was well and cheerful and had slept till 7.30 this morning. She only complained of slight pains in the radial region of her hand and in her head and face. What she tells me before the hypnosis becomes more and more significant. To-day she had scarcely anything dreadful to produce. She complained of pains and loss of sensation in her right leg. She told me that she had had an attack of abdominal inflammation in 1871; when she had hardly recovered from this, she had nursed her sick brother, and it was then that the pains first came on. They had even led to a temporary paralysis of her right leg.

During the hypnosis I asked her whether it would now be

[1] The visual memory of the big lizard had no doubt only attained its great importance owing to its coinciding in time with a powerful affect which she must have experienced during the theatrical performance. In treating the present patient, as I have already confessed [pp. 55 *n*. and 62 *n*.], I was often content to receive the most superficial explanations. In this instance, too, I failed to make any further investigation.— We shall be reminded, moreover, of hysterical macropsia. Frau Emmy was extremely short-sighted and astigmatic, and her hallucinations may often have been provoked by the indistinctness of her visual perceptions.

possible for her to take part in social life or whether she was still too much afraid. She said it was still disagreeable to have anyone standing behind her or just beside her. In this connection she told me of some more occasions on which she had been disagreeably surprised by someone suddenly appearing. Once, for instance, when she had been going for a walk with her daughters on the island of Rügen, two suspicious-looking individuals had come out from some bushes and insulted them. In Abbazia, while she was out for a walk one evening, a beggar had suddenly emerged from behind a rock and had knelt down in front of her. It seems that he was a harmless lunatic. Lastly, she told me of how her isolated country house had been broken into at night, which had very much alarmed her. It is easy to see, however, that the essential origin of this fear of people was the persecution to which she had been subjected after her husband's death.[1]

Evening.—Though she appeared to be in high spirits, she greeted me with the exclamation: 'I'm frightened to death; oh, I can hardly tell you, I hate myself!' I learned at last that she had had a visit from Dr. Breuer and that on his appearance she had given a start of alarm. As he noticed it, she had assured him that it was 'only this once'. She felt so very sorry on my account that she should have had to betray this relic of her former nervousness. I have more than once had occasion to notice during these last few days how hard she is on herself, how liable she is to blame herself severely for the least signs of neglect— if the towels for the massage are not in their usual place or if the newspaper for me to read when she is asleep is not instantly ready to hand. After the removal of the first and most superficial layer of tormenting recollections, her morally oversensitive personality, with its tendency to self-depreciation, has come into view. Both in her waking state and under hypnosis, I duly told her (what amounted to the old legal tag '*de minimis non curat lex*') that there is a whole multitude of indifferent, small things lying between what is good and what is evil— things about which no one need reproach himself. She did not take in my lesson, I fancy, any more than would an ascetic

---

[1] At the time I wrote this I was inclined to look for a *psychical* origin for all symptoms in cases of hysteria. I should now explain this sexually abstinent woman's tendency to anxiety as being due to *neurosis* (i.e. anxiety neurosis). [See below, p. 88.]

mediaeval monk, who sees the finger of God or a temptation of the Devil in every trivial event of his life and who is incapable of picturing the world even for a brief moment or in its smallest corner as being without reference to himself.

In her hypnosis she brought up some further horrifying images (in Abbazia, for instance, she saw bloody heads on every wave of the sea). I made her repeat the lessons I had given her while she was awake.

May 15, [morning].—She had slept till 8.30 a.m. but had become restless towards morning, and received me with some slight signs of her *tic*, clacking and speech-inhibition. 'I'm frightened to death,' she said once more. In reply to a question she told me that the Pension in which her children were staying was on the fourth floor of a building and reached by a lift. She had insisted yesterday that the children should make use of the lift for coming down as well as going up, and was now reproaching herself about this, because the lift was not entirely to be trusted. The owner of the Pension had said so himself. Had I heard, she asked, the story of the Countess Sch. who had been killed in Rome in an accident of that kind? I happen to be acquainted with the Pension and I know that the lift is the private property of the owner of the Pension; it does not seem to me very likely that this man, who makes a special point of the lift in an advertisement, would himself have warned anyone against using it. It seemed to me that we had here one of the paramnesias that are brought about by anxiety. I told her my view and succeeded without any difficulty in getting her herself to laugh at the improbability of her fears. For that very reason I could not believe that this was the cause of her anxiety and determined to put the question to her hypnotic consciousness. During massage, which I resumed to-day after a few days' interval, she told me a loosely connected string of anecdotes, which may have been true—about a toad which was found in a cellar, an eccentric mother who looked after her idiot child in a strange fashion, a woman who was shut up in an asylum because she had melancholia—and which showed the kind of recollections that passed through her head when she was in a disquieted frame of mind. When she had got these stories out she became very cheerful. She described her life on her estate and her contacts with prominent men in German Russia and

North Germany; and I really found it extremely hard to reconcile activities of this kind with the picture of such a severely neurotic woman.

I therefore asked her in hypnosis why she was so restless this morning. In place of her doubts about the lift, she informed me that she had been afraid that her period was going to start again and would again interfere with the massage.[1]

[1] The sequence of events had accordingly been as follows: When she woke up in the morning she found herself in an anxious mood, and to account for it she grasped at the first anxious idea that came to mind. On the previous afternoon she had had a conversation about the lift at the Pension. Over-careful of her children as usual, she had asked their governess whether her elder daughter, who could not walk much on account of ovarian neuralgia on the right side and pains in the right leg, used the lift for going down as well as up. A paramnesia then enabled her to link the anxiety she was conscious of with the idea of the lift. Her consciousness did not present her with the *real* cause of her anxiety; *that* only emerged—but now it did so without any hesitation —when I questioned her about it in hypnosis. The process was the same as that studied by Bernheim and others after him in persons who carry out in a post-hypnotic condition instructions given them during hypnosis. For instance, Bernheim (1886, 29) suggested to a patient that after he woke up he should put both his thumbs in his mouth. He did so, and excused his action by saying that his tongue had been giving him pain since the previous day when he had bitten it in an epileptiform attack. Again, in obedience to a suggestion, a girl made an attempt to murder a law-court officer who was totally unknown to her. When she was seized and questioned as to the motives of her act, she invented a story of a wrong done to her which called for revenge. There seems to be a necessity for bringing psychical phenomena of which one becomes conscious into causal connection with other conscious material. In cases in which the true causation evades conscious perception one does not hesitate to attempt to make another connection, which one believes, although it is false. It is clear that a split in the content of consciousness must greatly facilitate the occurrence of 'false connections' of this kind. [See below, p. 302 f.]

I shall dwell a little on this example I have given of a false connection, since in more than one respect it deserves to be described as typical. It is typical, in the first place, of the present patient's behaviour; for in the further course of the treatment she afforded me many opportunities of resolving such false connections by explanations arrived at in hypnosis, and of removing their effects. I will give a detailed account of one of these instances, since it throws a strong light on the psychological phenomenon in question. I had recommended Frau Emmy to try replacing her usual luke-warm bath by a hip-bath of cool water, which I told her would be more refreshing. She used to obey medical instructions implicitly, but never ceased to view them with profound mistrust. I

I then got her to tell me the history of her pains in the leg. She began in the same way as yesterday [about having nursed her brother] and then went on with a long series of instances of experiences, alternately distressing and irritating, which she

have already said that she had hardly ever derived any benefit from her medical treatment. My advice to her to take cool baths was not delivered in such an authoritative manner as to prevent her from having the courage to give open expression to her hesitations: 'Whenever I have taken a cool bath,' she said, 'it has made me melancholy for the rest of the day. But I will try it again, if you like; you mustn't think I won't do whatever you tell me to.' I pretended to give up my proposal, but in her next hypnosis I suggested to her that she should herself put forward the idea of cool baths—having thought it over, she would like to try the experiment after all, and so on. This in fact happened. Next day, she took up the idea of having cool hip-baths; she tried to convince me with all the arguments which I had previously used to her, and I agreed without much enthusiasm. But on the day after she had had the hip-bath I did in fact find her in a deep depression. 'Why are you like this to-day?' I asked. 'I knew beforehand that it would happen,' she answered, 'it's because of the cold bath; it always happens.' 'It was you yourself who asked for it,' I said. 'Now we know they don't suit you. We'll go back to the luke-warm ones.' Afterwards I asked her in her hypnosis, 'Was it really the cool bath that depressed you so much?' 'Oh,' was her answer, 'the cool bath had nothing to do with it. But I read in the paper this morning that a revolution had broken out in San Domingo. Whenever there is any unrest there the whites are always the sufferers; and I have a brother in San Domingo who has already caused us a lot of concern, and I am worried now in case something happens to him.' This brought to a close the issue between us. Next morning she took her cool hip-bath as though it were a matter of course and continued doing so for several weeks without ever attributing any depression to that source.

It will be agreed that this instance is typical also of the behaviour of a large number of neuropaths in regard to the therapeutic procedures recommended by their physicians. The patient who develops a symptom on a particular day—whether owing to unrest in San Domingo or elsewhere—is always inclined to attribute it to his doctor's latest advice. Of the two conditions necessary for bringing about a false connection of this kind, one, mistrust, seems always to be present; while the other, the splitting of consciousness, is replaced by the fact that most neuropaths have in part no knowledge of the true causes (or at any rate the releasing causes) of their disorder, and in part deliberately avoid such knowledge, because they are unwilling to be reminded of that share of the causes for which they themselves are to blame.

It might be thought that these psychical conditions which we have laid down for neuropaths as distinct from hysterics—namely, ignorance or deliberate overlooking—would necessarily be more favourable for

had had at the same time as her pains in the leg and the effect
of which had each time been to make them worse, even to the
point of her having bilateral paralysis of the legs with loss of
sensation in them. The same was true of the pains in her arm.

the production of a false connection than would be the presence of a
split in consciousness, which, after all, withdraws material for causal
connections from consciousness. The split, however, is rarely a clear-
cut one. As a rule, portions of the subconscious [cf. p. 45 n.] complex
of ideas intrude into the subject's ordinary consciousness, and it is
precisely they that provoke this kind of disturbance. What is usually
perceived consciously, as in the instances I have quoted above, is the
general feeling attached to the complex—a mood of anxiety, it may be,
or of grief; and it is this feeling that, by a kind of 'compulsion to associate', must have a connection found for it with some complex of ideas
which is present in consciousness. (Compare, too, the mechanism of
obsessional ideas, described in two papers, 1894a and 1895c.)

Not long ago I was able to convince myself of the strength of a compulsion of this kind towards association from some observations made
in a different field. For several weeks I found myself obliged to exchange
my usual bed for a harder one, in which I had more numerous or more
vivid dreams, or in which, it may be, I was unable to reach the normal
depth of sleep. In the first quarter of an hour after waking I remembered
all the dreams I had had during the night, and I took the trouble to
write them down and try to solve them. I succeeded in tracing all these
dreams back to two factors: (1) to the necessity for working out any
ideas which I had only dwelt upon cursorily during the day—which
had only been touched upon and not finally dealt with; and (2) to the
compulsion to link together any ideas that might be present in the same
state of consciousness. The senseless and contradictory character of the
dreams could be traced back to the uncontrolled ascendancy of this
latter factor.

It is a quite regular thing for the mood attaching to an experience
and the subject-matter of that experience to come into different relations to the primary consciousness. This was shown in the case of another
patient, Frau Cäcilie M., whom I got to know far more thoroughly than
any of the other patients mentioned in these studies. I collected from her
very numerous and convincing proofs of the existence of a psychical
mechanism of hysterical phenomena such as I have put forward above.
Personal considerations unfortunately make it impossible for me to
give a detailed case history of this patient, though I shall have occasion
to refer to it from time to time. Frau Cäcilie had latterly been in a
peculiar hysterical state. This state was certainly not a unique one,
though I do not know if it has hitherto been recognized. It might be
called a 'hysterical psychosis for the payment of old debts'. The patient
had experienced numerous psychical traumas and had spent many
years in a chronic hysteria which was attended by a great variety of
manifestations. The causes of all these states of hers were unknown to her

They too had come on while she was nursing someone who was ill, at the same time as the 'neck-cramps'. Concerning the latter, I only learnt that they succeeded some curious restless

and everyone else. Her remarkably well-stocked memory showed the most striking gaps. She herself complained that it was as though her life was chopped in pieces. One day an old memory suddenly broke in upon her clear and tangible and with all the freshness of a new sensation. For nearly three years after this she once again lived through all the traumas of her life—long-forgotten, as they seemed to her, and some, indeed, never remembered at all—accompanied by the acutest suffering and by the return of all the symptoms she had ever had. The 'old debts' which were thus paid covered a period of thirty-three years and made it possible to discover the origins, often very complicated, of all her abnormal states. The only way of relieving her was to give her an opportunity of talking off under hypnosis the particular reminiscence which was tormenting her at the moment, together with all its accompanying load of feelings and their physical expression. When I was prevented from doing so, so that she was obliged to say these things to a person in whose presence she felt embarrassed, it sometimes happened that she would tell him her story quite calmly and would subsequently, in hypnosis, produce for me all the tears, all the expressions of despair, with which she would have wished to accompany her recital. For a few hours after a purgation of this kind during hypnosis she used to be quite well and on the spot. After a short interval the next reminiscence of the series would break its way in. But this reminiscence would be preceded some hours earlier by the mood which was proper to it. She would become anxious or irritable or despairing without ever suspecting that this mood did not belong to the present moment but to the state to which she would next be subject. During this transition period she would habitually make a false connection to which she would obstinately cling until her next hypnosis. For instance, she once greeted me with the question: 'Am I not a worthless person? Is it not a sign of worthlessness that I said to you what I did yesterday?' What she had actually said to me the day before did not in fact seem to me to justify this damning verdict. After a short discussion, she clearly recognized this; but her next hypnosis brought to light a recollection of an occasion, twelve years earlier, which had aroused severe self-reproaches in her—though, incidentally, she no longer subcribed to them in the least.

[The last paragraph but one of this footnote gives us the earliest published report of a tentative approach by Freud to the problem of the interpretation of dreams. Both the two factors which he brings forward here were given a place in his ultimate analysis, though only a secondary one. The first of them was the theory championed by Robert and was discussed in Chapter I (G) of *The Interpretation of Dreams* (1900a), *Standard Ed.*, **4**, 78–80, and was partly accepted by Freud in Chapter VII (D), ibid., **5**, 579. The second of the factors brought forward here will be found mentioned in Chapter V (A), ibid., **4**, 179.]

states accompanied by depression which had been there previously. They consist in an 'icy grip' on the back of the neck,
together with an onset of rigidity and a painful coldness in all
her extremities, an incapacity to speak and complete prostra-
tion. They last from six to twelve hours. My attempts to show
that this complex of symptoms represented a recollection failed.
I put some questions to her with a view to discovering whether
her brother, while she was nursing him during his delirium, had
ever caught hold of her by the neck; but she denied this. She
said she did not know where these attacks came from.[1]

[1] On subsequent reflection, I cannot help thinking that these 'neck-
cramps' may have been determined organically and have been analogous to migraine. In medical practice we come across a number of
conditions of this kind which have not been described. These show such
a striking resemblance to the classical attack of hemicrania that we are
tempted to extend the concept of the latter and to attach only secondary
importance to the localization of the pain. As we know, many neuropathic women very often have hysterical attacks (spasms and deliria)
along with an attack of migraine. Every time I observed a 'neck-cramp'
in Frau Emmy it was accompanied by an attack of delirium. [Cf. p. 96.]

As regards the pains in her arm and leg, I am of opinion that what
we have here is the not very interesting and correspondingly common
case of determination by chance coincidence. She had pains of this kind
while she was in an agitated state nursing her sick brother; and, owing
to her exhaustion, she felt them more acutely than usual. These pains,
which were originally associated only accidentally with those experiences, were later repeated in her memory as the somatic symbol of the
whole complex of associations. I shall be able below [p. 174 ff.] to give
several more examples in confirmation of this process. It seems probable
that in the first instance these pains were rheumatic; that is to say, to
give a definite sense to that much misused term, they were of a kind
which resides principally in the muscles, involves a marked sensitiveness to pressure and modification of consistency in the muscles, is at its
most severe after a considerable period of rest and immobilization of
the extremity (i.e. in the morning), is improved by practising the
painful movement and can be dissipated by massage. These myogenic
pains, which are universally common, acquire great importance in
neuropaths. They themselves regard them as nervous and are encouraged in this by their physicians, who are not in the habit of examining
muscles by digital pressure. Such pains provide the material of countless
neuralgias and so-called sciaticas, etc. I will only refer briefly here to
the relation of these pains to the gouty diathesis. My patient's mother
and two of her sisters suffered very severely from gout (or chronic
rheumatism). Some part of the pains which she complained of at the
time of the treatment may, like her original pains, have been of contemporary origin. I cannot tell, since I had no experience then in
forming a judgement of this state of the muscles. [See below, p. 90.]

Evening.—She was in very good spirits and showed a great sense of humour. She told me incidentally that the affair of the lift was not as she had reported it. The proprietor had only said what he did in order to give an excuse for the lift not being used for downward journeys. She asked me a great many questions which had nothing pathological about them. She has had distressingly severe pains in her face, in her hand on the thumb side and in her leg. She gets stiff and has pains in her face if she sits without moving or stares at some fixed point for any considerable time. If she lifts anything heavy it brings on pains in her arm.—An examination of her right leg showed fairly good sensibility in her thigh, a high degree of anaesthesia in the lower part of the leg and in the foot and less in the region of the buttock and hip.

In hypnosis she informed me that she still occasionally has frightening ideas, such as that something might happen to her children, that they might fall ill or lose their lives, or that her brother, who is now on his honeymoon, might have an accident, or his wife might die (because the marriages of all her brothers and sisters had been so short). I could not extract any other fears from her. I forbad her any need to be frightened when there was no reason for it. She promised to give it up 'because you ask me to'. I gave her further suggestions for her pains, her leg, etc.

May 16, [morning].—She had slept well. She still complained of pains in her face, arms and legs. She was very cheerful. Her hypnosis yielded nothing. I applied a faradic brush to her anaesthetic leg.

Evening.—She gave a start as soon as I came in. 'I'm so glad you've come,' she said, 'I am so frightened.' At the same time she gave every indication of terror, together with stammering and *tic*. I first got her to tell me in her waking state what had happened. Crooking her fingers and stretching out her hands before her, she gave a vivid picture of her terror as she said: 'An enormous mouse suddenly whisked across my hand in the garden and was gone in a flash; things kept on gliding backwards and forwards.' (An illusion from the play of shadows?) 'A whole lot of mice were sitting in the trees.—Don't you hear the horses stamping in the circus?—There's a man groaning in the next room; he must be in pain after his operation.—Can I be in Rügen? Did I have a stove there like that?' She was confused by the multitude of thoughts crossing one another in her mind and by her efforts to sort out her actual surroundings from them. When I put questions to her about contemporary things, such as whether her daughters were here, she could make no answer.

I tried to disentangle the confusion of her mind under hypnosis. I asked her what it was that frightened her. She repeated the story of the mouse with every sign of terror, and added that as she went down the steps she saw a dreadful animal lying there, which vanished at once. I said that these were hallucinations and told her not to be frightened of mice; it was only drunkards who saw them (she disliked drunkards intensely). I told her the story of Bishop Hatto.[1] She knew it too, and listened to it with extreme horror.—'How did you come to think of the circus?' I went on to ask. She said that she had clearly heard the horses stamping in their stables near-by and getting tied up in their halters, which might injure them. When this happened Johann used to go out and untie them. I denied that there were stables near-by or that anyone in the next room had groaned. Did she know where she was? She said she knew *now*, but had thought earlier that she was in Rügen. I asked her how she got on to this memory. They had been talking in the garden, she said, of how hot it was in one part of it, and all at once the thought had come to her of the shadeless terrace in Rügen. Well then, I asked, what were her unhappy memories of her stay in Rügen? She produced a series of them. She had had the most frightful pains there in her legs and arms; when she was out on excursions there she had several times been caught in a fog and lost her way; twice, while she was on a walk, a bull had come after her, and so on. How was it that she had had this attack to-day?—How (she answered)? She had written a great many letters; it had taken her three hours and had given her a bad head.—I could assume, accordingly, that her attack of delirium was brought on by fatigue and that its content was determined by associations from such things as the shadeless place in the garden, etc. I repeated all the lessons I have been in the habit of giving her and left her composed to sleep.

May 17, [*morning*].—She had a very good night. In the bran bath which she had to-day, she gave some screams because she

[1] [Who, according to legend, was eaten by rats.]

took the bran for worms. I heard this from the nurse. She herself was reluctant to tell me about it. She was almost exaggeratedly cheerful, but she kept interrupting herself with cries of 'ugh!' and made faces expressive of terror. She also stammered more than she has for the last few days. She told me she had dreamt last night that she was walking on a lot of leeches. The night before she had had horrible dreams. She had had to lay out a number of dead people and put them in coffins, but would not put the lids on. (Obviously, a recollection of her husband.) She told me further that in the course of her life she had had a large number of adventures with animals. The worst had been with a bat which had got caught in her wardrobe, so that she had rushed out of the room without any clothes on. To cure her of this fear her brother had given her a lovely brooch in the form of a bat; but she had never been able to wear it.

Under hypnosis she explained that her fear of worms came from her having once been given a present of a pretty pincushion; but next morning, when she wanted to use it, a lot of little worms had crept out of it, because it had been filled with bran which was not quite dry. (A hallucination? Perhaps a fact.) I asked her to tell me some more animal stories. Once, she said, when she had been walking with her husband in a park in St. Petersburg, the whole path leading to a pond had been covered with toads, so that they had had to turn back. There had been times when she had been unable to hold out her hand to anyone, for fear of its turning into a dreadful animal, as had so often happened. I tried to free her from her fear of animals by going through them one by one and asking her if she was afraid of them. In the case of some of them she answered 'no'; in the case of others, 'I mustn't be afraid of them.'[1] I asked her why she had stammered and jerked about so much yesterday. She replied that she always did this when she was very frightened.[2]—But why *had* she been so frightened

---

[1] The procedure I was following here can scarcely be regarded as a good one: none of it was carried out exhaustively enough.

[2] Her stammering and clacking were not completely relieved after they had been traced back to the two initial traumas [the occasion of her daughter's illness and the frightened horses, cf. pp. 54 and 58], though from then on the two symptoms were strikingly improved. The patient herself explained the incompleteness of the success as follows. She had got into the habit of stammering and clacking whenever she

yesterday?—Because all kinds of oppressive thoughts had come into her head in the garden: in particular, how she could prevent something from heaping up again inside her after her treatment had come to an end. I repeated the three reasons for feeling reassured which I had already given her: (1) that she had become altogether healthier and more capable of resistance, (2) that she would get the habit of telling her thoughts to someone she was on close terms with, and (3) she would henceforth regard as indifferent a whole number of things which had hitherto weighed upon her. She went on to say that she had been worried as well because she had not thanked me for my visiting her late in the day; and she was afraid that I would lose patience with her on account of her recent relapse. She had been very much upset and alarmed because the house physician had asked a gentleman in the garden whether he was now able to face his operation. His wife had been sitting beside him, and she (the patient) could not help thinking that this might be the poor man's last evening.—After this last piece of information her depression seemed to be cleared up.[1]

Evening.—She was very cheerful and contented. The hypnosis produced nothing whatever. I devoted myself to dealing with her muscular pains and to restoring sensibility in her right leg. This was very easily accomplished in hypnosis, but her restored sensibility was in part lost again when she woke up. Before I left her she expressed her astonishment that it was such a long time since she had had any neck-cramps, though they usually came on before every thunderstorm.

May 18.—She had slept last night better than she had for years. But after her bath she complained of cold at the back of her

was frightened, so that in the end these symptoms had come to be attached not solely to the initial traumas but to a long chain of memories associated with them, which I had omitted to wipe out. This is a state of things which arises quite often and which always limits the beauty and completeness of the therapeutic outcome of the cathartic procedure.

[1] It was here that I learnt for the first time, what was confirmed on countless later occasions, that when one is resolving a current hysterical delirium, the patient's communications are given in a reverse chronological order, beginning with the most recent and least important impressions and connections of thought and only at the end reaching the primary impression, which is in all probability the most important one causally. [The same phenomenon is mentioned by Breuer, p. 35.]

neck, tightness and pains in the face, hands and feet. Her features were strained and her hands clenched. The hypnosis brought out no psychical content underlying her neck-cramp. I improved it by massage after she had woken up.[1]

I hope that this extract from the history of the first three weeks of the treatment will be enough to give a clear picture of the patient's state, of the character of my therapeutic efforts and of the measure of their success. I shall now proceed to amplify the case history.

The delirium which I have last described was also the last considerable disturbance in Frau Emmy von N.'s condition. Since I did not take the initiative in looking for the symptoms and their basis, but waited for something to come up in the patient or for her to tell me some thought that was causing her anxiety, her hypnoses soon ceased to produce material. I there-

---

[1] Her astonishment the evening before at its being so long since she had had a neck-cramp was thus a premonition of an approaching condition which was already in preparation at the time and was perceived in the unconscious [cf. p. 49 *n.*]. This curious kind of premonition occurred regularly in the case already mentioned [p. 69 *n.*] of Frau Cäcilie M. If, for instance, while she was in the best of health, she said to me, 'It's a long time since I've been frightened of witches at night', or, 'how glad I am that I've not had pains in my eyes for such a long time', I could feel sure that the following night a severe onset of her fear of witches would be making extra work for her nurse or that her next attack of pains in the eyes was on the point of beginning. On each occasion what was already present as a finished product in the unconscious was beginning to show through indistinctly. This idea, which emerged as a sudden notion, was worked over by the unsuspecting 'official' consciousness (to use Charcot's term) into a feeling of satisfaction, which swiftly and invariably turned out to be unjustified. Frau Cäcilie, who was a highly intelligent woman, to whom I am indebted for much help in gaining an understanding of hysterical symptoms, herself pointed out to me that events of this kind may have given rise to superstitions about the danger of being boastful or of anticipating evils. We must not vaunt our happiness on the one hand, nor, on the other, must we talk of the worst or it will happen. The fact is that we do not boast of our happiness until unhappiness is in the offing, and we become aware of our anticipation in the form of a boast, because in such cases the subject-matter of what we are recollecting emerges before the feeling that belongs to it—that is to say, because an agreeable contrasting idea is present in consciousness.—[An allusion to this same point will be found in a footnote near the beginning of a work of Freud's written some thirty years later: 'Negation' (1925*h*).]

fore made use of them principally for the purpose of giving her maxims which were to remain constantly present in her mind and to protect her from relapsing into similar conditions when she had got home. At that time I was completely under the sway of Bernheim's book on suggestion [1] and I anticipated more results from such didactic measures than I should to-day. My patient's condition improved so rapidly, that she soon assured me she had not felt so well since her husband's death. After a treatment lasting in all for seven weeks I allowed her to return to her home on the Baltic.

It was not I but Dr. Breuer who received news of her about seven months later. Her health had continued good for several months but had then broken down again as a result of a fresh psychical shock. Her elder daughter, during their first stay in Vienna, had already followed her mother in developing neck-cramps and mild hysterical states; but in particular, she had suffered from pains in walking owing to a retroverted uterus. On my advice she had gone for treatment to Dr. N., one of our most distinguished gynaecologists, who had put her uterus right by massage, and she had remained free from trouble for several months. Her trouble recurred, however, while they were at home, and her mother called in a gynaecologist from the neighbouring University town. He prescribed a combined local and general treatment for the girl, which, however, brought on a severe nervous illness (she was seventeen at the time). It is probable that this was already an indication of her pathological disposition which was to manifest itself a year later in a character-change. [See below, p. 83.] Her mother, who had handed the girl over to the doctors with her usual mixture of docility and mistrust, was overcome by the most violent self-reproaches after the unfortunate outcome of the treatment. A train of thought which I have not investigated brought her to the conclusion that Dr. N. and I were to-gether responsible for the girl's illness because we had made light of her serious condition. By an act of will as it were, she undid the effects of my treatment and promptly relapsed into the states from which I had freed her. A distinguished physician in her neighbourhood, to whom she went for advice, and Dr. Breuer, who was in correspondence with her, succeeded

[1] [Freud himself translated this book (Bernheim, 1886), and the translation was published in 1888–9.]

in convincing her of the innocence of the two targets of her accusations; but even after this was cleared up, the aversion to me which she formed at the time was left over as a hysterical residue, and she declared that it was impossible for her to take up her treatment with me again. On the advice of the same medical authority she turned for help to a Sanatorium in North Germany. At Breuer's desire I explained to the physician in charge the modifications of hypnotic therapy which I had found effective in her case.

This attempted transfer [1] failed completely. From the very first she seems to have been at cross-purposes with the doctor. She exhausted herself in resisting whatever was done for her. She went downhill, lost sleep and appetite, and only recovered after a woman friend of hers who visited her in the Sanatorium in effect secretly abducted her and looked after her in her house. A short time afterwards, exactly a year after her first meeting with me, she was again in Vienna and put herself once more into my hands.

I found her much better than I had expected from the accounts I had received by letter. She could get about and was free from anxiety; much of what I had accomplished the year before was still maintained. Her chief complaint was of frequent states of confusion—'storms in her head' as she called them. Besides this she suffered from sleeplessness, and was often in tears for hours at a time. She felt sad at one particular time of day (five o'clock). This was the regular hour at which, during the winter, she had been able to visit her daughter in the nursing home. She stammered and clacked a great deal and kept rubbing her hands together as though she was in a rage, and when I asked her if she saw a great many animals, she only replied: 'Oh keep still!'

At my first attempt to induce hypnosis she clenched her fists and exclaimed: 'I won't be given any antipyrin injections; I would rather have my pains! I don't like Dr. R.; he is antipathetic to me.' I perceived that she was involved in the memory of being hypnotized in the sanatorium, and she calmed down as soon as I brought her back to the present situation.

At the very beginning of the [resumed] treatment I had an

---

[1] [Though the German word here is *'Übertragung'*, it is evidently not used in the technical sense of 'transference' which is first found at the end of this volume, on p. 302.]

instructive experience. I had asked her how long she had had a recurrence of the stammering, and she had hesitatingly answered (under hypnosis) that it was ever since a shock she had at D—— during the winter. A waiter at the hotel in which she was staying had concealed himself in her bedroom. In the darkness, she said, she had taken the object for an overcoat and put out her hand to take hold of it; and the man had suddenly 'shot up into the air'. I took this memory-picture away, and in fact from that time on she ceased to stammer noticeably either in hypnosis or in waking life. I cannot remember what it was that led me to test the success of my suggestion, but when I returned the same evening I asked her in an apparently innocent voice how I could manage to fasten the door when I went away (while she was lying asleep) so that no one could slip into the room. To my astonishment she gave a violent start and began grinding her teeth and rubbing her hands. She indicated that she had had a severe shock of that kind at D——, but could not be persuaded to tell me the story. I observed that she had in mind the same story which she had told me that morning during the hypnosis and which I thought I had wiped out. In her next hypnosis she told me the story in greater detail and more truthfully. In her excitement she had been walking up and down the passage and found the door of her maid's bedroom open. She had tried to go in and sit down. Her maid had stood in the way, but she refused to be stopped and walked in, and then caught sight of the dark object against the wall which turned out to be a man. It was evidently the erotic factor in this little adventure which had caused her to give an untrue account of it. This taught me that an incomplete story under hypnosis produces no therapeutic effect. I accustomed myself to regarding as incomplete any story that brought about no improvement, and I gradually came to be able to read from patients' faces whether they might not be concealing an essential part of their confessions.

The work that I had to do with her this time consisted in dealing in hypnosis with the disagreeable impressions she had received during her daughter's treatment and during her own stay in the sanatorium. She was full of suppressed anger with the physician who had compelled her under hypnosis to spell out the word 't . . . o . . . a . . . d' and she made me promise never to make her say it. In this connection I ventured upon a practical joke in one of my suggestions to her. This was the only abuse of hypnosis—and a fairly innocent one at that—of which I have to plead guilty with this patient. I assured her that her stay in the sanatorium at '-tal' ['-'vale'] would become so remote to her that she would not even be able to recall its name and that whenever she wanted to refer to it she would hesitate between '-berg' ['-hill'], '-tal', '-wald' ['-wood'] and so on. This duly happened and presently the only remaining sign of her speech-inhibition was her uncertainty over this name. Eventually, following a remark by Dr. Breuer, I relieved her of this compulsive paramnesia.

I had a longer struggle with what she described as 'the storms in her head' than with the residues of these experiences. When I first saw her in one of these states she was lying on the sofa with her features distorted and her whole body unceasingly restless. She kept on pressing her hands to her forehead and calling out in yearning and helpless tones the name 'Emmy', which was her elder daughter's as well as her own. Under hypnosis she informed me that this state was a repetition of the many fits of despair by which she had been overcome during her daughter's treatment, when, after she had spent hours in trying to discover some means of correcting its bad effects, no way out presented itself. When, at such a time, she felt her thoughts becoming confused, she made it a practice to call out her daughter's name, so that it might help her back to clear-headedness. For, during the period when her daughter's illness was imposing fresh duties on her and she felt that her own nervous condition was once again gaining strength over her, she had determined that whatever had to do with the girl must be kept free from confusion, however chaotic everything else in her head was.

In the course of a few weeks we were able to dispose of these memories too and Frau Emmy remained under my observation for some time longer, feeling perfectly well. At the very end of her stay something happened which I shall describe in detail, since it throws the strongest light on the patient's character and the manner in which her states came about.

I called on her one day at lunch-time and surprised her in the act of throwing something wrapped up in paper into the garden, where it was caught by the children of the house-porter. In reply to my question, she admitted that it was her

(dry) pudding, and that this went the same way every day. This
led me to investigate what remained of the other courses and I
found that there was more than half left on the plates. When I
asked her why she ate so little she answered that she was not
in the habit of eating more and that it would be bad for her if
she did; she had the same constitution as her late father, who
had also been a small eater. When I enquired what she drank
she told me she could only tolerate thick fluids, such as milk,
coffee or cocoa; if she ever drank water or minerals it ruined her
digestion. This bore all the signs of a neurotic choice. I took a
specimen of her urine and found it was highly concentrated and
overcharged with urates.

I therefore thought it advisable to recommend her to drink
more and decided also to increase the amount of her food. It
is true that she did not look at all noticeably thin but I nevertheless thought it worth while to aim at feeding her up a little.
When on my next visit I ordered her some alkaline water and
forbad her usual way of dealing with her pudding, she showed
considerable agitation. 'I'll do it because you ask me to,' she
said, 'but I can tell you in advance that it will turn out badly,
because it is contrary to my nature, and it was the same with
my father.' When I asked her under hypnosis why it was that
she could not eat more or drink any water, she answered in a
rather sullen tone: 'I don't know.' Next day the nurse reported
that she had eaten the whole of her helpings and had drunk a
glass of the alkaline water. But I found Frau Emmy herself
lying in a profoundly depressed state and in a very ungracious
mood. She complained of having very violent gastric pains. 'I
told you what would happen,' she said. 'We have sacrificed all
the successful results that we have been struggling for so long.
I've ruined my digestion, as always happens if I eat more or
drink water, and I have to starve myself entirely for five days
to a week before I can tolerate anything.' I assured her that
there was no need to starve herself and that it was impossible
to ruin one's digestion in that way: her pains were only due to
the anxiety over eating and drinking. It was clear that this
explanation of mine made not the slightest impression on her.
For when, soon afterwards, I tried to put her to sleep, for the
first time I failed to bring about hypnosis; and the furious look
she cast at me convinced me that she was in open rebellion and
that the situation was very grave. I gave up trying to hypnotize

her, and announced that I would give her twenty-four hours to think things over and accept the view that her gastric pains came only from her fear. At the end of this time I would ask her whether she was still of the opinion that her digestion could be ruined for a week by drinking a glass of mineral water and eating a modest meal; if she said yes, I would ask her to leave. This little scene was in very sharp contrast to our normal relations, which were most friendly.

I found her twenty-four hours later, docile and submissive. When I asked her what she thought about the origin of her gastric pains, she answered, for she was incapable of prevarication: 'I think they come from my anxiety, but only because you say so.' I then put her under hypnosis and asked her once again: 'Why can't you eat more?'

The answer came promptly and consisted once more in her producing a series of chronologically arranged reasons from her store of recollections: 'I'm thinking how, when I was a child, it often happened that out of naughtiness I refused to eat my meat at dinner. My mother was very severe about this and under the threat of condign punishment I was obliged two hours later to eat the meat, which had been left standing on the same plate. The meat was quite cold by then and the fat was set so hard' (she showed her disgust) '. . . I can still see the fork in front of me . . . one of its prongs was a little bent. Whenever I sit down to a meal I see the plates before me with the cold meat and fat on them. And how, many years later, I lived with my brother who was an officer and who had that horrible disease. I knew it was contagious and was terribly afraid of making a mistake and picking up his knife and fork' (she shuddered) '. . . and in spite of that I ate my meals with him so that no one should know that he was ill. And how, soon after that, I nursed my other brother when he had consumption so badly. We sat by the side of his bed and the spittoon always stood on the table, open' (she shuddered again) '. . . and he had a habit of spitting across the plates into the spittoon. This always made me feel so sick, but I couldn't show it, for fear of hurting his feelings. And these spittoons are still on the table whenever I have a meal and they still make me feel sick.' I naturally made a thorough clearance of this whole array of agencies of disgust and then asked why it was that she could not drink water. When she was seventeen, she replied, the family had spent some months in Munich and almost all of them had contracted gastric catarrh owing to the bad drinking water. In the case of the others the trouble was quickly relieved by medical attention, but with her it had persisted. Nor had she been improved by the mineral water which she was recommended. When the doctor had prescribed it she had thought at once 'that won't be any use'. From that time onwards this intolerance both of ordinary water and mineral water had recurred on countless occasions.

The therapeutic effect of these discoveries under hypnosis was immediate and lasting. She did *not* starve herself for a week but the very next day she ate and drank without making any difficulty. Two months later she wrote in a letter: 'I am eating excellently and have put on a great deal of weight. I have already drunk forty bottles of the water. Do you think I should go on with it?'

I saw Frau von N. again in the spring of the following year at her estate near D——. At this time her elder daughter, whose name she had called out during her 'storms in the head', entered on a phase of abnormal development. She exhibited unbridled ambitions which were out of all proportion to the poverty of her gifts, and she became disobedient and even violent towards her mother. I still enjoyed her mother's confidence and was sent for to give my opinion on the girl's condition. I formed an unfavourable impression of the psychological change that had occurred in the girl, and in arriving at a prognosis I had also to take into account the fact that all her stepbrothers and sisters (the children of Herr von N. by his first marriage) had succumbed to paranoia. In her mother's family, too, there was no lack of a neuropathic heredity, although none of her more immediate relatives had developed a chronic psychosis. I communicated to Frau von N. without any reservation the opinion for which she had asked and she received it calmly and with understanding. She had grown stout, and looked in flourishing health. She had felt relatively very well during the nine months that had passed since the end of her last treatment. She had only been disturbed by slight neck-cramps and other minor ailments. During the several days which I spent in her house I came for the first time to realize the whole extent of her duties, occupations and intellectual interests. I also met the family doctor, who had not many complaints to make about the lady; so she had to some degree come to terms with the profession.

She was thus in very many respects healthier and more capable, but in spite of all my improving suggestions there had been little change in her fundamental character. She seemed not to have accepted the existence of a category of 'indifferent things'. Her inclination to torment herself was scarcely less than it had been at the time of her treatment. Nor had her hysterical disposition been quiescent during this good period. She complained, for instance, of an inability to make journeys of any length by train. This had come on during the last few months. A necessarily hurried attempt to relieve her of this difficulty resulted only in her producing a number of trivial disagreeable impressions left by some recent journeys she had made to D—— and its neighbourhood. She seemed reluctant, however, to be communicative under hypnosis, and even then I began to suspect that she was on the point of withdrawing once more from my influence and that the secret purpose of her railway inhibition was to prevent her making a fresh journey to Vienna.

It was during these days, too, that she made her complaints about gaps in her memory 'especially about the most important events' [p. 61 n.], from which I concluded that the work I had done two years previously had been thoroughly effective and lasting.—One day, she was walking with me along an avenue that led from the house to an inlet in the sea and I ventured to ask whether the path was often infested by toads. By way of reply she threw a reproachful glance at me, though unaccompanied by signs of horror; she amplified this a moment later with the words 'but the ones here are *real*'. During the hypnosis, which I induced in order to deal with her railway inhibition, she herself seemed dissatisfied with the answers she gave me, and she expressed a fear that in future she was likely to be less obedient under hypnosis than before. I determined to convince her of the contrary. I wrote a few words on a piece of paper, handed it to her and said: 'At lunch to-day you will pour me out a glass of red wine, just as you did yesterday. As I raise the glass to my lips you will say: "Oh, please pour me out a glass, too", and when I reach for the bottle, you will say: "No thank you, I don't think I will after all". You will then put your hand in your bag, draw out the piece of paper and find those same words written on it.' This was in the morning. A few hours later the little episode took place exactly as I had pre-arranged it, and so naturally that none of the many people present noticed anything. When she asked me for the wine she showed visible signs of an internal struggle—for she never drank wine—and after she had refused the drink with obvious relief, she put her hand into her bag and drew out the piece of paper on which appeared the last words she had spoken. She shook her head and stared at me in astonishment.

After my visit in May, 1890, my news of Frau von N. became gradually scantier. I heard indirectly that her daughter's deplorable condition, which caused her every kind of distress and agitation, did eventually undermine her health. Finally, in the summer of 1893, I had a short note from her asking my permission for her to be hypnotized by another doctor, since she was ill again and could not come to Vienna. At first I did not understand why my permission was necessary, till I remembered that in 1890 I had, at her own request, protected her against being hypnotized by anyone else, so that there should be no danger of her being distressed by coming under the control of a doctor who was antipathetic to her, as had happened at *-berg* (*-tal*, *-wald*). I accordingly renounced my exclusive prerogative in writing.

DISCUSSION

Unless we have first come to a complete agreement upon the terminology involved, it is not easy to decide whether a particular case is to be reckoned as a hysteria or some other neurosis (I am speaking here of neuroses which are not of a purely neurasthenic type); and we have still to await the directing hand which shall set up boundary-marks in the region of the commonly occurring mixed neuroses and which shall bring out the features essential for their characterization. If, accordingly, we are still accustomed to diagnosing a hysteria, in the narrower sense of the term, from its similarity to familiar typical cases, we shall scarcely be able to dispute the fact that the case of Frau Emmy von N. was one of hysteria. The mildness of her deliria and hallucinations (while her other mental activities remained intact), the change in her personality and store of memories when she was in a state of artificial somnambulism,

the anaesthesia in her painful leg, certain data revealed in her
anamnesis, her ovarian neuralgia, etc., admit of no doubt as
to the hysterical nature of the illness, or at least of the patient.
That the question can be raised at all is due only to one particular feature of the case, which also provides an opportunity
for a comment that is of general validity. As we have explained
in the 'Preliminary Communication' which appears at the
beginning of this volume, we regard hysterical symptoms as
the effects and residues of excitations which have acted upon
the nervous system as traumas. Residues of this kind are not
left behind if the original excitation has been discharged by
abreaction or thought-activity. It is impossible any longer at
this point to avoid introducing the idea of quantities (even
though not measurable ones). We must regard the process as
though a sum of excitation impinging on the nervous system is
transformed into chronic symptoms in so far as it has not been
employed for external action in proportion to its amount.[1] Now
we are accustomed to find in hysteria that a considerable part
of this 'sum of excitation' of the trauma is transformed into
purely somatic symptoms. It is this characteristic of hysteria
which has so long stood in the way of its being recognized as a
psychical disorder.

If, for the sake of brevity, we adopt the term 'conversion' [2]
to signify the transformation of psychical excitation into chronic
somatic symptoms, which is so characteristic of hysteria, then
we may say that the case of Frau Emmy von N. exhibited only
a small amount of conversion. The excitation, which was
originally psychical, remained for the most part in the psychical
sphere, and it is easy to see that this gives it a resemblance to
the other, non-hysterical neuroses. There are cases of hysteria
in which the whole surplus of stimulation undergoes conversion,
so that the somatic symptoms of hysteria intrude into what
appears to be an entirely normal consciousness. An incomplete
transformation is however more usual, so that some part at

---

[1] [For a detailed account of Freud's attempt at explaining psychology
on a quantitative basis see his posthumously published 'Project for a
Scientific Psychology' (1950a), written a few months after the present
work. He had already expressed these views briefly in the last paragraph but one of his first paper on the 'Neuro-Psychoses of Defence'
(1894a). See also the Editor's Introduction, p. xix ff.]

[2] [Freud had introduced this term in his first paper on the 'Neuro-
Psychoses of Defence' (1894a). See, however, p. 206 n.]

least of the affect that accompanies the trauma persists in consciousness as a component of the subject's state of feeling.

The psychical symptoms in our present case of hysteria with very little conversion can be divided into alterations of mood (anxiety, melancholic depression), phobias and abulias (inhibitions of will). The two latter classes of psychical disturbance are regarded by the French school of psychiatrists as stigmata of neurotic degeneracy, but in our case they are seen to have been adequately determined by traumatic experiences. These phobias and abulias were for the most part of traumatic origin, as I shall show in detail.

Some of the phobias, it is true, corresponded to the primary phobias of human beings, and especially of neuropaths—in particular, for instance, her fear of animals (snakes and toads, as well as all the vermin of which Mephistopheles boasted himself master[1]), and of thunderstorms and so on. But these phobias too were established more firmly by traumatic events. Thus her fear of toads was strengthened by her experience in early childhood of having a dead toad thrown at her by one of her brothers, which led to her first attack of hysterical spasms [p. 52]; and similarly, her fear of thunderstorms was brought out by the shock which gave rise to her clacking [p. 58], and her fear of fogs by her walk on the Island of Rügen [p. 73]. Nevertheless, in this group the primary—or, one might say, the instinctive—fear (regarded as a psychical stigma) plays the preponderant part.

The other, more specific phobias were also accounted for by particular events. Her dread of unexpected and sudden shocks was the consequence of the terrible impression made on her by seeing her husband, when he seemed to be in the best of health, succumb to a heart-attack before her eyes. Her dread of strangers, and of people in general, turned out to be derived from the time when she was being persecuted by her [husband's] family and was inclined to see one of their agents in every stranger and when it seemed to her likely that strangers knew of the things that were being spread abroad about her in writing and by word of mouth [p. 63]. Her fear of asylums and their inmates went back to a whole series of unhappy events

---

[1] [The lord of rats and eke of mice,
Of flies and bed-bugs, frogs and lice.
Goethe, *Faust*, Part I, Scene 3 (Bayard Taylor's translation).]

in her family and to stories poured into her listening ears by a stupid servant-girl [p. 55]. Apart from this, this phobia was supported on the one hand by the primary and instinctive horror of insanity felt by healthy people, and on the other hand by the fear, felt by her no less than by all neurotics, of going mad herself. Her highly specific fear that someone was standing behind her [p. 65] was determined by a number of terrifying experiences in her youth and later life. Since the episode in the hotel [p. 79], which was especially distressing to her because of its erotic implications, her fear of a stranger creeping into her room was greatly emphasized. Finally, her fear of being buried alive, which she shared with so many neuropaths, was entirely explained by her belief that her husband was not dead when his body was carried out—a belief which gave such moving expression to her inability to accept the fact that her life with the man she loved had come to a sudden end. In my opinion, however, all these psychical [1] factors, though they may account for the *choice* of these phobias, cannot explain their *persistence*. It is necessary, I think, to adduce a *neurotic* factor to account for this persistence—the fact that the patient had been living for years in a state of sexual abstinence. Such circumstances are among the most frequent causes of a tendency to anxiety. [2]

Our patient's abulias (inhibitions of will, inability to act) admit even less than the phobias of being regarded as psychical stigmata due to a general limitation of capacity. On the contrary, the hypnotic analysis of the case made it clear that her abulias were determined by a twofold psychical mechanism—which was at bottom a single one. In the first place an abulia may simply be the consequence of a phobia. This is so when the phobia is attached to an action of the subject's own instead of to an expectation [of an external event]—for instance, in our present case, the fear of going out or of mixing with people, as compared with the fear of someone creeping into the room. Here the inhibition of will is caused by the anxiety attendant

---

[1] [In the first German edition only, this word reads 'physical', which was clearly a misprint.]

[2] [See Freud's contemporary paper on anxiety neuroses (1895*b*).— In the previous sentence he is using the term 'neurotic', as he sometimes does at this period, in relation to what he later (1898*a*) termed the 'actual-neuroses'.]

upon the performance of the action. It would be wrong to regard abulias of this kind as symptoms distinct from the corresponding phobias, though it must be admitted that such phobias can exist (provided they are not too severe) without producing abulias. The second class of abulias depends on the presence of affectively-toned and unresolved associations which are opposed to linking up with other associations, and particularly with any that are incompatible with them. Our patient's anorexia offers a most brilliant instance of this kind of abulia [p. 82 f.]. She ate so little because she did not like the taste, and she could not enjoy the taste because the act of eating had from the earliest times been connected with memories of disgust whose sum of affect had never been to any degree diminished; and it is impossible to eat with disgust and pleasure at the same time. Her old-established disgust at meal-times had persisted undiminished because she was obliged constantly to suppress it, instead of getting rid of it by reaction. In her childhood she had been forced, under threat of punishment, to eat the cold meal that disgusted her, and in her later years she had been prevented out of consideration for her brothers from expressing the affects to which she was exposed during their meals together.

At this point I may perhaps refer to a short paper in which I have tried to give a psychological explanation of hysterical paralyses (Freud 1893c). I there arrived at a hypothesis that the cause of these paralyses lay in the inaccessibility to fresh associations of a group of ideas connected, let us say, with one of the extremities of the body; this associative inaccessibility depended in turn on the fact that the idea of the paralysed limb was involved in the recollection of the trauma—a recollection loaded with affect that had not been disposed of. I showed from examples from ordinary life that a cathexis [1] such as this of an idea whose affect is unresolved always involves a certain amount of associative inaccessibility and of incompatibility with new cathexes.

I have not hitherto succeeded in confirming, by means of hypnotic analysis, this theory about motor paralyses, but I can

[1] [This seems to be the first published appearance of the term 'Besetzung' ('cathexis') in the special sense in which Freud used it to denote one of the most fundamental concepts in his psychological theory. See the Editor's Introduction, p. xxiii.]

adduce Frau von N.'s anorexia as proving that this mechanism
is the operative one in certain abulias, and abulias are nothing
other than a highly specialized—or, to use a French expression,
'systematized'—kind of psychical paralysis.

Frau von N.'s psychical situation can be characterized in all
essentials by emphasizing two points. (1) The distressing affects
attaching to her traumatic experiences had remained unresolved—for instance, her depression, her pain (about her
husband's death), her resentment (at being persecuted by his
relatives), her disgust (at the compulsory meals), her fear
(about her many frightening experiences), and so on. (2) Her
memory exhibited a lively activity which, sometimes spontaneously, sometimes in response to a contemporary stimulus
(e.g. the news of the revolution in San Domingo [p. 68 *n.*]),
brought her traumas with their accompanying affects bit by bit
into her present-day consciousness. My therapeutic procedure
was based on the course of this activity of her memory and
endeavoured day by day to resolve and get rid of whatever
that particular day had brought to the surface, till the accessible
stock of her pathological memories seemed to be exhausted.

These two psychical characteristics, which I regard as generally present in hysterical paroxysms, opened the way to a
number of important considerations. I will, however, put off
discussing them till I have given some attention to the mechanism of the somatic symptoms.

It is not possible to assign the same origin to all the somatic
symptoms of these patients. On the contrary, even from this
case, which was not rich in them, we find that the somatic
symptoms of a hysteria can arise in a variety of ways. I will
venture, in the first place, to include pains among somatic
symptoms. So far as I can see, one set of Frau von N.'s pains
were certainly determined organically by the slight modifications (of a rheumatic kind) in the muscles, tendons or fascia
which cause so much more pain to neurotics than to normal
people. Another set of pains were in all probability *memories* of
pains—were mnemic symbols[1] of the times of agitation and

---

[1] [Cf. above, footnote, p. 71. Freud had already used this term in
Section I of his first paper on 'The Neuro-Psychoses of Defence' (1894*a*),
and he repeatedly uses it in the present work. It rarely occurs in his
later writings, though it is explained at some length in the first of his
Five Lectures (1910*a*).]

sick-nursing which played such a large part in the patient's life. These pains, too, may well have been originally justified on organic grounds but had since then been adapted for the purposes of the neurosis. I base these assertions about Frau von N.'s pains mainly on observations made elsewhere which I shall report on a later page.[1] On this particular point little information could be gathered from the patient herself.

Some of the striking motor phenomena exhibited by Frau von N. were simply an expression of the emotions and could easily be recognized in that light. Thus, the way in which she stretched her hands in front of her with her fingers spread out and crooked expressed horror, and similarly her facial play. This, of course, was a more lively and uninhibited way of expressing her emotions than was usual with women of her education and race. Indeed, she herself was restrained, almost stiff in her expressive movements when she was not in a hysterical state. Others of her motor symptoms were, according to herself, directly related to her pains. She played restlessly with her fingers (1888) [p. 49] or rubbed her hands against one another (1889) [p. 78] so as to prevent herself from screaming. This reason reminds one forcibly of one of the principles laid down by Darwin to explain the expression of the emotions —the principle of the overflow of excitation [Darwin, 1872, Chap. III], which accounts, for instance, for dogs wagging their tails. We are all of us accustomed, when we are affected by painful stimuli, to replace screaming by other sorts of motor innervations. A person who has made up his mind at the dentist's to keep his head and mouth still and not to put his hand in the way, may at least start drumming with his feet.[2]

A more complicated method of conversion is revealed by Frau von N.'s *tic*-like movements, such as clacking with the tongue and stammering, calling out the name 'Emmy' in confusional states [p. 80], using the composite formula 'Keep still! Don't say anything! Don't touch me!' (1888) [p. 49]. Of these motor manifestations, the stammering and clacking can be explained in accordance with a mechanism which I have described, in a short paper on the treatment of a case by

[1] [The subject of rheumatic pains and their relation to hysteria is discussed at some length in the case of Fräulein Elisabeth von R. below, p. 174. See also above, p. 71 *n*.]

[2] [Cf. Breuer's remarks on the same topic, p. 202.]

hypnotic suggestion (1892–3b), as 'the putting into effect of antithetic ideas'.[1] The process, as exemplified in our present instance [p. 54], would be as follows. Our hysterical patient, exhausted by worry and long hours of watching by the bedside of her sick child which had at last fallen asleep, said to herself: 'Now you must be perfectly still so as not to awaken the child.' This intention probably gave rise to an antithetic idea in the form of a fear that she might make a noise all the same that would wake the child from the sleep which she had so long hoped for. Similar antithetic ideas arise in us in a marked manner when we feel uncertain whether we can carry out some important intention.

Neurotics, in whose self-feeling we seldom fail to find a strain of depression or anxious expectation, form greater numbers of these antithetic ideas than normal people, or perceive them more easily; and they regard them as of more importance. In our patient's state of exhaustion the antithetic idea, which was normally rejected, proved itself the stronger. It is this idea which put itself into effect and which, to the patient's horror, actually produced the noise she dreaded. In order to explain the whole process it may further be assumed that her exhaustion was only a partial one; it affected, to use the terminology of Janet and his followers, only her 'primary' ego and did not result in a weakening of the antithetic idea as well.

It may further be assumed that it was her horror at the noise produced against her will that made the moment a traumatic one, and fixed the noise itself as a somatic mnemic symptom [2] of the whole scene. I believe, indeed, that the character of the *tic* itself, consisting as it did of a succession of sounds which were convulsively emitted and separated by pauses and which could be best likened to clackings, reveals traces of the process to which it owed its origin. It appears that a conflict had occurred between her intention and the antithetic idea (the counter-will) and that this gave the *tic* its discontinuous character and confined the antithetic idea to paths other than

---

[1] [The concept of antithetic ideas, as well as that of 'counter-will', which is mentioned just below, was discussed in this same paper.]

[2] ['*Symptom*' in all the German editions. It seems probable that this is a misprint for '*Symbol*'. 'Mnemic symbol' appears to give the better sense and is the term used throughout the book. (See footnote, p. 90.)]

the habitual ones for innervating the muscular apparatus of speech.

The patient's spastic inhibition of speech, her peculiar stammer, was the residue of an essentially similar exciting cause [p. 58]. Here, however, it was not the *outcome* of the final innervation—the exclamation—but the process of innervation itself—the attempted convulsive inhibition of the organs of speech—which was made into a symbol of the event for her memory.

These two symptoms, the clacking and the stammering, which were thus closely related through the history of their origin, continued to be associated and were turned into chronic symptoms after being repeated on a similar occasion. Thereafter they were put to a further use. Having originated at a moment of violent fright, they were thenceforward joined to *any* fright (in accordance with the mechanism of monosymptomatic hysteria which will be described in Case 5 [p. 149 f.]), even when the fright could not lead to an antithetic idea being put into effect.

The two symptoms were eventually linked up with so many traumas, had so much reason for being reproduced in memory, that they perpetually interrupted the patient's speech for no particular cause, in the manner of a meaningless *tic*.[1] Hypnotic analysis, however, was able to demonstrate how much meaning lay concealed behind this apparent *tic*; and if the Breuer procedure did not succeed in this case in getting rid of the two symptoms completely at a single blow, that was because the catharsis had extended only to the three principal traumas and not to the secondarily associated ones.[2]

[1] [Scarcely any references to *tic* occur in Freud's later writings. In a paper on the subject, Ferenczi (1921) writes: 'Professor Freud, whom I had occasion to question on the meaning and significance of *tic*, suggested that some organic factor might be at work in it.']

[2] I may here be giving an impression of laying too much emphasis on the details of the symptoms and of becoming lost in an unnecessary maze of sign-reading. But I have come to learn that the determination of hysterical symptoms does in fact extend to their subtlest manifestations and that it is difficult to attribute too much sense to them. Let me give an example to justify this statement. Some months ago I had under my treatment an eighteen-year-old girl belonging to a family with a bad heredity. Hysteria played its full part in her complex neurosis. The first thing I heard from her was a complaint that she suffered from attacks of despair of two varieties. In one variety she felt drawing and

In accordance with the rules governing hysterical attacks, the exclamation of 'Emmy' during her attacks of confusion reproduced, it will be remembered, her frequent states of helplessness during her daughter's treatment. This exclamation was linked to the content of the attack by a complex train of thought and was in the nature of a protective formula against the attack. The exclamation would probably, through a more extended application of its meaning, have degenerated into a *tic*, as had in fact already happened in the case of the complicated protective formula 'Don't touch me', etc. In both these instances hypnotic treatment prevented any further development of the symptoms; but the exclamation 'Emmy' had only just

pricking sensations in the lower part of her face, from her cheeks down towards her mouth; in the other variety the toes of both her feet were stretched out convulsively and kept on wriggling about. To begin with I myself was unwilling to attach much importance to these details, and there can be no doubt that earlier students of hysteria would have been inclined to regard these phenomena as evidence of the stimulation of cortical centres during a hysterical attack. It is true that we are ignorant of the locality of the centres for paraesthesias of this kind, but it is well known that such paraesthesias usher in partial epilepsy and constitute Charcot's sensory epilepsy. Symmetrical cortical areas in the immediate vicinity of the median fissure might be held responsible for the movement of the toes. But the explanation turned out to be a different one. When I had come to know the girl better I put a straight question to her as to what kind of thoughts came to her during these attacks. I told her not to be embarrassed and said that she must be able to give an explanation of the two phenomena. The patient turned red with shame, but I was able to persuade her in the end, without using hypnosis, to give the following account, the truth of which was fully confirmed by her companion, who was present at the time. From the time when her periods first set in she had suffered for years from *cephalalgia adolescentium* which had made any regular occupation impossible and had interfered with her education. When at last she was freed from this disability, this ambitious and rather simple-minded child was determined to work extremely hard at her own improvement, so as to catch up once more with her sisters and contemporaries. In doing so she made quite unreasonable efforts, and an effort of this kind usually ended in an outburst of despair at having over-estimated her powers. She also, of course, compared herself with other girls physically and felt unhappy when she discovered some physical disadvantage in herself. Her teeth projected noticeably, and she began to feel upset about this. She got the idea of correcting the defect by practising for a quarter of an hour at a time pulling down her upper lip over the projecting teeth. The failure of these childish efforts once led to a fit of despair; and thenceforward the drawing and pricking sensations from the cheek downwards were come into existence, and I caught it while it was still on its native soil, restricted to attacks of confusion.

As we have seen, these motor symptoms originated in various ways: by putting an antithetic idea into effect (as in the clacking), by a simple conversion of psychical excitation into motor activity (as in the stammering), or by a voluntary action during a hysterical paroxysm (as in the protective measures exemplified by the exclamation 'Emmy' and the longer formula). But however these motor symptoms may have originated, they all have one thing in common. They can be shown to have an original or long-standing connection with traumas, and stand as symbols for them in the activities of the memory.

established as the content of one of her two varieties of attack. The origin of the other variety—with its motor symptoms of stretching out and wriggling the toes—was no less easily found. I was told that her first attack of this kind followed after an excursion on the Schafberg near Ischl [in Upper Austria], and her relatives were naturally inclined to set it down to over-exertion. But the girl herself told me a different story. It seems that it was a favourite habit of the sisters to tease one another about the large size of their feet—an undeniable fact. The patient had long felt unhappy over this blemish and tried to force her feet into the tightest possible boots. Her observant father, however, would not allow this and saw to it that she only wore comfortably-fitting footgear. She was much dissatisfied with this regulation. She thought about it all the time and acquired the habit of wriggling her toes about in her shoes, as people do when they want to discover whether a shoe is much too large, how much smaller a size they could take, etc. During the excursion on the Schafberg (which she was far from finding an exertion) there was once again, of course, an opportunity for her attention to be drawn to the subject of shoes, in view of the shortened skirts she wore. One of her sisters said to her in the course of the walk: 'You've put extra big shoes on to-day.' She experimented by wriggling her toes and got the same impression. Thenceforward she could not escape from her agitation about the unlucky size of her feet, and when they got back from the walk her first attack came on; her toes curled up and moved about involuntarily as a mnemic symbol of the whole depressing train of thought.

I may point out that what we are dealing with here are attacks and not chronic symptoms. I may also add that after the patient's confession her first variety of symptoms ceased, but the second variety—her attacks of wriggling her toes—persisted. There must therefore have been something left over, which she had not confessed.

Postscript [in all editions]. I learnt later that the reason why the foolish girl worked so hard at beautifying herself was that she wanted to attract a young cousin of hers.—[*Added* 1924:] Some years later her neurosis turned into a dementia praecox.

Others of the patient's somatic symptoms were not of a hysterical nature at all. This is true, for example, of the neck-cramps, which I regard as a modified form of migraine [p. 71 n.] and which as such are not to be classed as a neurosis but as an organic disorder. Hysterical symptoms, however, regularly become attached to these. Frau von N.'s neck-cramps, for instance, were employed for the purpose of hysterical attacks, whereas she did not have the typical symptomatology of hysterical attacks at her disposal.

I will amplify this description of Frau von N.'s psychical state by considering the pathological changes of consciousness which could be observed in her. Like her neck-cramps, distressing present-day events (cf. her last delirium in the garden [p. 73]) or anything which powerfully recalled any of her traumas brought her into a state of delirium. In such states—and the few observations I made led me to no other conclusion—there was a limitation of consciousness and a compulsion to associate similar to that prevailing in dreams [p. 69 n.]; hallucinations and illusions were facilitated to the highest degree and feeble-minded or even nonsensical inferences were made. This state, which was comparable to one of hallucinatory alienation, probably represented an attack. It might be regarded as an acute psychosis (serving as the equivalent of an attack) which would be classified as a condition of 'hallucinatory confusion'. A further resemblance between such states of hers and a typical hysterical attack was shown by the fact that a portion of the old-established traumatic memories could usually be detected underlying the delirium. The transition from a normal state to a delirium often occurred quite imperceptibly. She would be talking quite rationally at one moment about matters of small emotional importance, and as her conversation passed on to ideas of a distressing kind I would notice, from her exaggerated gestures or the appearance of her regular formulas of speech, etc., that she was in a state of delirium. At the beginning of the treatment the delirium lasted all day long; so that it was difficult to decide with certainty whether any given symptoms—like her gestures—formed part of her psychical state merely as symptoms of an attack, or whether—like the clacking and stammering —they had become genuine chronic symptoms. It was often only possible *after the event* to distinguish between what had happened in a delirium and what had happened in her normal state. For the two states were separated in her memory, and she would sometimes be highly astonished to hear of the things which the delirium had introduced piecemeal into her normal conversation. My very first interview with her was the most remarkable instance of the way in which the two states were interwoven without paying any attention to each other. Only at one moment of this psychical see-sawing did it happen that her normal consciousness, in touch with the present day, was affected. This was when she gave me an answer which originated from her delirium and said she was 'a woman dating from last century' [p. 52 *n*.].

The analysis of these states of delirium in Frau von N. was not exhaustively carried out. This was mainly because her condition improved so rapidly that the deliria became sharply differentiated from her normal life and were restricted to the periods of her neck-cramps. On the other hand, I gathered a great deal of information about the patient's behaviour in a third state, that of artificial somnambulism. Whereas in her normal state she had no knowledge of the psychical experiences during her deliria and during her somnambulism, she had access during somnambulism to the memories of all three states. In point of fact, therefore, she was at her most normal in the state of somnambulism. Indeed, if I leave on one side the fact that in somnambulism she was far less reserved with me than she was at her best moments in ordinary life—that is, that in somnambulism she gave me information about her family and such things, while at other times she treated me as a stranger—and if, further, I disregard the fact that she exhibited the full degree of suggestibility characteristic of somnambulism, I am bound to say that during her somnambulism she was in a completely normal state. It was interesting to notice that on the other hand her somnambulism showed no trace of being super-normal, but was subject to all the mental failings that we are accustomed to associate with a normal state of consciousness.

The examples which follow throw light on the behaviour of her memory in somnambulism. In conversation one day she expressed her delight at the beauty of a plant in a pot which decorated the entrance hall of the nursing-home. 'But what is its name, doctor? Do you know? I used to know its German and its Latin names, but I've forgotten them both.' She had a wide knowledge of plants, while I was obliged on this occasion to admit my lack of botanical education. A few minutes later I asked her under hypnosis if she now knew the name of the plant in the hall. Without any hesitation she replied: 'The German name is "*Türkenlilie*" [Turk's-cap lily]; I really *have* forgotten the Latin one.' Another time, when she was feeling in good health, she told me of a visit she had paid to the Roman Catacombs, but could not recall two technical terms; nor could I help her with them. Immediately afterwards I asked her under hypnosis which words she had in mind. But she did not know them in hypnosis either. So I said to her: 'Don't bother about them any more now, but when you are in the garden to-morrow between five and six in the afternoon—nearer six than five— they will suddenly occur to you.' Next evening, while we were talking about something which had no connection with cata-combs, she suddenly burst out: ' "Crypt", doctor, and "Colum-barium".' 'Ah! those are the words you couldn't think of yesterday. When did they occur to you?' 'In the garden this afternoon just before I went up to my room.' I saw that she wanted to let me know in this way that she had followed out my instructions as to time exactly, as she was in the habit of leaving the garden at about six o'clock.

Thus we see that even in somnambulism she did not have access to the whole extent of her knowledge. Even in that state there was an actual and a potential consciousness. It used often to happen that when I asked her during her somnambulism where this or that phenomenon was derived from, she would wrinkle her forehead, and after a pause would answer in a deprecatory tone: 'I don't know.' On such occasions I had made it my practice to say: 'Think a moment; it will come to mind directly'; and after a short reflection she would be able to give me the desired information. But it sometimes happened that nothing came to her mind and that I was obliged to leave her with the task of remembering it by the next day; and this never failed to occur.

In her ordinary life Frau von N. scrupulously avoided any untruthfulness, nor did she ever lie to me under hypnosis. Occasionally, however, she would give me incomplete answers and keep back part of her story until I insisted a second time on her completing it. It was usually—as in the instance quoted on p. 79—the distaste inspired by the topic which closed her mouth in somnambulism no less than in ordinary life. Nevertheless, in spite of these restrictive traits, the impression made by her mental behaviour during somnambulism was, on the whole, one of an uninhibited unfolding of her mental powers and of a full command over her store of memories.

Though it cannot be denied that in a state of somnambulism she was highly suggestible, she was far from exhibiting a pathological absence of resistance. It can be asserted on the whole that I did not make more impression on her in that state than I might have expected to do if I were making an investigation of this kind into the psychical mechanisms of someone in full possession of his faculties who put complete confidence in what I said. The only difference was that Frau von N. was unable, in what passed as her normal state, to meet me with any such favourable mental attitude. If, as with her animal phobia, I failed to give her convincing reasons, or did not go into the psychical history of the origin of a symptom but tried to operate by the agency of authoritative suggestion, I invariably observed a strained and dissatisfied expression on her face; and when, at the end of the hypnosis, I asked her whether she would still be afraid of the animal, she would answer: 'No—since you insist.' A promise like this, based only on her obedience to me, never met with any success, any more than did the many general injunctions which I laid upon her, instead of which I might just as well have repeated the single suggestion that she should get well.

But this same person who clung so obstinately to her symptoms in the face of suggestion and would only abandon them in response to psychical analysis or personal conviction, was on the other hand as amenable as the best medium to be found in any hospital, so far as irrelevant suggestions were concerned— so far as it was a question of matters not connected with her illness. I have given instances of her post-hypnotic obedience in the course of the case history. There does not seem to me to be anything contradictory in this behaviour. Here, too, the stronger idea was bound to assert itself. If we go into the mechanism of '*idées fixes*', we find that they are based upon and supported by so many experiences operating with such intensity that we cannot be surprised to find that these ideas are able to put up a successful resistance against the opposing idea brought forward by suggestion, which is clothed with only limited powers.

It would have to be a truly pathological brain from which it was possible to blow away by mere suggestion such well-founded products of intense psychical events.[1]

[1] I have been deeply impressed in another of my patients by this interesting contrast during somnambulism between a most far-reaching obedience in everything unconnected with the symptoms and the obstinacy with which those symptoms persist because they are deeply rooted and inaccessible to analysis. A lively and gifted girl, who had suffered for eighteen months from severe disturbances of her power of walking, was under my treatment for more than five months without my being able to help her. She was analgesic and had painful areas in both legs and a rapid tremor in her hands. She walked bent forward, dragging her legs and with short steps; she staggered as though she was a cerebellar case and, indeed, often fell down. Her temperament was strikingly cheerful. One of the leading authorities in Vienna at the time was misled by this syndrome into diagnosing her case as one of multiple sclerosis. Another specialist recognized her as a hysteric—a diagnosis which was supported by the complicated picture presented by the disease in its beginnings (pains, fainting-fits, amaurosis)—and handed her on to me for treatment. I tried to improve her gait by suggestion, manipulation of her legs under hypnosis, etc., but I had no success in spite of her being an excellent subject for somnambulism. One day, after she once more came tottering into the room, one arm supported on her father's, the other on an umbrella whose tip was already much worn down, I lost patience and shouted at her in her hypnosis: 'This has gone on too long. To-morrow morning that umbrella of yours will break in your hands and you'll have to walk without it, and from that time on you will never need an umbrella again.' I cannot imagine how I came to be so foolish as to give a suggestion to an umbrella. Afterwards I felt ashamed of myself, and did not suspect that my clever patient would save my reputation in the eyes of her father, who was a physician and was present during her hypnoses. Next day her father said to me: 'What do you think she did yesterday? We were walking along the Ringstrasse [the main boulevard in Vienna] when she suddenly got into the highest spirits. She began singing—in the very middle of the street— "Ein freies Leben führen wir" ['We live a free life', from the popularly-sung robbers' chorus in Schiller's play, *Die Räuber*] and beat time on the pavement with her umbrella and broke it.' Of course she herself had no notion that she had wittily transformed a nonsensical suggestion into a brilliantly successful one. Since her condition was not improved by assurances, commands and treatment under hypnosis, I turned to psychical analysis and requested her to tell me what emotion had preceded the onset of her illness. She answered (under hypnosis but without any signs of feeling) that a short time previously a young relative of hers had died to whom she had for many years considered herself engaged. This piece of information, however, produced no alteration whatever in her condition. Accordingly, during her next hypnosis, I told her I was quite convinced that her cousin's death had had nothing at all to do

It was while I was studying Frau von N.'s abulias that I began for the first time to have grave doubts about the validity of Bernheim's assertion, 'tout est dans la suggestion' ['suggestion is everything'] and about his clever friend Delbœuf's inference: 'Comme quoi il n'y a pas d'hypnotisme' ['That being so, there is no such thing as hypnotism']. And to this day I cannot understand how it can be supposed that by merely holding up a finger and saying once 'go to sleep' I had created in the patient the peculiar psychical state in which her memory had access to all her psychical experiences. I may have called up the state by my suggestion but I did not create it, since its features—which are, incidentally, found universally—came as such a surprise to me.

The case history makes sufficiently plain the way in which therapeutic work was carried out during somnambulism. As is the usual practice in hypnotic psychotherapy, I fought against the patient's pathological ideas by means of assurances and prohibitions, and by putting forward opposing ideas of every sort. But I did not content myself with this. I investigated the genesis of the individual symptoms so as to be able to combat the premises on which the pathological ideas were erected. In the course of such an analysis it habitually happened that the patient gave verbal utterance with the most violent agitation to matters whose accompanying affect had hitherto only found outlet as an expression of emotion. [Cf. p. 91.] I cannot say how much of the therapeutic success each time was due to my suggesting the symptom away in statu nascendi and how much to my resolving the affect by abreaction, since I combined both these therapeutic factors. Accordingly, this case cannot strictly be used as evidence for the therapeutic efficacy of the cathartic procedure; at the same time I must add that only those symptoms of which I carried out a psychical analysis were really permanently removed.

The therapeutic success on the whole was considerable; but it was not a lasting one. The patient's tendency to fall ill in a similar way under the impact of fresh traumas was not got rid

with her state, but that something else had happened which she had not mentioned. At this she gave way to the extent of letting fall a single significant phrase; but she had hardly said a word before she stopped, and her old father, who was sitting behind her, began to sob bitterly. Naturally I pressed my investigation no further; but I never saw the patient again.

of. Anyone who wanted to undertake the definitive cure of a case of hysteria such as this would have to enter more thoroughly into the complex of phenomena than I attempted to do. Frau von N. was undoubtedly a personality with a severe neuropathic heredity. It seems likely that there can be no hysteria apart from a disposition of this kind. But on the other hand disposition alone does not make hysteria. There must be reasons that bring it about, and, in my opinion, these reasons must be appropriate: the aetiology is of a specific character. I have already mentioned that in Frau von N. the affects of a great number of traumatic experiences had been retained and that the lively activity of her memory brought now one and now another of these traumas to the surface of her mind. I shall now venture to put forward an explanation of the reason why she retained the affects in this way. That reason, it is true, was connected with her hereditary disposition. For, on the one hand, her feelings were very intense; she was of a vehement nature, capable of the strongest passions. On the other hand, since her husband's death, she had lived in complete mental solitude; her persecution by her relatives had made her suspicious of friends and she was jealously on guard against anyone acquiring too much influence over her actions. The circle of her duties was very wide, and she performed the whole of the mental work which they imposed on her by herself, without a friend or confidant, almost isolated from her family and handicapped by her conscientiousness, her tendency to tormenting herself and often, too, by the natural helplessness of a woman. In short the mechanism of the *retention of large sums of excitation*, apart from everything else, cannot be overlooked in this case. It was based partly on the circumstances of her life and partly on her natural disposition. Her dislike, for instance, of saying anything about herself was so great, that, as I noticed to my astonishment in 1891, none of the daily visitors to her house recognized that she was ill or were aware that I was her doctor.

Does this exhaust the aetiology of this case of hysteria? I do not think so. For at the time of her two treatments I had not yet raised in my own mind the questions which must be answered before an exhaustive explanation of such a case is possible. I am now of the opinion that there must have been some added factor to provoke the outbreak of illness precisely in these last years, considering that operative aetiological conditions had been present for many years previously. It has also struck me that amongst all the intimate information given me by the patient there was a complete absence of the sexual element, which is, after all, more liable than any other to provide occasion for traumas. It is impossible that her excitations in this field can have left no traces whatever; what I was allowed to hear was no doubt an *editio in usum delphini* [a bowdlerized edition] of her life-story. The patient behaved with the greatest and to all appearances with the most unforced sense of propriety, without a trace of prudishness. When, however, I reflect on the reserve with which she told me under hypnosis about her maid's little adventure in the hotel, I cannot help suspecting that this woman who was so passionate and so capable of strong feelings had not won her victory over her sexual needs without severe struggles, and that at times her attempts at suppressing this most powerful of all instincts had exposed her to severe mental exhaustion. She once admitted to me that she had not married again because, in view of her large fortune, she could not credit the disinterestedness of her suitors and because she would have reproached herself for damaging the prospects of her two children by a new marriage.

I must make one further remark before bringing Frau von N.'s case history to a close. Dr. Breuer and I knew her pretty well and for a fairly long time, and we used to smile when we compared her character with the picture of the hysterical psyche which can be traced from early times through the writings and the opinions of medical men. We had learnt[1] from our observations on Frau Cäcilie M. that hysteria of the severest type can exist in conjunction with gifts of the richest and most original kind—a conclusion which is, in any case, made plain beyond a doubt in the biographies of women eminent in history and literature. In the same way Frau Emmy von N. gave us an example of how hysteria is compatible with an unblemished character and a well-governed mode of life. The woman we came to know was an admirable one. The moral seriousness with which she viewed her duties, her intelligence and energy, which were no less than a man's, and her high degree of education and love of truth impressed both of us greatly; while her benevolent care for the welfare of all her dependents, her humility of mind and the refinement of her manners revealed

[1] [See Editor's Introduction, p. xi *n*.]

her qualities as a true lady as well. To describe such a woman as a 'degenerate' would be to distort the meaning of that word out of all recognition. We should do well to distinguish between the concepts of 'disposition' and 'degeneracy' as applied to people; otherwise we shall find ourselves forced to admit that humanity owes a large proportion of its great achievements to the efforts of 'degenerates'.

I must confess, too, that I can see no sign in Frau von N.'s history of the 'psychical inefficiency' [1] to which Janet attributes the genesis of hysteria. According to him the hysterical disposition consists in an abnormal restriction of the field of consciousness (due to hereditary degeneracy) which results in a disregard of whole groups of ideas and, later, to a disintegration of the ego and the organization of secondary personalities. If this were so, what remains of the ego after the withdrawal of the hysterically-organized psychical groups would necessarily also be less efficient than a normal ego; and in fact, according to Janet, the ego in hysteria is afflicted by psychical stigmata, condemned to mono-ideism and incapable of the volitional acts of ordinary life. Janet, I think, has made the mistake here of promoting what are after-effects of changes in consciousness due to hysteria to the rank of primary determinants of hysteria. The subject is one that deserves further consideration elsewhere;[2] but in Frau von N. there was no sign of any such inefficiency. During the times of her worst states she was and remained capable of playing her part in the management of a large industrial business, of keeping a constant eye on the education of her children, of carrying on her correspondence with prominent people in the intellectual world—in short, of fulfilling her obligations well enough for the fact of her illness to remain concealed. I am inclined to believe, then, that all this involved a considerable *excess* of efficiency, which could perhaps not be kept up in the long run and was bound to lead to exhaustion—to a secondary '*misère psychologique*' ['psychological impoverishment']. It seems likely that disturbances of this kind in her efficiency were beginning to make themselves felt

---

[1] [This passage seems to be based mainly on Janet, 1894, 300. (See footnote p. 230.) The German phrase '*psychische Minderleistung*', here translated as 'psychical inefficiency', is evidently Freud's version of Janet's '*insuffisance psychologique*'.]

[2] [It is discussed below by Breuer on p. 231 ff.]

at the time when I first saw her; but however that may be, severe hysteria had been present for many years before the appearance of the symptoms of exhaustion.[1]

---

[1] (*Footnote added* 1924:) I am aware that no analyst can read this case history to-day without a smile of pity. But it should be borne in mind that this was the first case in which I employed the cathartic procedure to a large extent. [Cf. p. 48.] For this reason I shall leave the report in its original form. I shall not bring forward any of the criticisms which can so easily be made on it to-day, nor shall I attempt to fill in any of the numerous gaps in it. I will only add two things: what I afterwards discovered about the immediate aetiology of the illness and what I heard of its subsequent course.

When, as I have mentioned, I spent a few days as Frau Emmy's guest in her country house, there was a stranger present at one of the meals who clearly tried to make himself agreeable. After his departure my hostess asked me how I had liked him and added as it were in passing: 'Only imagine, the man wants to marry me!' When I took this in connection with some other remarks which she had made, but to which I had not paid sufficient attention, I was led to conclude that she was longing at that time to be married again but found an obstacle to the realization of her purpose in the existence of her two daughters, who were the heiresses of their father's fortune.

A few years later at a Scientific Congress I met a prominent physician from Frau Emmy's part of the country. I asked him if he was acquainted with the lady and knew anything of her condition. Yes, he said, he knew her, and had himself given her hypnotic treatment. She had gone through the same performance with him—and with many other doctors—as she had with me. Her condition had become very bad; she had rewarded his hypnotic treatment of her by making a remarkable recovery, but had then suddenly quarrelled with him, left him, and once more set her illness going to its full extent. It was a genuine instance of the 'compulsion to repeat'.

It was not for another quarter of a century that I once more had news of Frau Emmy. Her elder daughter—the one of whom I had earlier made such an unfavourable prognosis—approached me with a request for a report on her mother's mental condition on the strength of my former treatment of her. She was intending to take legal proceedings against her mother, whom she represented as a cruel and ruthless tyrant. It seems that she had broken off relations with both her children and refused to assist them in their financial difficulties. The daughter who wrote to me had obtained a doctor's degree and was married.

[This case history had already been discussed briefly by Freud in his paper on 'A Case of Successful Treatment by Hypnotism' (1892–3*b*), and he made a short allusion to it in the first of his *Five Lectures* (1910*a*).]

CASE 3

Miss Lucy R., age 30 (Freud)

At the end of the year 1892 a colleague of my acquaintance referred a young lady to me who was being treated by him for chronically recurrent suppurative rhinitis. It subsequently turned out that the obstinate persistence of her trouble was due to caries of the ethmoid bone. Latterly she had complained of some new symptoms which the well-informed physician was no longer able to attribute to a local affection. She had entirely lost her sense of smell and was almost continuously pursued by one or two subjective olfactory sensations. She found these most distressing. She was, moreover, in low spirits and fatigued, and she complained of heaviness in the head, diminished appetite and loss of efficiency.

The young lady, who was living as a governess in the house of the managing director of a factory in Outer Vienna, came to visit me from time to time in my consulting hours. She was an Englishwoman. She had a delicate constitution, with a poor pigmentation, but was in good health apart from her nasal affection. Her first statements confirmed what the physician had told me. She was suffering from depression and fatigue and was tormented by subjective sensations of smell. As regards hysterical symptoms, she showed a fairly definite general analgesia, with no loss of tactile sensibility, and a rough examination (with the hand) revealed no restriction of the visual field. The interior of her nose was completely analgesic and without reflexes; she was sensitive to tactile pressure there, but the perception proper to it as a sense-organ was absent, alike for specific stimuli and for others (e.g. ammonia or acetic acid). The purulent nasal catarrh was just then in a phase of improvement.

In our first attempts at making the illness intelligible it was necessary to interpret the subjective olfactory sensations, since they were recurrent hallucinations, as chronic hysterical symptoms. Her depression might perhaps be the affect attaching to the trauma, and it should be possible to find an experience in which these smells, which had now become subjective, had been objective. This experience must have been the trauma which the recurring sensations of smell symbolized in memory. It might be more correct to regard the recurrent olfactory hallucinations, together with the depression which accompanied them, as equivalents of a hysterical *attack*. The nature of recurrent hallucinations makes them unsuitable in point of fact for playing the part of *chronic* symptoms. But this question did not really arise in a case like this which showed only a rudimentary development. It was essential, however, that the subjective sensations of smell should have had a specialized origin of a sort which would admit of their being derived from some quite particular real object.

This expectation was promptly fulfilled. When I asked her what the smell was by which she was most constantly troubled she answered: 'A smell of burnt pudding.' Thus I only needed to assume that a smell of burnt pudding had actually occurred in the experience which had operated as a trauma. It is very unusual, no doubt, for olfactory sensations to be chosen as mnemic symbols of traumas, but it was not difficult to account for this choice. The patient was suffering from suppurative rhinitis and consequently her attention was especially focused on her nose and nasal sensations. What I knew of the circumstances of the patient's life was limited to the fact that the two children whom she was looking after had no mother; she had died some years earlier of an acute illness.

I therefore decided to make the smell of burnt pudding the starting-point of the analysis. I will describe the course of this analysis as it might have taken place under favourable conditions. In fact, what should have been a single session spread over several. This was because the patient could only visit me in my consulting hours, when I could only devote a short time to her. Moreover, a single discussion of this sort used to extend over more than a week, since her duties would not allow her to make the long journey from the factory to my house very often. We used therefore to break our conversation off short and take up the thread at the same place next time.

Miss Lucy R. did not fall into a state of somnambulism when I tried to hypnotize her. I therefore did without somnambulism and conducted her whole analysis while she was in a state which may in fact have differed very little from a normal one.

I shall have to go into this point of my technical procedure in greater detail. When, in 1889, I visited the Nancy clinics, I heard Dr. Liébeault, the *doyen* of hypnotism, say: 'If only we had the means of putting every patient into a state of somnambulism, hypnotic therapy would be the most powerful of all.' In Bernheim's clinic it almost seemed as though such an art really existed and as though it might be possible to learn it from Bernheim. But as soon as I tried to practise this art on my own patients, I discovered that *my* powers at least were subject to severe limits, and that if somnambulism were not brought about in a patient at the first three attempts I had no means of inducing it. The percentage of cases amenable to somnambulism was very much lower in my experience than what Bernheim reported.

I was accordingly faced with the choice of either abandoning the cathartic method in most of the cases which might have been suitable for it, or of venturing on the experiment of employing that method without somnambulism and where the hypnotic influence was light or even where its existence was doubtful. It seemed to me a matter of indifference what degree of hypnosis—according to one or other of the scales that have been proposed for measuring it—was reached by this non-somnambulistic state; for, as we know, each of the various forms taken by suggestibility is in any case independent of the others, and the bringing about of catalepsy, automatic movements, and so on, does not work either for or against what I required for my purposes, namely that the awakening of forgotten memories should be made easier. Moreover, I soon dropped the practice of making tests to show the degree of hypnosis reached, since in quite a number of cases this roused the patients' resistance and shook their confidence in me, which I needed for carrying out the more important psychical work. Furthermore, I soon began to tire of issuing assurances and commands such as: 'You are going to sleep! . . . sleep!' and of hearing the patient, as so often happened when the degree of hypnosis was light, remonstrate with me: 'But, doctor, I'm *not* asleep', and of then having to make highly ticklish distinctions: 'I don't mean ordinary sleep; I mean hypnosis. As you see, you are hypnotized, you can't open your eyes', etc., 'and in any case, there's no need for you to go to sleep', and so on. I feel sure that many other physicians who practise psychotherapy can get out of such difficulties with more skill than I can. If so, they may adopt some procedure other than mine. It seems to me, however, that if one can reckon with such frequency on finding oneself in an embarrassing situation through the use of a particular word, one will be wise to avoid both the word and the embarrassment. When, therefore, my first attempt did not lead either to somnambulism or to a degree of hypnosis involving marked physical changes, I ostensibly dropped hypnosis, and only asked for 'concentration'; and I ordered the patient to lie down and deliberately shut his eyes as a means of achieving this 'concentration'. It is possible that in this way I obtained with only a slight effort the deepest degree of hypnosis that could be reached in the particular case.

But in doing without somnambulism I might be depriving myself of a precondition without which the cathartic method seemed unusable. For that method clearly rested on the patients in their changed state of consciousness having access to memories and being able to recognize connections which appeared not to be present in their normal state of consciousness. If the somnambulistic extension of memory were absent there could also be no possibility of establishing any determining causes which the patient could present to the physician as something unknown to him (the patient); and, of course, it is precisely the pathogenic memories which, as we have already said in our 'Preliminary Communication' [p. 9] are 'absent from the patients' memory, when they are in a normal psychical state, or are only present in a highly summary form'.

I was saved from this new embarrassment by remembering that I had myself seen Bernheim producing evidence that the memories of events during somnambulism are only *apparently* forgotten in the waking state and can be revived by a mild word of command and a pressure with the hand intended to indicate a different state of consciousness. He had, for instance, given a woman in a state of somnambulism a negative hallucination to the effect that he was no longer present, and had then endeavoured to draw her attention to himself in a great variety of ways, including some of a decidedly aggressive kind. He did not succeed. After she had been woken up he asked her to tell him what he had done to her while she thought he was not there. She replied in surprise that she knew nothing of it. But he did not accept this. He insisted that she could remember everything and laid his hand on her forehead to help her to recall it. And lo and behold! she ended by describing everything that she had ostensibly not perceived during her somnambulism and ostensibly not remembered in her waking state.

This astonishing and instructive experiment served as my model. I decided to start from the assumption that my patients knew everything that was of any pathogenic significance and that it was only a question of obliging them to communicate it. Thus when I reached a point at which, after asking a patient some question such as: 'How long have you had this symptom?' or: 'What was its origin?', I was met with the answer: 'I really don't know', I proceeded as follows. I placed my hand on the patient's forehead or took her head between my hands and said: 'You will think of it under the pressure of my hand. At the moment at which I relax my pressure you will see something in front of you or something will come into your head. Catch hold of it. It will be what we are looking for.—Well, what have you seen or what has occurred to you?'

On the first occasions on which I made use of this procedure (it was not with Miss Lucy R.[1]) I myself was surprised to find

---

[1] [Freud's first use of the 'pressure technique' seems to have been with Fräulein Elisabeth von R. (see below, p. 145), though his statement there is not completely unambiguous. Further accounts of this procedure, in addition to those in the text above and in the passage just referred to, will be found on pp. 155 f. and 270 ff. There is a slight apparent inconsistency in these accounts. In the present one, the patient is told that she will see something or have some idea 'at the moment at which I relax my pressure'; on p. 145, she is told that this will occur 'at the moment of the pressure'; and on p. 270 that it will occur 'all the time the pressure lasts'. It is not known exactly when Freud abandoned this pressure technique. He had certainly done so before 1904, since in his contribution of that date to Loewenfeld's book on obsessions he explicitly remarks that he avoids touching his patients in any way (1904a, Standard Ed., 7, 250). But it seems likely that he had already given up the practice before 1900, for he makes no mention of it in the short account of his procedure given near the beginning of Chapter II of *The Interpretation of Dreams* (1900a), Standard Ed., 4, 101. Incidentally, in this latter passage Freud still recommends that the patient should keep his eyes shut during analysis. This last remnant (apart from lying down) of the original hypnotic procedure was also explicitly disrecommended in the sentence already quoted from his contribution to Loewenfeld (1904a).—We have fairly exact information upon the period of Freud's use of hypnotism proper. In a letter to Fliess of December 28, 1887 (Freud, 1950a, Letter 2) he wrote: 'During the last

that it yielded me the precise results that I needed. And I can safely say that it has scarcely ever left me in the lurch since then. It has always pointed the way which the analysis should take and has enabled me to carry through every such analysis to an end without the use of somnambulism. Eventually I grew so confident that, if patients answered, 'I see nothing' or 'nothing has occurred to me', I could dismiss this as an impossibility and could assure them that they had certainly become aware of what was wanted but had refused to believe that that was so and had rejected it. I told them I was ready to repeat the procedure as often as they liked and they would see the same thing every time. I turned out to be invariably right. The patients had not yet learned to relax their critical faculty. They had rejected the memory that had come up or the idea that had occurred to them, on the ground that it was unserviceable and an irrelevant interruption; and after they had told it to me it always proved to be what was wanted. Occasionally, when, after three or four pressures, I had at last extracted the information, the patient would reply: 'As a matter of fact I knew that the first time, but it was just what I didn't want to say', or: 'I hoped that would not be it.'

This business of enlarging what was supposed to be a restricted consciousness was laborious—far more so, at least, than an investigation during somnambulism. But it nevertheless made me independent of somnambulism, and gave me insight into the motives which often determine the 'forgetting' of memories. I can affirm that this forgetting is often intentional and desired; and its success is never more than *apparent*.

I found it even more surprising perhaps that it was possible by the same procedure to bring back numbers and dates which, on the face of it, had long since been forgotten, and so to reveal how unexpectedly accurate memory can be.

The fact that in looking for numbers and dates our choice is so limited enables us to call to our help a proposition familiar

few weeks I have taken up hypnosis.' And in a lecture given before the Vienna 'Medizinisches Doktorencollegium' on December 12, 1904 (Freud, 1905*a*, *Standard Ed.*, **7**, 260) he declared: 'I have not used hypnosis for therapeutic purposes for some eight years (except for a few special experiments).' His use of hypnotism therefore fell approximately between the years 1887 and 1896.]

to us from the theory of aphasia, namely that recognizing something is a lighter task for memory than thinking of it spontaneously.[1] Thus, if a patient is unable to remember the year or month or day when a particular event occurred, we can repeat to him the dates of the possibly relevant years, the names of the twelve months and the thirty-one numbers of the days of the month, assuring him that when we come to the right number or the right name his eyes will open of their own accord or that he will feel which is the right one. In the great majority of cases the patient will in fact decide on a particular date. Quite often (as in the case of Frau Cäcilie M.) it is possible to prove from documents belonging to the period in question that the date has been recognized correctly; while in other cases and on other occasions the indisputable accuracy of the date thus chosen can be inferred from the context of the facts remembered. For instance, after a patient had had her attention drawn to the date which had been arrived at by this 'counting over' method, she said: 'Why, that's my father's birthday!' and added: 'Of course! It was because it was his birthday that I was expecting the event we were talking about.'

Here I can only touch upon the theme in passing. The conclusion I drew from all these observations was that experiences which have played an important pathogenic part, and all their subsidiary concomitants, are accurately retained in the patient's memory even when they seem to be forgotten—when he is unable to call them to mind.[2]

After this long but unavoidable digression I will return to

---

[1] [Freud had written his book on aphasia (1891b) not long before.]

[2] As an example of the technique which I have described above of carrying out investigations in non-somnambulistic states—that is, where there is no extension of consciousness—I will describe an instance which I happen to have analysed in the course of the last few days. I was treating a woman of thirty-eight, suffering from anxiety neurosis (agoraphobia, attacks of fear of death, etc.). Like so many such patients, she had a disinclination to admitting that she had acquired these troubles in her married life and would have liked to push them back into her early youth. Thus she told me that she was seventeen when she had had a first attack of dizziness, with anxiety and feelings of faintness, in the street in her small native town, and that these attacks had recurred from time to time, till a few years ago they had given place to her present disorder. I suspected that these first attacks of dizziness, in which the anxiety faded more and more into the background, were

the case of Miss Lucy R. As I have said, then, my attempts at
hypnosis with her did not produce somnambulism. She simply
lay quietly in a state open to some mild degree of influence,
with her eyes closed all the time, her features somewhat rigid,

hysterical and I made up my mind to embark on an analysis of them.
To begin with she only knew that this first attack came over her while
she was out shopping in the principal street. 'What were you going to
buy?'—'Different things, I believe; they were for a ball I had been
invited to.'—'When was this ball to take place?'—'Two days later, I
think.'—'Something must have happened to agitate you a few days
before, something that made an impression on you.'—'I can't think of
anything. After all, it was twenty-one years ago.'—'That makes no
difference; you will remember all the same. I shall press on your head,
and when I relax the pressure, you will think of something or see something, and you must tell me what that is.' I went through this procedure;
but she remained silent. 'Well, has nothing occurred to you?'—'I have
thought of something, but it can't have any connection with this.'—
'Tell it to me anyway.'—'I thought of a friend of mine, a girl, who is
dead. But she died when I was eighteen—a year later, that is.'—'We
shall see. Let's stick to this point. What about this friend of yours?'—
'Her death was a great shock to me, as I used to see a lot of her. A few
weeks earlier another girl had died, and that had made a great stir in the
town. So after all, I must have been seventeen at the time.'—'There,
you see, I told you we could rely on the things that come into your head
under the pressure of my hand. Now, can you remember what you were
thinking about when you felt dizzy in the street?'—'I wasn't thinking
of anything; I only felt dizzy.'—'That's not possible. States like that
never happen without being accompanied by some idea. I shall press
once more and the thought you had will come back to you. . . . Well,
what has occurred to you?'—'The idea that I am the third.'—'What
does that mean?'—'When I got the attack of dizziness I must have
thought: "Now I am dying, like the other two girls." '—'That was the
idea, then. As you were having the attack you thought of your friend.
So her death must have made a great impression on you.'—'Yes, it did.
I can remember now that when I heard of her death I felt it was dreadful to be going to a ball, while she was dead. But I was looking forward
so much to the ball and was so busy with preparations for it; I didn't
want to think of what had happened at all.' (We may observe here a
deliberate repression from consciousness, which rendered the patient's
memory of her friend pathogenic.)

The attack was now to some extent explained. But I still required to
know of some precipitating factor which had provoked the memory at
that particular time. I formed what happened to be a lucky conjecture.
'Do you remember the exact street you were walking along just then?'—
'Certainly. It was the principal street, with its old houses. I can see
them now.'—'And where was it that your friend lived?'—'In a house
in the same street. I had just passed it, and I had the attack a couple of
houses further on.'—'So when you went by the house it reminded you

and without moving hand or foot. I asked her if she could remember the occasion on which she first had the smell of burnt pudding. 'Oh yes, I know exactly. It was about two months ago, two days before my birthday. I was with the children in the schoolroom and was playing at cooking with them' (they were two little girls). 'A letter was brought in that had just been left by the postman. I saw from the postmark and the handwriting that it was from my mother in Glasgow and wanted to open it and read it; but the children rushed at me, tore the letter out of my hands and cried: "No, you shan't read it now! It must be for your birthday; we'll keep it for you!" While the children were having this game with me there was suddenly a strong smell. They had forgotten the pudding they were cooking and it was getting burnt. Ever since this I have been pursued by the smell. It is there all the time and becomes stronger when I am agitated.'

'Do you see this scene clearly before your eyes?'—'As large as life, just as I experienced it.'—'What could there be about it that was so agitating?'—'I was moved because the children of your dead friend, and you were once more overcome by the contrast which you did not want to think of.'

I was still not satisfied. There might, I thought, be something else at work as well that had aroused or reinforced the hysterical disposition of a girl who had till then been normal. My suspicions turned to her monthly periods as an appropriate factor, and I asked: 'Do you know at what time in the month your period came on?' The question was not a welcome one. 'Do you expect me to know that, too? I can only tell you that I had them very seldom then and very irregularly. When I was seventeen I only had one once.'—'Very well, then, we will find out when this once was by counting over.' I did the counting over, and she decided definitely on one particular month and hesitated between two days immediately preceding the date of a fixed holiday. 'Does that fit in somehow with the date of the ball?' She answered sheepishly: 'The ball was on the holiday. And now I remember, too, what an impression it made on me that my only period that year should have had to come on just before the ball. It was my first ball.'

There is no difficulty now in reconstructing the interconnection between the events, and we can now see into the mechanism of this hysterical attack. It is true that the achievement of this result had been a laborious business. It required complete confidence in my technique on my side, and the occurrence to the patient of a few key ideas, before it was possible to re-awaken, after an interval of twenty-one years, these details of a forgotten experience in a sceptical person who was, in fact, in a waking state. But once all this had been gone through, the whole thing fitted together.

were so affectionate to me.'—'Weren't they always?'—'Yes—
but just when I got the letter from my mother.'—'I don't understand why there is a contrast between the children's affection
and your mother's letter, for that's what you seem to be suggesting.'—'I was intending to go back to my mother's, and
the thought of leaving the dear children made me feel so sad.'—
'What's wrong with your mother? Has she been feeling lonely
and sent for you? Or was she ill at the time, and were you
expecting news of her?'—'No; she isn't very strong, but she's
not exactly ill, and she has a companion with her.'—'Then why
must you leave the children?'—'I couldn't bear it any longer
in the house. The housekeeper, the cook and the French
governess seem to have thought that I was putting myself above
my station. They joined in a little intrigue against me and said
all sorts of things against me to the children's grandfather, and
I didn't get as much support as I had expected from the two
gentlemen when I complained to them. So I gave notice to the
Director' (the children's father). 'He answered in a very friendly
way that I had better think the matter over for a couple of
weeks before I finally gave him my decision. I was in this state
of uncertainty at the time, and thought I should be leaving
the house; but I have stayed on.'—'Was there something particular, apart from their fondness for you, which attached you
to the children?'—'Yes. Their mother was a distant relation
of my mother's, and I had promised her on her death-bed
that I would devote myself with all my power to the children,
that I would not leave them and that I would take their
mother's place with them. In giving notice I had broken this
promise.'

This seemed to complete the analysis of the patient's subjective sensation of smell. It had turned out in fact to have
been an objective sensation originally, and one which was intimately associated with an experience—a little scene—in which
opposing affects had been in conflict with each other: her regret
at leaving the children and the slights which were nevertheless
urging her to make up her mind to do so. Her mother's letter
had not unnaturally reminded her of her reasons for this
decision, since it was her intention to join her mother on leaving here. The conflict between her affects had elevated the
moment of the letter's arrival into a trauma, and the sensation
of smell that was associated with this trauma persisted as its

symbol. It was still necessary to explain why, out of all the sense-perceptions afforded by the scene, she had chosen this smell as a symbol. I was already prepared, however, to use the chronic affection of her nose as a help in explaining the point. In response to a direct question she told me that just at that time she had once more been suffering from such a heavy cold in the nose that she could hardly smell anything. Nevertheless, while she was in her state of agitation she perceived the smell of the burnt pudding, which broke through the organically-determined loss of her sense of smell.

But I was not satisfied with the explanation thus arrived at. It all sounded highly plausible, but there was something that I missed, some adequate reason why these agitations and this conflict of affects should have led to hysteria rather than anything else. Why had not the whole thing remained on the level of normal psychical life? In other words, what was the justification for the conversion which occurred? Why did she not always call to mind the scene itself, instead of the associated sensation which she singled out as a symbol of the recollection? Such questions might be over-curious and superfluous if we were dealing with a hysteric of long standing in whom the mechanism of conversion was habitual. But it was not until this trauma, or at any rate this small tale of trouble, that the girl had acquired hysteria.

Now I already knew from the analysis of similar cases that before hysteria can be acquired for the first time one essential condition must be fulfilled: an idea must be *intentionally repressed from consciousness*[1] and excluded from associative modification. In my view this intentional repression is also the basis for the conversion, whether total or partial, of the sum of excitation. The sum of excitation, being cut off from psychical association, finds its way all the more easily along the wrong path to a somatic innervation. The basis for repression itself can only be a feeling of unpleasure, the incompatibility between the single idea that is to be repressed and the dominant mass of ideas constituting the ego. The repressed idea takes its revenge, however, by becoming pathogenic.

I accordingly inferred from Miss Lucy R.'s having succumbed to hysterical conversion at the moment in question that among the determinants of the trauma there must have

[1] [See footnote p. 10.]

been one which she had sought intentionally to leave in obscurity and had made efforts to forget. If her fondness for the children and her sensitiveness on the subject of the other members of the household were taken together, only one conclusion could be reached. I was bold enough to inform my patient of this interpretation. I said to her: 'I cannot think that these are all the reasons for your feelings about the children. I believe that really you are in love with your employer, the Director, though perhaps without being aware of it yourself, and that you have a secret hope of taking their mother's place in actual fact. And then we must remember the sensitiveness you now feel towards the servants, after having lived with them peacefully for years. You're afraid of their having some inkling of your hopes and making fun of you.'

She answered in her usual laconic fashion: 'Yes, I think that's true.'—'But if you knew you loved your employer why didn't you tell me?'—'I didn't know—or rather I didn't want to know. I wanted to drive it out of my head and not think of it again; and I believe latterly I have succeeded.' [1] 'Why was it that you were unwilling to admit this inclination? Were you ashamed of loving a man?'—'Oh no, I'm not unreasonably prudish. We're not responsible for our feelings, anyhow. It was distressing to me only because he is my employer and I am in his service and live in his house. I don't feel the same complete independence towards him that I could towards anyone else. And then I am only a poor girl and he is such a rich man of good family. People would laugh at me if they had any idea of it.'

[1] I have never managed to give a better description than this of the strange state of mind in which one knows and does not know a thing at the same time. It is clearly impossible to understand it unless one has been in such a state oneself. I myself have had a very remarkable experience of this sort, which is still clearly before me. If I try to recollect what went on in my mind at the time I can get hold of very little. What happened was that I saw something which did not fit in at all with my expectation; yet I did not allow what I saw to disturb my fixed plan in the least, though the perception should have put a stop to it. I was unconscious of any contradiction in this; nor was I aware of my feelings of repulsion, which must nevertheless undoubtedly have been responsible for the perception producing no psychical effect. I was afflicted by that blindness of the seeing eye which is so astonishing in the attitude of mothers to their daughters, husbands to their wives and rulers to their favourites.

She now showed no resistance to throwing light on the origin of this inclination. She told me that for the first few years she had lived happily in the house, carrying out her duties and free from any unfulfillable wishes. One day, however, her employer, a serious, overworked man whose behaviour towards her had always been reserved, began a discussion with her on the lines along which children should be brought up. He unbent more and was more cordial than usual and told her how much he depended on her for looking after his orphaned children; and as he said this he looked at her meaningly. . . . Her love for him had begun at that moment, and she even allowed herself to dwell on the gratifying hopes which she had based on this talk. But when there was no further development, and when she had waited in vain for a second hour's intimate exchange of views, she decided to banish the whole business from her mind. She entirely agreed with me that the look she had caught during their conversation had probably sprung from his thoughts about his wife, and she recognized quite clearly that there was no prospect of her feelings for him meeting with any return.

I expected that this discussion would bring about a fundamental change in her condition. But for the time being this did not occur. She continued to be in low spirits and depressed. She felt somewhat refreshed in the mornings by a course of hydropathic treatment which I prescribed for her at the same time. The smell of burnt pudding did not disappear completely, though it became less frequent and weaker. It only came on, she said, when she was very much agitated. The persistence of this mnemic symbol led me to suspect that, in addition to the main scene, it had taken over the representation of the many minor traumas subsidiary to that scene. We therefore looked about for anything else that might have to do with the scene of the burnt pudding; we went into the subject of the domestic friction, the grandfather's behaviour, and so on, and as we did so the burnt smell faded more and more. During this time, too, the treatment was interrupted for a considerable while, owing to a fresh attack of her nasal disorder, and this now led to the discovery of the caries of the ethmoid [p. 106].

On her return she reported that at Christmas she had received a great many presents from the two gentlemen of the house and even from the servants, as though they were all anxious to make it up with her and to wipe out her memory of the conflicts of the last few months. But these signs of good-will had not made any impression on her.

When I enquired once more about the smell of burnt pudding, she informed me that it had quite disappeared but that she was being bothered by another, similar smell, resembling cigar-smoke. It had been there earlier as well, she thought, but had, as it were, been covered by the smell of the pudding. Now it had emerged by itself.

I was not very well satisfied with the results of the treatment. What had happened was precisely what is always brought up against purely symptomatic treatment: I had removed one symptom only for its place to be taken by another. Nevertheless, I did not hesitate to set about the task of getting rid of this new mnemic symbol by analysis.

But this time she did not know where the subjective olfactory sensation came from—on what important occasion it had been an objective one. 'People smoke every day in our house,' she said, 'and I really don't know whether the smell I notice refers to some special occasion.' I then insisted that she should try to remember under the pressure of my hand. I have already mentioned [p. 114] that her memories had the quality of plastic vividness, that she was a 'visual' type. And in fact, at my insistence, a picture gradually emerged before her, hesitatingly and piecemeal to begin with. It was the dining-room in her house, where she was waiting with the children for the two gentlemen to return to luncheon from the factory. 'Now we are all sitting round the table, the gentlemen, the French governess, the housekeeper, the children and myself. But that's like what happens every day.'—'Go on looking at the picture; it will develop and become more specialized.'—'Yes, there is a guest. It's the chief accountant. He's an old man and he is as fond of the children as though they were his own grandchildren. But he comes to lunch so often that there's nothing special in that either.'—'Be patient and just keep looking at the picture; something's sure to happen.'—'Nothing's happening. We're getting up from the table; the children say their good-byes, and they go upstairs with us as usual to the second floor.'—'And then?' —'It *is* a special occasion, after all. I recognize the scene now. As the children say good-bye, the accountant tries to kiss them. My employer flares up and actually shouts at him:

"Don't kiss the children!" I feel a stab at my heart; and as the gentlemen are already smoking, the cigar-smoke sticks in my memory.'

This, then, was a second and deeper-lying scene which, like the first, operated as a trauma and left a mnemic symbol behind it. But to what did this scene owe its effectiveness? 'Which of the two scenes was the earlier,' I asked, 'this one or the one with the burnt pudding?'—'The scene I have just told you about was the earlier, by almost two months.'—'Then why did you feel this stab when the children's father stopped the old man? His reprimand wasn't aimed at you.'—'It wasn't right of him to shout at an old man who was a valued friend of his and, what's more, a guest. He could have said it quietly.' —'So it was only the violent way he put it that hurt you? Did you feel embarrassed on his account? Or perhaps you thought: "If he can be so violent about such a small thing with an old friend and guest, how much more so might he be with me if I were his wife".'—'No, that's not it.'—'But it had to do with his violence, hadn't it?'—'Yes, about the children being kissed. He has never liked that.'

And now, under the pressure of my hand, the memory of a third and still earlier scene emerged, which was the really operative trauma and which had given the scene with the chief accountant its traumatic effectiveness. It had happened a few months earlier still that a lady who was an acquaintance of her employer's came to visit them, and on her departure kissed the two children on the mouth. Their father, who was present, managed to restrain himself from saying anything to the lady, but after she had gone, his fury burst upon the head of the unlucky governess. He said he held her responsible if anyone kissed the children on the mouth, that it was her duty not to permit it and that she was guilty of a dereliction of duty if she allowed it; if it ever happened again he would entrust his children's upbringing to other hands. This had happened at a time when she still thought he loved her, and was expecting a repetition of their first friendly talk. The scene had crushed her hopes. She had said to herself: 'If he can fly out at me like this and make such threats over such a trivial matter, and one for which, moreover, I am not in the least responsible, I must have made a mistake. He can never have had any warm feelings for me, or they would have taught him to treat me with more consideration.'—It was obviously the recollection of this distressing scene which had come to her when the chief accountant had tried to kiss the children and had been reprimanded by their father.

After this last analysis, when, two days later, Miss Lucy visited me once more, I could not help asking her what had happened to make her so happy. She was as though transfigured. She was smiling and carried her head high. I thought for a moment that after all I had been wrong about the situation, and that the children's governess had become the Director's fiancée. But she dispelled my notion. 'Nothing has happened. It's just that you don't know me. You have only seen me ill and depressed. I'm always cheerful as a rule. When I woke yesterday morning the weight was no longer on my mind, and since then I have felt well.'—'And what do you think of your prospects in the house?'—'I am quite clear on the subject. I know I have none, and I shan't make myself unhappy over it.'—'And will you get on all right with the servants now?'—'I think my own oversensitiveness was responsible for most of that.'—'And are you still in love with your employer?'—'Yes, I certainly am, but that makes no difference. After all, I can have thoughts and feelings to myself.'

I then examined her nose and found that its sensitivity to pain and reflex excitability had been almost completely restored. She was also able to distinguish between smells, though with uncertainty and only if they were strong. I must leave it an open question, however, how far her nasal disorder may have played a part in the impairment of her sense of smell.

This treatment lasted in all for nine weeks. Four months later I met the patient by chance in one of our summer resorts. She was in good spirits and assured me that her recovery had been maintained.

Discussion

I am not inclined to under-estimate the importance of the case that I have here described, even though the patient was suffering only from a slight and mild hysteria and though only a few symptoms were involved. On the contrary it seems to me an instructive fact that even an illness such as this, so unproductive when regarded as a neurosis, called for so many psychical determinants. Indeed, when I consider this case history more closely, I am tempted to regard it as a model instance of one particular type of hysteria, namely the form of this illness which can be acquired even by a person of sound heredity, as a result of appropriate experiences. It should be understood that I do not mean by this a hysteria which is independent of *any* pre-existing disposition. It is probable that no such hysteria exists. But we do not recognize a disposition of this sort in a subject until he has actually become a hysteric; for previously there was no evidence of its existence. A neuropathic disposition, as generally understood, is something different. It is already marked out before the onset of the illness by the amount of the subject's hereditary taint or the sum of his individual psychical abnormalities. So far as my information goes, there was no trace in Miss Lucy R. of either of these factors. Her hysteria can therefore be described as an acquired one, and it presupposed nothing more than the possession of what is probably a very widespread proclivity—the proclivity to acquire hysteria. We have as yet scarcely a notion of what the features of this proclivity may be. In cases of this kind, however, the main emphasis falls upon the nature of the trauma, though taken in conjunction, of course, with the subject's reaction to it. It turns out to be a *sine qua non* for the acquisition of hysteria that an incompatibility should develop between the ego and some idea presented to it. I hope to be able to show elsewhere [1] how different neurotic disturbances arise from the different methods adopted by the 'ego' in order to escape from this incompatibility. The hysterical method of defence—for which, as we have seen, the possession of a particular proclivity is necessary—lies in the conversion of the excitation into a somatic innervation; and the advantage of this is that the incompatible idea is repressed from the ego's consciousness. In exchange, that consciousness now contains the physical reminiscence which has arisen through conversion (in our case, the patient's subjective sensations of smell) and suffers from the affect which is more or less clearly attached to pre-

---

[1] [Freud sketched out the distinction between the mechanisms used in hysteria, obsessions and paranoia in a communication to Fliess of January 1, 1896 (Freud, 1950a, Draft K); in the following May he published these findings in his second paper on 'The Neuro-Psychoses of Defence' (1896b).]

cisely that reminiscence. The situation which has thus been brought about is now not susceptible to further change; for the incompatibility which would have called for a removal of the affect no longer exists, thanks to the repression and conversion. Thus the mechanism which produces hysteria represents on the one hand an act of moral cowardice and on the other a defensive measure which is at the disposal of the ego. Often enough we have to admit that fending off increasing excitations by the generation of hysteria is, in the circumstances, the most expedient thing to do; more frequently, of course, we shall conclude that a greater amount of moral courage would have been of advantage to the person concerned.

The actual traumatic moment, then, is the one at which the incompatibility forces itself upon the ego and at which the latter decides on the repudiation of the incompatible idea. That idea is not annihilated by a repudiation of this kind, but merely repressed into the unconscious.[1] When this process occurs for the first time there comes into being a nucleus and centre of crystallization for the formation of a psychical group divorced from the ego—a group around which everything which would imply an acceptance of the incompatible idea subsequently collects. The splitting of consciousness in these cases of acquired hysteria is accordingly a deliberate and intentional one. At least it is often *introduced* by an act of volition; for the actual outcome is something different from what the subject intended. What he wanted was to do away with an idea, as though it had never appeared, but all he succeeds in doing is to isolate it psychically.

In the history of our present patient the traumatic moment was the moment of her employer's outburst against her about his children being kissed by the lady. For a time, however, that scene had no manifest effect. (It may be that her oversensitiveness and low spirits began from it, but I cannot say.) Her hysterical symptoms did not start until later, at moments which may be described as 'auxiliary'.[2] The characteristic feature of such an auxiliary moment is, I believe, that the two divided psychical groups temporarily converge in it, as they do in the extended consciousness which occurs in somnambulism. In

---

[1] [See footnote, p. 45 above.]

[2] [Freud had already discussed such 'auxiliary' traumatic moments in Section I of his first paper on 'The Neuro-Psychoses of Defence' (1894*a*).]

Miss Lucy R.'s case the first of the auxiliary moments, at which conversion took place, was the scene at table when the chief accountant tried to kiss the children. Here the traumatic memory was playing a part: she did not behave as though she had got rid of everything connected with her devotion to her employer. (In the history of other cases these different moments coincide; conversion occurs as an immediate effect of the trauma.)

The second auxiliary moment repeated the mechanism of the first one fairly exactly. A powerful impression temporarily reunited the patient's consciousness, and conversion once more took the path which had been opened out on the first occasion. It is interesting to notice that the second symptom to develop masked the first, so that the first was not clearly perceived until the second had been cleared out of the way. It also seems to me worth while remarking upon the reversed course which had to be followed by the analysis as well. I have had the same experience in a whole number of cases; the symptoms that had arisen later masked the earlier ones, and the key to the whole situation lay only in the last symptom to be reached by the analysis.

The therapeutic process in this case consisted in compelling the psychical group that had been split off to unite once more with the ego-consciousness. Strangely enough, success did not run *pari passu* with the amount of work done. It was only when the last piece of work had been completed that recovery suddenly took place.

CASE 4

KATHARINA —— (Freud)

IN the summer vacation of the year 189– I made an excursion into the Hohe Tauern [1] so that for a while I might forget medicine and more particularly the neuroses. I had almost succeeded in this when one day I turned aside from the main road to climb a mountain which lay somewhat apart and which was renowned for its views and for its well-run refuge hut. I reached the top after a strenuous climb and, feeling refreshed and rested, was sitting deep in contemplation of the charm of the distant prospect. I was so lost in thought that at first I did not connect it with myself when these words reached my ears: 'Are you a doctor, sir?' But the question was addressed to me, and by the rather sulky-looking girl of perhaps eighteen who had served my meal and had been spoken to by the landlady as 'Katharina'. To judge by her dress and bearing, she could not be a servant, but must no doubt be a daughter or relative of the landlady's.

Coming to myself I replied: 'Yes, I'm a doctor: but how did you know that?'

'You wrote your name in the Visitors' Book, sir. And I thought if you had a few moments to spare . . . The truth is, sir, my nerves are bad. I went to see a doctor in L—— about them and he gave me something for them; but I'm not well yet.'

So there I was with the neuroses once again—for nothing else could very well be the matter with this strong, well-built girl with her unhappy look. I was interested to find that neuroses could flourish in this way at a height of over 6,000 feet; I questioned her further therefore. I report the conversation that followed between us just as it is impressed on my memory and I have not altered the patient's dialect. [2]

'Well, what is it you suffer from?'

'I get so out of breath. Not always. But sometimes it catches me so that I think I shall suffocate.'

[1] [One of the highest ranges in the Eastern Alps.]
[2] [No attempt has been made in the English translation to imitate this dialect.]

125

This did not, at first sight, sound like a nervous symptom. But soon it occurred to me that probably it was only a description that stood for an anxiety attack: she was choosing shortness of breath out of the complex of sensations arising from anxiety and laying undue stress on that single factor.

'Sit down here. What is it like when you get "out of breath"?'

'It comes over me all at once. First of all it's like something pressing on my eyes. My head gets so heavy, there's a dreadful buzzing, and I feel so giddy that I almost fall over. Then there's something crushing my chest so that I can't get my breath.'

'And you don't notice anything in your throat?'

'My throat's squeezed together as though I were going to choke.'

'Does anything else happen in your head?'

'Yes, there's a hammering, enough to burst it.'

'And don't you feel at all frightened while this is going on?'

'I always think I'm going to die. I'm brave as a rule and go about everywhere by myself—into the cellar and all over the mountain. But on a day when that happens I don't dare to go anywhere; I think all the time someone's standing behind me and going to catch hold of me all at once.'

So it was in fact an anxiety attack, and introduced by the signs of a hysterical 'aura'[1]—or, more correctly, it was a hysterical attack the content of which was anxiety. Might there not probably be some other content as well?

'When you have an attack do you think of something? and always the same thing? or do you see something in front of you?'

'Yes. I always see an awful face that looks at me in a dreadful way, so that I'm frightened.'

Perhaps this might offer a quick means of getting to the heart of the matter.

'Do you recognize the face? I mean, is it a face that you've really seen some time?'

'No.'

'Do you know what your attacks come from?'

'No.'

'When did you first have them?'

[1] [The premonitory sensations preceding an epileptic or hysterical attack.]

'Two years ago, while I was still living on the other mountain with my aunt. (She used to run a refuge hut there, and we
moved here eighteen months ago.) But they keep on happening.'

Was I to make an attempt at an analysis? I could not venture
to transplant hypnosis to these altitudes, but perhaps I might
succeed with a simple talk. I should have to try a lucky guess.
I had found often enough that in girls anxiety was a consequence of the horror by which a virginal mind is overcome
when it is faced for the first time with the world of sexuality.[1]

So I said: 'If you don't know, I'll tell you how *I* think you
got your attacks. At that time, two years ago, you must have
seen or heard something that very much embarrassed you, and
that you'd much rather not have seen.'

'Heavens, yes!' she replied, 'that was when I caught my uncle
with the girl, with Franziska, my cousin.'

'What's this story about a girl? Won't you tell me all about it?'

'You can say *anything* to a doctor, I suppose. Well, at that
time, you know, my uncle—the husband of the aunt you've seen
here—kept the inn on the ——kogel.[2] Now they're divorced,
and it's my fault they were divorced, because it was through
me that it came out that he was carrying on with Franziska.'

'And how did you discover it?'

'This way. One day two years ago some gentlemen had
climbed the mountain and asked for something to eat. My aunt
wasn't at home, and Franziska, who always did the cooking,
was nowhere to be found. And my uncle was not to be found
either. We looked everywhere, and at last Alois, the little boy,
my cousin, said: "Why, Franziska must be in Father's room!"

---

[1] I will quote here the case in which I first recognized this causal
connection. I was treating a young married woman who was suffering
from a complicated neurosis and, once again [cf. p. 112 *n.*], was unwilling to admit that her illness arose from her married life. She objected
that while she was still a girl she had had attacks of anxiety, ending in
fainting fits. I remained firm. When we had come to know each other
better she suddenly said to me one day: 'I'll tell you now how I came
by my attacks of anxiety when I was a girl. At that time I used to sleep
in a room next to my parents'; the door was left open and a night-light
used to burn on the table. So more than once I saw my father get into
bed with my mother and heard sounds that greatly excited me. It was
then that my attacks came on.'—[Two cases of this kind are mentioned
by Freud in a letter to Fliess of May 30, 1893 (Freud, 1950*a*, Letter
12). Cf. also Section II of the first paper on anxiety neurosis (1895*b*).]

[2] [The name of the 'other' mountain.]

And we both laughed; but we weren't thinking anything bad. Then we went to my uncle's room but found it locked. That seemed strange to me. Then Alois said: "There's a window in the passage where you can look into the room." We went into the passage; but Alois wouldn't go to the window and said he was afraid. So I said: "You silly boy! I'll go. I'm not a bit afraid." And I had nothing bad in my mind. I looked in. The room was rather dark, but I saw my uncle and Franziska; he was lying on her.'

'Well?'

'I came away from the window at once, and leant up against the wall and couldn't get my breath—just what happens to me since. Everything went blank, my eyelids were forced together and there was a hammering and buzzing in my head.'

'Did you tell your aunt that very same day?'

'Oh no, I said nothing.'

'Then why were you so frightened when you found them together? Did you understand it? Did you know what was going on?'

'Oh no. I didn't understand anything at that time. I was only sixteen. I don't know what I was frightened about.'

'Fräulein Katharina, if you could remember now what was happening in you at that time, when you had your first attack, what you thought about it—it would help you.'

'Yes, if I could. But I was so frightened that I've forgotten everything.'

(Translated into the terminology of our 'Preliminary Communication' [p. 12], this means: 'The affect itself created a hypnoid state, whose products were then cut off from associative connection with the ego-consciousness.')

'Tell me, Fräulein. Can it be that the head that you always see when you lose your breath is Franziska's head, as you saw it then?'

'Oh no, she didn't look so awful. Besides, it's a man's head.'

'Or perhaps your uncle's?'

'I didn't see his face as clearly as that. It was too dark in the room. And why should he have been making such a dreadful face just then?'

'You're quite right.'

(The road suddenly seemed blocked. Perhaps something might turn up in the rest of her story.)

'And what happened then?'

'Well, those two must have heard a noise, because they came out soon afterwards. I felt very bad the whole time. I always kept thinking about it. Then two days later it was a Sunday and there was a great deal to do and I worked all day long. And on the Monday morning I felt giddy again and was sick, and I stopped in bed and was sick without stopping for three days.'

We [Breuer and I] had often compared the symptomatology of hysteria with a pictographic script which has become intelligible after the discovery of a few bilingual inscriptions. In that alphabet being sick means disgust. So I said: 'If you were sick three days later, I believe that means that when you looked into the room you felt disgusted.'

'Yes, I'm sure I felt disgusted,' she said reflectively, 'but disgusted at what?'

'Perhaps you saw something naked? What sort of state were they in?'

'It was too dark to see anything; besides they both of them had their clothes on. Oh, if only I knew what it was I felt disgusted at!'

I had no idea either. But I told her to go on and tell me whatever occurred to her, in the confident expectation that she would think of precisely what I needed to explain the case.

Well, she went on to describe how at last she reported her discovery to her aunt, who found that she was changed and suspected her of concealing some secret. There followed some very disagreeable scenes between her uncle and aunt, in the course of which the children came to hear a number of things which opened their eyes in many ways and which it would have been better for them not to have heard. At last her aunt decided to move with her children and niece and take over the present inn, leaving her uncle alone with Franziska, who had meanwhile become pregnant. After this, however, to my astonishment she dropped these threads and began to tell me two sets of older stories, which went back two or three years earlier than the traumatic moment. The first set related to occasions on which the same uncle had made sexual advances to her herself, when she was only fourteen years old. She described how she had once gone with him on an expedition down into the valley in the winter and had spent the night in the inn there. He sat in the bar drinking and playing cards, but she felt sleepy and went up to bed early in the room they were to share on the upper floor. She was not quite asleep when he came up; then she fell asleep again and woke up suddenly 'feeling his body' in the bed. She jumped up and remonstrated with him: 'What are you up to, Uncle? Why don't you stay in your own bed?' He tried to pacify her: 'Go on, you silly girl, keep still. You don't know how nice it is.'—'I don't like your "nice" things; you don't even let one sleep in peace.' She remained standing by the door, ready to take refuge outside in the passage, till at last he gave up and went to sleep himself. Then she went back to her own bed and slept till morning. From the way in which she reported having defended herself it seems to follow that she did not clearly recognize the attack as a sexual one. When I asked her if she knew what he was trying to do to her, she replied: 'Not at the time.' It had become clear to her much later on, she said; she had resisted because it was unpleasant to be disturbed in one's sleep and 'because it wasn't nice'.

I have been obliged to relate this in detail, because of its great importance for understanding everything that followed. —She went on to tell me of yet other experiences of somewhat later date: how she had once again had to defend herself against him in an inn when he was completely drunk, and similar stories. In answer to a question as to whether on these occasions she had felt anything resembling her later loss of breath, she answered with decision that she had every time felt the pressure on her eyes and chest, but with nothing like the strength that had characterized the scene of discovery.

Immediately she had finished this set of memories she began to tell me a second set, which dealt with occasions on which she had noticed something between her uncle and Franziska. Once the whole family had spent the night in their clothes in a hay loft and she was woken up suddenly by a noise; she thought she noticed that her uncle, who had been lying between her and Franziska, was turning away, and that Franziska was just lying down. Another time they were stopping the night at an inn at the village of N——; she and her uncle were in one room and Franziska in an adjoining one. She woke up suddenly in the night and saw a tall white figure by the door, on the point of turning the handle: 'Goodness, is that you, Uncle? What are you doing at the door?'—'Keep quiet. I was only

looking for something.'—'But the way out's by the *other* door.'
—'I'd just made a mistake' . . . and so on.

I asked her if she had been suspicious at that time. 'No, I
didn't think anything about it; I only just noticed it and
thought no more about it.' When I enquired whether she had
been frightened on these occasions too, she replied that she
thought so, but she was not so sure of it this time.

At the end of these two sets of memories she came to a stop.
She was like someone transformed. The sulky, unhappy face
had grown lively, her eyes were bright, she was lightened and
exalted. Meanwhile the understanding of her case had become
clear to me. The later part of what she had told me, in an
apparently aimless fashion, provided an admirable explanation
of her behaviour at the scene of the discovery. At that time
she had carried about with her two sets of experiences which
she remembered but did not understand, and from which she
drew no inferences. When she caught sight of the couple in
intercourse, she at once established a connection between the
new impression and these two sets of recollections, she began to
understand them and at the same time to fend them off. There
then followed a short period of working-out, of 'incubation',[1]
after which the symptoms of conversion set in, the vomiting
as a substitute for moral and physical disgust. This solved the
riddle. She had not been disgusted by the sight of the two people
but by the memory which that sight had stirred up in her. And,
taking everything into account, this could only be the memory of
the attempt on her at night when she had 'felt her uncle's body'.

So when she had finished her confession I said to her: 'I
know now what it was you thought when you looked into the
room. You thought: "Now he's doing with her what he wanted
to do with me that night and those other times." That was
what you were disgusted at, because you remembered the feeling when you woke up in the night and felt his body.'

'It may well be,' she replied, 'that that was what I was disgusted at and that that was what I thought.'

'Tell me just one thing more. You're a grown-up girl now
and know all sorts of things . . .'

'Yes, now I am.'

'Tell me just one thing. What part of his body was it that
you felt that night?'

[1] [Cf. below, p. 134.]

But she gave me no more definite answer. She smiled in an embarrassed way, as though she had been found out, like someone who is obliged to admit that a fundamental position has been reached where there is not much more to be said. I could imagine what the tactile sensation was which she had later learnt to interpret. Her facial expression seemed to me to be saying that she supposed that I was right in my conjecture. But I could not penetrate further, and in any case I owed her a debt of gratitude for having made it so much easier for me to talk to her than to the prudish ladies of my city practice, who regard whatever is natural as shameful.

Thus the case was cleared up.—But stop a moment! What about the recurrent hallucination of the head, which appeared during her attacks and struck terror into her? Where did it come from? I proceeded to ask her about it, and, as though *her* knowledge, too, had been extended by our conversation, she promptly replied: 'Yes, I know now. The head is my uncle's head—I recognize it now—but not from *that* time. Later, when all the disputes had broken out, my uncle gave way to a senseless rage against me. He kept saying that it was all my fault: if I hadn't chattered, it would never have come to a divorce. He kept threatening he would do something to me; and if he caught sight of me at a distance his face would get distorted with rage and he would make for me with his hand raised. I always ran away from him, and always felt terrified that he would catch me some time unawares. The face I always see now is his face when he was in a rage.'

This information reminded me that her first hysterical symptom, the vomiting, had passed away; the anxiety attack remained and acquired a fresh content. Accordingly, what we were dealing with was a hysteria which had to a considerable extent been abreacted. And in fact she had reported her discovery to her aunt soon after it happened.

'Did you tell your aunt the other stories—about his making advances to you?'

'Yes. Not at once, but later on, when there was already talk of a divorce. My aunt said: "We'll keep that in reserve. If he causes trouble in the Court, we'll say that too." '

I can well understand that it should have been precisely this last period—when there were more and more agitating scenes in the house and when her own state ceased to interest her aunt,

who was entirely occupied with the dispute—that it should
have been this period of accumulation and retention that left
her the legacy of the mnemic symbol [of the hallucinated face].

I hope this girl, whose sexual sensibility had been injured at
such an early age, derived some benefit from our conversation.
I have not seen her since.

DISCUSSION

If someone were to assert that the present case history is not
so much an analysed case of hysteria as a case solved by guess-
ing, I should have nothing to say against him. It is true that
the patient agreed that what I interpolated into her story was
probably true; but she was not in a position to recognize it as
something she had experienced. I believe it would have required hypnosis to bring that about. Assuming that my guesses
were correct, I will now attempt to fit the case into the schematic
picture of an 'acquired' hysteria on the lines suggested by
Case 3. It seems plausible, then, to compare the two sets of
erotic experiences with 'traumatic' moments and the scene of
discovering the couple with an 'auxiliary' moment. [Cf. p.123f.]
The similarity lies in the fact that in the former experiences
an element of consciousness was created which was excluded
from the thought-activity of the ego and remained, as it were,
in storage, while in the latter scene a new impression forcibly
brought about an associative connection between this separated
group and the ego. On the other hand there are dissimilarities
which cannot be overlooked. The cause of the isolation was not,
as in Case 3, an act of will on the part of the ego but *ignorance*
on the part of the ego, which was not yet capable of coping
with sexual experiences. In this respect the case of Katharina
is typical. In every analysis of a case of hysteria based on sexual
traumas we find that impressions from the pre-sexual period
which produced no effect on the child attain traumatic power
at a later date as memories, when the girl or married woman
has acquired an understanding of sexual life.[1] The splitting-off

---

[1] [Freud had discussed this at considerable length in the later sections
of Part II of his 1895 'Project' (Freud, 1950a) and expressed the same
view in Section I of his second paper on 'The Neuro-Psychoses of
Defence' (1896b). It was not until some years later that he came to
recognize the part played in the production of neuroses by sexual
impulses already present in early childhood. Cf. the Editor's Note to the
Three Essays (1905d), *Standard Ed.*, 7, 127–9.]

of psychical groups may be said to be a normal process in adolescent development; and it is easy to see that their later reception into the ego affords frequent opportunities for psychical disturbances. Moreover, I should like at this point to express a doubt as to whether a splitting of consciousness due to ignorance is really different from one due to conscious rejection, and whether even adolescents do not possess sexual knowledge far oftener than is supposed or than they themselves believe.

A further distinction in the psychical mechanism of this case lies in the fact that the scene of discovery, which we have described as 'auxiliary', deserves equally to be called 'traumatic'. It was operative on account of its own content and not merely as something that revived previous traumatic experiences. It combined the characteristics of an 'auxiliary' and a 'traumatic' moment. There seems no reason, however, why this coincidence should lead us to abandon a conceptual separation which in other cases corresponds also to a separation in time. Another peculiarity of Katharina's case, which, incidentally, has long been familiar to us, is seen in the circumstance that the conversion, the production of the hysterical phenomena, did not occur immediately after the trauma but after an interval of incubation. Charcot liked to describe this interval as the 'period of psychical working-out' [*élaboration*].[1]

The anxiety from which Katharina suffered in her attacks was a hysterical one; that is, it was a reproduction of the anxiety which had appeared in connection with each of the sexual traumas. I shall not here comment on the fact which I have found regularly present in a very large number of cases —namely that a mere suspicion of sexual relations calls up the affect of anxiety in virginal individuals.[2] [Cf. p. 127, *n.* 1.]

---

[1] [See Charcot 1888, **1**, 99. Cf. also Breuer's remarks on the subject on p. 213 below.]

[2] (*Footnote added* 1924:) I venture after the lapse of so many years to lift the veil of discretion and reveal the fact that Katharina was not the niece but the daughter of the landlady. The girl fell ill, therefore, as a result of sexual attempts on the part of her own father. Distortions like the one which I introduced in the present instance should be altogether avoided in reporting a case history. From the point of view of understanding the case, a distortion of this kind is not, of course, a matter of such indifference as would be shifting the scene from one mountain to another.

CASE 5

Fräulein Elisabeth von R. (Freud)

In the autumn of 1892 I was asked by a doctor I knew to examine a young lady who had been suffering for more than two years from pains in her legs and who had difficulties in walking. When making this request he added that he thought the çase was one of hysteria, though there was no trace of the usual indications of that neurosis. He told me that he knew the family slightly and that during the last few years it had met with many misfortunes and not much happiness. First the patient's father had died, then her mother had had to undergo a serious eye-operation and soon afterwards a married sister had succumbed to a heart-affection of long standing after a confinement. In all these troubles and in all the sick-nursing involved, the largest share had fallen to our patient.

My first interview with this young woman of twenty-four years of age did not help me to make much further progress in understanding the case. She seemed intelligent and mentally normal and bore her troubles, which interfered with her social life and pleasures, with a cheerful air—the *belle indifférence* of a hysteric,[1] I could not help thinking. She walked with the upper part of her body bent forward, but without making use of any support. Her gait was not of any recognized pathological type, and moreover was by no means strikingly bad. All that was apparent was that she complained of great pain in walking and of being quickly overcome by fatigue both in walking and in standing, and that after a short time she had to rest, which lessened the pains but did not do away with them altogether. The pain was of an indefinite character; I gathered that it was something in the nature of a painful fatigue. A fairly large, ill-defined area of the anterior surface of the right thigh was indicated as the focus of the pains, from which they most often radiated and where they reached their greatest intensity. In this area the skin and muscles were also particularly sensitive to pressure and pinching (though the prick of a needle was, if

[1] [Freud quotes this phrase again towards the end of his paper on repression (1915*d*), where he attributes it to Charcot.]

135

anything, met with a certain amount of unconcern). This hyperalgesia of the skin and muscles was not restricted to this area but could be observed more or less over the whole of both legs. The muscles were perhaps even more sensitive to pain than the skin; but there could be no question that the thighs were the parts most sensitive to both these kinds of pain. The motor power of the legs could not be described as small, and the reflexes were of medium strength. There were no other symptoms, so that there was no ground for suspecting the presence of any serious organic affection. The disorder had developed gradually during the previous two years and varied greatly in intensity.

I did not find it easy to arrive at a diagnosis, but I decided for two reasons to assent to the one proposed by my colleague, viz. that it was a case of hysteria. In the first place I was struck by the indefiniteness of all the descriptions of the character of her pains given me by the patient, who was nevertheless a highly intelligent person. A patient suffering from organic pains will, unless he is neurotic in addition, describe them definitely and calmly. He will say, for instance, that they are shooting pains, that they occur at certain intervals, that they extend from this place to that and that they seem to him to be brought on by one thing or another. Again, when a neurasthenic [1] describes his pains, he gives an impression of being engaged on a difficult intellectual task to which his strength is quite unequal. His features are strained and distorted as though under the influence of a distressing affect. His voice grows more shrill and he struggles to find a means of expression. He rejects any description of his pains proposed by the physician, even though it may turn out afterwards to have been unquestionably apt. He is clearly of opinion that language is too poor to find words for his sensations and that those sensations are something unique and previously unknown, of which it would be quite impossible to give an exhaustive description. For this reason he never tires of constantly adding fresh details, and when he is obliged to break off he is sure to be left with the conviction that he has not succeeded in making himself understood by the physician. All this is because his pains have attracted his whole attention to themselves. Fräulein von R.

---

[1] (A hypochondriac or a person affected with anxiety neurosis.) [These brackets are the author's.]

behaved in quite an opposite way; and we are driven to conclude that, since she nevertheless attached sufficient importance to her symptoms, her attention must be dwelling on something else, of which the pains were only an accessory phenomenon —probably on thoughts and feelings, therefore, which were connected with them.

But there is a second factor which is even more decisively in favour of this view of the pains. If one stimulates an area sensitive to pain in someone with an organic illness or in a neurasthenic, the patient's face takes on an expression of discomfort or physical pain. Moreover he flinches and draws back from the examination and resists it. In the case of Fräulein von R., however, if one pressed or pinched the hyperalgesic skin and muscles of her legs, her face assumed a peculiar expression, which was one of pleasure rather than pain. She cried out— and I could not help thinking that it was as though she was having a voluptuous tickling sensation—her face flushed, she threw back her head and shut her eyes and her body bent backwards. None of this was very exaggerated but it was distinctly noticeable, and it could only be reconciled with the view that her disorder was hysterical, and that the stimulation had touched upon a hysterogenic [1] zone.

Her expression of face did not fit in with the pain which was ostensibly set up by the pinching of her muscles and skin; it was probably more in harmony with the subject-matter of the thoughts which lay concealed behind the pain and which had been aroused in her by the stimulation of the parts of the body associated with those thoughts. I had repeatedly observed expressions of similar significance in undoubted cases of hysteria, when a stimulus was applied to their hyperalgesic zones. Her other gestures were evidently very slight hints of a hysterical attack.

To begin with there was no explanation of the unusual localization of her hysterogenic zone. The fact that the hyperalgesia mainly affected the muscles also gave food for thought. The disorder which is most usually responsible for diffuse and local sensitivity to pressure in the muscles is a rheumatic infiltration of those muscles—common chronic muscular rheumatism. I have already [p. 71 n.] spoken of its tendency to simulate

[1] [So in the first edition. All later editions have, no doubt erroneously, 'hysterical'.]

nervous affections. This possibility was not contradicted by the consistency of the patient's hyperalgesic muscles. There were numerous hard fibres in the muscular substance, and these seemed to be especially sensitive. Thus it was probable that an organic change in the muscles of the kind indicated was present and that the neurosis attached itself to this and made it seem of exaggerated importance.

Treatment proceeded on the assumption that the disorder was of this mixed kind. We recommended the continuation of systematic kneading and faradization of the sensitive muscles, regardless of the resulting pain, and I reserved to myself treatment of her legs with high tension electric currents, in order to be able to keep in touch with her. Her question whether she should force herself to walk was answered with a decided 'yes'.

In this way we brought about a slight improvement. In particular, she seemed to take quite a liking to the painful shocks produced by the high tension apparatus, and the stronger these were the more they seemed to push her own pains into the background. In the meantime my colleague was preparing the ground for psychical treatment, and when, after four weeks of my pretence treatment, I proposed the other method and gave her some account of its procedure and mode of operation, I met with quick understanding and little resistance.

The task on which I now embarked turned out, however, to be one of the hardest that I had ever undertaken, and the difficulty of giving a report upon it is comparable, moreover, with the difficulties that I had then to overcome. For a long time, too, I was unable to grasp the connection between the events in her illness and her actual symptom, which must nevertheless have been caused and determined by that set of experiences.

When one starts upon a cathartic treatment of this kind, the first question one asks oneself is whether the patient herself is aware of the origin and the precipitating cause of her illness. If so, no special technique is required to enable her to reproduce the story of her illness. The interest shown in her by the physician, the understanding of her which he allows her to feel and the hopes of recovery he holds out to her—all these will decide the patient to yield up her secret. From the beginning it seemed to me probable that Fräulein Elisabeth was conscious

of the basis of her illness, that what she had in her consciousness
was only a secret and not a foreign body. Looking at her, one
could not help thinking of the poet's words:

Das Mäskchen da weissagt verborgnen Sinn.[1]

In the first instance, therefore, I was able to do without
hypnosis, with the reservation, however, that I could make
use of it later if in the course of her confession material arose
to the elucidation of which her memory was unequal. Thus it
came about that in this, the first full-length analysis of a hysteria
undertaken by me, I arrived at a procedure which I later
developed into a regular method and employed deliberately.
This procedure was one of clearing away the pathogenic
psychical material layer by layer, and we liked to compare it
with the technique of excavating a buried city. I would begin
by getting the patient to tell me what was known to her and I
would carefully note the points at which some train of thought
remained obscure or some link in the causal chain seemed to
be missing. And afterwards I would penetrate into deeper
layers of her memories at these points by carrying out an
investigation under hypnosis or by the use of some similar
technique. The whole work was, of course, based on the expectation that it would be possible to establish a completely
adequate set of determinants for the events concerned. I shall
discuss presently the methods used for the deep investigation.

The story which Fräulein Elisabeth told of her illness was a
wearisome one, made up of many different painful experiences.
While she told it she was not under hypnosis; but I made her
lie down and keep her eyes shut, though I made no objection
to her occasionally opening them, changing her position, sitting
up, and so on. When she was more deeply moved than usual
by a part of her story she seemed to fall into a state more or
less resembling hypnosis. She would then lie motionless and
keep her eyes tightly shut.

I will begin by repeating what emerged as the most superficial layer of her memories. The youngest of three daughters,
she was tenderly attached to her parents and spent her youth
on their estate in Hungary. Her mother's health was frequently

[1] ['Her mask reveals a hidden sense.' Adapted from Goethe's *Faust*,
Part I (Scene 16).]—Nevertheless, it will be seen later that I was mistaken in this.

troubled by an affection of the eyes as well as by nervous states. Thus it came about that she found herself drawn into especially intimate contact with her father, a vivacious man of the world, who used to say that this daughter of his took the place of a son and a friend with whom he could exchange thoughts. Although the girl's mind found intellectual stimulation from this relationship with her father, he did not fail to observe that her mental constitution was on that account departing from the ideal which people like to see realized in a girl. He jokingly called her 'cheeky' and 'cock-sure', and warned her against being too positive in her judgements and against her habit of regardlessly telling people the truth, and he often said she would find it hard to get a husband. She was in fact greatly discontented with being a girl. She was full of ambitious plans. She wanted to study or to have a musical training, and she was indignant at the idea of having to sacrifice her inclinations and her freedom of judgement by marriage. As it was, she nourished herself on her pride in her father and in the prestige and social position of her family, and she jealously guarded everything that was bound up with these advantages. The unselfishness, however, with which she put her mother and elder sisters first, when an occasion arose, reconciled her parents completely to the harsher side of her character.

In view of the girls' ages it was decided that the family should move to the capital, where Elisabeth was able for a short time to enjoy a fuller and gayer life in the home circle. Then, however, the blow fell which destroyed the happiness of the family. Her father had concealed, or had perhaps himself overlooked, a chronic affection of the heart, and he was brought home unconscious one day suffering from a pulmonary oedema. He was nursed for eighteen months, and Elisabeth saw to it that she played the leading part at his sick-bed. She slept in his room, was ready to wake if he called her at night, looked after him during the day and forced herself to appear cheerful, while he reconciled himself to his hopeless state with uncomplaining resignation. The beginning of her illness must have been connected with this period of nursing, for she remembered that during its last six months she had taken to her bed for a day and a half on account of the pains we have described. She asserted, however, that these pains quickly passed off and had not caused her any uneasiness or attracted her attention. And in fact it was not until two years after her father's death that she felt ill and became incapable of walking on account of her pains.

The gap that was caused in the life of this family of four women by her father's death, their social isolation, the breaking-off of so many connections that had promised to bring her interest and enjoyment, her mother's ill-health which was now becoming more marked—all this cast a shadow over the patient's state of feeling; but at the same time it kindled a lively desire in her that her family might soon find something to replace their lost happiness, and led her to concentrate her whole affection and care on the mother who was still living.

When the year of mourning had passed, her elder sister married a gifted and energetic man. He occupied a responsible position and his intellectual powers seemed to promise him a great future. But to his closer acquaintances he exhibited a morbid sensitiveness and an egoistic insistence on his fads; and he was the first in the family circle to venture to show lack of consideration for the old lady. This was more than Elisabeth could bear. She felt called upon to take up the fight against her brother-in-law whenever he gave her occasion, while the other women did not take his temperamental outbursts to heart. It was a painful disappointment to her that the rebuilding of their former family happiness should be thus interrupted; and she could not forgive her married sister for the feminine pliancy with which she persistently avoided taking sides. Elisabeth retained a number of scenes in her memory in this connection, involving complaints, in part not expressed in words, against her first brother-in-law. But her chief reproach against him remained the fact that, for the sake of a prospective promotion, he moved with his small family to a remote town in Austria and thus helped to increase her mother's isolation. On this occasion Elisabeth felt acutely her helplessness, her inability to afford her mother a substitute for the happiness she had lost and the impossibility of carrying out the intention she had formed at her father's death.

The marriage of her second sister seemed to promise a brighter future for the family, for the second brother-in-law, though less outstanding intellectually, was a man after the heart of these cultivated women, brought up as they had been in a school of consideration for others. His behaviour reconciled

Elisabeth to the institution of marriage and to the thought of the sacrifices it involved. Moreover the second young couple remained in her mother's neighbourhood, and their child became Elisabeth's favourite. Unfortunately another event cast a shadow over the year in which this child was born. The treatment of her mother's eye-trouble necessitated her being kept in a dark room for several weeks, during which Elisabeth was with her. An operation was then pronounced unavoidable. The agitation at this prospect coincided with the preparations for her first brother-in-law's move. At last her mother came through the operation, which was performed by a master hand. The three families were united at a summer holiday resort, and it was hoped that Elisabeth, who had been exhausted by the anxieties of the last few months, would make a complete recovery during what was the first period of freedom from sorrows and fears that the family had enjoyed since her father's death.

It was precisely during this holiday, however, that Elisabeth's pains and locomotor weakness started. She had been to some extent aware of the pains for a short while, but they came on violently for the first time after she had had a warm bath in the bath establishment of the little watering-place. A few days earlier she had been for a long walk—in fact a regular tramp lasting half a day—and this they connected with the appearance of the pains, so that it was easy to take the view that Elisabeth had first been 'overtired' and had then 'caught cold'.

From this time on Elisabeth was the invalid of the family. She was advised by her doctor to devote the rest of the same summer to a course of hydropathic treatment at Gastein [in the Austrian Alps], and she went there with her mother. But a fresh anxiety now arose. Her second sister had become pregnant again and reports of her condition were most unfavourable, so that Elisabeth could hardly make up her mind to travel to Gastein. She and her mother had been there for barely a fortnight when they were called back by the news that her sister, who had now taken to her bed, was in a very bad state.

There followed an agonizing journey, during which Elisabeth was tormented not only by her pains but by dreadful expectations; on their arrival at the station there were signs that led them to fear the worst; and when they entered the sick-room there came the certainty that they had come too late to take their leave of a living person.

Elisabeth suffered not only from the loss of this sister, whom she had dearly loved, but almost as much from the thoughts provoked by her death and the changes which it brought along with it. Her sister had succumbed to an affection of the heart which had been aggravated by her pregnancy. The idea now presented itself that heart disease was inherited from the father's side of the family. It was then recalled that the dead sister had suffered during her early girlhood from chorea accompanied by a mild cardiac disorder. They blamed themselves and the doctors for having permitted the marriage, and it was impossible to spare the unhappy widower the reproach of having endangered his wife's health by bringing on two pregnancies in immediate succession. From that time onwards Elisabeth's thoughts were occupied without interruption with the gloomy reflection that when, for once in a way, the rare conditions for a happy marriage had been fulfilled, this happiness should have come to such an end. Furthermore, she saw the collapse once more of all she had desired for her mother. Her widowed brother-in-law was inconsolable and withdrew from his wife's family. It appeared that his own family, which had been estranged from him during his short, happy marriage, thought this was a favourable moment for drawing him back into their own circle. There was no way of preserving the unity that had existed formerly. It was not practicable for him to live with her mother in view of Elisabeth's unmarried state. Since, also, he refused to allow the two women to have the custody of the child, which was the dead woman's only legacy, he gave them occasion for the first time to accuse him of hard-heartedness. Lastly—and this was not the least distressing fact—a rumour reached Elisabeth that a dispute had arisen between her two brothers-in-law. She could only guess at its cause; it seemed, however, that the widower had put forward financial demands which the other declared were unjustifiable and which, indeed, in view of the mother's present sorrow, he was able to characterize as blackmail of the worst description.

Here, then, was the unhappy story of this proud girl with her longing for love. Unreconciled to her fate, embittered by the failure of all her little schemes for re-establishing the family's former glories, with those she loved dead or gone away or estranged, unready to take refuge in the love of some unknown man—she had lived for eighteen months in almost complete seclusion, with nothing to occupy her but the care of her mother and her own pains.

If we put greater misfortunes on one side and enter into a girl's feelings, we cannot refrain from deep human sympathy with Fräulein Elisabeth. But what shall we say of the purely medical interest of this tale of suffering, of its relations to her painful locomotor weakness, and of the chances of an explanation and cure afforded by our knowledge of these psychical traumas?

As far as the physician was concerned, the patient's confession was at first sight a great disappointment. It was a case history made up of commonplace emotional upheavals, and there was nothing about it to explain why it was particularly from hysteria that she fell ill or why her hysteria took the particular form of a painful abasia. It threw light neither on the causes nor the specific determination of her hysteria. We might perhaps suppose that the patient had formed an association between her painful mental impressions and the bodily pains which she happened to be experiencing at the same time, and that now, in her life of memories, she was using her physical feelings as a symbol of her mental ones. But it remained unexplained what her motives might have been for making a substitution of this kind and at what moment it had taken place. These, incidentally, were not the kind of questions that physicians were in the habit of raising. We were usually content with the statement that the patient was constitutionally a hysteric, liable to develop hysterical symptoms under the pressure of intense excitations *of whatever kind*.

Her confession seemed to offer even less help towards the cure of her illness than it did towards its explanation. It was not easy to see what beneficent influence Fräulein Elisabeth could derive from recapitulating the tale of her sufferings of recent years—with which all the members of her family were so familiar—to a stranger who received it with only a moderate sympathy. Nor was there any sign of the confession producing a curative effect of this kind. During this first period of her treatment she never failed to repeat that she was still feeling ill and that her pains were as bad as ever; and, when she looked at me as she said this with a sly look of satisfaction at my discomfiture, I could not help being reminded of old Herr von R.'s judgement about his favourite daughter—that she was often 'cheeky' and 'ill-behaved'. But I was obliged to admit that she was in the right.

If I had stopped the patient's psychical treatment at this stage, the case of Fräulein Elisabeth von R. would clearly have thrown no light on the theory of hysteria. But I continued my analysis because I firmly expected that deeper levels of her consciousness would yield an understanding both of the causes and the specific determinants of the hysterical symptoms. I therefore decided to put a direct question to the patient in an enlarged state of consciousness and to ask her what psychical impression it had been to which the first emergence of pains in her legs had been attached.

With this end in view I proposed to put the patient into a deep hypnosis. But, unfortunately, I could not help observing that my procedure failed to put her into any state other than the one in which she had made her recital. I was glad enough that on this occasion she refrained from triumphantly protesting: 'I'm not asleep, you know; I can't be hypnotized.' In this extremity the idea occurred to me of resorting to the device of applying pressure to the head, the origin of which I have described in full in the case history of Miss Lucy [p. 107 ff.]. I carried this out by instructing the patient to report to me faithfully whatever appeared before her inner eye or passed through her memory at the moment of the pressure. She remained silent for a long time and then, on my insistence, admitted that she had thought of an evening on which a young man had seen her home after a party, of the conversation that had taken place between them and of the feelings with which she had returned home to her father's sick-bed.

This first mention of the young man opened up a new vein of ideas the contents of which I now gradually extracted. It was a question here of a secret, for she had initiated no one, apart from a common friend, into her relations with the young man and the hopes attached to them. He was the son of a family with which they had long been on friendly terms and who lived near their former estate. The young man, who was himself an orphan, was devotedly attached to her father and followed his advice in pursuing his career. He had extended

M

his admiration for her father to the ladies of the family. Numerous recollections of reading together, of exchanging ideas, and of remarks made by him which were repeated to her by other people, bore witness to the gradual growth in her of a conviction that he loved her and understood her and that marriage with him would not involve the sacrifices on her part which she dreaded from marriage in general. Unluckily, he was scarcely any older than herself and was still far from being self-supporting. But she was firmly determined to wait for him.

After her father had fallen seriously ill and she had been so much taken up with looking after him, her meetings with her friend became more and more rare. The evening which she had first remembered represented what had actually been the climax of her feeling; but even then there had been no *éclaircissement* between them. On that occasion she had allowed herself to be persuaded, by the insistence of her family and of her father himself, to go to a party at which she was likely to meet him. She had wanted to hurry home early but had been pressed to stay and had given way when he promised to see her home. She had never had such warm feelings towards him as while he was accompanying her that evening. But when she arrived home late in this blissful frame of mind, she found her father was worse and reproached herself most bitterly for having sacrificed so much time to her own enjoyment. This was the last time she left her sick father for a whole evening. She seldom met her friend after this. After her father's death the young man seemed to keep away from her out of respect for her sorrow. The course of his life then took him in other directions. She had to familiarize herself by degrees with the thought that his interest in her had been displaced by others and that she had lost him. But this disappointment in her first love still hurt her whenever she thought of him.

It was therefore in this relationship and in the scene described above in which it culminated that I could look for the causes of her first hysterical pains. The contrast between the blissful feelings she had allowed herself to enjoy on that occasion and the worsening of her father's state which had met her on her return home constituted a conflict, a situation of incompatibility. The outcome of this conflict was that the erotic idea was repressed from association and the affect attaching to that idea was used to intensify or revive a physical pain which was present simultaneously or shortly before. Thus it was an instance of the mechanism of conversion for the purpose of defence, which I have described in detail elsewhere.[1]

A number of comments might of course be made at this point. I must emphasize the fact that I did not succeed in establishing from her memory that the conversion took place at the moment of her return home. I therefore looked about for similar experiences during the time she was nursing her father and elicited a number of them. Among these, special prominence attached, on account of their frequent occurrence, to scenes in which, at her father's call, she had jumped out of bed with bare feet in a cold room. I was inclined to attribute some importance to these factors, since in addition to complaining about the pain in her legs she also complained of tormenting sensations of cold. Nevertheless, even here I was unable to get hold of any scene which it was possible to identify as that at which the conversion had occurred. I was inclined for this reason to think that there was a gap in the explanation at this point, until I recollected that the hysterical pains in the legs had in fact not made their appearance during the period when she was nursing her father. She only remembered a single attack of pain, which had only lasted a day or two and had not attracted her attention [p. 140]. I now directed my enquiries to this first appearance of the pains. I succeeded in reviving the patient's memory of it with certainty. At that very time a relative had visited them and she had been unable to receive him, owing to being laid up in bed. This same man had been unlucky enough, when he visited them again two years later, to find her in bed once more. But in spite of repeated attempts we failed to trace any psychical cause for the first pains. I thought it safe to assume that they had in fact appeared without any psychical cause and were a mild rheumatic affection; and I was able to establish that this organic disorder, which was the model copied in her later hysteria, had in any case to be dated before the scene of her being accompanied back from the party. From the nature of things it is nevertheless possible that these pains, being of organic origin, may have persisted for some time to a mitigated degree without being very noticeable. The obscurity due to the fact that the analysis

[1] [See Freud's first paper on 'The Neuro-Psychoses of Defence' (1894a), and the footnote on p. 10 above.]

pointed to the occurrence of a conversion of psychical excitation into physical pain though that pain was certainly not perceived at the time in question or remembered afterwards—this is a problem which I hope to be able to solve later on the basis of further considerations and later examples.[1] [See below, p. 168 ff.]

The discovery of the reason for the first conversion opened a second, fruitful period of the treatment. The patient surprised me soon afterwards by announcing that she now knew why it was that the pains always radiated from that particular area of the right thigh and were at their most painful there: it was on this place that her father used to rest his leg every morning, while she renewed the bandage round it, for it was badly swollen. This must have happened a good hundred times, yet she had not noticed the connection till now. In this way she gave me the explanation that I needed of the emergence of what was an atypical hysterogenic zone. Further, her painful legs began to 'join in the conversation' during our analyses. [See p. 296.] What I have in mind is the following remarkable fact. As a rule the patient was free from pain when we started work. If, then, by a question or by pressure upon her head I called up a memory, a sensation of pain would make its first appearance, and this was usually so sharp that the patient would give a start and put her hand to the painful spot. The pain that was thus aroused would persist so long as she was under the influence of the memory; it would reach its climax when she was in the act of telling me the essential and decisive part of what she had to communicate, and with the last word of this it would disappear. I came in time to use such pains as a compass to guide me; if she stopped talking but admitted that she still had a pain, I knew that she had not told me everything, and insisted on her continuing her story till the pain had been talked away. Not until then did I arouse a fresh memory.

During this period of 'abreaction' the patient's condition, both physical and mental, made such a striking improvement that I used to say, only half-jokingly, that I was taking away a

---

[1] I cannot exclude the possibility, though I cannot establish the fact, that these pains, which chiefly affected the thighs, were of a *neurasthenic* nature. [Cf. p. 175 *n*.]

certain amount of her motives for pain every time and that when I had cleared them all away she would be well. She soon got to the point of being without pain most of the time; she allowed herself to be persuaded to walk about a great deal and to give up her former isolation. In the course of the analysis I sometimes followed the spontaneous fluctuations in her condition; and I sometimes followed my own estimate of the situation when I considered that I had not completely exhausted some portion of the story of her illness.

During this work I made some interesting observations, whose lessons I subsequently found confirmed in treating other patients. As regards the spontaneous fluctuations, in the first place, I found that in fact none had occurred which had not been provoked by association with some contemporary event. On one occasion she had heard of an illness of one of her acquaintances which reminded her of a detail of her father's illness; another time her dead sister's child had been on a visit to them, and its likeness to its mother had stirred up her feelings of grief; and yet another time a letter from her distant sister showed clear evidence of her unfeeling brother-in-law's influence and gave rise to a pain which required her to produce the story of a family scene which she had not yet told me about. Since she never brought up the same precipitating cause of a pain twice over, it seemed that we were justified in supposing that we should in this way exhaust the stock of them; and I therefore did not hesitate to get her into situations which were calculated to bring up fresh memories which had not yet reached the surface. For instance, I sent her to visit her sister's grave, and I encouraged her to go to a party at which she might once more come across the friend of her youth.

In the next place, I obtained some insight into the manner of origin of what might be described as a 'monosymptomatic' hysteria. For I found that her *right* leg became painful under hypnosis when the discussion turned on her nursing her sick father, on her relations with the friend of her youth or on other events falling within the first period of her pathogenic experiences; on the other hand, the pain made its appearance in her other, *left*, leg as soon as I stirred up a memory relating to her dead sister or her two brothers-in-law—in short, to an impression from the second half of the story of her illness. Having thus had my attention aroused by the regularity of this relation,

I carried my investigation further and formed an impression that this differentiation went still further and that every fresh psychical determinant of painful sensations had become attached to some fresh spot in the painful area of her legs. The original painful spot in her right thigh had related to her nursing her father; the area of pain had extended from this spot to neighbouring regions as a result of fresh traumas. Here, therefore, what we were dealing with was not strictly speaking a *single* physical symptom, linked with a variety of mnemic complexes in the mind, but a number of similar symptoms which appeared, on a superficial view, to be merged into one symptom. But I did not pursue further the delimitation of zones of pain corresponding to different psychical determinants, since I found that the patient's attention was directed away from this subject.

I did, however, turn my attention to the way in which the whole symptomatic complex of abasia might have been built up upon these painful zones, and in that connection I asked her various questions, such as what was the origin of her pains in walking? in standing? and in lying down? Some of these questions she answered spontaneously, some under the pressure of my hand. Two things emerged from this. In the first place she divided all the scenes with painful impressions attached to them into groups for me, according as she had experienced them while she was sitting or standing, and so on. For instance, she was *standing* by a door when her father was brought home with his heart attack [p. 140], and in her fright she stood stock still as though she was rooted to the ground. She went on to add a number of other memories to this first example of fright while she was standing, till she came to the fearful scene in which once again she *stood*, as though spellbound, by her sister's death-bed [pp. 142–3]. This whole chain of memories might be expected to show that there was a legitimate connection between her pains and standing up; and it might indeed be accepted as evidence of an association. But we must bear in mind that another factor must be proved to be present in all these events, one which directed her attention precisely to her standing (or, as the case may be, to her walking, sitting, etc.) and consequently led to conversion. The explanation of her attention taking this direction can scarcely be looked for elsewhere than in the circumstance that walking, standing and lying are functions and states of those parts of her body which in her case comprised the painful zones, namely, her legs. It was therefore easy in the present case to understand the connection between the astasia-abasia and the first occurrence of conversion.

Among the episodes which, according to this catalogue, seemed to have made *walking* painful, one received special prominence: a walk which she had taken at the health resort in the company of a number of other people [p. 142] and which was supposed to have been too long. The details of this episode only emerged with hesitation and left several riddles unsolved. She had been in a particularly yielding mood, and eagerly joined her party of friends. It was a fine day, not too hot. Her mother stopped at home and her elder sister had already gone away. Her younger sister felt unwell, but did not want to spoil her enjoyment; the brother-in-law began by saying that he would stay with his wife, but afterwards decided to join the party on Elisabeth's account. This scene seemed to have had a great deal to do with the first appearance of the pains, for she remembered being very tired and suffering from violent pain when she returned from the walk. She said, however, that she was not certain whether she had already noticed the pains before this. I pointed out to her that she was unlikely to have undertaken such a long walk if she had had any considerable pains. I asked her what it was in the walk that might have brought on the pain and she gave me the somewhat obscure reply that the contrast between her own loneliness and her sick sister's married happiness (which her brother-in-law's behaviour kept constantly before her eyes) had been painful to her.

Another scene, which was very close to the former one in time, played a part in linking the pains with *sitting*. It was a few days later. Her sister and brother-in-law had already left the place. She found herself in a restless, yearning mood. She rose early in the morning and climbed a small hill to a spot which they had often been to together and which afforded a lovely view. She sat down there on a stone bench and gave herself up to her thoughts. These were once again concerned with her loneliness and the fate of her family; and this time she openly confessed to a burning wish that she might be as happy as her sister. She returned from this morning meditation with violent pains, and that same evening had the bath after which the pains made their final and permanent appearance [p. 142].

It was further shown without any doubt that her pain in walking and standing used, to begin with, to be allayed when she was *lying down*. The pains were not linked to lying down as well until, after hearing the news of her sister's illness, she travelled back from Gastein [loc. cit.] and was tormented during the night alike by worry about her sister and by raging pains, as she lay, sleepless, stretched out in the railway carriage. And for quite a time after this, lying down was actually more painful to her than walking or standing.

In this way, firstly, the painful region had been extended by the addition of adjacent areas: every fresh theme which had a pathogenic effect had cathected a new region in the legs; secondly, each of the scenes which made a powerful impression on her had left a trace behind it, bringing about lasting and constantly accumulating cathexis of the various functions of the legs, a linking of these functions with her feelings of pain. But a third mechanism had unmistakably been involved in the building up of her astasia-abasia. The patient ended her description of a whole series of episodes by complaining that they had made the fact of her 'standing alone' painful to her. In another series of episodes, which comprised her unsuccessful attempts to establish a new life for her family, she was never tired of repeating that what was painful about them had been her feeling of helplessness, the feeling that she could not 'take a single step forward'. In view of this, I was forced to suppose that among the influences that went to the building up of her abasia, these reflections of hers played a part; I could not help thinking that the patient had done nothing more nor less than look for a *symbolic* expression of her painful thoughts and that she had found it in the intensification of her sufferings. The fact that somatic symptoms of hysteria can be brought about by symbolization of this kind was already asserted in our 'Preliminary Communication' [p. 5]. In the Discussion on the present case I shall bring forward two or three conclusive instances of this. [See p. 176 ff.] This psychical mechanism of symbolization did not play a prominent part with Fräulein Elisabeth von R. It did not *create* her abasia. But everything goes to show that the abasia which was already present received considerable reinforcement in this way. Accordingly, this abasia, at the stage of development at which I came across it, was to be equated not only with a functional paralysis based on psychical associations but also with one based on symbolization.

Before I resume my account of the case I will add a few words on the patient's behaviour during this second phase of the treatment. Throughout the analysis I made use of the technique of bringing out pictures and ideas by means of pressing on the patient's head, a method, that is, which would be unworkable without the patient's full co-operation and willing attention. [Cf. p. 110 f.] Sometimes, indeed, her behaviour fulfilled my highest expectations, and during such periods it was surprising with what promptitude the different scenes relating to a given theme emerged in a strictly chronological order. It was as though she were reading a lengthy book of pictures, whose pages were being turned over before her eyes. At other times there seemed to be impediments of whose nature I had no suspicion then. When I pressed her head she would maintain that nothing occurred to her. I would repeat my pressure and tell her to wait, but still nothing appeared. The first few times when this recalcitrance exhibited itself I allowed myself to be led into breaking off the work: it was an unfavourable day; we would try another time. Two observations, however, decided me to alter my attitude. I noticed, in the first place, that the method failed in this way only when I found Elisabeth in a cheerful state and free from pain, never when she was feeling badly. In the second place, that she often made such assertions as that she saw nothing, after she had allowed a long interval to pass during which her tense and preoccupied expression of face nevertheless betrayed the fact that a mental process was taking place in her. I resolved, therefore, to adopt the hypothesis that the procedure never failed: that on every occasion under the pressure of my hand some idea occurred to Elisabeth or some picture came before her eyes, but that she was not always prepared to communicate it to me, and tried to suppress once more what had been conjured up. I could think of two motives for this concealment. Either she was applying criticism to the idea, which she had no right to do, on the ground of its not being important enough or of its being an irrelevant reply to the question she had been asked; or she hesitated to produce it because—she found it too disagreeable to tell. I therefore proceeded as though I was completely convinced of the trustworthiness of my technique. I no longer accepted her declaration that nothing had occurred to her, but assured her that something *must* have occurred to her. Perhaps, I said, she had not been sufficiently attentive, in which case I should be glad to repeat my pressure. Or perhaps she thought that her idea was not the right one. This, I told her, was not her affair; she was under an obligation to remain completely objective and say what had come into her head, whether it was appropriate or not. Finally I declared that I knew very well that something *had* occurred to her and that she was concealing it from me; but she would never be free of her pains so long as she concealed anything. By thus insisting, I brought it about that from that time forward my pressure on her head never failed in its effect. I could not but conclude that I had formed a correct opinion of the state of affairs, and I derived from this analysis a literally unqualified reliance on my technique. It often happened that it was not until I had pressed her head three times that she produced a piece of information; but she herself would remark afterwards: 'I could have said it to you the first time.'—'And why didn't you?'—'I thought it wasn't what was wanted', or 'I thought I could avoid it, but it came back each time.' In the course of this difficult work I began to attach a deeper significance to the resistance offered by the patient in the reproduction of her memories and to make a careful collection of the occasions on which it was particularly marked.[1]

I have now arrived at the third period of the treatment. The patient was better. She had been mentally relieved and was now capable of successful effort. But her pains had manifestly not been removed; they recurred from time to time, and with all their old severity. This incomplete therapeutic result corresponded to an incompleteness in the analysis. I still did not know exactly at what moment and by what mechanism the pains had originated. During the reproduction of the great variety of scenes in the second period and while I was observing the patient's resistance to telling me about them, I had formed a particular suspicion. I did not venture yet, however, to adopt it as the basis of my further action. But a chance occurrence

---

[1] [This is the first mention of the important clinical fact of 'resistance'. It is discussed at greater length below, p. 268 ff.]

decided the matter. One day while I was working with the patient, I heard a man's footsteps in the next room and a pleasant voice which seemed to be asking some question. My patient thereupon got up and asked that we might break off for the day: she had heard her brother-in-law arrive and enquire for her. Up to that point she had been free from pain, but after the interruption her facial expression and gait betrayed the sudden emergence of severe pains. My suspicion was strengthened by this and I determined to precipitate the decisive explanation.

I therefore questioned her about the causes and circumstances of the first appearance of the pains. By way of answer her thoughts turned towards her summer visit to the health resort before her journey to Gastein, and a number of scenes turned up once more which had not been treated very completely. She recalled her state of feeling at the time, her exhaustion after her anxieties about her mother's eyesight and after having nursed her at the time of her operation, and her final despair of a lonely girl like her being able to get any enjoyment out of life or achieve anything in it. Till then she had thought herself strong enough to be able to do without the help of a man; but she was now overcome by a sense of her weakness as a woman and by a longing for love in which, to quote her own words, her frozen nature began to melt. In this mood she was deeply affected by her second sister's happy marriage—by seeing with what touching care he looked after her, how they understood each other at a single glance and how sure they seemed to be of each other. It was no doubt to be regretted that the second pregnancy followed so soon after the first, and her sister knew that this was the reason of her illness; but how willingly she bore it because he was its cause. On the occasion of the walk which was so intimately connected with Elisabeth's pains, her brother-in-law had at first been unwilling to join in it and had wanted to stay by his sick wife. She, however, persuaded him with a look to go with them, because she thought it would give Elisabeth pleasure. Elisabeth remained in his company all through the walk. They discussed every kind of subject, among them the most intimate ones. She found herself in complete agreement with everything he said, and a desire to have a husband like him became very strong in her. Then, a few days later, came the scene on the morning after the departure of her sister and brother-in-law when she made her way to the place with a view, which had been a favourite object of their walks. There she sat down and dreamt once again of enjoying such happiness as her sister's and of finding a husband who would know how to capture her heart like this brother-in-law of hers. She was in pain when she stood up, but it passed off once more. It was not until the afternoon, when she had had the warm bath, that the pains broke out, and she was never again free from them. I tried to discover what thoughts were occupying her mind while she was having the bath; but I learnt only that the bath-house had reminded her of the members of her family who had gone away, because that was the building in which they had stayed.

It had inevitably become clear to me long since what all this was about; but the patient, deep in her bitter-sweet memories, seemed not to notice the end to which she was steering, and continued to reproduce her recollections. She went on to her visit to Gastein, the anxiety with which she looked forward to every letter, finally the bad news about her sister, the long wait till the evening, which was the first moment at which they could get away from Gastein, then the journey, passed in tormenting uncertainty, and the sleepless night—all of these accompanied by a violent increase in her pains. I asked her whether during the journey she had thought of the grievous possibility which was afterwards realized. She answered that she had carefully avoided the thought, but she believed that her mother had from the beginning expected the worst.—Her memories now went on to their arrival in Vienna, the impression made on them by the relatives who met them, the short journey from Vienna to the summer resort in its neighbourhood where her sister lived, their reaching there in the evening, the hurried walk through the garden to the door of the small garden house, the silence within and the oppressive darkness; how her brother-in-law was not there to receive them, and how they stood before the bed and looked at her sister as she lay there dead. At that moment of dreadful certainty that her beloved sister was dead without bidding them farewell and without her having eased her last days with her care—at that very moment another thought had shot through Elisabeth's mind, and now forced itself irresistibly upon her once more, like a flash of lightning in the dark: 'Now he is free again and I can be his wife.'

Everything was now clear. The analyst's labours were richly rewarded. The concepts of the 'fending off' of an incompatible idea, of the genesis of hysterical symptoms through the conversion of psychical excitations into something physical and the formation of a separate psychical group through the act of will which led to the fending-off—all these things were, in that moment, brought before my eyes in concrete form. Thus and in no other way had things come about in the present case. This girl felt towards her brother-in-law a tenderness whose acceptance into consciousness was resisted by her whole moral being. She succeeded in sparing herself the painful conviction that she loved her sister's husband, by inducing physical pains in herself instead; and it was in the moments when this conviction sought to force itself upon her (on her walk with him, during her morning reverie, in the bath, by her sister's bedside) that her pains had come on, thanks to successful conversion. At the time when I started her treatment the group of ideas relating to her love had already been separated from her knowledge. Otherwise she would never, I think, have agreed to embarking on the treatment. The resistance with which she had repeatedly met the reproduction of scenes which operated traumatically corresponded in fact to the energy with which the incompatible idea had been forced out of her associations.

The period that followed, however, was a hard one for the physician. The recovery of this repressed idea had a shattering effect on the poor girl. She cried aloud when I put the situation drily before her with the words: 'So for a long time you had been in love with your brother-in-law.' She complained at this moment of the most frightful pains, and made one last desperate effort to reject the explanation: it was not true, I had talked her into it, it *could* not be true, she was incapable of such wickedness, she could never forgive herself for it. It was easy to prove to her that what she herself had told me admitted of no other interpretation. But it was a long time before my two pieces of consolation—that we are not responsible for our feelings, and that her behaviour, the fact that she had fallen ill in these circumstances, was sufficient evidence of her moral character—it was a long time before these consolations of mine made any impression on her.

In order to mitigate the patient's sufferings I had now to proceed along more than one path. In the first place I wanted to give her an opportunity of getting rid of the excitation that had been piling up so long, by 'abreacting' it. We probed into the first impressions made on her in her relations with her brother-in-law, the beginning of the feelings for him which she had kept unconscious. Here we came across all the little pre-monitory signs and intuitions of which a fully-grown passion can make so much in retrospect. On his first visit to the house he had taken her for the girl he was to marry and had greeted her before her elder but somewhat insignificant-looking sister. One evening they were carrying on such a lively conversation together and seemed to be getting on so well that his fiancée had interrupted them half-seriously with the remark: 'The truth is, you two would have suited each other splendidly.' Another time, at a party where they knew nothing of his en-gagement, the young man was being discussed and a lady criticized a defect in his figure which suggested that he had had a disease of the bones in his childhood. His fiancée herself litsened quietly, but Elisabeth flared up and defended the symmetry of her future brother-in-law's figure with a zeal which she herself could not understand. As we worked through these recollections it became clear to Elisabeth that her tender feeling for her brother-in-law had been dormant in her for a long time, perhaps even from the beginning of her acquaintance with him, and had lain concealed all that time behind the mask of mere sisterly affection, which her highly-developed family feeling could enable her to accept as natural.

This process of abreaction certainly did her much good. But I was able to relieve her still more by taking a friendly interest in her present circumstances. With this end in view I arranged for an interview with Frau von R. I found her an understanding and sensitive lady, though her vital spirits had been reduced by her recent misfortunes. I learned from her that on closer ex-amination the charge of unfeeling blackmail which had been brought by the elder brother-in-law against the widower and which had been so painful to Elisabeth had had to be with-drawn. No stain was left on the young man's character. It was a misunderstanding due to the different value which, as can readily be seen, would be attached to money by a business man, to whom money is a tool of his trade, and a civil servant. Nothing more than this remained of the painful episode. I begged her mother from that time forward to tell Elisabeth everything she needed to know, and in the future to give her the opportunity for unburdening her mind to which I should have accustomed her.

I was also, of course, anxious to learn what chance there was that the girl's wish, of which she was now conscious, would come true. Here the prospects were less favourable. Her mother told me that she had long ago guessed Elisabeth's fondness for the young man, though she had not known that the feeling had already been there during her sister's lifetime. No one seeing the two of them together—though in fact this had now become a rare event—could doubt the girl's anxiety to please him. But, she told me, neither she (the mother) nor the family advisers were particularly in favour of a marriage. The young man's health was by no means good and had received a fresh set-back from the death of his beloved wife. It was not at all certain, either, that his mental state was yet sufficiently recovered for him to contract a new marriage. This was perhaps why he was behaving with so much reserve; perhaps, too, it was because he was uncertain of his reception and wished to avoid comments that were likely to be made. In view of these reservations on both sides, the solution for which Elisabeth longed was unlikely to be achieved.

I told the girl what I had heard from her mother and had the satisfaction of benefiting her by giving her the explanation of the money affair. On the other hand I encouraged her to face with calmness the uncertainty about the future which it was impossible to clear up. But at this point the approach of summer made it urgent for us to bring the analysis to an end. Her condition was once more improved and there had been no more talk of her pains since we had been investigating their causes. We both had a feeling that we had come to a finish, though I told myself that the abreaction of the love she had so long kept down had not been carried out very fully. I regarded her as cured and pointed out to her that the solution of her difficulties would proceed on its own account now that the path had been opened to it. This she did not dispute. She left Vienna with her mother to meet her eldest sister and her family and to spend the summer together.

I have a few words to add upon the further course of Fräulein Elisabeth von R.'s case. Some weeks after we had separated I received a despairing letter from her mother. At her first attempt, she told me, to discuss her daughter's affairs of the heart with her, the girl had rebelled violently and had since then suffered from severe pains once more. She was indignant with me for having betrayed her secret. She was entirely inaccessible, and the treatment had been a complete failure. What was to be done now? she asked. Elisabeth would have nothing more to do with me. I did not reply to this. It stood to reason that Elisabeth after leaving my care would make one more attempt to reject her mother's intervention and once more take refuge in isolation. But I had a kind of conviction that everything would come right and that the trouble I had taken had not been in vain. Two months later they were back in Vienna, and the colleague to whom I owed the introduction of the case gave me news that Elisabeth felt perfectly well and was behaving as though there was nothing wrong with her, though she still suffered occasionally from slight pains. Several times since then she has sent me similar messages and each time promised to come and see me. But it is a characteristic of the personal relationship which arises in treatments of this kind that she has never done so. As my colleague assures me, she is to be regarded as cured. Her brother-in-law's connection with the family has remained unaltered.

In the spring of 1894 I heard that she was going to a private ball for which I was able to get an invitation, and I did not allow the opportunity to escape me of seeing my former patient whirl past in a lively dance. Since then, by her own inclination, she has married someone unknown to me.

DISCUSSION

I have not always been a psychotherapist. Like other neuropathologists, I was trained to employ local diagnoses and electro-prognosis, and it still strikes me myself as strange that the case histories I write should read like short stories and that, as one might say, they lack the serious stamp of science. I must console myself with the reflection that the nature of the subject is evidently responsible for this, rather than any preference of my own. The fact is that local diagnosis and electrical reactions lead nowhere in the study of hysteria, whereas a detailed description of mental processes such as we are accustomed to find in the works of imaginative writers enables me, with the use of a few psychological formulas, to obtain at least some kind of insight into the course of that affection. Case histories of this kind are intended to be judged like psychiatric ones; they have, however, one advantage over the latter, namely an intimate connection between the story of the patient's sufferings and the symptoms of his illness—a connection for which we still search in vain in the biographies of other psychoses.

In reporting the case of Fräulein Elisabeth von R. I have endeavoured to weave the explanations which I have been able to give of the case into my description of the course of her recovery. It may perhaps be worth while to bring together the important points once more. I have described the patient's character, the features which one meets with so frequently in hysterical people and which there is no excuse for regarding as a consequence of degeneracy: her giftedness, her ambition, her moral sensibility, her excessive demand for love which, to begin with, found satisfaction in her family, and the independence of her nature which went beyond the feminine ideal and found expression in a considerable amount of obstinacy, pugnacity and reserve. No appreciable hereditary taint, so my colleague told me, could be traced on either side of her family. It is true that her mother suffered for many years from a neurotic depression which had not been investigated; but her mother's brothers and sisters and her father and his family could be regarded as well-balanced people free from nervous trouble. No severe case of neuro-psychosis had occurred among her close relatives.

Such was the patient's nature, which was now assailed by painful emotions, beginning with the lowering effect of nursing her beloved father through a long illness.

There are good reasons for the fact that sick-nursing plays such a significant part in the prehistory of cases of hysteria. A number of the factors at work in this are obvious: the disturbance of one's physical health arising from interrupted sleep, the neglect of one's own person, the effect of constant worry on one's vegetative functions. But, in my view, the most important determinant is to be looked for elsewhere. Anyone whose mind is taken up by the hundred and one tasks of sick-nursing which follow one another in endless succession over a period of weeks and months will, on the one hand, adopt a habit of suppressing every sign of his own emotion, and on the other, will soon

divert his attention away from his own impressions, since he
has neither time nor strength to do justice to them. Thus he
will accumulate a mass of impressions which are capable of
affect, which are hardly sufficiently perceived and which, in
any case, have not been weakened by abreaction. He is creating
material for a 'retention hysteria'.[1] If the sick person recovers,
all these impressions, of course, lose their significance. But if he
dies, and the period of mourning sets in, during which the only
things that seem to have value are those that relate to the
person who has died, these impressions that have not yet been
dealt with come into the picture as well; and after a short
interval of exhaustion the hysteria, whose seeds were sown
during the time of nursing, breaks out.

We also occasionally come across this same fact of the traumas
accumulated during sick-nursing being dealt with subsequently,
where we get no general impression of illness but where the
mechanism of hysteria is nevertheless retained. Thus I am
acquainted with a highly-gifted lady who suffers from slight
nervous states and whose whole character bears evidence of
hysteria, though she has never had to seek medical help or been
unable to carry on her duties. She has already nursed to the
end three or four of those whom she loved. Each time she
reached a state of complete exhaustion; but she did not fall ill
after these tragic efforts. Shortly after her patient's death, however, there would begin in her a work of reproduction which
once more brought up before her eyes the scenes of the illness
and death. Every day she would go through each impression
once more, would weep over it and console herself—at her
leisure, one might say. This process of dealing with her impressions was dovetailed into her everyday tasks without the
two activities interfering with each other. The whole thing
would pass through her mind in chronological sequence. I
cannot say whether the work of recollection corresponded day
by day with the past. I suspect that this depended on the
amount of leisure which her current household duties allowed.[2]

In addition to these outbursts of weeping with which she
made up arrears and which followed close upon the fatal ter-

[1] [See p. 211 and footnote.]
[2] [In this account of the 'work of recollection' Freud seems to be
anticipating the 'work of mourning' which he described much later in
his paper 'Mourning and Melancholia' (1917e).]

mination of the illness, this lady celebrated annual festivals of remembrance at the period of her various catastrophes, and on these occasions her vivid visual reproduction and expressions of feeling kept to the date precisely. For instance, on one occasion I found her in tears and asked her sympathetically what had happened that day. She brushed aside my question half-angrily: 'Oh no,' she said, 'it is only that the specialist was here again to-day and gave us to understand that there was no hope. I had no time to cry about it then.' She was referring to the last illness of her husband, who had died three years earlier. I should be very much interested to know whether the scenes which she celebrated at these annual festivals of remembrance were always the same ones or whether different details presented themselves for abreaction each time, as I suspect in view of my theory.[1] But I cannot discover with certainty. The lady,

[1] I once learnt to my surprise that an 'abreaction of arrears' of this kind—though the impressions concerned were not derived from sicknursing—can form the subject-matter of an otherwise puzzling neurosis. This was so in the case of Fräulein Mathilde H., a good-looking, nineteen-year-old girl. When I first saw her she was suffering from a partial paralysis of the legs. Some months later, however, she came to me for treatment on account of a change in her character. She had become depressed to the point of a *taedium vitae*, utterly inconsiderate to her mother, irritable and inaccessible. The patient's picture as a whole forbad my assuming that this was a common melancholia. She was very easily put into a state of deep somnambulism, and I availed myself of this peculiarity of hers in order to give her commands and suggestions at every visit. She listened to these in deep sleep, to the accompaniment of floods of tears; but, apart from this, they caused very little change in her condition. One day she became talkative in her hypnosis and told me that the cause of her depression was the breaking off of her engagement, which had occurred several months earlier. Closer acquaintance with her fiancé had brought out more and more things that were unwelcome to her and her mother. On the other hand, the material advantages of the connection had been too obvious for it to be easy to decide to break it off. So for a long time they had both wavered and she herself had fallen into a state of indecision in which she regarded all that happened to her with apathy. In the end her mother uttered the decisive negative on her behalf. A little later she had woken up as though from a dream and begun to occupy her thoughts busily with the decision that had already been made and to weigh the pros and cons. This process, she told me, was still going on: she was living in the period of doubt, and every day she was possessed by the mood and thoughts which were appropriate to the day in the past with which she was occupied. Her irritability with her mother, too, had its basis only in the circumstances which prevailed at that

who had no less strength of character than intelligence, was ashamed of the violent effect produced in her by these reminiscences.

I must emphasize once more: this woman is not ill; her postponed abreaction was not a hysterical process, however much it resembled one. We may ask why it should be that one instance of sick-nursing should be followed by a hysteria and another not. It cannot be a matter of individual predisposition, for this was present to an ample degree in the lady I have in mind.

But I must now return to Fräulein Elisabeth von R. While she was nursing her father, as we have seen, she for the first time developed a hysterical symptom—a pain in a particular area of her right thigh. It was possible by means of analysis to find an adequate elucidation of the mechanism of the symptom. It happened at a moment when the circle of ideas embracing her duties to her sick father came into conflict with the content of the erotic desire she was feeling at the time. Under the pressure of lively self-reproaches she decided in favour of the former, and in doing so brought about her hysterical pain.

According to the view suggested by the conversion theory of hysteria what happened may be described as follows. She repressed her erotic idea from consciousness and transformed the amount of its affect into physical sensations of pain. It did not become clear whether she was presented with this first conflict on one occasion only or on several; the latter alternative is the more likely. An exactly similar conflict—though of higher ethical significance and even more clearly established by the analysis—developed once more some years later and led to an intensification of the same pains and to an extension beyond their original limits. Once again it was a circle of ideas of an erotic kind that came into conflict with all her moral ideas; for her inclinations centred upon her brother-in-law, and, both

time. In comparison with these activities of her thoughts, her present life seemed like a mere appearance of reality, like something in a dream.—I did not succeed in inducing the girl to talk again. I continued to address her while she was in deep somnambulism and saw her burst into tears each time without ever answering me; and one day, round about the anniversary of her engagement, her whole state of depression passed off—an event which brought me the credit of a great therapeutic success by hypnotism.

during her sister's lifetime and after her death, the thought of being attracted by precisely this man was totally unacceptable to her. The analysis provided detailed information about this conflict, which constituted the central point in the history of the illness. The germs of the patient's feeling for her brother-in-law may have been present for a long time; its development was favoured by physical exhaustion owing to more sick-nursing and by moral exhaustion owing to disappointments extending over many years. The coldness of her nature began to yield and she admitted to herself her need for a man's love. During the several weeks which she passed in his company at the health resort her erotic feelings as well as her pains reached their full height.

The analysis, moreover, gave evidence that during the same period the patient was in a special psychical state. The connection of this state with her erotic feelings and her pains seems to make it possible to understand what happened on the lines of the conversion theory. It is, I think, safe to say that at that time the patient did not become clearly conscious of her feelings for her brother-in-law, powerful though they were, except on a few occasions, and then only momentarily. If it had been otherwise, she would also inevitably have become conscious of the contradiction between those feelings and her moral ideas and would have experienced mental torments like those I saw her go through after our analysis. She had no recollection of any such sufferings; she had avoided them. It followed that her feelings themselves did not become clear to her. At that time, as well as during the analysis, her love for her brother-in-law was present in her consciousness like a foreign body, without having entered into relationship with the rest of her ideational life. With regard to these feelings she was in the peculiar situation of knowing and at the same time not knowing—a situation, that is, in which a psychical group was cut off. But this and nothing else is what we mean when we say that these feelings were not clear to her. We do not mean that their consciousness was of a lower quality or of a lesser degree, but that they were cut off from any free associative connection of thought with the rest of the ideational content of her mind.

But how could it have come about that an ideational group with so much emotional emphasis on it was kept so isolated? In general, after all, the part played in association by an idea increases in proportion to the amount of its affect.

We can answer this question if we take into account two facts which we can make use of as being established with certainty. (1) Simultaneously with the formation of this separate psychical group the patient developed her hysterical pains. (2) The patient offered strong resistance to the attempt to bring about an association between the separate psychical group and the rest of the content of her consciousness; and when, in spite of this, the connection was accomplished she felt great psychical pain. Our view of hysteria brings these two facts into relation with the splitting of her consciousness by asserting that the second of them indicates the *motive* for the splitting of consciousness, while the first indicates its *mechanism*. The motive was that of defence, the refusal on the part of the patient's whole ego to come to terms with this ideational group. The mechanism was that of conversion: i.e. in place of the mental pains which she avoided, physical pains made their appearance. In this way a transformation was effected which had the advantage that the patient escaped from an intolerable mental condition; though, it is true, this was at the cost of a psychical abnormality—the splitting of consciousness that came about—and of a physical illness—her pains, on which an astasia-abasia was built up.

I cannot, I must confess, give any hint of how a conversion of this kind is brought about. It is obviously not carried out in the same way as an intentional and voluntary action. It is a process which occurs under the pressure of the motive of defence in someone whose organization—or a temporary modification of it—has a proclivity in that direction.[1]

This theory calls for closer examination. We may ask: what *is* it that turns into physical pain here? A cautious reply would be: something that might have become, and should have become, *mental* pain. If we venture a little further and try to represent the ideational mechanism in a kind of algebraical picture, we may attribute a certain quota of affect to the ideational complex of these erotic feelings which remained unconscious, and say that this quantity (the quota of affect) is what was converted. It would follow directly from this description that the 'unconscious love' would have lost so much of its intensity through a conversion of this kind that it would have been reduced to

[1][Cf. p. 122. The term 'somatic compliance' used in the 'Dora' case (*Standard Ed.*, **7**, 40–2) may perhaps refer to this proclivity.]

no more than a weak idea. This reduction of strength would then have been the only thing which made possible the existence of these unconscious feelings as a separate psychical group. The present case, however, is not well fitted to give a clear picture of such a delicate matter. For in·this case there was probably only partial conversion; in others it can be shown with likelihood that complete conversion also occurs, and that in it the incompatible idea has in fact been 'repressed', as only an idea of very slight intensity can be. The patients concerned declare, after associative connection with the incompatible idea has been established, that their thoughts had not been concerned with it since the appearance of the hysterical symptoms.

I have asserted [p. 165] that on certain occasions, though only for the moment, the patient recognized her love for her brother-in-law consciously. As an example of this we may recall the moment when she was standing by her sister's bed and the thought flashed through her mind: 'Now he is free and you can be his wife' [p. 156]. I must now consider the significance of these moments in their bearing on our view of the whole neurosis. It seems to me that the concept of a 'defence hysteria' in itself implies that at least *one* moment of this kind must have occurred. Consciousness, plainly, does not know in advance when an incompatible idea is going to crop up. The incompatible idea, which, together with its concomitants, is later excluded and forms a separate psychical group, must originally have been in communication with the main stream of thought. Otherwise the conflict which led to their exclusion could not have taken place.[1] It is these moments, then, that are to be described as 'traumatic': it is at these moments that conversion takes place, of which the results are the splitting of consciousness and the hysterical symptom. In the case of Fräulein Elisabeth von R. everything points to there having been several such moments—the scenes of the walk, the morning reverie, the bath, and at her sister's bedside. It is even possible that new moments of the same kind happened during the treatment. What makes it possible for there to be *several* of these traumatic moments is that an experience similar to the one which originally introduced the incompatible idea adds

[1] It is otherwise in hypnoid hysteria, where the content of the separate psychical group would never have been in the ego-consciousness. [Cf. p. 286.]

fresh excitation to the separated psychical group and so puts a temporary stop to the success of the conversion. The ego is obliged to attend to this sudden flare-up of the idea and to restore the former state of affairs by a further conversion. Fräulein Elisabeth, who was much in her brother-in-law's company, must have been particularly liable to the occurrence of fresh traumas. From the point of view of my present exposition, I should have preferred a case in which the traumatic history lay wholly in the past.

I must now turn to a point which I have described [pp. 147–8] as offering a difficulty to the understanding of this case history. On the evidence of the analysis, I assumed that a first conversion took place while the patient was nursing her father, at the time when her duties as a nurse came into conflict with her erotic desires, and that what happened then was the prototype of the later events in the Alpine health resort which led to the outbreak of the illness. But it appeared from the patient's account that while she was nursing her father and during the time that followed—what I have described as the 'first period'—*she had no pains whatever and no locomotor weakness.* It is true that once during her father's illness she was laid up for a few days with pains in her legs, but it remained a question whether this attack was already to be ascribed to hysteria. No causal connection between these first pains and any psychical impression could be traced in the analysis. It is possible, and indeed probable, that what she was suffering from at that time were common rheumatic muscular pains. Moreover, even if we were inclined to suppose that this first attack of pains was the effect of a hysterical conversion as a result of the repudiation of her erotic thoughts at the time, the fact remains that the pains disappeared after only a few days, so that the patient had behaved differently in reality from what she seemed to indicate in the analysis. During her reproduction of what I have called the first period she accompanied all her stories about her father's illness and death, about her impressions of her dealings with her first brother-in-law, and so on, with manifestations of pain, whereas at the time of actually experiencing these impressions she had felt none. Is not this a contradiction which is calculated to reduce very considerably our belief in the explanatory value of an analysis such as this?

I believe I can solve this contradiction by assuming that the pains—the products of conversion—did not occur while the patient was experiencing the impressions of the first period, but only after the event, that is, in the second period, while she was reproducing those impressions in her thoughts. That is to say, the conversion did not take place in connection with her impressions when they were fresh, but in connection with her memories of them. I even believe that such a course of events is nothing unusual in hysteria and indeed plays a regular part in the genesis of hysterical symptoms. But since an assertion like this is not self-evident, I will try to make it more plausible by bringing forward some other instances.

It once happened to me that a new hysterical symptom developed in a patient during the actual course of an analytic treatment of this kind so that I was able to set about getting rid of it on the day after its appearance. I will interpolate the main features of the case at this point. It was a fairly simple one, yet not without interest.

Fräulein Rosalia H., aged twenty-three, had for some years been undergoing training as a singer. She had a good voice, but she complained that in certain parts of its compass it was not under her control. She had a feeling of choking and constriction in her throat so that her voice sounded tight. For this reason her teacher had not yet been able to consent to her appearing as a singer in public. Although this imperfection affected only her middle register, it could not be attributed to a defect in the organ itself. At times the disturbance was completely absent and her teacher expressed great satisfaction; at other times, if she was in the least agitated, and sometimes without any apparent cause, the constricted feeling would reappear and the production of her voice was impeded. It was not difficult to recognize a hysterical conversion in this very troublesome feeling. I did not take steps to discover whether there was in fact a contracture of some of the muscles of the vocal cords.[1] In the course of the hypnotic analysis which I

---

[1] I had another case of a singer under my observation in which a contracture of the masseters made it impossible for her to practise her art. This young woman had been obliged to go on the stage by unfortunate events in her family. She was singing at a rehearsal in Rome at a time when she was in a state of great emotional excitement, and suddenly had a feeling that she could not close her open mouth and fell to the floor in a faint. The doctor who was called in brought her

carried out with the girl, I learned the following facts about her history and consequently about the cause of her trouble. She lost her parents early in life and was taken to live with an aunt who herself had numerous children. In consequence of this she became involved in a most unhappy family life. Her aunt's husband, who was a manifestly pathological person, brutally ill-treated his wife and children. He wounded their feelings more particularly by the way in which he showed an open sexual preference for the servants and nursemaids in the house; and the more the children grew up the more offensive this became. After her aunt's death Rosalia became the protector of the multitude of children who were now orphaned and oppressed by their father. She took her duties seriously and fought through all the conflicts into which her position led her, though it required a great effort to suppress the hatred and contempt which she felt for her uncle.[1] It was at this time that the feeling of constriction in her throat started. Every time she had to keep back a reply, or forced herself to remain quiet in the face of some outrageous accusation, she felt a scratching in her throat, a sense of constriction, a loss of voice—all the sensations localized in her larynx and pharynx which now interfered with her singing. It was not to be wondered at that she sought an opportunity of making herself independent and escaping the agitations and distressing experiences which were of daily occurrence in her uncle's house. A highly competent teacher of singing came to her assistance disinterestedly and assured her that her voice justified her in choosing the profession of singer. She now began to take lessons with him in secret. But she used often to hurry off to her singing lesson while she still had the constriction in her throat that used to be left over after violent scenes at home. Consequently a connection was firmly established between her singing and her hysterical paraesthesia—a connection for which the way was prepared by the organic

jaws together forcibly. But thenceforward the patient was unable to open her jaws by more than a finger's breadth and had to give up her new profession. When, several years later, she came to me for treatment, the causes of her emotional excitement had obviously long since disappeared, for some massage while she was in a state of light hypnosis sufficed to enable her mouth to open wide. Since then the lady has sung in public.

[1] (*Footnote added* 1924:) In this instance, too [cf. p. 134 *n.* 2], it was in fact the girl's father, not her uncle.

sensations set up by singing. The apparatus over which she ought to have had full control when she was singing turned out to be cathected with residues of innervations left over from the numerous scenes of suppressed emotion. Since then, she had left her uncle's house and had moved to another town in order to be away from her family. But this did not get over her difficulty.

This good-looking and unusually intelligent girl exhibited no other hysterical symptoms.

I did my best to get rid of this 'retention hysteria' [1] by getting her to reproduce all her agitating experiences and to abreact them after the event. I made her abuse her uncle, lecture him, tell him the unvarnished truth, and so on, and this treatment did her good. Unfortunately, however, she was living in Vienna under very unfavourable conditions. She had no luck with her relatives. She was being put up by another uncle, who treated her in a friendly way; but for that very reason her aunt took a dislike to her. This woman suspected that her husband had a deeper interest in his niece, and therefore chose to make her stay in Vienna as disagreeable as possible. The aunt herself in her youth had been obliged to give up a desire for an artistic career and envied her niece for being able to cultivate her talent, though in the girl's case it was not her desire but her need for independence that had determined her decision. Rosalie [2] felt so constrained in the house that she did not venture, for instance, to sing or play the piano while her aunt was within earshot and carefully avoided singing or playing to her uncle (who, incidentally, was an old man, her mother's brother) when there was a possibility of her aunt coming in. While I was trying to wipe out the traces of old agitations, new ones arose out of these relations with her host and hostess, which eventually interfered with the success of my treatment as well as bringing it to a premature end.

One day the patient came for her session with a new symptom, scarcely twenty-four hours old. She complained of a disagreeable pricking sensation in the tips of her fingers, which, she said, had been coming on every few hours since the day before and compelled her to make a peculiar kind of twitching

---

[1] [See below, p. 211 and footnote.]

[2] [The name is given this form at this point and below in all the German editions.]

movement with her fingers. I was not able to observe an attack; otherwise I should no doubt have been able to guess from the nature of the movements what it was that had occasioned them. But I immediately tried to get on the track of the explanation of the symptom (it was in fact a minor hysterical attack) by hypnotic analysis. Since the whole thing had only been in existence such a short time I hoped that I should quickly be able to explain and get rid of the symptom. To my astonishment the patient produced a whole number of scenes, without hesitation and in chronological order, beginning with her early childhood.[1] They seemed to have in common her having had some injury done to her, against which she had not been able to defend herself, and which might have made her fingers jerk. They were such scenes, for instance, as of having had to hold out her hand at school and being struck on it with a ruler by her teacher. But they were quite ordinary occasions and I should have been prepared to deny that they could play a part in the aetiology of a hysterical symptom. But it was otherwise with one scene from her girlhood which followed. Her bad uncle, who was suffering from rheumatism, had asked her to massage his back and she did not dare to refuse. He was lying in bed at the time, and suddenly threw off the bed-clothes, sprang up and tried to catch hold of her and throw her down. Massage, of course, was at an end, and a moment later she had escaped and locked herself in her room. She was clearly loth to remember this and was unwilling to say whether she had seen anything when he suddenly uncovered himself. The sensations in her fingers might be explained in this case by a suppressed impulse to punish him, or simply by her having been engaged in massaging him at the time. It was only after relating this scene that she came to the one of the day before, after which the sensations and jerking in her fingers had set in as a recurrent mnemic symbol. The uncle with whom she was now living had asked her to play him something. She sat down to the piano and accompanied herself in a song, thinking that her aunt had gone out; but suddenly she appeared in the door. Rosalie jumped up, slammed the lid of the piano and threw the music away. We can guess what the memory was that rose in her mind and what the train of thought was that she was fending

---

[1] [Apparently an exception to the general rule of inverse chronological order stated in the footnote on p. 75.]

off at that moment: it was a feeling of violent resentment at the unjust suspicion to which she was subjected and which should have made her leave the house, while in fact she was obliged to stay in Vienna on account of the treatment and had nowhere else where she could be put up. The movement of her fingers which I saw her make while she was reproducing this scene was one of twitching something away, in the way in which one literally and figuratively brushes something aside—tosses away a piece of paper or rejects a suggestion.

She was quite definite in her insistence that she had not noticed this symptom previously—that it had not been occasioned by the scenes she had first described. We could only suppose, therefore, that the event of the previous day had in the first instance aroused the memory of earlier events with a similar subject-matter and that thereupon a mnemic symbol had been formed which applied to the whole group of memories. The energy for the conversion had been supplied, on the one hand, by freshly experienced affect and, on the other hand, by recollected affect.

When we consider the question more closely we must recognize that a process of this kind is the rule rather than the exception in the genesis of hysterical symptoms. Almost invariably when I have investigated the determinants of such conditions what I have come upon has not been a *single* traumatic cause but a group of similar ones. (This is well exemplified in the case of Frau Emmy—Case History 2.) In some of these instances it could be established that the symptom in question had already appeared for a short time after the first trauma and had then passed off, till it was brought on again and stabilized by a succeeding trauma. There is, however, in principle no difference between the symptom appearing in this temporary way after its first provoking cause and its being latent from the first. Indeed, in the great majority of instances we find that a first trauma has left no symptom behind, while a later trauma of the same kind produces a symptom, and yet that the latter could not have come into existence without the co-operation of the earlier provoking cause; nor can it be cleared up without taking all the provoking causes into account.

Stated in terms of the conversion theory, this incontrovertible fact of the summation of traumas and of the preliminary latency of symptoms tells us that conversion can result equally from fresh symptoms and from recollected ones. This hypothesis completely explains the apparent contradiction that we observed between the events of Fräulein Elisabeth von R.'s illness and her analysis. There is no doubt that the continued existence in consciousness of ideas whose affect has not been dealt with can be tolerated by healthy individuals up to a great amount. The view which I have just been putting forward does no more than bring the behaviour of hysterical people nearer to that of healthy ones. What we are concerned with is clearly a quantitative factor—the question of how much affective tension of this kind an organism can tolerate. Even a hysteric can retain a certain amount of affect that has not been dealt with; if, owing to the occurrence of similar provoking causes, that amount is increased by summation to a point beyond the subject's tolerance, the impetus to conversion is given. Thus when we say that the construction of hysterical symptoms can proceed on the strength of recollected affects as well as fresh ones, we shall not be making any unfamiliar assertion, but stating something that is almost accepted as a postulate.

I have now discussed the motives and mechanism of this case of hysteria; it remains for me to consider how precisely the hysterical symptom was determined. Why was it that the patient's mental pain came to be represented by pains in the legs rather than elsewhere? The circumstances indicate that this somatic pain was not *created* by the neurosis but merely used, increased and maintained by it. I may add at once that I have found a similar state of things in almost all the instances of hysterical pains into which I have been able to obtain an insight. [Cf. above, pp. 96–7.) There had always been a genuine, organically-founded pain present at the start. It is the commonest and most widespread human pains that seem to be most often chosen to play a part in hysteria: in particular, the periosteal and neuralgic pains accompanying dental disease, the headaches that arise from so many different sources and, not less often, the rheumatic muscular pains that are so often unrecognized [p. 71 *n.*]. In the same way I attribute an organic foundation to Fräulein Elisabeth von R.'s first attack of pain which occurred as far back as while she was nursing her father. I obtained no result when I tried to discover a psychical cause for it—and I am inclined, I must confess, to attribute a power of differential diagnosis to my method of evoking concealed memories, provided it is carefully handled. This pain, which was rheumatic in its origin,[1] then became a mnemic symbol of her painful psychical excitations; and this happened, so far as I can see, for more than one reason. The first and no doubt the most important of these reasons was that the pain was present in her consciousness at about the same time as the excitations. In the second place, it was connected, or could be connected, along a number of lines with the ideas in her mind at the time. The pain, indeed, may actually have been a consequence, though only a remote one, of the period of nursing—of the lack of exercise and reduced diet that her duties as a sick-nurse entailed. But the girl had no clear knowledge of this. More importance should probably be attached to the fact that she must have felt the pain during that time at significant moments, for instance, when she sprang out of bed in the cold of winter in response to a call from her father [p. 147]. But what must have had a positively decisive influence on the direction taken by the conversion was another line of associative connection [p. 148]: the fact that on a long succession of days one of her painful legs came into contact with her father's swollen leg while his bandages were being changed. The area on her right leg which was marked out by this contact remained thereafter the focus of her pains and the point from which they radiated. It formed an artificial hysterogenic zone whose origin could in the present case be clearly observed.

If anyone feels astonished at this associative connection between physical pain and psychical affect, on the ground of its being of such a multiple and artificial character, I should reply that this feeling is as little justified as astonishment at the fact that it is the rich people who own the most money.[2] Where there are no such numerous connections a hysterical symptom will not, in fact, be formed; for conversion will find no path open to it. And I can affirm that the example of Fräulein Elisabeth von R. was among the simpler ones as regards its determination. I have had the most tangled threads to unravel, especially in the case of Frau Cäcilie M.

[1] It may, however, have been of a spinal-neurasthenic sort. [Cf. p. 148 n.]

[2] [The allusion is to an epigram of Lessing's which Freud quotes again in *The Interpretation of Dreams* (Standard Ed., 4, 176).]

I have already discussed in the case history [p. 150 ff.] the way in which the patient's astasia-abasia was built up on these pains, after a particular path had been opened up for the conversion. In that passage, however, I also expressed my view that the patient had created, or increased, her functional disorder by means of symbolization, that she had found in the astasia-abasia a somatic expression for her lack of an independent position and her inability to make any alteration in her circumstances, and that such phrases as 'not being able to take a single step forward', 'not having anything to lean upon', served as the bridge for this fresh act of conversion [p. 152].

I shall try to support this view by other examples. Conversion on the basis of simultaneity, where there is also an associative link, seems to make the smallest demands on a hysterical disposition; conversion by symbolization, on the other hand, seems to call for the presence of a higher degree of hysterical modification. This could be observed in the case of Fräulein Elisabeth, but only in the later stage of her hysteria. The best examples of symbolization that I have seen occurred in Frau Cäcilie M., whose case I might describe as my most severe and instructive one. I have already explained [p. 69 n.] that a detailed report of her illness is unfortunately impossible.

Frau Cäcilie suffered among other things from an extremely violent facial neuralgia which appeared suddenly two or three times a year, lasted for from five to ten days, resisted any kind of treatment and then ceased abruptly. It was limited to the second and third branches of one trigeminal, and since an abnormal excretion of urates was undoubtedly present and a not quite clearly defined 'acute rheumatism' played some part in the patient's history, a diagnosis of gouty neuralgia was plausible enough. This diagnosis was confirmed by the different consultants who were called in at each attack. Treatment of the usual kind was ordered: the electric brush, alkaline water, purges; but each time the neuralgia remained unaffected until it chose to give place to another symptom. Earlier in her life— the neuralgia was fifteen years old—her teeth were accused of being responsible for it. They were condemned to extraction, and one fine day, under narcosis, the sentence was carried out on seven of the criminals. This was not such an easy matter; her teeth were so firmly attached that the roots of most of them had to be left behind. This cruel operation had no result, either temporary or permanent. At that time the neuralgia raged for months on end. Even at the time of my treatment, at each attack of neuralgia the dentist was called in. On each occasion he diagnosed the presence of diseased roots and began to get to work on them; but as a rule he was soon interrupted. For the neuralgia would suddenly cease, and at the same time the demand for the dentist's services. During the interval her teeth did not ache at all. One day, when an attack was raging once more, the patient got me to give her hypnotic treatment. I laid a very energetic prohibition on her pains, and from that moment they ceased. I began at that time to harbour doubts of the genuineness of the neuralgia.

About a year after this successful hypnotic treatment Frau Cäcilie's illness took a new and surprising turn. She suddenly developed new pathological states, different from those that had characterized the last few years. But after some reflection the patient declared that she had had all of them before at various times during the course of her long illness, which had lasted for thirty years. There now developed a really surprising wealth of hysterical attacks which the patient was able to assign to their right place in her past. And soon, too, it was possible to follow the often highly involved trains of thought that determined the order in which these attacks occurred. They were like a series of pictures with explanatory texts. Pitres must have had something of the sort in mind in putting forward his description of what he termed '*délire ecmnésique*'.[1] It was most remarkable to see the way in which a hysterical state of this kind belonging to the past was reproduced. There first came on, while the patient was in the best of health, a pathological mood with a particular colouring which she regularly misunderstood and attributed to some commonplace event of the last few hours. Then, to the accompaniment of an increasing clouding of consciousness, there followed hysterical symptoms: hallucinations, pains, spasms and long declamatory speeches. Finally, these were succeeded by the emergence in a hallucinatory form of an experience from the past which made it possible to explain her

---

[1] ['*Ecmnesia*', according to Pitres (1891, **2**, 290), 'is a form of partial amnesia, in which the memory of events prior to a particular period in the patient's life is preserved in its entirety, whereas the memory of events subsequent to that period is completely abolished.']

initial mood and what had determined the symptoms of her present attack. With this last piece of the attack her clarity of mind returned. Her troubles disappeared as though by magic and she felt well once again—till the next attack, half a day later. As a rule I was sent for at the climax of the attack, induced a state of hypnosis, called up the reproduction of the traumatic experience and hastened the end of the attack by artificial means. Since I assisted at several hundreds of such cycles with the patient, I gained the most instructive information on the way in which hysterical symptoms are determined. Indeed, it was the study of this remarkable case, jointly with Breuer, that led directly to the publication of our 'Preliminary Communication' [of 1893, which introduces the present volume].

In this phase of the work we came at last to the reproduction of her facial neuralgia, which I myself had treated when it appeared in contemporary attacks. I was curious to discover whether this, too, would turn out to have a psychical cause. When I began to call up the traumatic scene, the patient saw herself back in a period of great mental irritability towards her husband. She described a conversation which she had had with him and a remark of his which she had felt as a bitter insult. Suddenly she put her hand to her cheek, gave a loud cry of pain and said: 'It was like a slap in the face.' With this her pain and her attack were both at an end.

There is no doubt that what had happened had been a symbolization. She had felt as though she had actually been given a slap in the face. Everyone will immediately ask how it was that the sensation of a 'slap in the face' came to take on the outward forms of a trigeminal neuralgia, why it was restricted to the second and third branches, and why it was made worse by opening the mouth and chewing—though, incidentally, not by talking.

Next day the neuralgia was back again. But this time it was cleared up by the reproduction of *another* scene, the content of which was once again a supposed insult. Things went on like this for nine days. It seemed to be the case that for years insults, and particularly spoken ones, had, through symbolization, brought on fresh attacks of her facial neuralgia.

But ultimately we were able to make our way back to her first attack of neuralgia, more than fifteen years earlier. Here there was no symbolization but a conversion through simultaneity. She saw a painful sight which was accompanied by feelings of self-reproach, and this led her to force back another set of thoughts. Thus it was a case of conflict and defence. The generation of the neuralgia at that moment was only explicable on the assumption that she was suffering at the time from slight toothache or pains in the face, and this was not improbable, since she was just then in the early months of her first pregnancy.

Thus the explanation turned out to be that this neuralgia had come to be indicative of a particular psychical excitation by the usual method of conversion, but that afterwards it could be set going through associative reverberations from her mental life, or symbolic conversion. In fact, the same behaviour that we found in Fräulein Elisabeth von R.

I will give a second example which demonstrates the action of symbolization under other conditions. At a particular period, Frau Cäcilie was afflicted with a violent pain in her right heel— a shooting pain at every step she took, which made walking impossible. Analysis led us in connection with this to a time when the patient had been in a sanatorium abroad. She had spent a week in bed and was going to be taken down to the common dining-room for the first time by the house physician. The pain came on at the moment when she took his arm to leave the room with him; it disappeared during the reproduction of the scene, when the patient told me she had been afraid at the time that she might not 'find herself on a right footing' with these strangers.

This seems at first to be a striking and even a comic example of the genesis of hysterical symptoms through symbolization by means of a verbal expression. Closer examination of the circumstances, however, favours another view of the case. The patient had been suffering at the time from pains in the feet generally, and it was on their account that she had been confined to bed so long. All that could be claimed on behalf of symbolization was that the fear which overcame the patient, as she took her first steps, picked out from among all the pains that were troubling her at the time the one particular pain which was symbolically appropriate, the pain in her right heel, and developed it into a psychical pain and gave it special persistence.

In these examples the mechanism of symbolization seems to be reduced to secondary importance, as is no doubt the general rule. But I have examples at my disposal which seem to prove the genesis of hysterical symptoms through symbolization alone. The following is one of the best, and relates once more to Frau

Cäcilie. When a girl of fifteen, she was lying in bed, under the watchful eye of her strict grandmother. The girl suddenly gave a cry; she had felt a penetrating pain in her forehead between her eyes, which lasted for weeks. During the analysis of this pain, which was reproduced after nearly thirty years, she told me that her grandmother had given her a look so 'piercing' that it had gone right into her brain. (She had been afraid that the old woman was viewing her with suspicion.) As she told me this thought she broke into a loud laugh, and the pain once more disappeared. In this instance I can detect nothing other than the mechanism of symbolization, which has its place, in some sense, midway between autosuggestion and conversion.

My observation of Frau Cäcilie M. gave me an opportunity of making a regular collection of symbolizations of this kind. A whole set of physical sensations which would ordinarily be regarded as organically determined were in her case of psychical origin or at least possessed a psychical meaning. A particular series of experiences of hers were accompanied by a stabbing sensation in the region of the heart (meaning 'it stabbed me to the heart'). The pain that occurs in hysteria of nails being driven into the head was without any doubt to be explained in her case as a pain related to thinking. ('Something's come into my head.') Pains of this kind were always cleared up as soon as the problems involved were cleared up. Running parallel to the sensation of a hysterical 'aura' [1] in the throat, when that feeling appeared after an insult, was the thought 'I shall have to swallow this'. She had a whole quantity of sensations and ideas running parallel with each other. Sometimes the sensation would call up the idea to explain it, sometimes the idea would create the sensation by means of symbolization, and not infrequently it had to be left an open question which of the two elements had been the primary one.

I have not found such an extensive use of symbolization in any other patient. It is true that Frau Cäcilie M. was a woman who possessed quite unusual gifts, particularly artistic ones, and whose highly developed sense of form was revealed in some poems of great perfection. It is my opinion, however, that when a hysteric creates a somatic expression for an emotionally-coloured idea by symbolization, this depends less than one

[1] [See footnote, p. 126.]

would imagine on personal or voluntary factors. In taking a verbal expression literally and in feeling the 'stab in the heart' or the 'slap in the face' after some slighting remark as a real event, the hysteric is not taking liberties with words, but is simply reviving once more the sensations to which the verbal expression owes its justification. How has it come about that we speak of someone who has been slighted as being 'stabbed to the heart' unless the slight had in fact been accompanied by a precordial sensation which could suitably be described in that phrase and unless it was identifiable by that sensation? What could be more probable than that the figure of speech 'swallowing something', which we use in talking of an insult to which no rejoinder has been made, did in fact originate from the innervatory sensations which arise in the pharynx when we refrain from speaking and prevent ourselves from reacting to the insult? All these sensations and innervations belong to the field of 'The Expression of the Emotions', which, as Darwin [1872] has taught us, consists of actions which originally had a meaning and served a purpose. These may now for the most part have become so much weakened that the expression of them in words seems to us only to be a figurative picture of them, whereas in all probability the description was once meant literally; and hysteria is right in restoring the original meaning of the words in depicting its unusually strong innervations. Indeed, it is perhaps wrong to say that hysteria creates these sensations by symbolization. It may be that it does not take linguistic usage as its model at all, but that both hysteria and linguistic usage alike draw their material from a common source.[1]

[1] In states in which mental alteration goes deeper, we clearly also find a symbolic version in concrete images and sensations of more artificial turns of speech. Frau Cäcilie M. passed through a period during which she transformed every thought she had into a hallucination, the explanation of which often called for much ingenuity. She complained to me at that time of being troubled by a hallucination that her two doctors—Breuer and I—were hanging on two trees next each other in the garden. The hallucination disappeared after the analysis had brought out the following explanation. The evening before, Breuer had refused to give her a drug she had asked for. She had then set her hopes on me but had found me equally hard-hearted. She was furious with us over this, and in her anger she thought to herself: 'There's nothing to choose between the two of them; one's the *pendant* [match] of the other.'—[A short summary of the case history of Fräulein Elisabeth was given by Freud in the second of his *Five Lectures* (1910a).]

III

THEORETICAL

(BREUER)

III

THEORETICAL

(BREUER)

In the 'Preliminary Communication' which introduces this work we laid down the conclusions to which we were led by our observations, and I think that I can stand by them in the main. But the 'Preliminary Communication' is so short and concise that for the most part it was only possible in it to hint at our views. Now, therefore, that the case histories have brought forward evidence in support of our conclusions it may be permissible to state them at greater length. Even here, there is, of course, no question of dealing with the *whole* field of hysteria. But we may give a somewhat closer and clearer account (with some added reservations, no doubt) of those points for which insufficient evidence was adduced or which were not given enough prominence in the 'Preliminary Communication'.

In what follows little mention will be made of the brain and none whatever of molecules. Psychical processes will be dealt with in the language of psychology; and, indeed, it cannot possibly be otherwise. If instead of 'idea' we chose to speak of 'excitation of the cortex', the latter term would only have any meaning for us in so far as we recognized an old friend under that cloak and tacitly reinstated the 'idea'. For while ideas are constant objects of our experience and are familiar to us in all their shades of meaning, 'cortical excitations' are on the contrary rather in the nature of a postulate, objects which we hope to be able to identify in the future. The substitution of one term for another would seem to be no more than a pointless disguise. Accordingly, I may perhaps be forgiven if I make almost exclusive of psychological terms.

There is another point for which I must ask in advance for the reader's indulgence. When a science is making rapid advances, thoughts which were first expressed by single individuals quickly become common property. Thus no one who attempts to put forward to-day his views on hysteria and its

185

psychical basis can avoid repeating a great quantity of other people's thoughts which are in the act of passing from personal into general possession. It is scarcely possible always to be certain who first gave them utterance, and there is always a danger of regarding as a product of one's own what has already been said by someone else. I hope, therefore, that I may be excused if few quotations are found in this discussion and if no strict distinction is made between what is my own and what originates elsewhere. Originality is claimed for very little of what will be found in the following pages.

(1) Are All Hysterical Phenomena Ideogenic?

In our 'Preliminary Communication' we discussed the psychical mechanism of 'hysterical phenomena', not of 'hysteria', because we did not wish to claim that this psychical mechanism or the psychical theory of hysterical symptoms in general has unlimited validity. We are not of the opinion that all the phenomena of hysteria come about in the manner described by us in that paper, nor do we believe that they are all ideogenic, that is, determined by ideas. In this we differ from Moebius, who in 1888 proposed to define as hysterical all pathological phenomena that are caused by ideas. This statement was later elucidated to the effect that only a part of the pathological phenomena correspond in their content to the ideas that cause them—those phenomena, namely, that are produced by allo- or auto-suggestion, as, for instance, when the idea of not being able to move one's arm causes a paralysis of it; while another part of the hysterical phenomena, though caused by ideas, do not correspond to them in their content—as, for instance, when in one of our patients a paralysis of the arm was caused by the sight of snake-like objects [p. 39].

In giving this definition, Moebius is not merely proposing a modification in nomenclature and suggesting that in future we should only describe as hysterical those pathological phenomena which are ideogenic (determined by ideas); what he thinks is that all hysterical symptoms are ideogenic. 'Since ideas are very frequently the cause of hysterical phenomena, I believe that they always are.' He terms this an inference by analogy. I prefer to call it a generalization, the justification for which must first be tested.

Before any discussion of the subject, we must obviously decide what we understand by hysteria. I regard hysteria as a clinical picture which has been empirically discovered and is based on observation, in just the same way as tubercular pulmonary phthisis. Clinical pictures of this kind that have been arrived at empirically are made more precise, deeper and clearer by the progress of our knowledge; but they ought not to be and cannot be disrupted by it. Aetiological research has shown that the various constituent processes of pulmonary phthisis have various causes: the tubercle is due to *bacillus Kochii*, and the disintegration of tissue, the formation of cavities and the septic fever are due to other microbes. In spite of this, tubercular phthisis remains a clinical unity and it would be wrong to break it up by attributing to it only the 'specifically tubercular' modifications of tissue caused by Koch's bacillus and by detaching the other modifications from it. In the same way hysteria must remain a clinical unity even if it turns out that its phenomena are determined by various causes, and that some of them are brought about by a psychical mechanism and others without it.

It is my conviction that this is in fact so; only a part of the phenomena of hysteria are ideogenic, and the definition put forward by Moebius tears in half the clinical unity of hysteria, and indeed the unity of one and the same symptom in the same patient.

We should be drawing an inference completely analogous to Moebius's 'inference by analogy' if we were to say that because ideas and perceptions very often give rise to erections we may assume that they alone ever do so and that peripheral stimuli set this vasomotor process in action only by a roundabout path through the psyche. We know that this inference would be false, yet it is based on at least as many facts as Moebius's assertion about hysteria. In conformity with our experience of a large number of physiological processes, such as the secretion of saliva or tears, changes in the action of the heart, etc., it is possible and plausible to assume that one and the same process may be set in motion equally by ideas and by peripheral and other non-psychical stimuli. The contrary would need to be proved and we are very far short of that. Indeed, it seems certain that many phenomena which are described as hysterical are not caused by ideas alone.

Let us consider an everyday instance. A woman may, whenever an affect arises, produce on her neck, breast and face an erythema appearing first in blotches and then becoming confluent. This is determined by ideas and therefore according to Moebius is a hysterical phenomenon. But this same erythema appears, though over a less extensive area, when the skin is irritated or touched, etc. This would *not* be hysterical. Thus a phenomenon which is undoubtedly a complete unity would on one occasion be hysterical and on another occasion not. It may of course be questioned whether this phenomenon, the erethism of the vasomotors, should be regarded as a specifically hysterical one or whether it should not be more properly looked upon simply as 'nervous'. But on Moebius's view the breaking up of the unity would necessarily result in any case and the affectively-determined erythema would alone be called hysterical.

This applies in exactly the same way to the hysterical pains which are of so much practical importance. No doubt these are often determined directly by ideas. They are 'hallucinations of pain'. If we examine these rather more closely it appears that the fact of an idea being very vivid is not enough to produce them but that there must be a special abnormal condition of the apparatuses concerned with the conduction and sensation of pain, just as in the case of affective erythema an abnormal excitability of the vasomotors must be present. The phrase 'hallucinations of pain' undoubtedly gives the most pregnant description of the nature of these neuralgias, but it compels us, too, to carry over to them the views that we have formed on hallucinations in general. A detailed discussion of these views would not be in place here. I subscribe to the opinion that 'ideas', mnemic images pure and simple, without any excitation of the perceptual apparatus, never, even at their greatest vividness and intensity, attain the character of objective existence which is the mark of hallucinations.[1]

---

[1] This perceptual apparatus, including the sensory areas of the cortex, must be different from the organ which stores up and reproduces sense-impressions in the form of mnemic images. For the basic essential of the function of the perceptual apparatus is that its *status quo ante* should be capable of being restored with the greatest possible rapidity; otherwise no proper further perception could take place. The essential of memory, on the other hand, is that no such restoration should occur but that every perception should create changes that are permanent. It is impossible for one and the same organ to fulfil these two contra-

This applies to sensory hallucinations and still more to hallucinations of pain. For it does not seem possible for a healthy person to endow the memory of a physical pain with even the degree of vividness, the distant approximation to the real sensation, which can, after all, be attained by optical and acoustic mnemic images. Even in the normal hallucinatory state of healthy people which occurs in sleep there are never, I believe, dreams of pain unless a real sensation of pain is present. This 'retrogressive' excitation,[1] emanating from the organ of memory and acting on the perceptual apparatus by means of ideas, is therefore in the normal course of things still more difficult in the case of pain than in that of visual or auditory sensations. Since hallucinations of pain arise so easily in hysteria, we must posit an abnormal excitability of the apparatus concerned with sensations of pain.

This excitability makes its appearance not only under the spur of ideas but of peripheral stimuli in just the same way as the erethism of the vasomotors which we discussed above.

It is a matter of daily observation to find that in people with normal nerves peripheral pains are brought on by pathological processes, not in themselves painful, in other organs. Thus

dictory conditions. The mirror of a reflecting telescope cannot at the same time be a photographic plate. I am in agreement with Meynert, in the sense of believing, as I have said, that what gives hallucinations their objective character is an excitation of the perceptual apparatus (though I do not agree with him when he speaks of an excitation of the subcortical centres). If the perceptual organ is excited by a mnemic image, we must suppose that that organ's excitability has been changed in an abnormal direction, and that this change is what makes hallucination possible. [The thesis that a single apparatus could not perform the functions both of perception and memory was adopted by Freud in the seventh chapter of his *Interpretation of Dreams* (1900a), *Standard Ed.*, **5**, 538. He had already accepted it in his posthumous 'Project' (1950a, Part I, Section 3), written a few months after the publication of the present work, as well as in a letter to Fliess of December 6, 1896, and he recurred to it in Chapter IV of *Beyond the Pleasure Principle* (1920g, *Standard Ed.*, **18**, 25) and in his paper on the 'mystic writing-pad' (1925a). In the last but one of these he explicitly attributes this line of thought to Breuer.]

[1] [This idea of the retrogressive nature of hallucination was adopted by Freud in his discussion of dreams in the posthumous 'Project', Part I, Section 20. It will also be found in the seventh chapter of *The Interpretation of Dreams*, *Standard Ed.*, **5**, 542 ff., where the term 'regression' is used.]

headaches arise from relatively insignificant changes in the nose or neighbouring cavities, and again, neuralgias of the intercostal and brachial nerves from the heart, etc. If the abnormal excitability, which we have been obliged to postulate as a necessary condition of hallucinations of pain, is present in a patient, that excitability is also at the disposal, so to speak, of the irradiations that I have just mentioned. The irradiations that occur also in non-neurotic people are made more intense, and irradiations are formed of a sort which, it is true, we only find in neurotic patients but which are based on the same mechanism as the others. Thus, ovarian neuralgia depends, I believe, on states of the genital apparatus. That its causes are psychical would have to be proved, and this is not achieved by showing that that particular kind of pain, like any other, can be produced under hypnosis as a hallucination, or that its causes *can* be psychical. Like erythema or one of the normal secretions, it arises both from psychical and from purely somatic causes. Are we to describe only the first kind as hysterical—cases which we know have a psychical origin? If so, the commonly observed cases of ovarian neuralgia would have to be excluded from the hysterical syndrome, and this will hardly do.

If a slight injury to a joint is gradually followed by a severe arthralgia, no doubt the process involves a psychical element, viz. a concentration of attention on the injured part, which intensifies the excitability of the nerve tracts concerned. But this can hardly be expressed by saying that the hyperalgesia has been caused by ideas.

The same is true of the pathological *diminution* of sensation. It is quite unproved and improbable that general analgesia or analgesia of individual parts of the body unaccompanied by anaesthesia is caused by ideas. And even if the discoveries of Binet and Janet were to be fully confirmed to the effect that hemi-anaesthesia is determined by a peculiar psychical condition, by a splitting of the psyche, the phenomenon would be a psychogenic but not an ideogenic one, and therefore, according to Moebius, should not be termed hysterical.

If, therefore, there are a large number of characteristic hysterical phenomena which we cannot suppose to be ideogenic, it would seem right to limit the application of Moebius's thesis. We shall not define as hysterical those pathological phenomena which are caused by ideas, but only assert that a great number of hysterical phenomena, probably more than we suspect to-day, are ideogenic. But the fundamental pathological change which is present in every case and enables ideas as well as non-psychological stimuli to produce pathological effects lies in an abnormal excitability of the nervous system.[1] How far this excitability is itself of psychical origin is another question.

Yet even though only some of the phenomena of hysteria are ideogenic, nevertheless it is precisely they that may be described as the specifically hysterical ones, and it is the investigation of them, the discovery of their psychical origin, which constitutes the most important recent step forward in the theory of the disorder. The further question then arises: how do these phenomena come about? What is their 'psychical mechanism'?

This question requires a quite different answer in the case of each of the two groups into which Moebius divides ideogenic symptoms [p. 186]. Those pathological phenomena which correspond in their content to the instigating idea are relatively understandable and clear. If the idea of a heard voice does not merely cause it to echo faintly in the 'inward ear', as it does in healthy people, but causes it to be perceived in a hallucinatory manner as a real, objective acoustic sensation, this may be equated with familiar phenomena of normal life—with dreams —and is quite intelligible on the hypothesis of abnormal excitability. We know that with every voluntary movement it is the idea of the result to be achieved which initiates the relevant muscular contraction; and it is not very hard to see that the idea that this contraction is impossible will impede the movement (as happens in paralysis by suggestion).

The situation is otherwise with those phenomena which have no logical connection with the determining idea. (Here, too, normal life offers parallels, as, for instance, blushing for shame.) How do they arise? Why does an idea in a sick man evoke one particular entirely irrational movement or hallucination which does not in any way correspond to it?

In our 'Preliminary Communication' we felt able to say

[1] Attributed by Oppenheim [1890] to 'instability of the molecules'. It may be possible at a later stage to replace the very vague statement in the text above by a more precise and significant formula. [Cf. below, p. 241 ff.]

something about this causal relation on the basis of our observations. In our exposition of the subject, however, we introduced and employed without apology the concept of 'excitations which flow away or have to be abreacted'.[1] This concept is of fundamental importance for our theme and for the theory of the neuroses in general, and it seems to demand and to deserve a more detailed examination. Before I proceed to this, I must ask to be forgiven for taking the reader back to the basic problems of the nervous system. A feeling of oppression is bound to accompany any such descent to the 'Mothers' [i.e., exploration of the depths].[2]

But any attempt at getting at the roots of a phenomenon inevitably leads in this way to basic problems which cannot be evaded. I hope therefore that the abstruseness of the following discussion may be viewed with indulgence.

(2) INTRACEREBRAL TONIC EXCITATIONS—AFFECTS

(A)

We know two extreme conditions of the central nervous system: a clear waking state and dreamless sleep. A transition between these is afforded by conditions of every degree of decreasing clarity. What interests us here is not the question of the purpose of sleep and its physical basis (its chemical or vasomotor determinants) but the question of the essential distinction between the two conditions.

We can give no direct information about the deepest, dreamless sleep, for the very reason that all observations and experiences are excluded by the state of total unconsciousness. But as regards the neighbouring condition of sleep accompanied by dreams, the following assertions can be made. In the first place, when in that condition we intend to make voluntary movements —of walking, speaking, etc.—this does not result in the corresponding contractions of the muscles being voluntarily initiated, as they are in waking life. In the second place, sensory stimuli

---

[1] [This is not an actual quotation from the 'Preliminary Communication', where this underlying hypothesis is nowhere explicitly mentioned. Cf. the remarks on this in the Editor's Introduction, p. xix ff.]

[2] [An allusion to Faust's mysterious researches (in Goethe's *Faust*, Part II, Act I).]

are perhaps perceived (for they often make their way into dreams) but they are not apperceived, i.e. do not become conscious perceptions. Again, ideas that emerge do not, as in waking life, activate all the ideas which are connected with them and which are present in potential consciousness; a great number of the latter remain unexcited. (For instance, we find ourselves talking to a dead person without remembering that he is dead.) Furthermore, incompatible ideas can be present simultaneously without mutually inhibiting each other, as they do in waking life. Thus, association is defective and incomplete. We may safely assume that in the deepest sleep this severance of connections between the psychical elements is carried still further and becomes total.

On the other hand, when we are fully awake every act of will initiates the corresponding movement; sense-impressions become conscious perceptions; and ideas are associated with the whole store present in potential consciousness. In that condition the brain functions as a unit with complete internal connections.

We shall perhaps only be describing these facts in other words if we say that in sleep the paths of connection and conduction in the brain are not traversable by excitations of the psychical elements (? cortical cells), whereas in waking life they are completely so traversable.

The existence of these two different conditions of the paths of conduction can, it seems, only be made intelligible if we suppose that in waking life those paths are in a state of tonic excitation (what Exner [1894, 93] calls 'intercellular tetanus'), that this intracerebral excitation is what determines their conductive capability, and that the diminution and disappearance of that excitation is what sets up the state of sleep.

We ought not to think of a cerebral path of conduction as resembling a telephone wire which is only excited electrically at the moment at which it has to function (that is, in the present context, when it has to transmit a signal). We ought to liken it to a telephone line through which there is a constant flow of galvanic current and which can no longer be excited if that current ceases. Or better, let us imagine a widely-ramified electrical system for lighting and the transmission of motor power; what is expected of this system is that simple establishment of a contact shall be able to set any lamp or machine in operation. To make this possible, so that everything shall be ready to work, there must be a certain tension present throughout the entire network of lines of conduction, and the dynamo engine must expend a given quantity of energy for this purpose. In just the same way there is a certain amount of excitation present in the conductive paths of the brain when it is at rest but awake and prepared to work.[1]

This view of the matter is supported by the fact that merely being awake, without doing any work, gives rise to fatigue and produces a need for sleep. The state of waking in itself causes a consumption of energy.

Let us imagine a man in a state of intense expectation, which is not, however, directed to any particular sensory field. We then have before us a brain which is quiescent but prepared for

---

[1] I may perhaps venture here to indicate briefly the notion on which the above statements are based. We usually think of the sensory nerve-cells as being passive receptive organs. This is a mistake. For the mere existence of a system of associative fibres proves that these sensory nerve-cells also send out excitation into the nerve-fibres. If excitation from two sensory cells flows into a nerve-fibre that connects them— whether *per continuitatem* or *per contiguitatem* [i.e. whether it is an extension of them or is in contact with them]—then a state of tension must exist in it. This state of tension has the same relation to the excitation flowing away in, for instance, a peripheral motor fibre as hydrostatic pressure has to the living force of flowing water or as electric tension has to an electric current. If all the nerve-cells are in a state of mean excitation and are exciting their nerve-processes [axones], the whole immense network forms a single reservoir of 'nervous tension'. Apart then from a potential energy which lies quiescent in the chemical substance of the cell and an unknown form of kinetic energy which is discharged when the fibres are in a state of excitation, we must assume the existence of yet another quiescent state of nervous excitation: tonic excitation or nervous tension. [This footnote and the corresponding passage in the text above seem to have been regarded by Freud as his ground for attributing to Breuer the distinction between the 'free' and 'bound' forms of psychical energy and the allied distinction between the primary and secondary systems of psychical functioning. In his paper on 'The Unconscious' (1915e, end of Section V) and in *Beyond the Pleasure Principle* (1920g, Chapter IV, *Standard Ed.*, **18**, 26-7) he definitely asserts that these ideas are derived from Breuer's contribution to *Studies on Hysteria*, but he gives no more precise reference. Freud had already adopted the idea in Chapter VII of *The Interpretation of Dreams* (1900a, *Standard Ed.*, **5**, 599 ff.); but the question is discussed at greater length towards the end of the first Section of Part III of the posthumously-published 'Project' (1950a).]

action. We may rightly suppose that in such a brain all the paths of conduction are at the maximum of their conductive capability—that they are in a state of tonic excitation. It is a significant fact that in ordinary language we speak of such a state as one of tension. Experience teaches us what a strain this state is and how fatiguing, though no actual motor or psychical work is performed in it.

This is an exceptional state, which, precisely on account of the great consumption of energy involved, cannot be tolerated for long. But even the normal state of being wide awake calls for an amount of intracerebral excitation varying between limits that are not very widely separated. Every diminishing degree of wakefulness down to drowsiness and true sleep is accompanied by correspondingly lower degrees of excitation.

When the brain is performing actual work, a greater consumption of energy is no doubt required than when it is merely *prepared* to perform work. (In just the same way the electrical system described above by way of comparison must cause a greater amount of electrical energy to flow into the conducting lines when a large number of lamps or motors are switched into the circuit.) Where functioning is normal no more energy is liberated than is immediately employed in activity. The brain, however, behaves like one of those electrical systems of restricted capability which are unable to produce both a large amount of light and of mechanical work at the same time. If it is transmitting power, only a little energy is available for lighting, and *vice versa*. Thus we find that if we are making great muscular efforts we are unable to engage in continuous thought, or that if we concentrate our attention in one sensory field the efficiency of the other cerebral organs is reduced—that is to say, we find that the brain works with a varying but limited amount of energy.

The non-uniform distribution of energy is no doubt determined by what Exner [1894, 165] calls 'facilitation by attention'—by an increase in the conductive capability of the paths in use and a decrease in that of the others; and thus in a working brain the 'intracerebral tonic excitation', too, is non-uniformly distributed.'[1]

[1] The conception of the energy of the central nervous system as being a quantity distributed over the brain in a changing and fluctuating manner is an old one. 'La sensibilité', wrote Cabanis [1824, **3**, 153],

We wake up a person who is sleeping—that is, we suddenly raise the quantity of his tonic intracerebral excitation—by bringing a lively sensory stimulus to bear upon him. Whether alterations in the blood-circulation in the brain are essential links here in the causal chain, and whether the blood-vessels are directly dilated by the stimulus, or whether the dilatation is a consequence of the excitation of the cerebral elements—all this is undecided. What is certain is that the state of excitation, entering through a gateway of the senses, spreads over the brain from that point, becomes diffused and brings all the paths of conduction into a state of higher facilitation.

It is still not in the least clear, of course, how *spontaneous* awakening occurs—whether it is always one and the same portion of the brain that is the first to enter a state of waking excitation and the excitation then spreads from there, or whether sometimes one and sometimes another group of elements acts as the awakener. Nevertheless spontaneous awakening, which, as we know, can take place in complete quiet and darkness without any external stimulus, proves that the development of energy is based on the vital process of the cerebral elements themselves. A muscle remains unstimulated, quiescent, however long it has been in a state of rest and even though it has accumulated a maximum of tensile force. This is not so with the cerebral elements. We are no doubt right in supposing that during sleep the latter regain their previous condition and gather tensile force. When this has happened to a certain degree, when, as we may say, a certain level has been reached, the surplus flows away into the paths of conduction, facilitates them and sets up the intracerebral excitation of the waking state.

We can find an instructive example of the same thing in waking life. When the waking brain has been quiescent for a considerable time without transforming tensile force into live energy by functioning, there arises a need and an urge for activity. Long motor quiescence creates a need for movement

'semble se comporter à la manière d'une fluide dont la quantité totale est déterminée et qui, toutes les fois qu'il se jette en plus grande abondance dans un de ses canaux, diminue proportionellement dans le-autres.' (Quoted from Janet, 1894, 277.) ['Sensibility seems to behave like a fluid whose total quantity is fixed and which, whenever it pours into one of its channels in greater abundance, becomes proportionally less in the others.']

(compare the aimless running round of a caged animal) and if this need cannot be satisfied a distressing feeling sets in. Lack of sensory stimuli, darkness and complete silence become a torture; mental repose, lack of perceptions, ideas and associative activity produce the torment of boredom. These unpleasurable feelings correspond to an 'excitement', to an increase in normal intracerebral excitation.

Thus the cerebral elements, after being completely restored, liberate a certain amount of energy even when they are at rest; and if this energy is not employed functionally it increases the normal intracerebral excitation. The result is a feeling of unpleasure. Such feelings are always generated when one of the organism's needs fails to find satisfaction. Since these feelings disappear when the surplus quantity of energy which has been liberated is employed functionally, we may conclude that the removal of such surplus excitation is a need of the organism. And here for the first time we meet the fact that there exists in the organism a *'tendency to keep intracerebral excitation constant'* (Freud),[1]

Such a surplus of intracerebral excitation is a burden and a nuisance, and an urge to use it up arises in consequence. If it cannot be used in sensory or ideational activity, the surplus flows away in purposeless motor action, in walking up and down, and so on, and this we shall meet with later as the commonest method of discharging excessive tensions.

We are familiar with the great individual variations which are found in this respect: the great differences between lively people and inert and lethargic ones, between those who 'cannot sit still' and those who have an 'innate gift for lounging on sofas' and between mentally agile minds and dull ones which can tolerate intellectual rest for an unlimited length of time.

[1] [This seems to be the first explicit enunciation of Freud's 'principle of constancy'. It had been used previously by him in writings that were only posthumously published (1941a [1892] and 1940d [1892]). Freud developed the subject further in another posthumously published work, his 'Project' (1950a), which was written a few months after the publication of the present *Studies*, and in which he names the hypothesis 'the principle of neuronic inertia'. (See, in particular, Section 1 of Part I of that work.) He had, however, stated its essence in the lecture (1893h) which he delivered at about the time of publication of the 'Preliminary Communication'. The subject is discussed more fully in the Editor's Introduction, p. xix ff.]

These differences, which make up a man's 'natural temperament', are certainly based on profound differences in his nervous
system—on the degree to which the functionally quiescent
cerebral elements liberate energy.

We have spoken of a tendency on the part of the organism
to keep tonic cerebral excitation constant. A tendency of
this kind is, however, only intelligible if we can see what need
it fulfils. We can understand the tendency in warm-blooded
animals that to keep a constant mean temperature, because our
experience has taught us that that temperature is an optimum
for the functioning of their organs. And we make a similar
assumption in regard to the constancy of the water-content
of the blood; and so on. I think that we may also assume that
there is an optimum for the height of the intracerebral tonic
excitation. At that level of tonic excitation the brain is accessible
to all external stimuli, the reflexes are facilitated, though only
to the extent of normal reflex activity, and the store of ideas
is capable of being aroused and open to association in the
mutual relation between individual ideas which corresponds to
a clear and reasonable state of mind. It is in this state that the
organism is best prepared for work.

The situation is already altered by the uniform [pp. 194–5]
heightening of tonic excitation which constitutes 'expectation'.
This makes the organism hyperaesthetic towards sensory
stimuli, which quickly become distressing, and also increases
its reflex excitability above what is useful (proneness to fright).
No doubt this state is useful for some situations and purposes;
but if it appears spontaneously and not for any such reasons,
it does not improve our efficiency but impairs it. In ordinary
life we call this being 'nervous'. In the great majority of forms
of increase in excitation, however, the over-excitation is *not*
uniform, and this is always detrimental to efficiency. We call
this 'excitement'. That the organism should tend to maintain
the optimum of excitation and to return to that optimum after
it has been exceeded is not surprising, but quite in keeping
with other regulating factors in the organism.

I shall venture once more to recur to my comparison with an
electrical lighting system. The tension in the network of lines
of conduction in such a system has an optimum too. If this is
exceeded its functioning may easily be impaired; for instance,
the electric light filaments may be quickly burned through. I

shall speak later of the damage done to the system itself through a break-down of its insulation or through 'short-circuiting'.

(B)

Our speech, the outcome of the experience of many generations, distinguishes with admirable delicacy between those forms and degrees of heightening of excitation which are still useful for mental activity [i.e. in spite of rising above the optimum (see last paragraph but one)] because they raise the free energy of all cerebral functions uniformly, and those forms and degrees which restrict that activity because they partly increase and partly inhibit these psychical functions in a manner that is *not* uniform. The first are given the name of 'incitement', and the second 'excitement'.[1] An interesting conversation, or a cup of tea or coffee has an 'inciting' [stimulating] effect; a dispute or a considerable dose of alcohol has an 'exciting' one. While incitement only arouses the urge to employ the increased excitation functionally, excitement seeks to discharge itself in more or less violent ways which are almost or even actually pathological. Excitement constitutes the psycho-physical basis of the effects, and these will be discussed below. But I must first touch briefly on some physiological and endogenous causes of increases of excitation.

Among these, in the first place, are the organism's major physiological needs and instincts: need for oxygen, craving for food, and thirst. Since the excitement which they set going is linked to certain sensations and purposive ideas, it is not such a pure example of increase of excitation as the one discussed above [pp. 196–7], which arose solely from the quiescence of the cerebral elements. The former always has its special colouring. But it is unmistakable in the anxious agitation which accompanies dyspnoea and in the restlessness of a starving man.

The increase of excitation that comes from these sources is determined by the chemical change in the cerebral elements themselves, which are short of oxygen, of tensile force or of water. It flows away along preformed motor paths, which lead to the satisfaction of the need that set it going: dyspnoea leads to breathing with effort, and hunger and thirst to a search for and attainment of food and water. The principle of the

[1] [In German '*Anregung*' = 'incitement', 'stimulation'; '*Aufregung*' = 'excitement', 'agitation'.]

constancy of excitation scarcely comes into operation as far as this kind of excitation is concerned; for the interests which are served by the increase in excitation in these cases are of far greater importance to the organism than the re-establishment of normal conditions of functioning in the brain. It is true that we see animals in a zoo running backwards and forwards excitedly before feeding-time; but this may no doubt be regarded as a residue of the preformed motor activity of looking for food, which has now become useless owing to their being in captivity, and not as a means of freeing the nervous system of excitement.

If the chemical structure of the nervous system has been permanently altered by a persistent introduction of foreign substances, then a lack of these substances will cause states of excitation, just as the lack of normal nutritive substances does in healthy people. We see this in the excitement occurring in abstinence from narcotics.

A transition between these endogenous increases of excitation and the psychical affects in the narrower sense is provided by sexual excitation and sexual affect. Sexuality at puberty appears in the first of these forms, as a vague, indeterminate, purposeless heightening of excitation. As development proceeds, this endogenous heightening of excitation, determined by the functioning of the sex-glands, becomes firmly linked (in the normal course of things) with the perception or idea of the other sex—and, indeed, with the idea of a particular individual, where the remarkable phenomenon of falling in love occurs. This idea takes over the whole quantity of excitation liberated by the sexual instinct. It becomes an 'affective idea'; that is to say, when it is actively present in consciousness it sets going the increase of excitation which in point of fact originated from another source, namely the sex-glands.

The sexual instinct is undoubtedly the most powerful source of persisting increases of excitation (and consequently of neuroses). Such increases are distributed very unevenly over the nervous system. When they reach a considerable degree of intensity the train of ideas becomes disturbed and the relative value of the ideas is changed; and in orgasm [1] thought is almost completely extinguished.

[1] ['*Orgasmus*' in the first and second editions. In later editions this is misprinted '*Organismus*'.]

Perception too—the psychical interpretation of sense-impressions—is impaired. An animal which is normally timid and cautious becomes blind and deaf to danger. On the other hand, at least in males, there is an intensification of the aggressive instinct. Peaceable animals become dangerous until their excitation has been discharged in the motor activities of the sexual act.

(C)

A disturbance like this of the dynamic equilibrium of the nervous system—a non-uniform distribution of increased excitation—is what makes up the psychical side of affects.

No attempt will be made here to formulate either a psychology or a physiology of the affects. I shall only discuss a single point, which is of importance for pathology, and moreover only for ideogenic affects—those which are called up by perceptions and ideas. (Lange, 1885 [62 ff.], has rightly pointed out that affects can be caused by toxic substances, or, as psychiatry teaches us, above all by pathological changes, almost in the same way as they can by ideas.)

It may be taken as self-evident that all the disturbances of mental equilibrium which we call acute affects go along with an increase of excitation. (In the case of *chronic* affects, such as sorrow and care, that is to say protracted anxiety, the complication is present of a state of severe fatigue which, though it maintains the non-uniform distribution of excitation, nevertheless reduces its height.) But this increased excitation cannot be employed in psychical activity. All powerful affects restrict association—the train of ideas. People become 'senseless' with anger or fright. Only the group of ideas which provoked the affect persists in consciousness, and it does so with extreme intensity. Thus the excitement cannot be levelled out by associative activity.

Affects that are 'active' or 'sthenic' do, however, level out the increased excitation by *motor* discharge. Shouting and jumping for joy, the increased muscular tone of anger, angry words and retaliatory deeds—all these allow the excitation to flow away in movements. Mental pain discharges it in difficult breathing and in an act of secretion: in sobs and tears. It is a matter of everyday experience that such reactions reduce excitement and allay it. As we have already remarked [p. 8], ordinary language expresses this in such phrases as 'to cry oneself out', 'to blow off steam', etc. What is being got rid of is nothing else than the increased cerebral excitation.

Only some of these reactions, such as angry deeds and words, serve a purpose in the sense of making any change in the actual state of affairs. The rest serve no purpose whatever, or rather their only purpose is to level out the increase of excitation and to establish psychical equilibrium. In so far as they achieve this they serve the 'tendency to keep [intra-]cerebral excitation constant' [p. 197].

The 'asthenic' affects of fright and anxiety do not bring about this reactive discharge. Fright paralyses outright the power of movement as well as of association, and so does anxiety if the single useful reaction of running away is excluded by the cause of the affect of anxiety or by circumstances. The excitation of fright disappears only by a gradual levelling out.

Anger has adequate reactions corresponding to its cause. If these are not feasible, or if they are inhibited, they are replaced by substitutes. Even angry words are substitutes of this kind. But other, even quite purposeless, acts may appear as substitutes. When Bismarck had to suppress his angry feelings in the King's presence, he relieved himself afterwards by smashing a valuable vase on the floor. This deliberate replacement of one motor act by another corresponds exactly to the replacement of natural pain-reflexes by other muscular contractions. When a tooth is extracted the preformed reflex is to push away the dentist and utter a cry; if, instead of that, we contract the muscles of our arms and press against the sides of the chair, we are shifting the quantum of excitation that has been generated by the pain from one group of muscles to another. [Cf. p. 91.] In the case of violent spontaneous toothache, where there is no preformed reflex apart from groaning, the excitation flows off in aimless pacing up and down. In the same way we transpose the excitation of anger from the adequate reaction to another one, and we feel relieved provided it is used up by *any* strong motor innervation.

If, however, the affect can find no discharge of excitation of any kind along these lines, then the situation is the same with anger as with fright and anxiety. The intracerebral excitation is powerfully increased, but is employed neither in associative nor in motor activity. In normal people the disturbance is gradually levelled out. But in some, abnormal reactions appear. An 'abnormal expression of the emotions', as Oppenheim [1890] says, is formed.

(3) HYSTERICAL CONVERSION

I shall scarcely be suspected of identifying nervous excitation with electricity, if I return once more to the comparison with an electrical system. If the tension in such a system becomes excessively high, there is danger of a break occurring at weak points in the insulation. Electrical phenomena then appear at abnormal points; or, if two wires lie close beside each other, there is a short circuit. Since a permanent change has been produced at these points, the disturbance thus brought about may constantly recur if the tension is sufficiently increased. An abnormal 'facilitation' has taken place.

That the conditions applying in the nervous system are to some extent similar can well be maintained. It forms throughout an interconnected whole; but at many points in it great, though not insurmountable, resistances are interposed, which prevent the general, uniform distribution of excitation. Thus in normal people in a waking state excitation in the organ of ideation does not pass over to the organs of perception: such people do not hallucinate [cf. p. 189]. In the interests of the safety and efficiency of the organism, the nervous apparatuses of the complexes of organs which are of vital importance— the circulatory and digestive organs—are separated by strong resistances from the organs of ideation. Their independence is assured. They are not affected directly by ideas. But the resistances which prevent the passage of intracerebral excitation to the circulatory and digestive apparatuses vary in strength from one individual to another. All degrees of affective excitability are to be found between, on the one hand, the ideal (which is rarely met with to-day) of a man who is absolutely free from 'nerves', whose heart-action remains constant in every situation and is only affected by the particular work it has to perform, the man who has a good appetite and digestion, whatever danger he is in—between a man of this kind and, on the other hand, a 'nervous' man who has palpitations and diarrhoea on the smallest provocation.

However this may be, there are resistances in normal people

against the passage of cerebral excitation to the vegetative organs. These resistances correspond to the insulation of electrical conducting lines. At points at which they are abnormally weak they are broken through when the tension of cerebral excitation is high, and this—the affective excitation—passes over to the peripheral organs. There ensues an 'abnormal expression of emotion'.

Of the two factors which we have mentioned as being responsible for this result, one has already been discussed by us in detail. This first factor is a high degree of intracerebral excitation which has failed to be levelled down either by ideational activities or by motor discharge, or which is too great to be dealt with in this way.

The second factor is an abnormal weakness of the resistances in particular paths of conduction. This may be determined by the individual's initial constitution (innate disposition); or it may be determined by states of excitation of long duration which, as one might say, loosen the whole structure of his nervous system and lower all its resistances (pubertal disposition); or it may be determined by weakening influences, such as illness and under-nourishment (disposition due to states of exhaustion). The resistance of particular paths of conduction may be lowered by a previous illness of the organ concerned, which has facilitated the paths to and from the brain. A diseased heart is more susceptible to the influence of an affect than is a healthy one. 'I have a sounding-board in my abdomen', I was told by a woman who suffered from parametritis, 'if anything happens, it starts up my old pain.' (Disposition through local illness.)

The motor actions in which the excitation of affects is normally discharged are ordered and co-ordinated even though they are often useless. But an excessively strong excitation may by-pass or break through the co-ordinative centres and flow off in primitive movements. In infants, apart from the respiratory action of screaming, affects only produce and find expression in unco-ordinated contractions of the muscles of this primitive kind—in arching the body and kicking about. As development proceeds, the musculature passes more and more under the control of the power of co-ordination and the will. But the opisthotonus, which represents the maximum of motor effort of the total somatic musculature, and the clonic movements of kicking and threshing about, persist throughout life as the form of reaction for the maximal excitation of the brain— for the purely physical excitation in epileptic attacks as well as for the discharge of maximal affects in the shape of more or less epileptoid convulsions (viz. the purely motor part of hysterical attacks).

It is true that abnormal affective reactions of this kind are characteristic of hysteria. But they also occur apart from that illness. What they indicate is a more or less high degree of nervous disorder, not hysteria. Such phenomena cannot be described as hysterical if they appear as consequences of an affect which, though of great intensity, has an objective basis, but only if they appear with apparent spontaneity as manifestations of an illness. These latter, as many observations, including our own, have shown, are based on recollections which revive the original affect—or rather, *which would revive it if those reactions did not, in fact, occur instead.*

It may be taken for granted that a stream of ideas and recollections runs through the consciousness of any reasonably intelligent person while his mind is at rest. These ideas are so little vivid that they leave no trace behind in the memory and it is impossible afterwards to say how the associations occurred. If, however, an idea comes up that originally had a strong affect attached to it, that affect is revived with more or less intensity. The idea which is thus 'coloured' by affect emerges in consciousness clearly and vividly. The strength of the affect which can be released by a memory is very variable, according to the amount to which it has been exposed to 'wearing-away' by different influences, and especially according to the degree to which the original affect has been 'abreacted'. We pointed out in our 'Preliminary Communication' [p. 8] to what a varying extent the affect of anger at an insult, for instance, is called up by a recollection, according to whether the insult has been repaid or endured in silence. If the psychical reflex was fully achieved on the original occasion, the recollection of it releases a far smaller quantity of excitation.[1] If not, the

[1] The instinct of revenge, which is so powerful in the natural man and is disguised rather than repressed by civilization, is nothing whatever but the excitation of a reflex that has not been released. To defend oneself against injury in a fight and, in doing so, to injure one's

recollection is perpetually forcing on to the subject's lips the abusive words which were originally suppressed and which would have been the psychical reflex to the original stimulus.

If the original affect was discharged not in a normal but in an 'abnormal' reflex, this latter is equally released by recollection. The excitation arising from the affective idea is 'converted' (Freud) [1] into a somatic phenomenon.

Should this abnormal reflex become completely facilitated by frequent repetition, it may, it seems, drain away the operative force of the releasing ideas so totally that the affect itself emerges to a minimal extent only, or not at all. In such a case the 'hysterical conversion' is complete. The idea, moreover, which now no longer produces any psychical consequences, may be overlooked by the subject, or may be promptly forgotten if it emerges, like any other idea which is unaccompanied by affect.

It may be easier to accept the possibility of a cerebral excitation which should have given rise to an idea being replaced in this way by an excitation of some peripheral path, if we call to mind the inverse course of events which follows when a preformed reflex fails to occur. I will select an extremely trivial example—the sneezing reflex. If a stimulus of the mucous membrane of the nose fails for any reason to release this preformed

opponent is the adequate and preformed psychical reflex. If it has been carried out insufficiently or not at all, it is constantly released again by recollection, and the 'instinct of revenge' comes into being as an irrational volitional impulse, just as do all other 'instincts'. The proof of this lies precisely in the irrationality of the impulse, its divorce from any question of usefulness or expediency, indeed in its disregard of all considerations of the subject's own safety. As soon as the reflex has been released, the irrational nature of the impulse can become conscious.

> Ein andres Antlitz, eh sie geschehen,
> Ein anderes zeigt die vollbrachte Tat.

[Literally: 'A deed shows one countenance before it has happened and another after it has been accomplished.' Schiller, *Die Braut von Messina*, III, 5.]

[1] [Freud comments, near the beginning of his 'History of the Psycho-Analytic Movement' (1914*d*), on the appearance here of his name in brackets. He remarks that Breuer seemed to be implying that the priority for this piece of theory belonged to Freud. 'I believe,' he goes on, 'that actually the distinction relates only to the name, and that the conception came to us simultaneously and together.'—See also footnote 2, p. 86.]

reflex, a feeling of excitation and tension arises, as we all know. The excitation, which has been unable to flow off along motor paths, now, inhibiting all other activity, spreads over the brain. This everyday example gives us the pattern of what happens when a psychical reflex, even the most complicated one, fails to occur. The excitement which we have discussed above [pp. 205–6 n.] as characteristic of the instinct of revenge is in essentials the same. And we can follow the same process even up to the highest regions of human achievement. Goethe did not feel he had dealt with an experience till he had discharged it in creative artistic activity. This was in his case the preformed reflex belonging to affects, and so long as it had not been carried out the distressing increase in his excitation persisted.

Intracerebral excitation and the excitatory process in peripheral paths are of reciprocal magnitudes: the former increases if and so long as no reflex is released; it diminishes and disappears when it has been transformed into peripheral nervous excitation. Thus it seems understandable that no observable affect is generated if the idea that should have given rise to it immediately releases an abnormal reflex into which the excitation flows away as soon as it is generated. The 'hysterical conversion' is then complete. The original intracerebral excitation belonging to the affect has been transformed into the excitatory process in the peripheral paths. What was originally an affective idea now no longer provokes the affect but only the abnormal reflex.[1]

We have now gone a step beyond the 'abnormal expression of the emotions'. Hysterical phenomena (abnormal reflexes) do not seem to be ideogenic even to intelligent patients who are good observers, because the idea that gave rise to them is no longer coloured with affect and no longer marked out among

---

[1] I am anxious not to drive the analogy with an electrical system to death. In view of the totally dissimilar conditions it can scarcely illustrate the processes in the nervous system, and can certainly not explain them. But I may once more recall the case in which, owing to excessively high tension, the insulation of the wires in a lighting system breaks down and a 'short circuit' occurs at some point in it. If electrical phenomena (such as overheating or sparking) occur at this point, the lamp to which the wire leads fails to light. In just the same way, the affect fails to appear if the excitation flows away in an abnormal reflex and is converted into a somatic phenomenon.

other ideas and memories. They emerge as purely somatic phenomena, apparently without psychical roots.

What is it that determines the discharge of affect in such a way that one particular abnormal reflex is produced rather than some other? Our observations answer this question in many instances by showing that here again the discharge follows the 'principle of least resistance' and takes place along those paths whose resistances have already been weakened by concurrent circumstances. This covers the case which we have already mentioned [p. 204] of a particular reflex being facilitated by already-existing somatic illness. If, for instance, someone suffers often from cardiac pains, these will also be provoked by affects. Alternatively, a reflex may be facilitated by the fact that the muscular innervation concerned was deliberately intended at the moment at which the affect originally occurred. Thus, Anna O. (in our first case history) [p. 38] tried, in her fright, to stretch out her right arm that had gone to sleep owing to pressure against the back of the chair, in order to ward off the snake; and from that time on the tetanus in her right arm was provoked by the sight of any snake-like object. Or again [pp. 39–40], in her emotion, she brought her eyes forcibly together in order to read the hands of the watch, and thereupon a convergent squint became one of the reflexes of that affect. And so on.

This is due to the operation of simultaneity, which, indeed, governs our normal associations. Every sense-perception calls back into consciousness any other sense-perception that appeared originally at the same time. (Cf. the text-book example of the visual image of a sheep and the sound of its bleating, etc.) If the original affect was accompanied by a vivid sense-impression, the latter is called up once more when the affect is repeated; and since it is a question of discharging excessively great excitation, the sense-impression emerges, not as a recollection, but as a hallucination. Almost all our case histories provide instances of this. It is also what happened in the case of a woman who experienced a painful affect at a time when she was having violent toothache due to periostitis, and who thenceforward suffered from infra-orbital neuralgia whenever the affect was renewed or even recollected [pp. 176–9].

What we have here is the facilitation of abnormal reflexes

according to the general laws of association. But sometimes (though, it must be admitted, only in higher degrees of hysteria) true sequences of associated ideas lie between the affect and its reflex. Here we have *determination through symbolism*. What unites the affect and its reflex is often some ridiculous play upon words or associations by sound, but this only happens in dream-like states when the critical powers are low and lies outside the group of phenomena with which we are here dealing.

In a large number of cases the path taken by the train of determination remains unintelligible to us, because we often have a very incomplete insight into the patient's mental state and an imperfect knowledge of the ideas which were active at the time of the origin of the hysterical phenomenon. But we may assume that the process is not entirely unlike what we can observe clearly in more favourable cases.

The experiences which released the original affect, the excitation of which was then converted into a somatic phenomenon, are described by us as *psychical traumas*, and the pathological manifestation arising in this way, as *hysterical symptoms of traumatic origin*. (The term 'traumatic hysteria' has already been applied to phenomena which, as being consequences of physical injuries—traumas in the narrowest sense of the word—form part of the class of 'traumatic neuroses'.)

The genesis of hysterical phenomena that are determined by traumas finds a perfect analogy in the hysterical conversion of the psychical excitation which originates, not from external stimuli nor from the inhibition of normal psychical reflexes, but from the inhibition of the course of association. The simplest example and model of this is afforded by the excitation which arises when we cannot recollect a name or cannot solve a riddle, and so on. If someone tells us the name or gives us the answer to the riddle, the chain of associations is ended, and the excitation vanishes, just as it does on the ending of a reflex chain. The strength of the excitation caused by the blocking of a line of associations is in direct ratio to the interest which we take in them—that is, to the degree to which they set our will in motion. Since, however, the search for a solution of the problem, or whatever it may be, always involves a large amount of work, though it may be to no purpose, even a powerful excitation finds employment and does not press for discharge, and consequently never becomes pathogenic.

It does, however, become pathogenic if the course of associations is inhibited owing to ideas of equal importance being irreconcilable—if, for instance, fresh thoughts come into conflict with old-established ideational complexes. Such are the torments of religious doubt to which many people succumb and many more succumbed in the past. Even in such cases, however, the excitation and the accompanying psychical pain (the feeling of unpleasure) only reach any considerable height if some volitional interest of the subject's comes into play—if, for instance, a doubter feels himself threatened in the matter of his happiness or his salvation. Such a factor is always present, however, when the conflict is one between firmly-rooted complexes of moral ideas in which one has been brought up and the recollection of actions or merely thoughts of one's own which are irreconcilable with them; when, in other words, one feels the pangs of conscience. The volitional interest in being pleased with one's own personality and satisfied with it comes into operation here and increases to the highest degree the excitation due to the inhibition of associations. It is a matter of everyday experience that a conflict like this between irreconcilable ideas has a pathogenic effect. What are mostly in question are ideas and processes connected with sexual life: masturbation in an adolescent with moral sensibilities; or, in a strictly conscientious married woman, becoming aware of an attraction to a man who is not her husband. Indeed, the first emergence of sexual feelings and ideas is very often in itself enough to bring about an intense state of excitation, owing to its conflicting with a deeply-rooted idea of moral purity.[1]

A state of excitation of this kind is usually followed by psychical consequences, such as pathological depression and anxiety-states (Freud [1895b]). Sometimes, however, concurrent circumstances bring about an abnormal somatic phenomenon in which the excitation is discharged. Thus there may be vomiting when the feeling of uncleanness produces a physical feeling of nausea, or a *tussis nervosa*, as in Anna O. (Case History 1 [pp. 43–4]), when moral anxiety provokes a spasm of the glottis, and so on.[2]

---

[1] Cf. on this point some interesting observations and comments by Benedikt [1894, 51 ff.].

[2] Compare a passage in Mach's 'Bewegungsempfindungen' [1875] which deserves to be recalled in this connection: 'It has often been found during the experiments (on giddiness) which I have described,

There is a normal, appropriate reaction to excitation caused by very vivid and irreconcilable ideas—namely, to communicate them by speech. An amusingly exaggerated picture of the urge to do this is given in the story of Midas's barber, who spoke his secret aloud to the reeds.[1] We meet the same urge as one of the basic factors of a major historical institution—the Roman Catholic confessional. Telling things is a relief; it discharges tension even when the person to whom they are told is not a priest and even when no absolution follows. If the excitation is denied this outlet it is sometimes converted into a somatic phenomenon, just as is the excitation belonging to traumatic affects. The whole group of hysterical phenomena that originate in this way may be described, with Freud, as *hysterical phenomena of retention*.[2]

The account that we have hitherto given of the mechanism by which hysterical phenomena originate is open to the criticism that it is too schematic and simplifies the facts. In order that a healthy person who is not initially neuropathic may develop a genuine hysterical symptom, with its apparent independence of the mind and with a somatic existence in its own right, there must always be a number of concurrent circumstances.

The following case will serve as an example of the complicated nature of the process. A twelve-year-old boy, who had previously suffered from *pavor nocturnus* and whose father was highly neurotic, came home from school one day feeling unwell. He complained of difficulty in swallowing and headache.

that in general a feeling of nausea set in if it was difficult to bring the sensations of movement into harmony with the optical impressions. It appeared as though a part of the stimulus proceeding from the labyrinth had been compelled to leave the optic tracts, which were closed to it on account of another stimulus, and to enter upon quite other tracts . . . I have also repeatedly observed a feeling of nausea in making an attempt to combine stereoscopic images which are widely separated.'

Here we have nothing less than the physiological pattern for the generation of pathological, hysterical phenomena as a result of the co-existence of vivid ideas which are irreconcilable with one another.

[1] [Viz.: 'King Midas has ass's ears.']

[2] [The first publication in which Freud used the term 'retention hysteria' was his first paper on the 'Neuro-Psychoses of Defence' (1894a, Section I). It was briefly mentioned on pp. 162 and 171 above, and is discussed at greater length below on pp. 285–6, where Freud appears to attribute the term jointly to Breuer and himself, and where, incidentally, he throws doubts on the importance of the concept.]

The family doctor assumed that the cause was a sore throat. But the condition did not improve even after several days. The boy refused food and vomited when it was pressed on him. He moved about listlessly, without energy or enjoyment; he wanted to lie in bed all the time and was very much run down physically. When I saw him five weeks later, he gave the impression of being a shy and shut-in child, and I became convinced that his condition had a psychical basis. On being questioned closely, he brought up a trivial explanation—a severe reproof given by his father—which had clearly not been the real cause of his illness. Nor could anything be learnt from his school. I promised that I would extract the information later under hypnosis. This, however, turned out to be unnecessary. In response to strong appeals from his clever and energetic mother, he burst into tears and told the following story. While he was on his way home from school he had gone into a urinal, and a man had held out his penis to him and asked him to take it into his mouth. He had run away in terror, and nothing else had happened to him. But he was ill from that instant. As soon as he had made his confession he recovered completely.—In order to produce the anorexia, the difficulty in swallowing and the vomiting, several factors were required: the boy's innate neurotic nature, his severe fright, the irruption of sexuality in its crudest form into his childish temperament and, as the specifically determining factor, the idea of disgust. The illness owed its persistence to the boy's silence, which prevented the excitation from finding its normal outlet.

In all other cases, as in this one, there must be a convergence of several factors before a hysterical symptom can be generated in anyone who has hitherto been normal. Such symptoms are invariably 'overdetermined', to use Freud's expression.[1]

It may be assumed that an overdetermination of this sort is also present when the same affect has been called out by a series of several provoking causes. The patient and those about him

[1] [This seems to be the first published appearance of the term 'überdeterminiert', which is used by Freud himself below on p. 263. On p. 290 he uses the synonymous German word 'überbestimmt', and this already occurs in his monograph on aphasia (1891b, 76) in a passage on learning to speak which will be found translated in an appendix to the paper on 'The Unconscious' (1915e), Standard Ed., 14. It is, it must be added, unlikely that the notion of multiple causation should never have been expressed earlier by other writers in similar terminology.]

attribute the hysterical symptom only to the last cause, though that cause has as a rule merely brought to light something that had already been almost accomplished by other traumas.

A girl of seventeen[1] had her first hysterical attack (which was followed by a number of others) when a cat jumped on her shoulder in the dark. The attack seemed simply to be the result of fright. Closer investigation showed, however, that the girl, who was particularly good-looking and was not properly looked after, had recently had a number of more or less brutal attempts made on her, and had herself been sexually excited by them. (Here we have the factor of disposition.) A few days before, a young man had attacked her on the same dark staircase and she had escaped from him with difficulty. This was the actual psychical trauma, which the cat did no more than make manifest. But it is to be feared that in many such cases the cat is regarded as the *causa efficiens*.

In order for the repetition of an affect to bring about a conversion in this way, it is not always necessary that there should be a number of *external* provoking causes; the renewal of the affect in *memory* is often also enough, if the recollection is repeated rapidly and frequently, immediately after the trauma and before its affect has become weakened. This is enough if the affect was a very powerful one. Such is the case in traumatic hysteria, in the narrower sense of the word. During the days following a railway accident, for instance, the subject will live through his frightful experiences again both in sleeping and waking, and always with the renewed affect of fright, till at last, after this period of 'psychical working-out [*élaboration*]' (in Charcot's phrase [cf. p. 134]) or of 'incubation', conversion into a somatic phenomenon takes place. (Though there is another factor concerned which we shall have to discuss later.)

As a rule, however, an affective idea is promptly subjected to 'wearing away', to all the influences touched on in our 'Preliminary Communication' (p. 9), which deprive it little by little of its quota of affect.[2] Its revival causes an

[1] I have to thank Herr Assistent Dr. Paul Karplus for this case.

[2] ['*Affektwert*' (here and a few lines lower down), literally 'affective value'. This is an approximate synonym for '*Affektbetrag*', as is shown by a sentence in Freud's paper in French on organic and hysterical paralyses (1893c). He there uses the words '*valeur affective*' and adds in parenthesis the German '*Affektbetrag*'. This latter term is regularly translated here as 'quota of affect', e.g. on p. 166.]

ever-diminishing amount of excitation, and the recollection thus loses the capacity to contribute to the production of a somatic phenomenon. The facilitation of the abnormal reflex disappears and the *status quo ante* is thereupon re-established.

The 'wearing-away' influences, however, are all of them effects of association, of thinking, of corrections by reference to other ideas. This process of correction becomes impossible if the affective idea is withdrawn from 'associative contact'. When this happens the idea retains its whole quota of affect. Since at every renewal the whole sum of excitation of the original affect is liberated once more, the facilitation of the abnormal reflex that was started at the time is finally completed; or, if the facilitation was already complete, it is maintained and stabilized. The phenomenon of hysterical conversion is in this way permanently established.

Our observations show two ways in which affective ideas can be excluded from association.

The first is 'defence',[1] the deliberate suppression of distressing ideas which seem to the subject to threaten his happiness or his self-esteem. In his [first] paper on 'The Neuro-Psychoses of Defence' (1894*a*) and in his case histories in the present volume, Freud has discussed this process, which undoubtedly possesses very high pathological significance. We cannot, it is true, understand how an idea can be deliberately repressed from consciousness. But we are perfectly familiar with the corresponding positive process, that of concentrating attention on an idea, and we are just as unable to say how we effect *that*. Ideas, then, from which consciousness is diverted, which are not thought about, are also withdrawn from the wearing-away process and retain their quota of affect undiminished.

We have further found that there is another kind of idea that remains exempt from being worn away by thought. This may happen, not because one does not *want* to remember the idea, but because one *cannot* remember it: because it originally emerged and was endowed with affect in states in respect of which there is amnesia in waking consciousness—that is, in hypnosis or in states similar to it. The latter seem to be of the highest importance for the theory of hysteria, and accordingly deserve a somewhat fuller examination.[2]

[1] [See footnote, p. 10.]

[2] When, here and later on, we speak of ideas that are currently present

(4) Hypnoid States

When, in our 'Preliminary Communication' [p. 12] we put forward the thesis that the basis and *sine qua non* of hysteria is the existence of hypnoid states, we were overlooking the fact that Moebius had already said exactly the same thing in 1890. 'The necessary condition for the (pathogenic) operation of ideas is, on the one hand, an innate—that is, hysterical—disposition and, on the other, a special frame of mind. We can only form an imprecise idea of this frame of mind. It must resemble a state of hypnosis; it must correspond to some kind of vacancy of consciousness in which an emerging idea meets with no resistance from any other—in which, so to speak, the field is clear for the first comer. We know that a state of this kind can be brought about not only by hypnotism but by emotional shock (fright, anger, etc.) and by exhausting factors (sleeplessness, hunger, and so on).' [Moebius, 1894, 17.]

The problem to whose solution Moebius was here making a tentative approach is that of the generating of somatic phenomena by ideas. He here recalls the ease with which this can occur under hypnosis, and regards the operation of affects as analogous. Our own, somewhat different, view on the operation of the affects has been fully explained above [p. 201 ff.]. I need not, therefore, enter further into the difficulty involved in Moebius's assumption that in anger there is a 'vacancy of consciousness' [1] (which admittedly exists in fright and prolonged anxiety) or into the more general difficulty of drawing an analogy between the state of excitation in an affect and the quiescent state in hypnosis. We shall come back later [p. 220], however, to these remarks by Moebius, which in my opinion embody an important truth.

and operative but yet unconscious, we are seldom concerned with *single* ideas (such as the big snake hallucinated by Anna O. which started her contracture). It is almost always a question of *complexes* of ideas, of recollections of external events and trains of thought of the subject's own. It may sometimes happen that every one of the individual ideas comprised in such a complex of ideas is thought of consciously, and that what is exiled from consciousness is only the particular combination of them.

[1] It is possible that by this description Moebius means nothing else than the inhibition of the current of ideas—an inhibition which certainly occurs in the case of affects, though owing to entirely different causes from those operating in hypnosis.

For us, the importance of these states which resemble hypnosis—'hypnoid' states—lies, in addition and most especially, in the amnesia that accompanies them and in their power to bring about the splitting of the mind which we shall discuss presently and which is of fundamental significance for 'major hysteria'. We still attribute this importance to hypnoid states. But I must add a substantial qualification to our thesis. Conversion—the ideogenic production of somatic phenomena—can also come about apart from hypnoid states. Freud has found in the deliberate amnesia of defence a second source, independent of hypnoid states, for the construction of ideational complexes which are excluded from associative contact. But, accepting this qualification, I am still of opinion that hypnoid states are the cause and necessary condition of many, indeed of most, major and complex hysterias.

First and foremost, of course, among hypnoid states are to be numbered true auto-hypnoses, which are distinguished from artificial hypnoses only by the fact of their originating spontaneously. We find them in a number of fully-developed hysterias, occurring with varying frequency and duration, and often alternating rapidly with normal waking states (cf. Case Histories 1 and 2). On account of the dream-like nature of their content, they often deserve the name of '*delirium hystericum*'. What happens during auto-hypnotic states is subject to more or less total amnesia in waking life (whereas it is completely remembered in artificial hypnosis). The amnesia withdraws the psychical products of these states, the associations that have been formed in them, from any correction during waking thought; and since in auto-hypnosis criticism and supervision by reference to other ideas is diminished, and, as a rule, disappears almost completely, the wildest delusions may arise from it and remain untouched for long periods. Thus it is almost only in these states that there arises a somewhat complicated irrational 'symbolic relation between the precipitating cause and the pathological phenomenon' [p. 5], which, indeed, is often based on the most absurd similarities of sound and verbal associations. The absence of criticism in auto-hypnotic states is the reason why auto-suggestions so frequently arise from them— as, for instance, when a paralysis remains behind after a hysterical attack. But, and this may be merely by chance, we have scarcely ever in our analyses come across an instance of a hysterical phenomenon originating in this manner. We have always found it happen, in auto-hypnosis no less than outside it, as a result of the same process—namely, conversion of an affective excitation.

In any case, this 'hysterical conversion' takes place more easily in auto-hypnosis than in the waking state, just as suggested ideas are realized physically as hallucinations and movements so much more easily in artificial hypnosis. Nevertheless the process of conversion of excitation is essentially the same as has been described above. When once it has taken place, the somatic phenomenon is repeated if the affect and the auto-hypnosis occur simultaneously. And in that case it seems as though the hypnotic state has been called up by the affect itself. Accordingly, so long as there is a clear-cut alternation between hypnosis and full waking life, the hysterical symptom remains restricted to the hypnotic state and is strengthened there by repetition; moreover, the idea that gave rise to it is exempt from correction by waking thoughts and their criticism, precisely because it never emerges in clear waking life.

Thus with Anna O. (Case History 1) the contracture of her right arm, which was associated in her auto-hypnosis with the affect of anxiety and the idea of the snake, remained for four months restricted to the moments during which she was in a hypnotic state (or, if we consider this term inappropriate for *absences* of very short duration, a hypnoid one), though it recurred frequently. The same thing happened with other conversions that were carried out in her hypnoid state; and in this way the great complex of hysterical phenomena grew up in a condition of complete latency and came into the open when her hypnoid state became permanent. [Cf. p. 42 f.]

The phenomena which have arisen in this way emerge into clear consciousness only when the split in the mind, which I shall discuss later, has been completed, and when the alternation between waking and hypnoid states has been replaced by a co-existence between the normal and the hypnoid complexes of ideas.

Are hypnoid states of this kind in existence before the patient falls ill, and how do they come about? I can say very little about this, for apart from the case of Anna O. we have no observations at our disposal which might throw light on the point. It seems certain that with her the auto-hypnosis had the way paved for it by habitual reveries and that it was fully established by an affect of protracted anxiety, which, indeed, would itself be the basis for a hypnoid state. It seems not improbable that this process holds good fairly generally.

A great variety of states lead to 'absence of mind' but only a few of them predispose to auto-hypnosis or pass over immediately into it. An investigator who is deep in a problem is also no doubt anaesthetic to a certain degree, and he has large groups of sensations of which he forms no conscious perception; and the same is true of anyone who is using his creative imagination actively (cf. Anna O.'s 'private theatre' [p. 22]). But in such states energetic mental work is carried on, and the excitation of the nervous system which is liberated is used up in this work. In states of abstraction and dreaminess, on the other hand, intracerebral excitation sinks below its clear waking level. These states border on sleepiness and pass over into sleep. If during such a state of absorption, and while the flow of ideas is inhibited, a group of affectively-coloured ideas is active, it creates a high level of intracerebral excitation which is not used up by mental work and is at the disposal of abnormal functioning, such as conversion.

Thus neither 'absence of mind' during energetic work nor unemotional twilight states are pathogenic; on the other hand, reveries that are filled with emotion and states of fatigue arising from protracted affects *are* pathogenic. The broodings of a care-ridden man, the anxiety of a person watching at the sick-bed of someone dear to him, the day-dreams of a lover— these are states of this second kind. Concentration on the affective group of ideas begins by producing 'absence of mind'. The flow of ideas grows gradually slower and at last almost stagnates; but the affective idea and its affect remain active, and so consequently does the great quantity of excitation which is not being used up functionally. The similarity between this situation and the determinants of hypnosis seems unmistakable. The subject who is to be hypnotized must not really go to sleep, that is to say, his intracerebral excitation must not sink to the level of sleep; but his flow of ideas must be inhibited. When this is so, the whole mass of excitation is at the disposal of the suggested idea.

This is the way in which pathogenic auto-hypnosis would seem to come about in some people—by affect being introduced into a habitual reverie. This is perhaps one of the reasons why in the anamnesis of hysteria we so often come across the two great pathogenic factors of being in love and sick-nursing. In the former, the subject's longing thoughts about his absent loved one create in him a 'rapt' state of mind, cause his real environment to grow dim, and then bring his thinking to a standstill charged with affect; while in sick-nursing the quiet by which the subject is surrounded, his concentration on an object, his attention fixed on the patient's breathing—all this sets up precisely the conditions demanded by many hypnotic procedures and fills the twilight state produced in this way with the affect of anxiety. It is possible that these states differ only quantitatively from true auto-hypnoses and that they pass over into them.

Once this has happened, the hypnosis-like state is repeated again and again when the same circumstances arise; and the subject, instead of the normal *two* conditions of mind, has three: waking, sleeping and the hypnoid state. We find the same thing happening when deep artificial hypnosis has been frequently brought on.

I cannot say whether spontaneous hypnotic states may also be generated without an affect intervening in this way, as a result of an innate disposition; but I consider it very probable. When we see the difference in susceptibility to artificial hypnosis both among healthy and sick people and how easily it is brought on in some, it seems reasonable to suppose that in such people it can also appear spontaneously. And a disposition for this is perhaps necessary before a reverie can turn into an auto-hypnosis. I am therefore far from attributing to all hysterical patients the generating mechanism which we have been taught by Anna O.

I speak of hypnoid states rather than of hypnosis itself because it is so difficult to make a clear demarcation of these states, which play such an important part in the genesis of hysteria. We do not know whether reveries, which were described above as preliminary stages of auto-hypnosis, may not themselves be able to produce the same pathological effect as auto-hypnosis, and whether the same may not also be true of a protracted affect of anxiety. It is certainly true of fright. Since fright inhibits the flow of ideas at the same time at which an affective idea (of danger) is very active, it offers a complete parallel to a reverie charged with affect; and since the recollection of the affective idea, which is constantly being renewed, keeps on re-establishing this state of mind, 'hypnoid fright' comes into being, in which conversion is either brought about or stabilized. Here we have the incubation stage of 'traumatic hysteria' in the strict sense of the words.

In view of the fact that states of mind which are so different though they agree with one another in the most important respect can be classed with auto-hypnosis, it seems desirable to adopt the expression 'hypnoid', which lays stress on this internal similarity. It sums up the view put forward by Moebius in the passage quoted above [p. 215]. Most of all, however, it points to auto-hypnosis itself, the importance of which in the genesis of hysterical phenomena rests on the fact that it makes conversion easier and protects (by amnesia) the converted ideas from wearing-away—a protection which leads, ultimately, to an increase in the psychical splitting.

If a somatic symptom is caused by an idea and is repeatedly set going by it, we should expect that intelligent patients capable of self-observation would be conscious of the connection; they would know by experience that the somatic phenomenon appeared at the same time as the memory of a particular event. The underlying causal nexus is, it is true, unknown to them; but all of us always know what the idea is which makes us cry or laugh or blush, even though we have not the slightest understanding of the nervous mechanism of these ideogenic phenomena. Sometimes patients do really observe the connection and are conscious of it. For instance, a woman may say that her mild hysterical attack (trembling and palpitations, perhaps) comes from some great emotional disturbance and is repeated when, and only when, some event reminds her of it. But this is not the case with very many or indeed the majority of hysterical symptoms. Even intelligent patients are unaware that their symptoms arise as the result of an idea and regard them as physical phenomena on their own account. If it were otherwise the psychical theory of hysteria must already have reached a respectable age.

It would be plausible to believe that, though the symptoms in question were ideogenic in the first instance, the repetition of them has, to use Romberg's phrase [1840, 192], 'imprinted' them into the body, and they would now no longer be based on a psychical process but on modifications in the nervous system which have occurred in the meantime: they would have become self-sufficient, genuinely somatic symptoms.

This view is in itself neither untenable nor improbable. But I believe that the new light which our observations have thrown on the theory of hysteria lies precisely in its having shown that this view is inadequate to meet the facts, at any rate in many instances. We have seen that hysterical symptoms of the most various kinds which have lasted for many years 'immediately and permanently disappeared when we had succeeded in bringing clearly to light the memory of the event by which they were provoked and in arousing their accompanying affect, and when the patient had described that event in the greatest possible detail and had put the affect into words' [p. 6]. The case histories which have been reported in these pages provide some pieces of evidence in support of these assertions. 'We may reverse the dictum *"cessante causa cessat effectus"* ["when the cause ceases the effect ceases"], and conclude from these observations that the determining process' (that is, the recollection of it) 'continues to operate for years—not indirectly, through a chain of intermediate causal links, but as a *directly* releasing cause— just as a psychical pain that is remembered in waking consciousness still provokes a lachrymal secretion long after the event. Hysterics suffer mainly from reminiscences.' [P. 7.] But if this is so—if the memory of the psychical trauma must be regarded as operating as a contemporary agent, like a foreign body, long after its forcible entrance, and if nevertheless the patient has no consciousness of such memories or their emergence—then we must admit that *unconscious ideas exist and are operative*.

Moreover, when we come to analyse hysterical phenomena we do not only find such unconscious ideas *in isolation*. We must recognize the fact that in reality, as has been shown by the valuable work carried out by French investigators, large complexes of ideas and involved psychical processes with important consequences remain completely unconscious in a number of patients and co-exist with conscious mental life; we must recognize that there is such a thing as a splitting of psychical activity, and that this is of fundamental value for our understanding of complicated hysterias.

I may perhaps be allowed to explore this difficult and obscure region rather more fully. The need to establish the meaning of the terminology that has been used may to some extent excuse the theoretical discussion which follows.

(5) Unconscious Ideas and Ideas Inadmissible to Consciousness—Splitting of the Mind

We call those ideas conscious which we are aware of. There exists in human beings the strange fact of self-consciousness. We are able to view and observe, as though they were objects, ideas that emerge in us and succeed one another. This does not happen always, since occasions for self-observation are rare. But the capacity for it is present in everyone, for everyone can say: 'I thought this or that.' We describe as conscious those ideas which we observe as active in us, or which we should so observe if we attended to them. At any given moment of time there are very few of them; and if others, apart from those, should be current at the time, we should have to call them *unconscious* ideas.

It hardly seems necessary any longer to argue in favour of the existence of current ideas that are unconscious or sub-conscious.[1] They are among the commonest facts of everyday life. If I have forgotten to make one of my medical visits, I have feelings of lively unrest. I know from experience what this feeling means: that I have forgotten something. I search my memories in vain; I fail to discover the cause, till suddenly, hours later perhaps, it enters my consciousness. But I have been uneasy the whole time. Accordingly, the idea of the visit has been all the time operative, that is to say present, but not in my consciousness. Or again, a busy man may have been annoyed by something one morning. He is entirely absorbed by his office work; while he is doing it his conscious thoughts are fully occupied, and he gives no thought to his annoyance. But his decisions are influenced by it and he may well say 'no' where he would otherwise have said 'yes'. So in spite of everything this memory is operative, that is to say present. A great deal of what we describe as 'mood' comes from sources of this kind, from ideas that exist and are operative beneath the threshold

[1] [See footnote, p. 45.]

of consciousness. Indeed, the whole conduct of our life is constantly influenced by subconscious ideas. We can see every day how, where there is mental degeneration, as for instance in the initial stages of general paralysis, the inhibitions which normally restrain certain actions become weaker and disappear. But the patient who now makes indecent jokes in the presence of women was not, in his healthy days, prevented from doing so by conscious memories and reflections; he avoided it 'instinctively' and 'automatically'—that is to say, he was restrained by ideas which were called up by the impulse to behave in this way, but which remained beneath the threshold of consciousness, though they nevertheless inhibited the impulse.—All intuitive activity is directed by ideas which are to a large extent subconscious. For only the clearest and most intense ideas are perceived by self-consciousness, whilst the great mass of current but weaker ideas remains unconscious.

The objections that are raised against 'unconscious ideas' existing and being operative seem for the most part to be juggling with words. No doubt 'idea' is a word belonging to the terminology of conscious thinking, and 'unconscious idea' is therefore a self-contradictory expression. But the physical process which underlies an idea is the same in content and form (though not in quantity) whether the idea rises above the threshold of consciousness or remains beneath it. It would only be necessary to construct some such term as 'ideational substratum' in order to avoid the contradiction and to counter the objection.

Thus there seems to be no theoretical difficulty in also recognizing unconscious ideas as causes of pathological phenomena. But if we go into the matter more closely we come upon other difficulties. As a rule, when the intensity of an unconscious idea increases it enters consciousness *ipso facto*. Only when its intensity is slight does it remain unconscious. What seems hard to understand is how an idea can be sufficiently intense to provoke a lively motor act, for instance, and at the same time not intense enough to become conscious.

I have already [p. 205 f.] mentioned a view which should not, perhaps, be dismissed out of hand. On this view the clarity of our ideas, and consequently their capacity for being observed by our self-consciousness—that is, for being conscious—is determined, among other things, by the feelings of pleasure or unpleasure which they arouse, by their quota of affect.[1] When an idea immediately produces lively somatic consequences, this implies that the excitation engendered by it flows off into the paths concerned in these consequences, instead of, as would happen otherwise, becoming diffused in the brain; and precisely *because* this idea has physical consequences, because its sums of psychical stimuli have been 'converted' into somatic ones, it loses the clarity which would otherwise have marked it out in the stream of ideas. Instead of this it is lost among the rest.

Suppose, for instance, that someone has had a violent affect during a meal and has not 'abreacted' it. When subsequently he attempts to eat he is overtaken by choking and vomiting and these seem to him purely somatic symptoms. His hysterical vomiting continues for some considerable time. It disappears after the affect has been revived, described and reacted to under hypnosis. There can be no doubt that every attempt to eat called up the memory concerned. This memory started the vomiting but did not appear clearly in consciousness, because it was now without affect, whereas the vomiting absorbed the attention completely.

It is conceivable that the reason which has just been given explains why *some* ideas that release hysterical phenomena are not recognized as their causes. But this reason—the fact that ideas that have lost their affect because they have been converted are overlooked—cannot possibly explain why, in other cases, ideational complexes that are anything but devoid of affect do not enter consciousness. Numerous examples of this are to be found in our case histories.

In patients like these we found that it was the rule for the emotional disturbance—apprehensiveness, angry irritability, grief—to precede the appearance of the somatic symptom or to follow it immediately, and to increase, either until it was cleared up by being given utterance in words or until the affect and the somatic phenomenon gradually disappeared again. Where the former happened the quality of the affect always

---

[1] [Breuer seems here to be using the term 'affect', in a sense quite exceptional in the present volume (though one sometimes employed by other psychologists), to indicate specifically feelings of pleasure and unpleasure. The same word '*Affektwert*' is used by him above (p. 213f.) in his regular sense of an unspecified emotion or feeling.]

became quite understandable, even though its intensity could not fail to seem to a normal person (and to the patient himself, after it had been cleared up) to be out of all proportion. These, then, were ideas which were intense enough not merely to cause powerful somatic phenomena but also to call out the appropriate affect and to influence the course of association by bringing allied ideas into prominence—but which, in spite of all this, remained outside consciousness themselves. In order to bring them into consciousness hypnosis was necessary (as in Case Histories 1 and 2), or (as in Case Histories 4 and 5) a laborious search had to be made with strenuous help from the physician.

Ideas such as these which, though current, are unconscious, not because of their relatively small degree of liveliness, but in spite of their great intensity, may be described as ideas that are 'inadmissible to consciousness'.[1]

The existence of ideas of this kind that are inadmissible to consciousness is pathological. In normal people all ideas that can become current at all enter consciousness as well if they are sufficiently intense. In our patients we find a large complex of ideas that are admissible to consciousness existing side by side with a smaller complex of ideas that are not. Thus in them the field of ideational psychical activity does not coincide with potential consciousness. The latter is more restricted than the former. Their psychical ideational activity is divided into a conscious and an unconscious part, and their ideas are divided into some that are admissible and some that are inadmissible to consciousness. We cannot, therefore, speak of a splitting of consciousness, though we can of a *splitting of the mind*.

Conversely, these subconscious ideas cannot be influenced or corrected by conscious thought. They are very often concerned with experiences which have in the meantime lost their meaning—dread of events which did not occur, fright that turned

---

[1] This expression [*'Bewusstseinsunfähig'*] is not unambiguous and for that reason leaves much to be desired. It is, however, constructed on the analogy of *'Hoffähig'* ['admissible to Court', 'having the *entrée*'] and may in the meantime be used for lack of a better term. [Though on the analogy of *'Hoffähig'* the word is here translated *'inadmissible* to consciousness', its literal meaning is *'incapable* of consciousness'. It could equally well be translated 'incapable of being (or becoming) conscious'. The word was adopted by Freud and frequently used by him, and the context then often calls for one of these other renderings.]

to laughter or joy after a rescue. Such subsequent developments deprive the memory of all its affect so far as consciousness is concerned; but they leave the subconscious idea, which provokes somatic phenomena, completely untouched.

Perhaps I may be allowed to quote another example. A young married woman was for some time very much worried about her younger sister's future. As a result of this her period, normally regular, lasted for two weeks; she was tender in the left hypogastrium, and twice she found herself lying stiff on the floor, coming out of a 'faint'. There followed an ovarian neuralgia on the left side, with signs of a severe peritonitis. The absence of fever, and a contracture of the left leg (and of her back), showed that the illness was a *pseudo*-peritonitis; and when, a few years later, the patient died and an autopsy was performed, all that was found was a 'microcystic degeneration' of *both* ovaries without any traces of an old peritonitis. The severe symptoms disappeared by degrees and left behind an ovarian neuralgia, a contracture of the muscles of the back, so that her trunk was as stiff as a board, and a contracture of the left leg. The latter was got rid of under hypnosis by direct suggestion. The contracture of her back was unaffected by this. Meanwhile her younger sister's difficulties had been completely smoothed out and all her fears on that score had vanished. But the hysterical phenomena, which could only have been derived from them, persisted unaltered. It was tempting to suppose that what we were faced by were changes in innervation, which had assumed an independent status and were no longer attached to the idea that had caused them. But after the patient had been compelled under hypnosis to tell the whole story up to the time when she had fallen ill of 'peritonitis'— which she did most unwillingly—she immediately sat up in bed without assistance, and the contracture of her back disappeared for ever. (Her ovarian neuralgia, which was undoubtedly much older in its origin, remained unaffected.) Thus we see that her pathogenic anxious idea had persisted in active operation for months on end, and that it had been completely inaccessible to any correction by actual events.

If we are obliged to recognize the existence of ideational complexes that never enter consciousness and are not influenced by conscious thought, we shall have admitted that, even in such simple cases of hysteria as the one I have just described, there is a splitting of the mind into two relatively independent portions. I do not assert that everything that we call hysterical has a splitting of this kind as its basis and necessary condition; but I *do* assert that 'the splitting of psychical activity which is so striking in the well-known cases in the form of *"double conscience"* is present to a rudimentary degree in every major hysteria', and that 'the liability and tendency to such a dissociation is the basic phenomenon of this neurosis'.[1]

But before entering into a discussion of this subject, I must add a comment with regard to the unconscious ideas which produce somatic effects. Many hysterical phenomena last continuously for a long time, like the contracture in the case described above. Should we and may we suppose that during all this time the causative idea is perpetually active and currently present? I think so. It is true that in healthy people we see their psychical activity going forward to the accompaniment of a rapid change of ideas. But we find sufferers from severe melancholia immersed continuously for long periods in the same distressing idea which is perpetually active and present. Indeed, we may well believe that even when a healthy person has a great care on his mind it is present all the time, since it governs his facial expression even when his consciousness is filled with other thoughts. But the portion of psychical activity which is separated off in hysterical subjects and which we think of as filled with unconscious ideas contains as a rule such a meagre store of them and is so inaccessible to interchange with external impressions that it is easy to believe that a single idea can be permanently active in it.

If it seems to us, as it does to Binet and Janet, that what lies at the centre of hysteria is a splitting off of a portion of psychical activity, it is our duty to be as clear as possible on this subject. It is only too easy to fall into a habit of thought which assumes that every substantive has a substance behind it—which gradually comes to regard 'consciousness' as standing for some actual thing; and when we have become accustomed to make use metaphorically of spatial relations, as in the term

---

[1] [This passage, which is in inverted commas in the original but has no page reference, is a slightly modified version of a sentence which will be found in italics on p. 12 of the 'Preliminary Communication'.]

'sub-consciousness', we find as time goes on that we have actually formed an idea which has lost its metaphorical nature and which we can manipulate easily as though it was real. Our mythology is then complete.

All our thinking tends to be accompanied and aided by spatial ideas, and we talk in spatial metaphors. Thus when we speak of ideas which are found in the region of clear consciousness and of unconscious ones which never enter the full light of self-consciousness, we almost inevitably form pictures of a tree with its trunk in daylight and its roots in darkness, or of a building with its dark underground cellars. If, however, we constantly bear in mind that all such spatial relations are metaphorical and do not allow ourselves to be misled into supposing that these relations are literally present in the brain, we may nevertheless speak of a consciousness and a subconsciousness. But only on this condition.

We shall be safe from the danger of allowing ourselves to be tricked by our own figures of speech if we always remember that after all it is in the same brain, and most probably in the same cerebral cortex, that conscious and unconscious ideas alike have their origin.[1] How this is possible we cannot say. But then we know so little of the psychical activity of the cerebral cortex that one puzzling complication the more scarcely increases our limitless ignorance. We must take it as a fact that in hysterical patients a part of their psychical activity is inaccessible to perception by the self-consciousness of the waking individual and that their mind is thus split.

A universally known example of a division of psychical activity like this is to be seen in hysterical attacks in some of their forms and stages. At their beginning, conscious thought is often extinguished; but afterwards it gradually awakens. Many intelligent patients admit that their conscious ego was quite lucid during the attack and looked on with curiosity and surprise at all the mad things they did and said. Such patients have, furthermore, the (erroneous) belief that with a little goodwill they could have inhibited the attack, and they are inclined to blame themselves for it. 'They need not have behaved like that.' (Their self-reproaches of being guilty of simulation are

----

[1] [Cf. some remarks to a similar effect towards the end of the last paragraph but one of Freud's preface to his translation of Bernheim's *De la suggestion* (Freud, 1888–9).]

also to a great extent based on this feeling.)[1] But when the next
attack comes on, the conscious ego is as little able to control
what happens as in earlier ones.—Here we have a situation
in which the thought and ideation of the conscious waking ego
stands alongside of the ideas which normally reside in the darkness of the unconscious but which have now gained control
over the muscular apparatus and over speech, and indeed even
over a large part of ideational activity itself: the splitting of the
mind is manifest.

It may be remarked that the findings of Binet and Janet
deserve to be described as a splitting not merely of psychical
activity but of consciousness. As we know, these observers have
succeeded in getting into contact with their patients' 'subconsciousness', with the portion of psychical activity of which
the conscious waking ego knows nothing; and they have been
able in some of their cases to demonstrate the presence of all
the psychical functions, including self-consciousness, in that
portion, since it has access to the memory of earlier psychical
events. This half of a mind is therefore quite complete and
conscious in itself. In our cases the part of the mind which is
split off is 'thrust into darkness',[2] as the Titans are imprisoned
in the crater of Etna, and can shake the earth but can never
emerge into the light of day. In Janet's cases the division of the
realm of the mind has been a total one. Nevertheless, there is
still inequality in status. But this, too, disappears when the
two halves of consciousness alternate, as they do in the well-
known cases of *double conscience*, and when they do not differ in
their functional capability.

But let us return to the ideas which we have shown in our
patients as the causes of their hysterical phenomena. It is far
from being possible for us simply to describe them all as being
'unconscious' and 'inadmissible to consciousness'. They form
an almost unbroken scale, passing through every gradation of
vagueness and obscurity, between perfectly conscious ideas
which release an unusual reflex and those which never enter
consciousness in waking life but only in hypnosis. In spite of
this, we regard it as established that a splitting of psychical

[1] [These points are exemplified in the case of Anna O. See above,
p. 46.]

[2] ['*In die Finsternis gebracht*', a phrase used by Mephistopheles of himself, in *Faust*, Part I (Scene 4).]

activity occurs in the more severe degrees of hysteria and that it alone seems to make a psychical theory of the illness possible.

What, then, can be asserted or suspected with probability about the causes and origin of this phenomenon?

Janet, to whom the theory of hysteria owes so very much and with whom we are in agreement in most respects, has expressed a view on this point which we are unable to accept.

Janet's view is the following.[1] He considers that the 'splitting of a personality' rests on an innate psychological weakness ('*insuffisance psychologique*'). All normal mental activity pre-supposes a certain capacity for 'synthesis', the ability to unite several ideas into a complex. The combination of the various sense-perceptions into a picture of the environment is already a synthetic activity of this kind. This mental function is found to be far below the normal in hysterical patients. If a normal person's attention is directed as fully as possible upon some point, e.g. upon a perception by a single sense, it is true that he temporarily loses the capacity to apperceive impressions from the other senses—that is, to take them up into his conscious thought. But in hysterical subjects this happens without any special concentration of the attention. As soon as they perceive anything they are inaccessible to other sense-perceptions. Indeed, they are not even in a position to take in together a number of impressions coming from a *single* sense. They can, for instance, only apperceive tactile sensations in one half of the body; those from the other side reach the centre and are used for the co-ordination of movement, but are not apperceived. A person like this is hemi-anaesthetic. In normal people, an idea calls into consciousness a great number of others by association; these may be related to the first one, for instance, in a confirmatory or an inhibiting manner, and only the most vivid ideas are so extremely powerful that their associations remain below the threshold of consciousness. In hysterical people this is always the case. Every idea takes possession of the whole of their limited mental activity, and this accounts

[1] [The account of Janet's views which follows seems to be derived principally from the concluding chapter of Janet, 1894. This chapter was a reprint of a paper published in the *Archives de Neurologie* in 1893 (June and July) which was largely concerned with the Breuer and Freud 'Preliminary Communication'. Cf. also above, p. 104.]

for their excessive affectivity. This characteristic of their mind is described by Janet as the 'restriction of the field of consciousness' of hysterical patients, on the analogy of a 'restriction of the field of vision'. For the most part the sense-impressions that are not apperceived and the ideas that are aroused but do not enter consciousness cease without producing further consequences. Sometimes, however, they accumulate and form complexes [1]—mental strata withdrawn from consciousness; they form a subconsciousness. Hysteria, which is essentially based on this splitting of the mind, is a *'maladie par faiblesse'* ['disease due to weakness'], and that is why it develops most readily when a mind which is innately weak is submitted to influences that weaken it still further or is faced by heavy demands in relation to which its weakness stands out still more.

Janet's opinions, as thus summarized, already give his answer to the important question as to the disposition to hysteria—as to the nature of the *typus hystericus* (taking the term in the sense in which we speak of a *typus phthisicus*, by which we understand the long narrow thorax, the small heart, etc.). Janet regards a particular form of congenital mental weakness as the disposition to hysteria. In reply, we should like to formulate our own view briefly as follows. It is not the case that the splitting of consciousness occurs because the patients are weak-minded; they appear to be weak-minded because their mental activity is divided and only a part of its capacity is at the disposal of their conscious thought. We cannot regard mental weakness as the *typus hystericus*, as the essence of the disposition to hysteria.

An example makes plain what is intended by the first of these two sentences. We were frequently able to observe the following course of events with one of our patients (Frau Cäcilie M.). While she was feeling comparatively well a hysterical symptom would appear—a tormenting, obsessive hallucination, a neuralgia, or something of the kind—and would for some time increase in intensity. Simultaneously the patient's mental capacity would continuously decrease, and after a few days any uninitiated observer would have been bound to call her weak-minded. She would then be relieved of the unconscious idea

---

[1] [This use of the word 'complex' seems to come very close to that which Jung is generally regarded as having introduced some ten years later. Cf. Part II of Freud's 'History of the Psycho-Analytic Movement' (1914*d*).]

(the memory of a psychical trauma, often belonging to the remote past), either by the physician under hypnosis or by her suddenly describing the event in a state of agitation and to the accompaniment of a lively emotion. When this had happened she did not merely become quiet and cheerful and free from the tormenting symptom; it was always astonishing to observe the width and clarity of her intellect and the acuteness of her understanding and judgement. Chess, which she played excellently, was a favourite occupation of hers, and she enjoyed playing two games at a time, which can scarcely be regarded as indicating a lack of mental synthesis. It was impossible to escape the impression that during a course of events such as we have just described the unconscious idea drew to itself an ever-increasing portion of her psychical activity and that the more this happened the smaller became the part played by conscious thought, till it was reduced to total imbecility; but that when, to use the remarkably apt Viennese expression, she was '*beisammen*' [literally 'together', meaning 'in one's right mind'], she possessed quite remarkable mental powers.

As a comparable state in normal people we would adduce, not concentration of attention, but *preoccupation*. If someone is 'preoccupied' by some vivid idea, such as a worry, his mental capacity is similarly reduced.

Every observer is largely under the influence of the subjects of his observation, and we are inclined to believe that Janet's views were mainly formed in the course of a detailed study of the feeble-minded hysterical patients who are to be found in hospitals or institutions because they have not been able to hold their own in life on account of their illness and the mental weakness caused by it. Our own observations, carried out on educated hysterical patients, have forced us to take an essentially different view of their minds. In our opinion 'among hysterics may be found people of the clearest intellect, strongest will, greatest character and highest critical power' [cf. p. 13]. No amount of genuine, solid mental endowment is excluded by hysteria, though actual achievements are often made impossible by the illness. After all, the patron saint of hysteria, St. Theresa, was a woman of genius with great practical capacity.

But on the other hand no degree of silliness, incompetence and weakness of will is a protection against hysteria. Even if we disregard what is merely a *result* of the illness, we must recognize the type of feeble-minded hysteric as a common one. Yet even so, what we find here is not torpid, phlegmatic stupidity but an excessive degree of mental mobility which leads to inefficiency. I shall discuss later the question of innate disposition. Here I merely propose to show that Janet's opinion that mental weakness is in any way at the root of hysteria and splitting of the mind is untenable.[1]

In complete opposition to Janet's views, I believe that in a great many cases what underlies dissociation is an *excess* of efficiency, the habitual co-existence of two heterogeneous trains of ideas. It has frequently been pointed out that we are often not merely 'mechanically' active while our conscious thought is occupied by trains of ideas which have nothing in common with our activity, but that we are also capable of what is undoubtedly psychical functioning while our thoughts are 'busy elsewhere'—as, for instance, when we read aloud correctly and with the appropriate intonation, but afterwards have not the slightest idea of what we have been reading.

There are no doubt a whole number of activities, from mechanical ones such as knitting or playing scales, to some requiring at least a small degree of mental functioning, all of which are performed by many people with only half their mind on them. This is specially true of people who are of a very lively disposition, to whom monotonous, simple and uninteresting occupation is a torture, and who actually begin by deliberately amusing themselves with thinking of something different (cf. Anna O.'s 'private theatre' [p. 22]). Another situation, but a similar one, occurs when an interesting set of ideas, derived for instance from books or plays, forces itself upon the subject's attention and intrudes into his thoughts. This intrusion is still more vigorous if the extraneous set of ideas is strongly coloured with affect (e.g. worry or the longing of someone in love). We then have the state of preoccupation that I have touched upon above, which, however, does not prevent many people from performing fairly complicated actions. Social circumstances often necessitate a duplication of this kind even when the thoughts involved are of an exacting kind, as for instance when a woman who is in the throes of extreme worry or of passionate

[1] [Cf. in this connection Freud's remarks on Frau Emmy von N. (p. 103 ff.).]

excitement carries out her social duties and the functions of an affable hostess. We all of us manage minor achievements of this kind in the course of our work; and self-observation seems always to show that the affective group of ideas are not merely aroused from time to time by association but are present in the mind all the time and enter consciousness unless it is taken up with some external impression or act of will.

Even in people who do not habitually allow day-dreams to pass through their minds alongside their usual activity, some situations give rise during considerable periods of time to this simultaneous existence of changing impressions and reactions from external life on the one hand, and an affectively-coloured group of ideas on the other. *Post equitem sedet atra cura* ['black care sits behind the rider'].[1] Among these situations the most prominent are those of looking after someone dear to us who is ill, and of being in love. Experience shows that sick-nursing and sexual affects also play the principal part in the majority of the more closely analysed case histories of hysterical patients.

I suspect that the duplication of psychical functioning, whether this is habitual or caused by emotional situations in life, acts as a substantial *predisposition* to a genuine pathological splitting of the mind. This duplication passes over into the latter state if the content of the two co-existing sets of ideas is no longer of the same kind, if one of them contains ideas which are inadmissible to consciousness—which have been fended off, that is, or have arisen from hypnoid states. When this is so, it is impossible for the two temporarily divided streams to re-unite, as is constantly happening in healthy people, and a region of unconscious psychical activity becomes permanently split off. This hysterical splitting of the mind stands in the same relation to the 'double ego' of a healthy person as does the hypnoid state to a normal reverie. In this latter contrast what determines the pathological quality is amnesia, and in the former what determines it is the inadmissibility of the ideas to consciousness.

Our first case history, that of Anna O., to which I am obliged to keep on returning, affords a clear insight into what happens. The girl was in the habit, while she was in perfect health, of allowing trains of imaginative ideas to pass through her mind

[1] [Horace, *Odes*, III, 1.]

during her ordinary occupations. While she was in a situation that favoured auto-hypnosis, the affect of anxiety entered into her reverie and created a hypnoid state for which she had amnesia. This was repeated on different occasions and its ideational content gradually became richer and richer; but it continued to alternate with states of completely normal waking thought. After four months the hypnoid state gained entire control of the patient. The separate attacks ran into one another and thus an *état de mal* arose, an acute hysteria of the most severe type. This lasted for several months in various forms (the period of somnambulism); it was then forcibly interrupted [p. 27], and thereafter alternated once again with normal psychical behaviour. But even during her normal behaviour there was a persistence of somatic and psychical phenomena (contractures, hemi-anaesthesia and changes in speech) of which in this case we know as a fact that they were based on ideas belonging to the hypnoid state. This proves that even during her normal behaviour the ideational complex belonging to the hypnoid state, the 'subconsciousness', was in existence and that the split in her mind persisted.

I have no second example to offer of a similar course of development. I think, however, that the case throws some light also on the growth of *traumatic* neuroses. During the first few days after the traumatic event, the state of hypnoid fright is repeated every time the event is recalled. While this state recurs more and more often, its intensity so far diminishes that it no longer *alternates* with waking thought but only exists side by side with it. It now becomes continuous, and the somatic symptoms, which earlier were only present during the attack of fright, acquire a permanent existence. I can, however, only *suspect* that this is what happens, as I have never analysed a case of this kind.

Freud's observations and analyses show that the splitting of the mind can also be caused by 'defence', by the deliberate deflection of consciousness from distressing ideas: only, how-ever, in some people, to whom we must therefore ascribe a mental idiosyncrasy. In normal people, such ideas are either successfully suppressed, in which case they vanish completely, or they are not, in which case they keep on emerging in con-sciousness. I cannot tell what the nature of this idiosyncrasy is. I only venture to suggest that the assistance of the hypnoid state is necessary if defence is to result not merely in single converted ideas being made into unconscious ones, but in a genuine splitting of the mind. Auto-hypnosis has, so to speak, created the space or region of unconscious psychical activity into which the ideas which are fended off are driven. But, however this may be, the fact of the pathogenic significance of 'defence' is one that we must recognize.

I do not think, however, that the genesis of splitting of the mind is anything like covered by the half-understood processes that we have discussed. Thus, in their initial stages hysterias of a severe degree usually exhibit for a time a syndrome that may be described as acute hysteria. (In the anamnesis of male cases of hysteria we generally come across this form of illness represented as being 'encephalitis'; in female cases ovarian neuralgia leads to a diagnosis of 'peritonitis'.) In this acute stage of hysteria psychotic traits are very distinct, such as manic and angry states of excitement, rapidly changing hysterical phenomena, hallucinations, and so on. In states of this kind the splitting of the mind may perhaps take place in a different manner from that which we have tried to describe above. Perhaps the whole of this stage is to be regarded as a long hypnoid state, the residues of which provide the nucleus of the unconscious ideational complex, while waking thought is amnesic for it. Since we are for the most part ignorant of the causes that lead to an acute hysteria of this kind (for I do not venture to regard the course of events with Anna O. as having general application), there would seem to be another sort of psychical splitting which, in contrast to those discussed above, might be termed irrational.[1] And no doubt yet other forms of this process exist, which are still concealed from our young psychological science; for it is certain that we have only taken the first steps in this region of knowledge, and our present views will be substantially altered by further observations.

Let us now enquire what the knowledge of splitting of the mind that has been gained during the last few years has

[1] I must, however, point out that precisely in the best-known and clearest example of major hysteria with manifest '*double conscience*'—precisely in the case of Anna O.—no residue of the acute stage was carried over into the chronic one, and all the phenomena of the latter had already been produced during the 'incubation period' in hypnoid and affective states.

achieved towards an understanding of hysteria. It seems to have been great in amount and in importance.

These discoveries have in the first place made it possible for what are apparently purely somatic symptoms to be traced back to ideas, which, however, are not discoverable in the patients' consciousness. (It is unnecessary to enter into this again.) In the second place, they have taught us to understand hysterical attacks, in part at least, as being products of an unconscious ideational complex. (Cf. Charcot.) But, besides this, they have also explained some of the psychical characteristics of hysteria, and this point perhaps deserves a more detailed discussion.

It is true that 'unconscious ideas' never, or only rarely and with difficulty, enter waking thought; but they influence it. They do so, first, through their consequences—when, for instance, a patient is tormented by a hallucination which is totally unintelligible and senseless, but whose meaning and motivation become clear under hypnosis. Further, they influence association by making certain ideas more vivid than they would have been if they had not been thus reinforced from the unconscious. So particular groups of ideas constantly force themselves on the patient with a certain amount of compulsion and he is obliged to think of them. (The case is similar with Janet's hemi-anaesthetic patients. When their anaesthetic hand is repeatedly touched they feel nothing; but when they are told to name any number they like, they always choose the one corresponding to the number of times they have been touched.) Again, unconscious ideas govern the patient's emotional tone, his state of feeling. When, in the course of unrolling her memories, Anna O. approached an event which had originally been bound up with a lively affect, the corresponding feeling made its appearance several days in advance and before the recollection appeared clearly even in her hypnotic consciousness.

This makes the patients' 'moods' intelligible—their inexplicable, unreasonable changes of feeling which seem to waking thought without motive. The impressionability of hysterical patients is indeed to a large extent determined simply by their innate excitability; but the lively affects into which they are thrown by relatively trivial causes become more intelligible if we reflect that the 'split-off mind' acts like a sounding-board

to the note of a tuning-fork. Any event that provokes unconscious memories liberates the whole affective force of these
ideas that have not undergone a wearing-away, and the affect
that is called up is then quite out of proportion to any that
would have arisen in the conscious mind alone.

I have spoken above (p. 231 f.) of a patient whose psychical
functioning always stood in inverse ratio to the vividness of
her unconscious ideas. The diminution of her conscious thinking was based partly, but only partly, on a peculiar kind of
abstraction. After each of her momentary '*absences*'—and
these were constantly occurring—she did not know what she
had thought of in the course of it. She oscillated between her
'*conditions primes*' and '*secondes*', between the conscious and the
unconscious ideational complexes. But it was not only on that
account that her psychical functioning was reduced, nor on
account of the affect which dominated her from the unconscious.
While she was in this state her waking thought was without
energy, her judgement was childish and she seemed, as I have
said, positively imbecile. I believe that this was due to the fact
that waking thought has less energy at its disposal if a great
amount of psychical excitation is appropriated by the unconscious.

If this state of things is not merely temporary, if the split-off
mind is in a *constant* state of excitation, as it was with Janet's
hemi-anaesthetic patients—in whom, moreover, all the sensations in no less than one half of the body were perceived only
by the unconscious mind—if this is the case, so little cerebral
functioning is left over for waking thought that the weakness
of mind which Janet describes and regards as innate is fully
accounted for. There are only very few people of whom it could
be said, as of Uhland's Bertrand de Born, that they never
need more than half their mind.[1] Such a reduction in their
psychical energy does make the majority of people weak-
minded.

This weakness of mind caused by a splitting of the psyche
seems also to be a basis of a momentous characteristic of *some*
hysterical patients—their suggestibility. (I say 'some', since it
is certain that among hysterical patients are to be found people
of the soundest and most critical judgement as well.)

By suggestibility we understand, in the first instance, only an

[1] [A famous troubadour about whom Uhland wrote a ballad.]

inability to criticize ideas and complexes of ideas (judgements) which emerge in the subject's own consciousness or are introduced into it from outside through the spoken word or through reading. All criticism of ideas like these which come freshly into consciousness is based on the fact that they awaken other ideas by association and amongst them some that are irreconcilable with the fresh ones. The resistance to these latter is thus dependent on the store of antagonistic ideas in potential consciousness, and the strength of the resistance corresponds to the ratio between the vividness of the fresh ideas and that of those aroused from memory. Even in normal intellects this ratio is very various. What we describe as an intellectual temperament depends on it to a great extent. A 'sanguine' man is always delighted by new people and things, and this is no doubt so because the intensity of his mnemic images is less in comparison with that of new impressions than it is in a quieter, 'phlegmatic' man. In pathological states the preponderance of fresh ideas and the lack of resistance to them increases in proportion to the fewness of the mnemic images aroused—that is, in proportion to the weakness and poorness of their associative powers. This is already what happens in sleep and dreams, in hypnosis and whenever there is a reduction in mental energy, so long as this does not also reduce the vividness of the fresh ideas.

The unconscious, split-off mind in hysteria is pre-eminently suggestible on account of the poverty and incompleteness of its ideational content. But the suggestibility of the conscious mind, too, in some hysterical patients seems to be based on this. They are excitable from their innate disposition; in them, fresh ideas are very vivid. In contrast to this, their intellectual activity proper, their associative function, is reduced, because only a part of their psychical energy is at the disposal of their waking thought, owing to a splitting-off of an 'unconscious'. As a result of this their power of resistance both to auto- and allo-suggestions is diminished and sometimes abolished. The suggestibility of their *will* also seems to be due to this alone. On the other hand, *hallucinatory* suggestibility, which promptly changes every idea of a sense-perception into an actual perception, demands, like all hallucinations, an abnormal degree of excitability of the perceptual organ and cannot be traced back solely to a splitting of the mind.

(6) INNATE DISPOSITION—DEVELOPMENT OF HYSTERIA

At almost every stage of these discussions I have been obliged to recognize that most of the phenomena which we have been endeavouring to understand can be based, among other things, on an innate idiosyncrasy. This defies any explanation that seeks to go beyond a mere statement of the facts. But the *capacity to acquire* hysteria is also undoubtedly linked with an idiosyncrasy of the person concerned, and an attempt to define it more accurately will perhaps not be entirely unprofitable.

I have explained above why I cannot accept Janet's view that the disposition to hysteria is based on innate psychical weakness. The medical practitioner who, in his capacity as family doctor, observes the members of hysterical families at all ages will certainly be inclined to regard this disposition as lying in an excess rather than in a defect. Adolescents who are later to become hysterical are for the most part lively, gifted and full of intellectual interests before they fall ill. Their energy of will is often remarkable. They include girls who get out of bed at night so as secretly to carry on some study that their parents have forbidden from fear of their overworking. The capacity for forming sound judgements is certainly not more abundant in them than in other people; but it is rare to find in them simple, dull intellectual inertia and stupidity. The overflowing productivity of their minds has led one of my friends to assert that hysterics are the flower of mankind, as sterile, no doubt, but as beautiful as double flowers.

Their liveliness and restlessness, their craving for sensations and mental activity, their intolerance of monotony and boredom, may be formulated thus: they are among those people whose nervous system while it is at rest liberates excess of excitation which requires to be made use of (cf. p. 197). During development at puberty, and in consequence of it, this original excess is supplemented by the powerful increase in excitation which arises from the awakening of sexuality, from the sex-glands. From then on there is a surplus quantity of free nervous energy available for the production of pathological phenomena.

But in order for these phenomena to appear in the form of hysterical symptoms there must evidently also be another, specific idiosyncrasy in the individual concerned. For after all, the great majority of lively and excitable people do not become hysterical. I was only able, above [p. 191], to describe this idiosyncracy in the vague and unenlightening phrase, 'abnormal excitability of the nervous system'. But it may be possible to go further and say that this abnormality lies in the fact that in such people the excitation of the central organ can flow into the sensory nervous apparatuses which are normally accessible only to peripheral stimuli, as well as into the nervous apparatuses of the vegetative organs which are isolated from the central nervous system by powerful resistances. It may be that this idea of there being a surplus of excitation constantly present which has access to the sensory, vasomotor and visceral apparatuses already accounts for some pathological phenomena.

In people of this kind, as soon as their attention is forcibly concentrated on some part of the body, what Exner [1894, 165 ff.] speaks of as the 'facilitation of attention' in the sensory path of conduction concerned exceeds the normal amount. The free, floating excitation is, as it were, diverted into this path, and a local hyperalgesia is produced. As a result, every pain, however caused, reaches maximum intensity, every ailment is 'fearful' and 'unbearable'. Further, whereas in normal people a quantity of excitation, after cathecting a sensory path, always leaves it again, this is not so in these cases. That quantity, moreover, not only remains behind but is constantly increased by the influx of fresh excitations. A slight injury to a joint thus leads to arthralgia, and the painful sensations due to ovarian swelling lead to chronic ovarian neuralgia; and since the nervous apparatuses of the circulation are more accessible to cerebral influence than in normal people, we find nervous palpitation of the heart, a tendency to fainting, proneness to excessive blushing and turning pale, and so on.

However, it is not only in regard to *central* influences that the peripheral nervous apparatuses are more easily excitable. They also react in an excessive and perverse fashion to appropriate, functional stimuli. Palpitations follow from moderate effort no less than from emotional excitement, and the vasomotor nerves cause the arteries to contract ('dead fingers'), apart from any psychical influence. And just as a slight injury leaves behind an arthralgia, a short attack of bronchitis is followed by nervous asthma, and indigestion by frequent cardiac pains. We must accordingly recognize that accessibility to sums of excitation of central origin is no more than a special case of general abnormal excitability,[1] even though it is the most important one from the point of view of our present topic.

It seems to me, therefore, that the old 'reflex theory' of these symptoms, which would perhaps be better described simply as 'nervous' ones but which form part of the empirical clinical picture of hysteria, should not be completely rejected. The vomiting, which of course accompanies the dilatation of the uterus in pregnancy, may, where there is abnormal excitability, quite well be set going in a reflex manner by trivial uterine stimuli, or perhaps even by the periodic changes in size of the ovaries. We are acquainted with so many remote effects resulting from organic changes, so many strange instances of 'referred pain', that we cannot reject the possibility that a host of nervous symptoms which are sometimes determined psychically may in other cases be remote effects of reflex action. Indeed, I venture to put forward the highly unmodern heresy that even motor weakness in a leg may sometimes be determined by a genital affection, not psychically, but by direct reflex action. I think we shall do well not to insist too much on the exclusiveness of our new discoveries or to seek to apply them in all cases.

Other forms of abnormal sensory excitability still escape our understanding completely: general analgesia, for instance, anaesthetic areas, real restriction of the field of vision, and so on. It is possible and perhaps probable that further observations will prove the psychical origin of one or other of these stigmata[2] and so explain the symptom; but this has not yet happened (for I do not venture to generalize the findings presented by our first case history), and I do not think it is justifiable to presume that this is their origin before it has been properly traced.

On the other hand the idiosyncrasy of the nervous system and of the mind which we have been discussing seems to explain one or two very familiar properties of many hysterical patients. The surplus of excitation which is liberated by their nervous system when in a state of rest determines their incapacity to tolerate a monotonous life and boredom—their craving for sensations which drives them, after the onset of their illness, to interrupt the monotony of their invalid life by all kinds of 'incidents', of which the most prominent are from the nature

[1] Oppenheim's 'instability of the molecules'. [See footnote, p. 191.]
[2] [See footnote, p. 15.]

of things pathological phenomena. They are often supported in this by autosuggestion. They are led further and further along this road by their need for being ill, a remarkable trait which is as pathognomonic for hysteria as is *fear* of being ill for hypochondria.[1] I know a hysterical woman who inflicted on herself injuries which were often quite severe, merely for her own use and without those about her or her physician learning of them. If she did nothing else she used to play all kinds of tricks while she was alone in her room simply to prove to herself that she was not normal. For she had in fact a distinct feeling of not being well and could not discharge her duties satisfactorily, and she tried to justify herself in her own eyes by actions such as these. Another patient, a very sick woman suffering from pathological conscientiousness and full of distrust of herself, felt every hysterical phenomenon as something guilty, because, she said, she need not have had it if she had really wanted not to. When a paresis of her legs was wrongly diagnosed as a disease of the spine she felt it as an immense relief, and when she was told that it was 'only nervous' and would pass off, that was enough to bring on severe pangs of conscience. The need to be ill arises from the patient's desire to convince herself and other people of the reality of her illness. When this need is further associated to the distress caused by the monotony of a sick-room, the inclination to produce more and more new symptoms is developed to its fullest.

If, however, this turns into deceitfulness and actual simulation (and I think that we now err just as far on the side of denying simulation as we used to on the side of accepting it), that is based, not on the hysterical disposition but, as Moebius has so aptly said, on its being complicated by other forms of degeneracy—by innate, moral inferiority. In just the same way the 'malicious hysteric' comes into existence when someone who is innately excitable but poor in emotion is also a victim to the egoistic stunting of character which is so easily produced by chronic ill-health. Incidentally, the 'malicious hysteric' is scarcely commoner than the malicious patient in the later stages of tabes.

A surplus of excitation also gives rise to pathological phenomena in the motor sphere. Children having this characteristic very easily develop *tic*-like movements. These may be started

[1] [Cf. a remark of Freud's, p. 258.]

in the first instance by some sensation in the eyes or face or by an uncomfortable article of clothing, but they become permanent unless they are promptly checked. The reflex paths are very easily and quickly dug in deep.

Nor can the possibility be dismissed of there being purely motor convulsive attacks which are independent of any psychical factor and in which all that happens is that the mass of excitation accumulated by summation is discharged, in just the same way as the mass of stimuli caused by anatomical modifications is discharged in an epileptic fit. Here we should have the non-ideogenic hysterical convulsion.

We so often find adolescents who had previously been healthy, though excitable, falling ill of hysteria during pubertal development, that we must ask ourselves whether that process may not create the disposition to hysteria where it was not present innately. And in any case we must attribute more to it than a simple raising of the quantity of excitation. Sexual maturation impinges on the whole nervous system, increasing excitability and reducing resistances everywhere. We are taught this from the observation of adolescents who are not hysterical and we are thus justified in believing that sexual maturation also establishes the hysterical disposition in so far as it consists precisely in this characteristic of the nervous system. In saying this we are already recognizing sexuality as one of the major components of hysteria. We shall see that the part it plays in it is very much greater still and that it contributes in the most various ways to the constitution of the illness.

If the stigmata spring directly from this innate breeding-ground of hysteria and are not of ideogenic origin, it is also impossible to give ideogenesis such a central position in hysteria as is sometimes done nowadays. What could be more genuinely hysterical than the stigmata? They are pathognomonic findings which establish the diagnosis; and yet precisely they seem not to be ideogenic. But if the basis of hysteria is an idiosyncracy of the whole nervous system, the complex of ideogenic, psychically determined symptoms is erected on it as a building is on its foundations. And it is a building *of several storeys.* Just as it is only possible to understand the structure of such a building if we distinguish the plans of the different floors, it is, I think, necessary in order to understand hysteria for us to pay attention to the various kinds of complication in the causation of the symptoms. If we disregard them and try to carry through an explanation of hysteria by employing a single causal nexus, we shall always find a very large residue of unexplained phenomena left over. It is just as though we tried to insert the different rooms of a many-storeyed house into the plan of a single storey.

Like the stigmata, a number of other nervous symptoms—some pains and vasomotor phenomena and perhaps purely motor convulsive attacks—are, as we have seen, not caused by ideas but are direct results of the fundamental abnormality of the nervous system.

Closest to them are the ideogenic phenomena which are simply conversions of affective excitation (p. 203). They arise as the consequences of affects in people with a hysterical disposition and in the first instance they are only an 'abnormal expression of the emotions' (Oppenheim [1890]).[1] This becomes by repetition a genuine and apparently purely somatic hysterical symptom, while the idea that gave rise to it becomes unnoticeable (p. 206) or is fended off and therefore repressed from consciousness. The most numerous and important of the ideas that are fended off and converted have a sexual content. They are at the bottom of a great deal of the hysteria of puberty. Girls who are approaching maturity—and it is they who are chiefly concerned—behave very differently towards the sexual ideas and feelings which crowd in on them. Some girls meet them with complete unembarrassment, among whom a few ignore and overlook the whole subject. Others accept them like boys, and this is no doubt the rule with peasant and working-class girls. Others again, with more or less perverse curiosity, run after anything sexual that they can get hold of in talk or books. And lastly there are natures of a refined organization who, though their sexual excitability is great, have an equally great moral purity and who feel that anything sexual is something incompatible with their ethical standards, something dirtying and smirching.[2] They repress sexuality from their

---

[1] This disposition is nothing else than what Strümpell [1892] speaks of as the 'disturbance in the psycho-physical sphere' which underlies hysteria.

[2] Some observations lead us to believe that the fear of touching, or, more properly, the fear of being dirtied, which compels women to keep on washing their hands all the time, very often has this derivation. Their washing is derived from the same mental process as Lady Macbeth's.

consciousness, and the affective ideas with a content of this kind which have caused the somatic phenomena are fended off and thus become unconscious.

The tendency towards fending off what is sexual is further intensified by the fact that in young unmarried women sensual excitation has an admixture of anxiety, of fear of what is coming, what is unknown and half-suspected, whereas in normal and healthy young men it is an unmixed aggressive instinct. The girl senses in Eros the terrible power which governs and decides her destiny and she is frightened by it. All the greater, then, is her inclination to look away and to repress from her consciousness the thing that frightens her.

Marriage brings fresh sexual traumas. It is surprising that the wedding night does not have pathogenic effects more frequently, since unfortunately what it involves is so often not an erotic seduction but a violation. But indeed it is not rare to find in young married women hysterias which can be traced back to this and which vanish if in the course of time sexual enjoyment emerges and wipes out the trauma. Sexual traumas also occur in the later course of many marriages. The case histories from whose publication we have been obliged to refrain include a great number of them—perverse demands made by the husband, unnatural practices, etc. I do not think I am exaggerating when I assert that *the great majority of severe neuroses in women have their origin in the marriage bed*.[1]

Certain sexual noxae, which consist essentially in insufficient satisfaction (*coitus interruptus*, *ejaculatio praecox*, etc.), result according to the discovery of Freud (1895*b*) not in hysteria but in an anxiety neurosis. I am of opinion, however, that even in such cases the excitation of the sexual affect is quite frequently converted into hysterical somatic phenomena.

It is self-evident and is also sufficiently proved by our observations that the non-sexual affects of fright, anxiety and anger lead to the development of hysterical phenomena. But it is perhaps worth while insisting again and again that the sexual

[1] It is a most unfortunate thing that clinical medicine ignores one of the most important of all the pathogenic factors or at least only hints at it delicately. This is certainly a subject in which the acquired knowledge of experienced physicians should be communicated to their juniors, who as a rule blindly overlook sexuality—at all events so far as their patients are concerned.

factor is by far the most important and the most productive
of pathological results. The unsophisticated observations of our
predecessors, the residue of which is preserved in the term
'hysteria' [derived from the Greek word for 'uterus'], came
nearer the truth than the more recent view which puts sexuality
almost last, in order to save the patients from moral reproaches.
The sexual needs of hysterical patients are no doubt just as
variable in degree from individual to individual as in healthy
people and are no stronger than in them; but the former fall
ill from them, and, for the most part, precisely owing to struggling against them, owing to their *defence* against sexuality.

Alongside sexual hysteria we must at this point recall hysteria
due to fright—traumatic hysteria proper—which constitutes
one of the best known and recognized forms of hysteria.

In what may be called the same stratum as the phenomena
which arise from the conversion of affective excitation are to
be found those which owe their origin to suggestion (mostly
auto-suggestion) in individuals who are innately suggestible.
A high degree of suggestibility—that is to say, the unrestricted
preponderance of ideas that have been freshly aroused—is not
among the essential features of hysteria. It can, however, be
present as a complication in people with a hysterical disposition,
in whom this very idiosyncrasy of the nervous system makes
possible the somatic realization of supervalent [1.] ideas. Moreover, it is for the most part only *affective* ideas which are realized
in somatic phenomena by suggestion, and consequently the
process may often be regarded as a conversion of the accompanying affect of fright or anxiety.

These processes—the conversion of affect, and suggestion—
remain identical even in the complicated forms of hysteria
which we must now consider. They merely find more favourable
conditions in such cases: it is invariably through one of these
two processes that psychically-determined hysterical phenomena come into being.

The third constituent of the hysterical disposition, which
appears in some cases in addition to those that have been
already discussed, is the hypnoid state, the tendency to auto-
hypnosis (p. 215). This state favours and facilitates in the

---

[1] ['*Überwertig.*' Freud attributes this term to Wernicke in his analysis
of 'Dora' (1905e), *Standard Ed.*, **7**, 54.]

greatest degree both conversion and suggestion; and in this way it erects, as we might say, on the top of the minor hysterias, the higher storey of major hysteria. The tendency to auto-hypnosis is a state which is to begin with only temporary and which alternates with the normal one. We may attribute to it the same increase of mental influence on the body that we observe in artificial hypnosis. This influence is all the more intense and deep-going here in that it is acting upon a nervous system which even outside hypnosis is abnormally excitable.[1] We cannot tell how far and in what cases the tendency to auto-hypnosis is an innate property of the organism. I have expressed the view above (pp. 218–19) that it develops from reveries that are charged with affect. But there can be no doubt that innate disposition plays a part in this as well. If this view is correct, it will be clear here once again how great an influence on the development of hysteria is to be ascribed to sexuality. For, apart from sick-nursing, no psychical factor is so well-calculated to produce reveries charged with affect as are the longings of a person in love. And over and above this the sexual orgasm [2] itself, with its wealth of affect and its restriction of consciousness, is closely akin to hypnoid states.

The hypnoid element is most clearly manifested in hysterical attacks and in those states which can be described as acute hysteria and which, it seems, play such an important part in the development of hysteria (p. 236). These are obviously psychotic states which persist for a long time, often for several months and which it is frequently necessary to describe as hallucinatory confusion. Even if the disturbance does not go as far as this, a great variety of hysterical phenomena emerge in it, a few of which actually persist after it is over. The psychical content of these states consists partly in precisely the ideas which have been fended off in waking life and repressed from

---

[1] It is tempting to identify the disposition to hypnosis with innate abnormal excitability; for artificial hypnosis, too, exhibits ideogenic changes in secretion and local blood-supply, formation of vesicles, etc. This seems to be the view held by Moebius. But in my opinion it would involve us in a vicious circle. The miraculous workings of hypnosis are, so far as I can see, only observable in hysterical patients. What we should be doing would be first to assign the phenomena of hysteria to hypnosis, and then to assert that hypnosis is the cause of those phenomena.

[2] ['*Orgasmus.*' In the first edition only this is misprinted '*Organismus*'.]

consciousness. (Cf. the 'hysterical deliria in saints and nuns, continent women and well-brought-up children' [p. 11].)

Since these states are so often nothing less than psychoses and are yet derived immediately and exclusively from hysteria, I cannot agree with Moebius's opinion that 'apart from the deliria attached to attacks, it is impossible to speak of an actual hysterical insanity' (1895, 18). In many cases these states constitute an insanity of this kind; and psychoses like these also recur in the further course of a hysteria. It is true that essentially they are nothing other than the psychotic stage of an attack, but since they last for months they can nevertheless hardly be described as attacks.

How does one of these acute hysterias arise? In the best-known case (Case History 1) it developed out of an accumulation of hypnoid attacks; in another case (where there was already a complicated hysteria present) it arose in association with a withdrawal of morphine. The process is for the most part completely obscure and awaits clarification from further observations.

Accordingly, we may apply to the hysterias which have been discussed here Moebius's pronouncement (ibid., 16): 'The essential change that occurs in hysteria is that the mental state of the hysterical patient becomes temporarily or permanently similar to that of a hypnotized subject.'

The persistence in the normal state of the symptoms that have arisen during the hypnoid one corresponds entirely to our experiences with post-hypnotic suggestion. But this already implies that complexes of ideas that are inadmissible to consciousness co-exist with the trains of ideas that pursue a conscious course, that the splitting of the mind has taken place (p. 229). It seems certain that this can happen even without a hypnoid state, from the wealth of thoughts which have been fended off and repressed from consciousness but not suppressed. In one way or another there comes into existence a region of mental life—sometimes poor in ideas and rudimentary, sometimes more or less on a par with waking thought—our knowledge of which we owe, above all, to Binet and Janet. The splitting of the mind is the consummation of hysteria. I have shown above (in Section 5) how it explains the principal characteristics of the disorder. One part of the patient's mind is in the hypnoid state, permanently, but with a varying degree of

vividness in its ideas, and is always prepared whenever there
is a lapse in waking thought to assume control over the whole
person (e.g. in an attack or delirium). This occurs as soon as
a powerful affect interrupts the normal course of ideas, in twilight states and states of exhaustion. Out of this persisting
hypnoid state unmotivated ideas, alien to normal association,
force their way into consciousness, hallucinations are introduced into the perceptual system and motor acts are innervated
independently of the conscious will. This hypnoid mind is in
the highest degree susceptible to conversion of affects and to
suggestion, and thus fresh hysterical phenomena appear easily,
which without the split in the mind would only have come
about with great difficulty and under the pressure of repeated
affects. The split-off mind is the devil with which the unsophisticated observation of early superstitious times believed
that these patients were possessed. It is true that a spirit alien
to the patient's waking consciousness holds sway in him; but
the spirit is not in fact an alien one, but a part of his own.

The attempt that has been made here to make a synthetic
construction of hysteria out of what we know of it to-day is
open to the reproach of eclecticism, if such a reproach can be
justified at all. There were so many formulations of hysteria,
from the old 'reflex theory' to the 'dissociation of personality',
which have had to find a place in it. But it can scarcely be
otherwise; for so many excellent observers and acute minds
have concerned themselves with hysteria. It is unlikely that
any of their formulations was without a portion of the truth.
A future exposition of the true state of affairs will certainly
include them all and will merely combine all the one-sided
views of the subject into a corporate reality. Eclecticism, therefore, seems to me nothing to be ashamed of.

But how far we still are to-day from the possibility of any
such complete understanding of hysteria! With what uncertain
strokes have its outlines been drawn in these pages, with what
clumsy hypotheses have the gaping lacunas been concealed
rather than bridged! Only one consideration is to some extent
consoling: that this defect attaches, and must attach, to all
physiological expositions of complicated psychical processes.
We must always say of them what Theseus in *A Midsummer
Night's Dream* says of tragedy: 'The best in this kind are but

shadows.' And even the weakest is not without value if it honestly and modestly tries to hold on to the outlines of the shadows which the unknown real objects throw upon the wall. For then, in spite of everything, the hope is always justified that there may be some degree of correspondence and similarity between the real processes and our idea of them.

IV

THE PSYCHOTHERAPY OF HYSTERIA

(FREUD)

IV

THE PSYCHOTHERAPY OF HYSTERIA

(FREUD)

IN our 'Preliminary Communication' we reported how, in the course of our investigation into the aetiology of hysterical symptoms, we also came upon a therapeutic method which seemed to us of practical importance. For 'we found, to our great surprise at first, that *each individual hysterical symptom immediately and permanently disappeared when we had succeeded in bringing clearly to light the memory of the event by which it was provoked and in arousing its accompanying affect, and when the patient had described that event in the greatest possible detail and had put the affect into words'.* (P. 6.)

We further endeavoured to explain the way in which our psychotherapeutic method works. '*It brings to an end the operative force of the idea which was not abreacted in the first instance, by allowing its strangulated affect to find a way out through speech; and it subjects it to associative correction by introducing it into normal consciousness (under light hypnosis) or by removing it through the physician's suggestion, as is done in somnambulism accompanied by amnesia.*' (P. 17.)

I will now try to give a connected account of how far this method carries us, of the respects in which it achieves more than other methods, of the technique by which it works and of the difficulties it meets with. Much of the substance of this is already contained in the case histories printed in the earlier portion of this book, and I shall not be able to avoid repeating myself in the account which follows.

(1)

For my own part, I too may say that I can still hold by what is contained in the 'Preliminary Communication'. None the less I must confess that during the years which have since passed —in which I have been unceasingly concerned with the problems touched upon in it—fresh points of view have forced themselves on my mind. These have led to what is in part at least

255

a different grouping and interpretation of the factual material known to me at that time. It would be unfair if I were to try to lay too much of the responsibility for this development upon my honoured friend Dr. Josef Breuer. For this reason the considerations which follow stand principally under my own name.

When I attempted to apply to a comparatively large number of patients Breuer's method of treating hysterical symptoms by an investigation and abreaction of them under hypnosis, I came up against two difficulties, in the course of dealing with which I was led to an alteration both in my technique and in my view of the facts. (1) I found that not everyone could be hypnotized who exhibited undoubted hysterical symptoms and who, it was highly probable, was governed by the same psychical mechanism. (2) I was forced to take up a position on the question of what, after all, essentially characterizes hysteria and what distinguishes it from other neuroses.

I will put off until later my account of how I got over the first of these two difficulties and what I have learnt from it, and I will begin by describing the attitude I adopted in my daily practice towards the second problem. It is very hard to obtain a clear view of a case of neurosis before one has submitted it to a thorough analysis—an analysis which can, in fact, only be brought about by the use of Breuer's method; but a decision on the diagnosis and the form of therapy to be adopted has to be made before any such thorough knowledge of the case has been arrived at. The only course open to me, therefore, was to select for cathartic treatment such cases as could be provisionally diagnosed as hysteria, which exhibited one or more of the stigmata or characteristic symptoms of hysteria. It then sometimes happened that in spite of the diagnosis of hysteria the therapeutic results turned out to be very scanty and that even analysis brought nothing significant to light. On other occasions again, I tried applying Breuer's method of treatment to neuroses which no one could have mistaken for hysteria, and I found that in that manner they could be influenced and indeed cleared up. I had this experience, for instance, with obsessional ideas, genuine obsessional ideas of the Westphal type,[1] in cases without a single trait which recalled hysteria.

[1] [Westphal (1877) had given a detailed descriptive classification of these.]

Consequently, the psychical mechanism revealed by the 'Preliminary Communication' could not be pathognomonic for hysteria. Nor could I resolve, merely for the sake of preserving that mechanism as a criterion of it, to lump all these other neuroses in with hysteria. I eventually found a way out of all these emerging doubts by the plan of treating all the other neuroses in question in the same way as hysteria. I determined to investigate their aetiology and the nature of their psychical mechanism in every case and to let the decision as to whether the diagnosis of hysteria was justified depend upon the outcome of that investigation.

Thus, starting out from Breuer's method, I found myself engaged in a consideration of the aetiology and mechanism of the neuroses in general. I was fortunate enough to arrive at some serviceable findings in a relatively short time.[1] In the first place I was obliged to recognize that, in so far as one can speak of determining causes which lead to the *acquisition* of neuroses, their aetiology is to be looked for in *sexual* factors. There followed the discovery that different sexual factors, in the most general sense, produce different pictures of neurotic disorders. And it then became possible, in the degree to which this relation was confirmed, to venture on using aetiology for the purpose of characterizing the neuroses and of making a sharp distinction between the clinical pictures of the various neuroses. Where the aetiological characteristics coincided regularly with the clinical ones, this was of course justified.

In this manner I found that neurasthenia presented a monotonous clinical picture in which, as my analyses showed, a 'psychical mechanism' played no part. There was a sharp distinction between neurasthenia and 'obsessional neurosis', the

[1] [The findings reported in this and the next three paragraphs had already been published by Freud in his first paper on 'The Neuro-Psychoses of Defence' (1894a) and his first paper on anxiety neurosis (1895b).—In reading what follows, it should be borne in mind that Freud subsequently separated off a further clinical entity to which he gave the name 'anxiety hysteria' and which, though anxiety was its most obvious feature, had a traceable psychical mechanism parallel to that of conversion hysteria. Freud's first lengthy discussion of anxiety hysteria appeared in the case history of 'Little Hans' (1909b), *Standard Ed.*, **10**, 115–7. The distinction between 'anxiety neurosis' and 'anxiety hysteria' is brought out very clearly in the paper on 'wild' psychoanalysis (1910k).]

neurosis of obsessional ideas proper. In this latter one I was able to recognize a complicated psychical mechanism, an aetiology similar to that of hysteria and an extensive possibility of reducing it by psychotherapy. On the other hand, it seemed to me absolutely necessary to detach from neurasthenia a complex of neurotic symptoms which depend on a quite different and indeed at bottom a *contrary* aetiology. The component symptoms of this complex are united by a characteristic which has already been recognized by Hecker (1893). For they are either symptoms or equivalents and rudiments of *manifestations of anxiety*; and for this reason I have given to this complex which is to be detached from neurasthenia the name of 'anxiety neurosis'. I have maintained [Freud 1895*b*] that it arises from an accumulation of physical tension, which is itself once more of sexual origin. This neurosis, too, has no psychical mechanism, but it invariably influences mental life, so that 'anxious expectation', phobias, hyperaesthesia to pains, etc., are among its regular manifestations. This anxiety neurosis, in my sense of the term, no doubt coincides in part with the neurosis which, under the name of 'hypochondria', finds a place in not a few descriptions alongside hysteria and neurasthenia. But I cannot regard the delimitation of hypochondria in any of the works in question as being the correct one, and the applicability of its name seems to me to be prejudiced by the fixed connection of that term with the symptom of 'fear of illness'.[1]

After I had in this way fixed the simple pictures of neurasthenia, anxiety neurosis and obsessional ideas, I went on to consider the cases of neurosis which are commonly included under the diagnosis of hysteria. I reflected that it was not right to stamp a neurosis as a whole as hysterical because a few hysterical signs were prominent in its complex of symptoms. I could well understand this practice, since after all hysteria is the oldest, best-known and most striking of the neuroses under consideration; but it was an abuse, for it put down to the

---

[1] [Cf. above, p. 243.—Freud had already considered the relations between hypochondria, neurasthenia and anxiety neurosis in Part I of his first paper on anxiety neurosis (1895*b*). Much later, in the course of his closing remarks in a discussion on masturbation (1912*f*), he suggested that hypochondria should be regarded, together with neurasthenia and anxiety neurosis, as a third 'actual neurosis'—that is, as having a purely physical aetiology. He took up this idea at much greater length at the beginning of Section II of his paper on narcissism (1914*c*).]

account of hysteria so many traits of perversion and degeneracy. Whenever a hysterical sign, such as an anaesthesia or a characteristic attack, was found in a complicated case of psychical degeneracy, the whole condition was described as one of 'hysteria', so that it is not surprising that the worst and the most contradictory things were found together under this label. But just as it was certain that *this* diagnosis was incorrect, it was equally certain that we ought also to separate out the various neuroses; and since we were acquainted with neurasthenia, anxiety neurosis, etc., in a pure form, there was no longer any need to overlook them in the combined picture.

The following view, therefore, seemed to be the more probable one. The neuroses which commonly occur are mostly to be described as 'mixed'. Neurasthenia and anxiety neuroses are easily found in pure forms as well, especially in young people. Pure forms of hysteria and obsessional neurosis are rare; as a rule these two neuroses are combined with anxiety neurosis. The reason why mixed neuroses occur so frequently is that their aetiological factors are so often intermixed, sometimes only by chance, sometimes as a result of causal relations between the processes from which the aetiological factors of the neuroses are derived. There is no difficulty in tracing this out and demonstrating it in detail. As regards hysteria, however, it follows that that disorder can scarcely be segregated from the nexus of the sexual neuroses for the purposes of study, that as a rule it represents only a single side, only one aspect, of a complicated case of neurosis, and that it is only in marginal cases that it can be found and treated in isolation. We may perhaps say in a number of instances: *a potiori fit denominatio* [i.e. it has been given its name from its more important feature].

I will now examine the case histories that have been reported here, with a view to seeing whether they speak in favour of my opinion that hysteria is not an independent clinical entity.

Breuer's patient, Anna O., seems to contradict my opinion and to be an example of a pure hysterical disorder. This case, however, which has been so fruitful for our knowledge of hysteria, was not considered at all by its observer from the point of view of a sexual neurosis, and is now quite useless for this purpose. When I began to analyse the second patient, Frau Emmy von N., the expectation of a sexual neurosis being the basis of hysteria was fairly remote from my mind. I had come fresh from the school of Charcot, and I regarded the linking of hysteria with the topic of sexuality as a sort of insult—just as the women patients themselves do. When I go through my notes on this case to-day there seems to me no doubt at all that it must be looked on as a case of severe anxiety neurosis accompanied by anxious expectation and phobias—an anxiety neurosis which originated from sexual abstinence and had become combined with hysteria. Case 3, that of Miss Lucy R., can perhaps best be described as a marginal case of pure hysteria. It was a short hysteria which ran an episodic course and had an unmistakable sexual aetiology, such as would correspond to an anxiety neurosis. The patient was an over-mature girl with a need to be loved, whose affections had been too hastily aroused through a misunderstanding. The anxiety neurosis, however, did not become visible, or it escaped me. Case 4, Katharina, was nothing less than a model of what I have described as 'virginal anxiety'.[1] It was a combination of anxiety neurosis and hysteria. The former created the symptoms, while the latter repeated them and operated with them. Incidentally, it was a case typical of a large number of neuroses in young people that are described as 'hysteria'. Case 5, that of Fräulein Elisabeth von R., was once again not investigated as a sexual neurosis. I was only able to express, without confirming it, a suspicion that a spinal neurasthenia may have been its basis [p. 175, footnote].

I must add, though, that in the meantime pure hysterias have become even rarer in my experience. If it was possible for me to bring together these four cases as hysterias and if in reporting them I was able to overlook the points of view that were of importance as regards sexual neuroses, the reason is that these histories date some distance back, and that I did not at that time as yet submit such cases to a deliberate and searching investigation of their neurotic sexual foundation. And if, instead of these four, I did not report *twelve* cases whose analysis provides a confirmation of the psychical mechanism of hysterical phenomena put forward by us, this reticence was necessitated by the very circumstance that the analysis revealed these cases as being simultaneously sexual neuroses, although certainly no diagnostician would have refused them the name

[1] [See footnote 1, p. 127.]

of hysteria. But an elucidation of these sexual neuroses would overstep the bounds of the present joint publication.

I should not like it to be wrongly thought that I do not wish to allow that hysteria is an independent neurotic affection, that I regard it merely as a psychical manifestation of anxiety neurosis and that I attribute to it 'ideogenic' symptoms only and am transferring the somatic symptoms (such as hysterogenic points and anaesthesias) to anxiety neurosis. Nothing of the sort. In my opinion it is possible to deal with hysteria, freed from any admixture, as something independent; and to do so in every respect except in that of therapeutics. For in therapeutics we are concerned with a practical aim, with getting rid of the pathological state as a whole. And if hysteria generally appears as a component of a mixed neurosis, the situation resembles that in which there is a mixed infection, where preserving life sets a problem which does not coincide with that of combating the operation of one particular pathogenic agent.

It is very important for me to distinguish the part played by hysteria in the picture of the mixed neuroses from that played by neurasthenia, anxiety neurosis and so on, because, once I have made this distinction, I shall be able to express concisely the therapeutic value of the cathartic method. For I am inclined to venture the assertion that that method is—as a matter of theory—very well able to get rid of any hysterical symptom, whereas, as will be easily understood, it is completely powerless against the phenomena of neurasthenia and is only able rarely and in roundabout ways to influence the psychical effects of anxiety neurosis. Its therapeutic effectiveness in any particular case will accordingly depend on whether the hysterical components of the clinical picture do or do not assume a position of practical importance in comparison with the other neurotic components.

There is another obstacle in the way of the effectiveness of the cathartic method, which we have already indicated in the 'Preliminary Communication' [p. 17]. It cannot affect the underlying causes of hysteria: thus it cannot prevent fresh symptoms from taking the place of the ones which had been got rid of. On the whole, then, I must claim a prominent place for our therapeutic method as employed within the framework of a therapy of the neuroses; but I should like to advise against assessing its value or applying it outside this framework. Since, however, I cannot in these pages offer a 'therapy of the neuroses' of the sort needed by practitioners, what I have just said is equivalent to postponing my account of the subject to a possible later publication. But I am able, I think, to add the following remarks by way of expansion and elucidation.

(1) I do not maintain that I have actually got rid of all the hysterical symptoms that I have undertaken to influence by the cathartic method. But it is my opinion that the obstacles have lain in the personal circumstances of the patients and have not been due to any question of theory. I am justified in leaving these unsuccessful cases out of account in arriving at a judgement, just as a surgeon disregards cases of death which occur under anaesthesia, owing to post-operational haemorrhage, accidental sepsis, etc., in making a decision about a new technique. When I come to deal with the difficulties and drawbacks of the procedure later on, I shall return to a consideration of failures from this source. [See p. 301.]

(2) The cathartic method is not to be regarded as worthless because it is a symptomatic and not a causal one. For a causal therapy is in fact as a rule only a prophylactic one; it brings to a halt any further effects of the noxious agency, but does not therefore necessarily get rid of the results which that agency has already brought about. As a rule a second phase of treatment is required to perform this latter task, and in cases of hysteria the cathartic method is quite invaluable for this purpose.

(3) Where a period of hysterical production, an acute hysterical paroxysm, has been overcome and all that is left over are hysterical symptoms in the shape of residual phenomena, the cathartic method suffices for every indication and brings about complete and permanent successes. A favourable therapeutic constellation of this kind is not seldom to be found precisely in the region of sexual life, owing to the wide oscillations in the intensity of sexual needs and the complications of the conditions necessary in order to bring about a sexual trauma. Here the cathartic method does all that can be asked of it, for the physician cannot set himself the task of altering a constitution such as the hysterical one. He must content himself with getting rid of the troubles to which such a constitution is inclined and which may arise from it with the conjunction of external circumstances. He will feel satisfied if the patient

regains her working capacity. Moreover, he is not without consolation for the future when he considers the possibility of a relapse. He is aware of the principal feature in the aetiology of the neuroses—that their genesis is as a rule overdetermined,[1] that several factors must come together to produce this result; and he may hope that this convergence will not be repeated at once, even though a few individual aetiological factors remain operative.

It might be objected that, in cases of hysteria like this, in which the illness has run its course, the residual symptoms in any case pass away spontaneously. It may be said in reply, however, that a spontaneous cure of this kind is very often neither rapid nor complete enough and that it can be assisted to an extraordinary degree by our therapeutic intervention. We may readily leave it for the moment as an unresolved question whether by means of the cathartic therapy we cure only what is capable of spontaneous cure or sometimes also what would not have been cleared up spontaneously.

(4) Where we meet with an acute hysteria, a case which is passing through the period of the most active production of hysterical symptoms and in which the ego is being constantly overwhelmed by the products of the illness (i.e. during a hysterical psychosis), even the cathartic method will make little change in the appearance and course of the disorder. In such circumstances we find ourselves in the same position as regards the neurosis as a physician faced by an acute infectious disease. The aetiological factors have performed their work sufficiently at a time which has now passed and is beyond the reach of any influence; and now, after the period of incubation has elapsed, they have become manifest. The illness cannot be broken off short. We must wait for it to run its course and in the meantime make the patient's circumstances as favourable as possible. If, during an acute period like this, we get rid of the products of the illness, the freshly generated hysterical symptoms, we must also be prepared to find that those that have been got rid of will promptly be replaced by others. The physician will not be spared the depressing feeling of being faced by a Sisyphean task. The immense expenditure of labour, and the dissatisfaction of the patient's family, to whom the inevitable length of an acute neurosis is not likely to be as familiar as the

[1] [See footnote, p. 212.]

analogous case of an acute infectious disease—these and other difficulties will probably make a systematic application of the cathartic method as a rule impossible in any given case. Nevertheless, it remains a matter for serious consideration whether it may not be true that even in an acute hysteria the regular clearing up of the products of the illness exercises a curative influence, by supporting the patient's normal ego which is engaged in the work of defence, and by preserving it from being overwhelmed and falling into a psychosis and even perhaps into a permanent state of confusion.

What the cathartic method is able to accomplish even in acute hysteria, and how it even restricts the fresh production of pathological symptoms in a manner that is of practical importance, is quite clearly revealed by the case history of Anna O., in which Breuer first learnt to employ this psychotherapeutic procedure.

(5) Where it is a question of hysterias which run a chronic course, accompanied by a moderate but constant production of hysterical symptoms, we find the strongest reason for regretting our lack of a therapy which is effective causally, but we also have most ground for the appreciation of the value of the cathartic procedure as a *symptomatic* therapy. In such cases we have to do with the mischief produced by an aetiology that persists chronically. Everything depends on reinforcing the patient's nervous system in its capacity to resist; and we must reflect that the existence of a hysterical symptom means a weakening of the resistance of that nervous system and represents a factor predisposing to hysteria. As can be seen from the mechanism of monosymptomatic hysteria, a new hysterical symptom is most easily formed in connection with, and on the analogy of, one that is already present. The point at which a symptom has already broken through once (see p. 203) forms a weak spot at which it will break through again the next time. A psychical group that has once been split off plays the part of a 'provoking' crystal from which a crystallization which would otherwise not have occurred will start with the greatest facility [p. 123]. To get rid of the symptoms which are already present, to undo the psychical changes which underlie them, is to give back to patients the whole amount of their capacity for resistance, so that they can successfully withstand the effects of the noxious agency. A very great deal can be done for such

patients by means of prolonged supervision and occasional 'chimney-sweeping' (p. 30).

(6) It remains for me to mention the apparent contradiction between the admission that not all hysterical symptoms are psychogenic and the assertion that they can all be got rid of by a psychotherapeutic procedure. The solution lies in the fact that some of these non-psychogenic symptoms (stigmata, for instance) are, it is true, indications of illness, but cannot be described as ailments; and consequently it is not of practical importance if they persist after the successful treatment of the illness. As regards other such symptoms, it seems to be the case that in some roundabout way they are carried off along with the psychogenic symptoms, just as, perhaps, in some roundabout way they are after all dependent on a psychical causation.

I must now consider the difficulties and disadvantages of our therapeutic procedure, so far as they do not become obvious to everyone from the case histories reported above or from the remarks on the technique of the method which follow later. I will enumerate and indicate these difficulties rather than elaborate them.

The procedure is laborious and time-consuming for the physician. It presupposes great interest in psychological happenings, but personal concern for the patients as well. I cannot imagine bringing myself to delve into the psychical mechanism of a hysteria in anyone who struck me as low-minded and repellent, and who, on closer acquaintance, would not be capable of arousing human sympathy; whereas I can keep the treatment of a tabetic or rheumatic patient apart from personal approval of this kind. The demands made on the patient are not less. The procedure is not applicable at all below a certain level of intelligence, and it is made very much more difficult by any trace of feebleness of mind. The complete consent and complete attention of the patients are needed, but above all their confidence, since the analysis invariably leads to the disclosure of the most intimate and secret psychical events. A good number of the patients who would be suitable for this form of treatment abandon the doctor as soon as the suspicion begins to dawn on them of the direction in which the investigation is leading. For patients such as these the doctor has remained a stranger. With others, who have decided to put themselves in his hands and place their confidence in him—a step which in other such situations is only taken voluntarily and never at the doctor's request—with these other patients, I say, it is almost inevitable that their personal relation to him will force itself, for a time at least, unduly into the foreground. It seems, indeed, as though an influence of this kind on the part of the doctor is a *sine qua non* to a solution of the problem.[1] I do not think any essential difference is made in this respect whether hypnosis can be used or whether it has to be by-passed and replaced by something else. But reason demands that we should emphasize the fact that these drawbacks, though they are inseparable from our procedure, cannot be laid at its door. On the contrary, it is quite clear that they are based on the predetermining conditions of the neuroses that are to be cured and that they must attach to any medical activity which involves intense preoccupation with the patient and leads to a psychical change in him. I have not been able to attribute any deleterious effects or danger to the employment of hypnosis, though I made copious use of it in some of my cases. Where I caused damage, the reasons lay elsewhere and deeper. If I survey my therapeutic efforts during the last few years since the communications made by my honoured teacher and friend Josef Breuer showed me the use of the cathartic method, I believe that in spite of everything, I have done much more, and more frequent, good than harm and have accomplished some things which no other therapeutic procedure could have achieved. It has on the whole, as the 'Preliminary Communication' put it, brought 'considerable therapeutic advantages' [p. 17].

There is one other advantage in the use of this procedure which I must emphasize. I know of no better way of getting to understand a severe case of complicated neurosis with a greater or lesser admixture of hysteria than by submitting it to an analysis by Breuer's method. The first thing that happens is the disappearance of whatever exhibits a hysterical mechanism. In the meantime I have learnt in the course of the analysis to interpret the residual phenomena and to trace their aetiology; and in this way I have secured a firm basis for deciding which of the weapons in the therapeutic armoury against the neuroses is indicated in the case concerned. When

---

[1] [This topic is discussed at greater length below, p. 301 ff.]

I reflect on the difference that I usually find between my judgement on a case of neurosis *before* and *after* an analysis of this kind, I am almost inclined to regard an analysis as essential for the understanding of a neurotic illness. Moreover, I have adopted the habit of combining cathartic psychotherapy with a rest-cure which can, if need be, be extended into a complete treatment of feeding-up on Weir Mitchell lines. This gives me the advantage of being able on the one hand to avoid the very disturbing introduction of new psychical impressions during a psychotherapy, and on the other hand to remove the boredom of a rest-cure, in which the patients not infrequently fall into the habit of harmful day-dreaming. It might be expected that the often very considerable psychical work imposed on the patients during a cathartic treatment, and the excitations resulting from the reproduction of traumatic experiences, would run counter to the intentions of the Weir Mitchell rest-cure and would hinder the successes which we are accustomed to see it bring about. But the opposite is in fact the case. A combination such as this between the Breuer and Weir Mitchell procedures produces all the physical improvement that we expect from the latter, as well as having a far-reaching psychical influence such as never results from a rest-cure without psychotherapy.[1]

(2)

I will now return to my earlier remark [p. 256] that in my attempts to apply Breuer's method more extensively I came upon the difficulty that a number of patients could not be hypnotized, although their diagnosis was one of hysteria and it seemed probable that the psychical mechanism described by us operated in them. I needed hypnosis to extend their memory in order to find the pathogenic recollections which were not present in their ordinary consciousness. I was obliged therefore either to give up the idea of treating such patients or to endeavour to bring about this extension in some other way.

I was able as little as anyone else to explain why it is that one person can be hypnotized and another not, and thus I

---

[1] [Weir Mitchell's book on *The Treatment of Certain Forms of Neurasthenia and Hysteria* had been favourably reviewed by Freud (1887*b*).]

could not adopt a causal method of meeting the difficulty. I noticed, however, that in some patients the obstacle lay still further back: they refused even any *attempt* at hypnosis. The idea then occurred to me one day that the two cases might be identical and that both might signify an unwillingness; that people who were not hypnotizable were people who had a psychical objection to hypnosis, whether their objection was expressed as unwillingness or not. I am not clear in my mind whether I can maintain this view.

The problem was, however, how to by-pass hypnosis and yet obtain the pathogenic recollections. This I succeeded in doing in the following manner.

When, at our first interview, I asked my patients if they remembered what had originally occasioned the symptom concerned, in some cases they said they knew nothing of it, while in others they brought forward something which they described as an obscure recollection and could not pursue further. If, following the example of Bernheim when he awoke in his patients impressions from their somnambulistic state which had ostensibly been forgotten (cf. p. 109 f.), I now became insistent—if I assured them that they *did* know it, that it would occur to their minds,—then, in the first cases, something did actually occur to them, and, in the others, their memory went a step further. After this I became still more insistent; I told the patients to lie down and deliberately close their eyes in order to 'concentrate'—all of which had at least some resemblance to hypnosis. I then found that without any hypnosis new recollections emerged which went further back and which probably related to our topic. Experiences like this made me think that it would in fact be possible for the pathogenic groups of ideas, that were after all certainly present, to be brought to light by mere insistence; and since this insistence involved effort on my part and so suggested the idea that I had to overcome a resistance, the situation led me at once to the theory that *by means of my psychical work I had to overcome a psychical force in the patients which was opposed to the pathogenic ideas becoming conscious (being remembered)*. A new understanding seemed to open before my eyes when it occurred to me that this must no doubt be the same psychical force that had played a part in the generating of the hysterical symptom and had at that time prevented the pathogenic idea from becoming conscious. What kind of force could one suppose was operative here, and what motive could have put it into operation? I could easily form an opinion on this. For I already had at my disposal a few completed analyses in which I had come to know examples of ideas that were pathogenic, and had been forgotten and put out of consciousness. From these I recognized a universal characteristic of such ideas: they were all of a distressing nature, calculated to arouse the affects of shame, of self-reproach and of psychical pain, and the feeling of being harmed; they were all of a kind that one would prefer not to have experienced, that one would rather forget. From all this there arose, as it were automatically, the thought of *defence*. It has indeed been generally admitted by psychologists that the acceptance of a new idea (acceptance in the sense of believing or of recognizing as real) is dependent on the nature and trend of the ideas already united in the ego, and they have invented special technical names for this process of censorship [1] to which the new arrival must submit. The patient's ego had been approached by an idea which proved to be incompatible, which provoked on the part of the ego a repelling force of which the purpose was defence against this incompatible idea. This defence was in fact successful. The idea in question was forced out of consciousness and out of memory. The psychical trace of it was apparently lost to view. Nevertheless that trace must be there. If I endeavoured to direct the patient's attention to it, I became aware, in the form of *resistance*, of the same force as had shown itself in the form of *repulsion* when the symptom was generated. If, now, I could make it appear probable that the idea had become pathogenic precisely as a result of its expulsion and repression, the chain would seem complete. In several of the discussions on our case histories, and in a short paper on 'The Neuro-Psychoses of Defence' (1894a), I have attempted to sketch out the psychological hypotheses by the help of which this causal connection—the fact of conversion—can be demonstrated.

Thus a psychical force, aversion on the part of the ego, had originally driven the pathogenic idea out of association and was now [2] opposing its return to memory. The hysterical

---

[1] [This appears to be Freud's first published use of the term.]

[2] ['*Jetzt.*' This word is found only in the first edition. It is omitted, probably by accident, in all the later editions.]

patient's 'not knowing' was in fact a 'not wanting to know'—a not wanting which might be to a greater or less extent conscious. The task of the therapist, therefore, lies in overcoming by his psychical work this resistance to association. He does this in the first place by 'insisting', by making use of psychical compulsion to direct the patients' attention to the ideational traces of which he is in search. His efforts, however, are not exhausted by this, but, as I shall show, they take on other forms in the course of an analysis and call in other psychical forces to assist them.

I must dwell on the question of insistence a little longer. Simple assurances such as 'of course you know it', 'tell me all the same', 'you'll think of it in a moment' do not carry us very far. Even with patients in a state of 'concentration' the thread breaks off after a few sentences. It should not be forgotten, however, that it is always a question here of a *quantitative* comparison, of a struggle between motive forces of different degrees of strength or intensity. Insistence on the part of a strange doctor who is unfamiliar with what is happening is not powerful enough to deal with the resistance to association in a serious case of hysteria. We must think of stronger means.

In these circumstances I make use in the first instance of a small technical device.[1] I inform the patient that, a moment later, I shall apply pressure to his forehead, and I assure him that, all the time the pressure lasts, he will see before him a recollection in the form of a picture or will have it in his thoughts in the form of an idea occurring to him; and I pledge him to communicate this picture or idea to me, whatever it may be. He is not to keep it to himself because he may happen to think it is not what is wanted, not the right thing, or because it would be too disagreeable for him to say it. There is to be no criticism of it, no reticence, either for emotional reasons or because it is judged unimportant. Only in this manner can we find what we are in search of, but in this manner we shall find it infallibly. Having said this, I press for a few seconds on the forehead of the patient as he lies in front of me; I then leave go and ask quietly, as though there were no question of a disappointment: 'What did you see?' or 'What occurred to you?'

This procedure has taught me much and has also invariably achieved its aim. To-day I can no longer do without it. I am

[1] [See p. 110 and footnote.]

of course aware that a pressure on the forehead like this could be replaced by any other signal or by some other exercise of physical influence on the patient; but since the patient is lying in front of me, pressure on his forehead, or taking his head between my two hands, seems to be the most convenient way of applying suggestion for the purpose I have in view. It would be possible for me to say by way of explaining the efficacy of this device that it corresponded to a 'momentarily intensified hypnosis'; but the mechanism of hypnosis is so puzzling to me that I would rather not make use of it as an explanation. I am rather of opinion that the advantage of the procedure lies in the fact that by means of it I dissociate the patient's attention from his conscious searching and reflecting—from everything, in short, on which he can employ his will—in the same sort of way in which this is effected by staring into a crystal ball, and so on.[1] The conclusion which I draw from the fact that what I am looking for always appears under the pressure of my hand is as follows. The pathogenic idea which has ostensibly been forgotten is always lying ready 'close at hand' and can be reached by associations that are easily accessible. It is merely a question of getting some obstacle out of the way. This obstacle seems once again to be the subject's will, and different people can learn with different degrees of ease to free themselves from their intentional thinking and to adopt an attitude of completely objective observation towards the psychical processes taking place in them.[2]

What emerges under the pressure of my hand is not always a 'forgotten' recollection; it is only in the rarest cases that the actual pathogenic recollections lie so easily to hand on the surface. It is much more frequent for an idea to emerge which is an intermediate link in the chain of associations between the idea from which we start and the pathogenic idea which we are in search of; or it may be an idea which forms the starting point of a new series of thoughts and recollections at the end

[1] [The part played in the technique of hypnotism by distracting conscious attention was discussed by Freud much later, in Chapter X of his *Group Psychology* (1921c), *Standard Ed.*, **18**, 126. Further references to the use of the same mechanism in telepathy and in joking are enumerated in a footnote to that passage.]

[2] [The difficulty felt by some people in adopting this non-critical attitude was discussed by Freud at some length in Chapter II of *The Interpretation of Dreams* (1900a), *Standard Ed.*, **4**, 101–3.]

of which the pathogenic idea will be found. It is true that where this happens my pressure has not revealed the pathogenic idea —which would in any case be incomprehensible, torn from its context and without being led up to—but it has pointed the way to it and has shown the direction in which further investigation is to be made. The idea that is first provoked by the pressure may in such cases be a familiar recollection which has never been repressed. If on our way to the pathogenic idea the thread is broken off once more, it only needs a repetition of the procedure, of the pressure, to give us fresh bearings and a fresh starting-point.

On yet other occasions the pressure of the hand provokes a memory which is familiar in itself to the patient, but the appearance of which astonishes him because he has forgotten its relation to the idea from which we started. This relation is then confirmed in the further course of the analysis. All these consequences of the pressure give one a deceptive impression of there being a superior intelligence outside the patient's consciousness which keeps a large amount of psychical material arranged for particular purposes and has fixed a planned order for its return to consciousness. I suspect, however, that this unconscious second intelligence is no more than an appearance.

In every fairly complicated analysis the work is carried on by the repeated, indeed continuous, use of this procedure of pressure on the forehead. Sometimes this procedure, starting from where the patient's waking retrospection breaks off, points the further path through memories of which he has remained aware; sometimes it draws attention to connections which have been forgotten; sometimes it calls up and arranges recollections which have been withdrawn from association for many years but which can still be recognized as recollections; and sometimes, finally, as the climax of its achievement in the way of reproductive thinking, it causes thoughts to emerge which the patient will never recognize as his own, which he never *remembers*, although he admits that the context calls for them inexorably, and while he becomes convinced that it is precisely these ideas that are leading to the conclusion of the analysis and the removal of his symptoms.

I will try to enumerate a few instances of the excellent results brought about by this technical procedure.

I treated a girl suffering from an intolerable *tussis nervosa* which had dragged on for six years. It obviously drew nourishment from every common catarrh, but must nevertheless have had strong psychical motives. All other kinds of therapy had long proved impotent against it. I therefore tried to remove the symptom by means of psychical analysis. All she knew was that her nervous cough began when, at the age of fourteen, she was boarding with an aunt. She maintained that she knew nothing of any mental agitations at that time and did not believe that there was any motive for her complaint. Under the pressure of my hand she first of all remembered a big dog. She then recognized the picture in her memory: it was a dog of her aunt's which became attached to her, followed her about everywhere, and so on. And it now occurred to her, without further prompting, that this dog died, that the children gave it a solemn burial and that her cough started on the way back from the funeral. I asked why, but had once more to call in the help of a pressure. The thought then came to her: 'Now I am quite alone in the world. No one here loves me. This creature was my only friend, and now I have lost him.' She continued her story. 'The cough disappeared when I left my aunt's, but it came on again eighteen months later.' 'Why was that?' 'I don't know.' I pressed again. She recalled the news of her uncle's death, when the cough started again, and also recalled having a similar train of thought. Her uncle seems to have been the only member of the family who had shown any feeling for her, who had loved her. Here, then, was the pathogenic idea. No one loved her, they preferred everyone else to her, she did not deserve to be loved, and so on. But there was something attaching to the idea of 'love' which there was a strong resistance to her telling me. The analysis broke off before this was cleared up.

Some time ago I was asked to relieve an elderly lady of her attacks of anxiety, though judging by her traits of character she was scarcely suitable for treatment of this kind. Since her menopause she had become excessively pious, and she used to receive me at each visit armed with a small ivory crucifix concealed in her hand, as though I were the Evil One. Her anxiety attacks, which were of a hysterical character, went back to her early girlhood and, according to her, originated from the use of a preparation of iodine intended to reduce a moderate

swelling of her thyroid gland. I naturally rejected this derivation and tried to find another instead of it which would har-
monize better with my views on the aetiology of the neuroses.
I asked her first for an impression from her youth which stood
in a causal relation to her anxiety attacks, and, under the
pressure of my hand, a memory emerged of her reading what
is known as an 'edifying' book, in which there occurred a
mention, in a sufficiently pious strain, of the sexual processes.
The passage in question made an impression on the girl which
was quite the reverse of the author's intention: she burst into
tears and flung the book away. This was *before* her first anxiety
attack. A second pressure on the patient's forehead conjured
up a further reminiscence—the recollection of a tutor of her
brothers who had manifested a great admiration for her and
towards whom she herself had had feelings of some warmth.
This recollection culminated in the reproduction of an evening
in her parents' house when they had all sat round the table
with the young man and had enjoyed themselves immensely in
an entertaining conversation. During the night following that
evening she was woken up by her first anxiety attack which,
it is safe to say, had more to do with a repudiation of a sensual
impulse than with any contemporary doses of iodine.—What
prospect should I have had by any other method of revealing
such a connection, against her own views and assertions, in this
recalcitrant patient who was so prejudiced against me and every
form of mundane therapy?

Another example concerns a young, happily-married woman.
As long ago as in her early girlhood she used for some time to
be found every morning in a stuporose condition, with her
limbs rigid, her mouth open and her tongue protruding; and
now once again she was suffering, on waking, from attacks
which were similar though not so severe. Since deep hypnosis
turned out not to be obtainable, I began to investigate while
she was in a state of concentration. At my first pressure I assured
her that she would see something that was directly related to
the causes of her condition in her childhood. She was quiet and
co-operative. She saw once more the house in which she had
spent her early girlhood, her own room, the position of her bed,
her grandmother, who had lived with them at that time, and
one of her governesses of whom she had been very fond. A
number of small scenes, all of them unimportant, which took

place in these rooms and between these people followed one after the other; they were concluded by the departure of the governess, who left in order to get married. I could make nothing at all of these reminiscences; I could not establish any relation between them and the aetiology of the attacks. Various circumstances showed, however, that they belonged to the same period at which the attacks first appeared. But before I was able to proceed with the analysis I had occasion to talk to a colleague who in former years had been the family doctor of my patient's parents. He gave me the following information. At the time at which he was treating the girl, who was approaching maturity and very well developed physically, for her first attacks, he was struck by the excessive affectionateness of the relation between her and the governess who was at that time in the house. He became suspicious and induced the grandmother to keep an eye on this relationship. After a short time the old lady was able to report to him that the governess was in the habit of visiting the child in bed at night and that after such nights the child was invariably found next morning in an attack. They did not hesitate after this to arrange for the silent removal of this corrupter of youth. The children and even the mother were encouraged to believe that the governess had left in order to get married.—My therapy, which was immediately successful, consisted in giving the young woman the information I had received.

The revelations which one obtains through the procedure of pressing occasionally appear in a very remarkable form and in circumstances which make the assumption of there being an unconscious intelligence even more tempting. Thus I remember a lady who had suffered for many years from obsessions and phobias and who referred me to her childhood for the genesis of her illness but was also quite unable to say what might be to blame for it. She was frank and intelligent and she put up only a remarkably small conscious resistance. (I may remark in parenthesis that the psychical mechanism of obsessions has a very great deal of internal kinship with hysterical symptoms and that the technique of analysis is the same for both of them.) When I asked this lady whether she had seen anything or had any recollection under the pressure of my hand, she replied: 'Neither the one nor the other, but a word has suddenly occurred to me.' 'A single word?' 'Yes, but it sounds too silly.'

'Say it all the same.' 'Concierge.' 'Nothing else?' 'No.' I pressed a second time and once more an isolated word shot through her mind: 'Night-gown.' I saw now that this was a new sort of method of answering, and by pressing repeatedly I brought out what seemed to be a meaningless series of words: 'Concierge' —'night-gown'—'bed'—'town'—'farm-cart.' 'What does all this mean?' I asked. She reflected for a moment and the following thought occurred to her: 'It must be the story that has just come into my head. When I was ten years old and my next elder sister was twelve, she went raving mad one night and had to be tied down and taken into the town on a farm-cart. I remember perfectly that it was the concierge who overpowered her and afterwards went with her to the asylum as well.' We pursued this method of investigation and our oracle produced another series of words, which, though we were not able to interpret all of them, made it possible to continue this story and lead on from it to another one. Soon, moreover, the meaning of this reminiscence became clear. Her sister's illness had made such a deep impression on her because the two of them shared a secret; they slept in one room and on a particular night they had both been subjected to sexual assaults by a certain man. The mention of this sexual trauma in the patient's childhood revealed not only the origin of her first obsessions but also the trauma which subsequently produced the pathogenic effects.

The peculiarity of this case lay only in the emergence of isolated key-words which we had to work into sentences; for the appearance of disconnectedness and irrelevance which characterized the words emitted in this oracular fashion applies equally to the complete ideas and scenes which are normally produced under my pressure. When these are followed up, it invariably turns out that the apparently disconnected reminiscences are closely linked in thought and that they lead quite straight to the pathogenic factor we are looking for. For this reason I am glad to recall a case of analysis in which my confidence in the products of pressure were first put to a hard test but afterwards brilliantly justified.

A very intelligent and apparently happy young married woman had consulted me about an obstinate pain in her abdomen which was resistant to treatment. I recognized that the pain was situated in the abdominal wall and must be referred to palpable muscular indurations, and I ordered local treatment. Some months later I saw the patient again and she said to me: 'The pain I had then passed off after the treatment you recommended, and it stayed away for a long time; but now it has come back in a nervous form. I know that is so, because I no longer have it, as I used to, when I make certain movements, but only at particular times—for instance, when I wake up in the morning and when I am agitated in certain ways.' The lady's diagnosis was quite correct. It was now a question of finding out the cause of the pain, and she could not help me about this while she was in an uninfluenced state. When I asked her, in concentration and under the pressure of my hand, whether anything occurred to her or whether she saw anything, she decided in favour of seeing and began to describe her visual pictures. She saw something like a sun with rays, which I naturally took to be a phosphene, produced by pressure on the eyes. I expected that something more serviceable would follow. But she went on: 'Stars of a curious pale blue light, like moonlight' and so on, all of which I took to be no more than flickering, flashes and bright specks before her eyes. I was already prepared to regard this experiment as a failure and I was wondering how I could make an inconspicuous retreat from the affair, when my attention was attracted by one of the phenomena which she described. She saw a large black cross, leaning over, which had round its edges the same shimmer of light with which all her other pictures had shone, and on whose cross-beam a small flame flickered. Clearly there could no longer be any question of a phosphene here. I now listened carefully. Quantities of pictures appeared bathed in the same light, curious signs looking rather like Sanskrit; figures like triangles, among them a large triangle; the cross once more. . . . This time I suspected an allegorical meaning and asked what the cross could be. 'It probably means pain,' she replied. I objected that by 'cross' one usually meant a moral burden. What lay concealed behind the pain? She could not say, and went on with her visions: a sun with golden rays. And this she was also able to interpret. 'It's God, the primaeval force.' Then came a gigantic lizard which regarded her enquiringly but not alarmingly. Then a heap of snakes. Then once more a sun, but with mild, silver rays; and in front of her, between her and this source of light, a grating which hid the centre of

the sun from her. I had known for some time that what I had
to deal with were allegories and at once asked the meaning of
this last picture. She answered without hesitation: 'The sun is
perfection, the ideal, and the grating represents my weaknesses
and faults which stand between me and the ideal.' 'Are you
reproaching yourself, then? Are you dissatisfied with yourself?'
'Yes indeed.' 'Since when?' 'Since I have been a member of
the Theosophical Society and have been reading its publications. I always had a low opinion of myself.' 'What has made
the strongest impression on you recently?' 'A translation from
the Sanskrit which is just now coming out in instalments.' A
minute later I was being initiated into her mental struggles
and her self-reproaches, and was hearing about a small episode
which gave rise to a self-reproach—an occasion on which what
had previously been an organic pain now for the first time
appeared as the consequence of the conversion of an excitation.
The pictures which I had first taken for phosphenes were
symbols of trains of thought influenced by the occult and were
perhaps actually emblems from the title-pages of occult books.

Hitherto I have been so warm in my praises of the achievements of pressure as an auxiliary procedure, and I have the
whole time so greatly neglected the aspect of defence or resistance, that I may no doubt have created an impression that this
little device has put us in a position to master the psychical
obstacles to a cathartic treatment. But to believe this would be
to make a serious mistake. Gains of this kind, so far as I can
see, are not to be looked for in treatment. Here, as elsewhere,
a large change requires a large amount of work. The procedure
by pressure is no more than a trick for temporarily taking
unawares an ego which is eager for defence. In all fairly serious
cases the ego recalls its aims once more and proceeds with its
resistance.

I must mention the different forms in which this resistance
appears. One is that, as a rule, the pressure procedure fails on
the first or second occasion. The patient then declares, very
disappointedly: 'I expected something would occur to me, but
all I thought was how tensely I was expecting it. Nothing
came.' The fact of the patient putting himself on his guard
like this does not yet amount to an obstacle. We can say in
reply: 'It's precisely because you were too curious; it will work

next time.' And in fact it does work. It is remarkable how often patients, even the most docile and intelligent, can completely forget their undertaking, though they had agreed to it beforehand. They promised to say whatever occurred to them under the pressure of my hand, irrespectively of whether it seemed to them relevant or not, and of whether it was agreeable to them to say it or not—to say it, that is, without selecting and without being influenced by criticism or affect. But they do not keep this promise; it is evidently beyond their strength to do so. The work keeps on coming to a stop and they keep on maintaining that this time nothing has occurred to them. We must not believe what they say, we must always assume, and tell them, too, that they have kept something back because they thought it unimportant or found it distressing. We must insist on this, we must repeat the pressure and represent ourselves as infallible, till at last we are really told something. The patient then adds: 'I could have told you that the first time.' 'Why didn't you say it?' 'I couldn't believe it could be that. It was only when it came back every time that I made up my mind to say it.' Or else: 'I hoped it wouldn't be that of all things. I could well do without saying that. It was only when it refused to be repressed that I saw I shouldn't be let off.' Thus after the event the patient betrays the motives for a resistance which he refused to admit to begin with. He is evidently quite unable to do anything but put up resistance.

This resistance often conceals itself behind some remarkable excuses. 'My mind is distracted to-day; the clock (or the piano in the next room) is disturbing me.' I have learned to answer such remarks: 'Not at all. You have at this moment come up against something that you had rather not say. It won't do any good. Go on thinking about it.' The longer the pause between my hand-pressure and the patient's beginning to speak, the more suspicious I become and the more it is to be feared that the patient is re-arranging what has occurred to him and is mutilating it in his reproduction of it. A most important piece of information is often announced as being a redundant accessory, like an opera prince disguised as a beggar. 'Something has occurred to me now, but it has nothing to do with the subject. I'm only saying it because you want to know everything.' Accompanying words such as these usually introduce the long-sought solution. I always prick up my ears when I hear a patient speak so disparagingly of something that has occurred to him. For it is an indication that defence has been successful if the pathogenic ideas seem, when they re-emerge, to have so little importance. From this we can infer in what the process of defence consisted: it consisted in turning a strong idea into a weak one, in robbing it of its affect.

A pathogenic recollection is thus recognizable, among other things, by the fact that the patient describes it as unimportant and nevertheless only utters it under resistance. There are cases, too, in which the patient tries to disown it even after its return. 'Something has occurred to me now, but you obviously put it into my head.' Or, 'I know what you expect me to answer. Of course you believe I've thought this or that.' A particularly clever method of disavowal lies in saying: 'Something has occurred to me now, it's true, but it seems to me as if I'd put it in deliberately. It doesn't seem to be a reproduced thought at all.' In all such cases, I remain unshakably firm. I avoid entering into any of these distinctions but explain to the patient that they are only forms of his resistance and pretexts raised by it against reproducing this particular memory, which we must recognize in spite of all this.

When memories return in the form of pictures our task is in general easier than when they return as thoughts. Hysterical patients, who are as a rule of a 'visual' type, do not make such difficulties for the analyst as those with obsessions.

Once a picture has emerged from the patient's memory, we may hear him say that it becomes fragmentary and obscure in proportion as he proceeds with his description of it. *The patient is, as it were, getting rid of it by turning it into words.* We go on to examine the memory picture itself in order to discover the direction in which our work is to proceed. 'Look at the picture once more. Has it disappeared?' 'Most of it, yes, but I still see this detail.' 'Then this residue must still mean something. Either you will see something new in addition to it, or something will occur to you in connection with it.' When this work has been accomplished, the patient's field of vision is once more free and we can conjure up another picture. On other occasions, however, a picture of this kind will remain obstinately before the patient's inward eye, in spite of his having described it; and this is an indication to me that he still has something important to tell me about the topic of the picture. As soon as this has been done the picture vanishes, like a ghost that has been laid.

It is of course of great importance for the progress of the analysis that one should always turn out to be in the right *vis-à-vis* the patient, otherwise one would always be dependent on what he chose to tell one. It is therefore consoling to know that the pressure technique in fact never fails, apart from a single case, which I shall have to discuss later [p. 301 ff.] but of which I can at once say that it corresponds to a particular motive for resistance. It can of course happen that one makes use of the procedure in circumstances in which there is nothing for it to reveal. For instance, we may ask for the further aetiology of a symptom when we already have it completely before us, or we may investigate a psychical genealogy of a symptom, such as a pain, which is in fact a somatic one. In such cases the patient will equally assert that nothing has occurred to him and this time he will be in the right. We can avoid doing the patient an injustice if we make it a quite general rule all through the analysis to keep an eye on his facial expression as he lies quietly before us. We can then learn to distinguish without any difficulty the restful state of mind that accompanies the real absence of a recollection from the tension and signs of emotion with which he tries to disavow the emerging recollection, in obedience to defence. Moreover, experiences like these make it possible also to use the pressure technique for purposes of differential diagnosis.

Thus even with the assistance of the pressure technique the work is by no means easy. The one advantage that we gain is of learning from the results of this procedure the direction in which we have to conduct our enquiries and the things that we have to insist upon to the patient. With some cases this suffices. The principal point is that I should guess the secret and tell it to the patient straight out; and he is then as a rule obliged to abandon his rejection of it. In other cases more is required. The patient's persisting resistance is indicated by the fact that connections are broken, solutions fail to appear, the pictures are recalled indistinctly and incompletely. Looking back from a later period of an analysis to an earlier one, we are often astonished to realize in what a mutilated manner all the ideas and scenes emerged which we extracted from the patient by the procedure of pressing. Precisely the essential elements of the picture were missing—its relation to himself or to the main contents of his thoughts—and that is why it remained unintelligible.

I will give one or two examples of the way in which a censoring of this kind operates when pathogenic recollections first emerge. For instance, the patient sees the upper part of a woman's body with the dress not properly fastened—out of carelessness, it seems. It is not until much later that he fits a head to this torso and thus reveals a particular person and his relation to her. Or he brings up a reminiscence from his childhood of two boys. What they look like is quite obscure to him, but they are said to have been guilty of some misdeed. It is not until many months later and after the analysis has made great advances that he sees this reminiscence once more and recognizes himself in one of the children and his brother in the other.

What means have we at our disposal for overcoming this continual resistance? Few, but they include almost all those by which one man can ordinarily exert a psychical influence on another. In the first place, we must reflect that a psychical resistance, especially one that has been in force for a long time, can only be resolved slowly and by degrees, and we must wait patiently. In the next place, we may reckon on the intellectual interest which the patient begins to feel after working for a short time. By explaining things to him, by giving him information about the marvellous world of psychical processes into which we ourselves only gained insight by such analyses, we make him himself into a collaborator, induce him to regard himself with the objective interest of an investigator, and thus push back his resistance, resting as it does on an affective basis. But lastly—and this remains the strongest lever—we must endeavour, after we have discovered the motives for his defence, to deprive them of their value or even to replace them by more powerful ones. This no doubt is where it ceases to be possible to state psychotherapeutic activity in formulas. One works to the best of one's power, as an elucidator (where ignorance has given rise to fear), as a teacher, as the representative of a freer or superior view of the world, as a father confessor who gives absolution, as it were, by a continuance of his sympathy and respect after the confession has been made. One tries to give the patient human assistance, so far as this is allowed by the capacity of one's own personality and by the amount of sympathy that one can feel for the particular case. It is an essential precondition for such psychical activity that we should have more or less divined the nature of the case and the motives of the defence operating in it, and fortunately the technique of insistence and pressure takes us as far as this. The more such riddles we have already solved, the easier we may find it to guess a new one and the sooner we shall be able to start on the truly curative psychical work. For it is well to recognize this clearly: the patient only gets free from the hysterical symptom by reproducing the pathogenic impressions that caused it and by giving utterance to them with an expression of affect, and thus the therapeutic task *consists solely in inducing him to do so*; when once this task has been accomplished there is nothing left for the physician to correct or to remove. Whatever may be required for this purpose in the way of counter-suggestions has already been expended during the struggle against the resistance. The situation may be compared with the unlocking of a locked door, after which opening it by turning the handle offers no further difficulty.

Besides the intellectual motives which we mobilize to overcome the resistance, there is an affective factor, the personal influence of the physician, which we can seldom do without, and in a number of cases the latter alone is in a position to remove the resistance. The situation here is no different from what it is elsewhere in medicine and there is no therapeutic procedure of which one may say that it can do entirely without the co-operation of this personal factor.

(3)

In view of what I have said in the preceding section about the difficulties of my technique, which I have unsparingly exposed (I brought them together, incidentally, from the severest cases; things often turn out very much more conveniently)—in view of all this, then, everyone will no doubt feel inclined to ask whether it would not be more expedient, instead of putting up with all these troubles, to make a more energetic use of hypnosis or to restrict the use of the cathartic method to patients who can be put under deep hypnosis. As regards the latter proposal I should have to answer that in that case the number of suitable patients, so far as *my* skill is concerned, would dwindle far too much; and I would meet the first piece of advice with the suspicion that the forcible imposition of hypnosis might not spare us much resistance. My experiences on this point, oddly enough, have not been numerous, and I cannot, therefore, go beyond a suspicion. But where I have carried out a cathartic treatment under hypnosis instead of under concentration, I did not find that this diminished the work I had to do. Not long ago I completed a treatment of this kind in the course of which I caused a hysterical paralysis of the legs to clear up. The patient passed into a state which was very different psychically from waking and which was characterized physically by the fact that it was impossible for her to open her eyes or get up till I had called out to her: 'Now wake up!' None the less I have never come across greater resistance than in this case. I attached no importance to these physical signs, and towards the end of the treatment, which lasted ten months, they had ceased to be noticeable. But in spite of this the patient's state while we were working lost none of its psychical[1] characteristics—the capacity she possessed for remembering unconscious material and her quite special relation to the figure of the physician. On the other hand, I have given an example in the case history of Frau Emmy von N. of a cathartic treatment in the deepest somnambulism in which resistance played scarcely any part. But it is also true that I learnt from that lady nothing whose telling might have called for any special overcoming of objections, nothing that she could not have told me even in a waking state, supposing we had been acquainted for some time and she had thought fairly highly of me. I never reached the true causes of her illness, which were no doubt identical with the causes of her relapse after my treatment (for this was my first attempt with this method); and the only occasion on which I happened to ask her for a reminiscence which involved an erotic element [p. 79] I found her just as reluctant and untrustworthy in what she told me as I did later with any of my non-somnambulistic patients. I have already spoken in that lady's case history of the resistance which she put up even during somnambulism to other requests and suggestions of mine. I have become altogether sceptical about the value of hypnosis in facilitating cathartic

[1] ['Psychical' in the first edition only; omitted in all the later editions.]

treatments, since I have experienced instances in which during deep somnambulism there has been absolute *therapeutic* recalcitrance, where in other respects the patient has been perfectly obedient. I reported a case of this kind briefly on p. 100 *n.*, and I could add others. I may admit, too, that this experience has corresponded pretty well to the requirement I insist upon that there shall be a quantitative relation between cause and effect in the psychical field as well [as in the physical one].[1]

In what I have hitherto said the idea of resistance has forced its way into the foreground. I have shown how, in the course of our therapeutic work, we have been led to the view that hysteria originates through the repression of an incompatible idea from a motive of defence. On this view, the repressed idea would persist as a memory trace that is weak (has little intensity), while the affect that is torn from it would be used for a somatic innervation. (That is, the excitation is 'converted'.) It would seem, then, that it is precisely through its repression that the idea becomes the cause of morbid symptoms—that is to say, becomes pathogenic. A hysteria exhibiting this psychical mechanism may be given the name of 'defence hysteria'.

Now both of us, Breuer and I, have repeatedly spoken of two other kinds of hysteria, for which we have introduced the terms 'hypnoid hysteria' and 'retention hysteria'. It was hypnoid hysteria which was the first of all to enter our field of study. I could not, indeed, find a better example of it than Breuer's first case, which stands at the head of our case histories.[2] Breuer has put forward for such cases of hypnoid hysteria a psychical mechanism which is substantially different from that of defence by conversion. In his view what happens in hypnoid hysteria is that an idea becomes pathogenic because it has been received during a special psychical state and has from the first remained outside the ego. No psychical force has therefore been required in order to keep it apart from the ego and no resistance need be aroused if we introduce it into the ego with the help of mental activity during somnambulism. And

---

[1] [Some remarks on the length of the period during which Freud made use of the techniques of 'pressure' and hypnotism respectively will be found above in a footnote on p. 110 f.]

[2] [The last nine words are omitted in the German collected editions, *G.S.*, 1925 and *G.W.*, 1952, in which the case of Anna O. is not included.]

Anna O.'s case history in fact shows no sign of any such resistance.

I regard this distinction as so important that, on the strength of it, I willingly adhere to this hypothesis of there being a hypnoid hysteria. Strangely enough, I have never in my own experience met with a genuine hypnoid hysteria. Any that I took in hand has turned into a defence hysteria. It is not, indeed, that I have never had to do with symptoms which demonstrably arose during dissociated states of consciousness and were obliged for that reason to remain excluded from the ego. This was sometimes so in my cases as well; but I was able to show afterwards that the so-called hypnoid state owed its separation to the fact that in it a psychical group had come into effect which had previously been split off by defence. In short, I am unable to suppress a suspicion that somewhere or other the roots of hypnoid and defence hysteria come together, and that there the primary factor is defence. But I can say nothing about this.

My judgement is for the moment equally uncertain as regards 'retention hysteria',[1] in which the therapeutic work is supposed equally to proceed without resistance. I had a case which I looked upon as a typical retention hysteria and I rejoiced in the prospect of an easy and certain success. But this success did not occur, though the work was in fact easy. I therefore suspect, though once again subject to all the reserve which is proper to ignorance, that at the basis of retention hysteria, too, an element of defence is to be found which has forced the whole process in the direction of hysteria. It is to be hoped that fresh observations will soon decide whether I am running the risk of falling into one-sidedness and error in thus favouring an extension of the concept of defence to the whole of hysteria.

I have dealt so far with the difficulties and technique of the cathartic method, and I should like to add a few indications as to the form assumed by an analysis when this technique is adopted. For me this is a highly interesting subject, but I cannot expect it to arouse similar interest in others, who have not yet carried out an analysis of this kind. I shall, it is true, once more be talking about the technique, but this time it

[1] [Cf. above, p. 211 and footnote.]

will be about inherent difficulties for which we cannot hold the patients responsible and which must be partly the same in a hypnoid or retention hysteria as in the defence hysterias which I have before my eyes as a model. I approach this last part of my exposition with the expectation that the psychical characteristics which will be revealed in it may one day acquire a certain value as raw material for the dynamics of ideation.

The first and most powerful impression made upon one during such an analysis is certainly that the pathogenic psychical material which has ostensibly been forgotten, which is not at the ego's disposal and which plays no part in association and memory, nevertheless in some fashion lies ready to hand and in correct and proper order. It is only a question of removing the resistances that bar the way to the material. In other respects this material is known,[1] in the same way in which we are able to know anything; the correct connections between the separate ideas and between them and the non-pathogenic ones, which are frequently remembered, are in existence; they have been completed at some time and are stored up in the memory. The pathogenic psychical material appears to be the property of an intelligence which is not necessarily inferior to that of the normal ego. The appearance of a second personality is often presented in the most deceptive manner.

Whether this impression is justified, or whether in thinking this we are not dating back to the period of the illness an arrangement of the psychical material which in fact was made after recovery—these are questions which I should prefer not to discuss as yet, and not in these pages. The observations made during such analyses can in any case be most conveniently and clearly described if we regard them from the position that we are able to assume after recovery for the purpose of surveying the case as a whole.

As a rule, indeed, the situation is not as simple as we have represented it in particular cases—for instance, where there is one symptom only, which has arisen from one major trauma. We do not usually find a *single* hysterical symptom, but a number of them, partly independent of one another and partly linked together. We must not expect to meet with a *single*

---

[1] ['*Gewusst*' ('known') in the first edition only. In all later German editions '*bewusst*' ('conscious') which seems to make much less good sense.]

traumatic memory and a *single* pathogenic idea as its nucleus; we must be prepared for *successions* of *partial* traumas and *concatenations* of pathogenic trains of thought. A monosymptomatic traumatic hysteria is, as it were, an elementary organism, a unicellular creature, as compared with the complicated structure of such comparatively severe [1] neuroses as we usually meet with.

The psychical material in such cases of hysteria presents itself as a structure in several dimensions which is stratified in at least three different ways. (I hope I shall presently be able to justify this pictorial mode of expression.) To begin with there is a nucleus consisting in memories of events or trains of thought in which the traumatic factor has culminated or the pathogenic idea has found its purest manifestation. Round this nucleus we find what is often an incredibly profuse amount of other mnemic material which has to be worked through in the analysis and which is, as we have said, arranged in a threefold order.

In the first place there is an unmistakable linear chronological order which obtains within each separate theme. As an example of this I will merely quote the arrangement of the material in Breuer's analysis of Anna O. Let us take the theme of becoming deaf, of not hearing. This was differentiated according to seven sets of determinants, and under each of these seven headings ten to over a hundred individual memories were collected in chronological series (p. 36). It was as though we were examining a dossier that had been kept in good order. The analysis of my patient Emmy von N. contained similar files of memories though they were not so fully enumerated and described. These files form a quite general feature of every analysis and their contents always emerge in a chronological order which is as infallibly trustworthy as the succession of days of the week or names of the month in a mentally normal person. They make the work of analysis more difficult by the peculiarity that, in reproducing the memories, they reverse the order in which these originated. The freshest and newest experience in the file appears first, as an outer cover, and last of all comes the experience with which the series in fact began.

I have described such groupings of similar memories into

---

[1] ['*Schwereren*' ('comparatively severe') in the first and second editions only; '*schweren*' ('severe') in all later editions.]

collections arranged in linear sequences (like a file of documents, a packet, etc.) as constituting 'themes'. These themes exhibit a second kind of arrangement. Each of them is—I cannot express it in any other way—stratified concentrically round the pathogenic nucleus. It is not hard to say what produces this stratification, what diminishing or increasing magnitude is the basis of this arrangement. The contents of each particular stratum are characterized by an equal degree of resistance, and that degree increases in proportion as the strata are nearer to the nucleus. Thus there are zones within which there is an equal degree of modification of consciousness, and the different themes extend across these zones. The most peripheral strata contain the memories (or files), which, belonging to different themes, are easily remembered and have always been clearly conscious. The deeper we go the more difficult it becomes for the emerging memories to be recognized, till near the nucleus we come upon memories which the patient disavows even in reproducing them.

It is this peculiarity of the concentric stratification of the pathogenic psychical material which, as we shall hear, lends to the course of these analyses their characteristic features. A third kind of arrangement has still to be mentioned—the most important, but the one about which it is least easy to make any general statement. What I have in mind is an arrangement according to thought-content, the linkage made by a logical thread which reaches as far as the nucleus and tends to take an irregular and twisting path, different in every case. This arrangement has a dynamic character, in contrast to the morphological one of the two stratifications mentioned previously. While these two would be represented in a spatial diagram by a continuous line, curved or straight, the course of the logical chain would have to be indicated by a broken line which would pass along the most roundabout paths from the surface to the deepest layers and back, and yet would in general advance from the periphery to the central nucleus, touching at every intermediate halting-place—a line resembling the zig-zag line in the solution of a Knight's Move problem, which cuts across the squares in the diagram of the chess-board.

I must dwell for a moment longer on this last simile in order to emphasize a point in which it does not do justice to the characteristics of the subject of the comparison. The logical chain corresponds not only to a zig-zag, twisted line, but rather to a ramifying system of lines and more particularly to a converging one. It contains nodal points at which two or more threads meet and thereafter proceed as one; and as a rule several threads which run independently, or which are connected at various points by side-paths, debouch into the nucleus. To put this in other words, it is very remarkable how often a symptom is determined in several ways, is 'overdetermined'.[1]

My attempt to demonstrate the organization of the pathogenic psychical material will be complete when I have introduced one more complication. For it can happen that there is more than one nucleus in the pathogenic material—if, for instance, we have to analyse a second outbreak of hysteria which has an aetiology of its own but is nevertheless connected with a first outbreak of acute hysteria which was got over years earlier. It is easy to imagine, if this is so, what additions there must be to the strata and paths of thought in order to establish a connection between the two pathogenic nuclei.

I shall now make one or two further remarks on the picture we have just arrived at of the organization of the pathogenic material. We have said that this material behaves like a foreign body, and that the treatment, too, works like the removal of a foreign body from the living tissue. We are now in a position to see where this comparison fails. A foreign body does not enter into any relation with the layers of tissue that surround it, although it modifies them and necessitates a reactive inflammation in them. Our pathogenic psychical group, on the other hand, does not admit of being cleanly extirpated from the ego. Its external strata pass over in every direction into portions of the normal ego; and, indeed, they belong to the latter just as much as to the pathogenic organization. In analysis the boundary between the two is fixed purely conventionally, now at one point, now at another, and in some places it cannot be laid down at all. The interior layers of the pathogenic organization are increasingly alien to the ego, but once more without there being any visible boundary at which the pathogenic material begins. In fact the pathogenic organization does not behave like a foreign body, but far more like an infiltrate. In this simile the resistance must be regarded as what is infiltrating.

[1] ['*Überbestimmt.*' See footnote, p. 212.]

Nor does the treatment consist in extirpating something—psychotherapy is not able to do this for the present—but in causing the resistance to melt and in thus enabling the circulation to make its way into a region that has hitherto been cut off.

(I am making use here of a number of similes, all of which have only a very limited resemblance to my subject and which, moreover, are incompatible with one another. I am aware that this is so, and I am in no danger of over-estimating their value. But my purpose in using them is to throw light from different directions on a highly complicated topic which has never yet been represented. I shall therefore venture to continue in the following pages to introduce similes in the same manner, though I know this is not free from objection.)

If it were possible, after the case had been completely cleared up, to demonstrate the pathogenic material to a third person in what we now know is its complicated and multi-dimensional organization, we should rightly be asked how a camel like this got through the eye of the needle. For there is some justification for speaking of the 'defile' of consciousness. The term gains meaning and liveliness for a physician who carries out an analysis like this. Only a single memory at a time can enter ego-consciousness. A patient who is occupied in working through such a memory sees nothing of what is pushing after it and forgets what has already pushed its way through. If there are difficulties in the way of mastering this single pathogenic memory—as, for instance, if the patient does not relax his resistance against it, if he tries to repress or mutilate it—then the defile is, so to speak, blocked. The work is at a standstill, nothing more can appear, and the single memory which is in process of breaking through remains in front of the patient until he has taken it up into the breadth of his ego. The whole spatially-extended mass of psychogenic material is in this way drawn through a narrow cleft and thus arrives in consciousness cut up, as it were, into pieces or strips. It is the psychotherapist's business to put these together once more into the organization which he presumes to have existed. Anyone who has a craving for further similes may think at this point of a Chinese puzzle.

If we are faced with starting such an analysis, in which we have reason to expect an organization of pathogenic material like this, we shall be assisted by what experience has taught us, namely that *it is quite hopeless to try to penetrate directly to the nucleus of the pathogenic organization.* Even if we ourselves could guess it, the patient would not know what to do with the explanation offered to him and would not be psychologically changed by it.

There is nothing for it but to keep at first to the periphery of the psychical structure. We begin by getting the patient to tell us what he knows and remembers, while we are at the same time already directing his attention and overcoming his slighter resistances by the use of the pressure procedure. Whenever we have opened a new path by thus pressing on his forehead, we may expect him to advance some distance without fresh resistance.

After we have worked in this way for some time, the patient begins as a rule to co-operate with us. A great number of reminiscences now occur to him, without our having to question him or set him tasks. What we have done is to make a path to an inner stratum within which the patient now has spontaneously at his disposal material that has an equal degree of resistance attaching to it. It is best to allow him for a time to reproduce such material without being influenced. It is true that he himself is not in a position to uncover important connections, but he may be left to clear up material lying within the same stratum. The things that he brings up in this way often seem disconnected, but they offer material which will be given point when a connection is discovered later on.

Here we have in general to guard against two things. If we interfere with the patient in his reproduction of the ideas that pour in on him, we may 'bury' things that have to be freed later with a great deal of trouble. On the other hand we must not over-estimate the patient's unconscious 'intelligence' and leave the direction of the whole work to it. If I wanted to give a diagrammatic picture of our mode of operation, I might perhaps say that we ourselves undertake the opening up of inner strata, advancing *radially*, whereas the patient looks after the *peripheral* extension of the work.

Advances are brought about, as we know, by overcoming resistance in the manner already indicated. But before this, we have as a rule another task to perform. We must get hold of a piece of the logical thread, by whose guidance alone we may hope to penetrate to the interior. We cannot expect that the free communications made by the patient, the material from the most superficial strata, will make it easy for the analyst to recognize at what points the path leads into the depths or where he is to find the starting-points of the connections of thought of which he is in search. On the contrary. This is precisely what is carefully concealed; the account given by the patient sounds as if it were complete and self-contained. It is at first as though we were standing before a wall which shuts out every prospect and prevents us from having any idea whether there is anything behind it, and if so, what.

But if we examine with a critical eye the account that the patient has given us without much trouble or resistance, we shall quite infallibly discover gaps and imperfections in it. At one point the train of thought will be visibly interrupted and patched up by the patient as best he may, with a turn of speech or an inadequate [1] explanation; at another point we come upon a motive which would have to be described as a feeble one in a normal person. The patient will not recognize these deficiencies when his attention is drawn to them. But the physician will be right in looking behind the weak spots for an approach to the material in the deeper layers and in hoping that he will discover precisely there the connecting threads for which he is seeking with the pressure procedure. Accordingly, we say to the patient: 'You are mistaken; what you are putting forward can have nothing to do with the present subject. We must expect to come upon something else here, and this will occur to you under the pressure of my hand.'

For we may make the same demands for logical connection and sufficient motivation in a train of thought, even if it extends into the unconscious, from a hysterical patient as we should from a normal individual. It is not within the power of a neurosis to relax these relations. If the chains of ideas in neurotic and particularly in hysterical patients produce a different impression, if in them the relative intensity of different ideas seems inexplicable by psychological determinants alone, we have already found out the reason for this and can attribute it to *the existence of hidden unconscious motives*. We may thus suspect the presence of such secret motives wherever a breach of this kind in a train of thought is apparent or when the force ascribed by the patient to his motives goes far beyond the normal.

[1] [In the first edition only, 'a quite inadequate'.]

In carrying out this work we must of course keep free from the theoretical prejudice that we are dealing with the abnormal brains of '*dégénérés*' and '*déséquilibrés*',[1] who are at liberty, owing to a stigma, to throw overboard the common psychological laws that govern the connection of ideas and in whom one chance idea may become exaggeratedly intense for no motive and another may remain indestructible for no psychological reason. Experience shows that the contrary is true of hysteria. Once we have discovered the concealed motives, which have often remained unconscious, and have taken them into account, nothing that is puzzling or contrary to rule remains in hysterical connections of thought, any more than in normal ones.

In this way, then, by detecting lacunas in the patient's first description, lacunas which are often covered by 'false connections' [see below, p. 302], we get hold of a piece of the logical thread at the periphery, and from this point on we clear a further path by the pressure technique.

In doing this, we very seldom succeed in making our way right into the interior along one and the same thread. As a rule it breaks off half-way: the pressure fails and either produces no result or one that cannot be clarified or carried further in spite of every effort. We soon learn, when this happens, to avoid the mistakes into which we might fall. The patient's facial expression must decide whether we have really come to an end, or whether this is an instance which requires no psychical elucidation, or whether what has brought the work to a standstill is excessive resistance. In the last case, if we cannot promptly overcome the resistance we may assume that we have followed the thread into a stratum which is for the time being still impenetrable. We drop it and take up another thread, which we may perhaps follow equally far. When we have arrived at this stratum along all the threads and have discovered the entanglements on account of which the separate threads could not be followed any further in isolation, we can think of attacking the resistance before us afresh.

It is easy to imagine how complicated a work of this kind can become. We force our way into the internal strata, overcoming resistances all the time; we get to know the themes accumulated in one of these strata and the threads running

---

[1] ['Degenerate' and 'unbalanced' persons. The view then currently held by French psychopathologists.]

through it, and we experiment how far we can advance with our present means and the knowledge we have acquired; we obtain preliminary information about the contents of the next strata by means of the pressure technique; we drop threads and pick them up again; we follow them as far as nodal points; we are constantly making up arrears; and every time that we pursue a file of memories we are led to some side-path, which nevertheless eventually joins up again. By this method we at last reach a point at which we can stop working in strata and can penetrate by a main path straight to the nucleus of the pathogenic organization. With this the struggle is won, though not yet ended. We must go back and take up the other threads and exhaust the material. But now the patient helps us energetically. His resistance is for the most part broken.

In these later stages of the work it is of use if we can guess the way in which things are connected up and tell the patient before we have uncovered it. If we have guessed right, the course of the analysis will be accelerated; but even a wrong hypothesis helps us on, by compelling the patient to take sides and by enticing him into energetic denials which betray his undoubted better knowledge.

We learn with astonishment from this that *we are not in a position to force anything on the patient about the things of which he is ostensibly ignorant or to influence the products of the analysis by arousing an expectation.* I have never once succeeded, by foretelling something, in altering or falsifying the reproduction of memories or the connection of events; for if I had, it would inevitably have been betrayed in the end by some contradiction in the material. If something turned out as I had foretold, it was invariably proved by a great number of unimpeachable reminiscences that I had done no more than guess right. We need not be afraid, therefore, of telling the patient what we think his next connection of thought is going to be. It will do no harm.

Another observation, which is constantly repeated, relates to the patient's spontaneous reproductions. It may be asserted that every single reminiscence which emerges during an analysis of this kind has significance. An intrusion of *irrelevant* mnemic images (which happen in some way or other to be associated with the important ones) in fact never occurs. An exception which does not contradict this rule may be postulated for memories which, unimportant in themselves, are nevertheless indispensable as a bridge, in the sense that the association between two important memories can only be made through them.

The length of time during which a memory remains in the narrow defile in front of the patient's consciousness is, as has already been explained [p. 291], in direct proportion to its importance. A picture which refuses to disappear is one which still calls for consideration, a thought which cannot be dismissed is one that needs to be pursued further. Moreover, a recollection never returns a second time once it has been dealt with; an image that has been 'talked away' is not seen again. If nevertheless this does happen we can confidently assume that the second time the image will be accompanied by a new set of thoughts, or the idea will have new implications. In other words, they have not been completely dealt with. Again, it frequently happens that an image or thought will re-appear in different degrees of intensity, first as a hint and later with complete clarity. This, however, does not contradict what I have just asserted.

Among the tasks presented by analysis is that of getting rid of symptoms which are capable of increasing in intensity or of returning: pains, symptoms (such as vomiting) which are due to stimuli, sensations or contractures. While we are working at one of these symptoms we come across the interesting and not undesired phenomenon of 'joining in the conversation'.[1] The problematical symptom re-appears, or appears with greater intensity, as soon as we reach the region of the pathogenic organization which contains the symptom's aetiology, and thenceforward it accompanies the work with characteristic oscillations which are instructive to the physician. The intensity of the symptom (let us take for instance a desire to vomit) increases the deeper we penetrate into one of the relevant pathogenic memories; it reaches its climax shortly before the patient gives utterance to that memory; and when he has finished doing so it suddenly diminishes or even vanishes completely for a time. If, owing to resistance, the patient delays his telling for a long time, the tension of the sensation—of the desire to vomit—becomes unbearable, and if we cannot force him to speak he actually begins to vomit. In this way we obtain

---

[1] [An example of this will be found in the case history of Fräulein Elisabeth von R. (p. 148). It is also mentioned by Breuer on p. 37.]

a plastic impression of the fact that 'vomiting' takes the place of a psychical act (in this instance, the act of utterance), exactly as the conversion theory of hysteria maintains.

This oscillation in intensity on the part of the hysterical symptom is then repeated every time we approach a fresh memory which is pathogenic in respect of it. The symptom, we might say, is on the agenda all the time. If we are obliged temporarily to drop the thread to which this symptom is attached, the symptom, too, retires into obscurity, to emerge once more at a later period of the analysis. This performance goes on until the working-over of the pathogenic material disposes of the symptom once and for all.

In all this, strictly speaking, the hysterical symptom is not behaving in any way differently from the memory-picture or the reproduced thought which we conjure up under the pressure of our hand. In both cases we find the same obsessionally obstinate recurrence in the patient's memory, which has to be disposed of. The difference lies only in the apparently spontaneous emergence of the hysterical symptoms, while, as we very well remember, we ourselves provoked the scenes and ideas. In fact, however, there is an uninterrupted series, extending from the unmodified *mnemic residues* of affective experiences and acts of thought to the hysterical symptoms, which are the *mnemic symbols* of those experiences and thoughts.

The phenomenon of hysterical symptoms joining in the conversation during the analysis involves a practical drawback, to which we ought to be able to reconcile the patient. It is quite impossible to effect an analysis of a symptom at a single stretch or to distribute the intervals in our work so that they fit in precisely with pauses in the process of dealing with the symptom. On the contrary, interruptions which are imperatively prescribed by incidental circumstances in the treatment, such as the lateness of the hour, often occur at the most inconvenient points, just as one may be approaching a decision or just as a new topic emerges. Every newspaper reader suffers from the same drawback in reading the daily instalment of his serial story, when, immediately after the heroine's decisive speech or after the shot has rung out, he comes upon the words: 'To be continued.' In our own case the topic that has been raised but not dealt with, the symptom that has become temporarily intensified and has not yet been explained, persists in the patient's mind and may perhaps be more troublesome to him than it has otherwise been. He [1] will simply have to make the best of this; there is no other way of arranging things. There are patients who, in the course of an analysis, simply cannot get free of a topic that has once been raised and who are obsessed by it in the interval between two treatments; since by themselves they cannot take any steps towards getting rid of it, they suffer more, to begin with, than they did before the treatment. But even such patients learn in the end to wait for the doctor and to shift all the interest that they feel in getting rid of the pathogenic material on to the hours of treatment, after which they begin to feel freer in the intervals.

The general condition of patients during an analysis of this kind also deserves notice. For a time it is uninfluenced by the treatment and continues to be an expression of the factors that were operative earlier. But after this there comes a moment when the treatment takes hold of the patient; it grips his interest, and thenceforward his general condition becomes more and more dependent on the state of the work. Every time something new is elucidated or an important stage in the process of the analysis is reached, the patient, too, feels relieved and enjoys a foretaste, as it were, of his approaching liberation. Every time the work halts and confusion threatens, the psychical burden by which he is oppressed increases; his feeling of unhappiness and his incapacity for work grow more intense. But neither of these things happens for more than a short time. For the analysis proceeds, disdaining to boast because the patient feels well for the time being and going on its way regardless of his periods of gloom. We feel glad, in general, when we have replaced the spontaneous oscillations in his condition by oscillations which we ourselves have provoked and which we understand, just as we are glad when we see the spontaneous succession of symptoms replaced by an order of the day which corresponds to the state of the analysis.

To begin with, the work becomes more obscure and difficult, as a rule, the deeper we penetrate into the stratified psychical

---

[1] ['*Er*' ('he') in the first and second editions. '*Es*' ('it', evidently a misprint) in the third edition. This was changed to '*Man*' ('one') in the 1924 edition, perhaps in order to make sense of the '*es*'; but the meaning was now somewhat changed from the original one.]

structure which I have described above. But once we have worked our way as far as the nucleus, light dawns and we need not fear that the patient's general condition will be subject to any severe periods of gloom. But the reward of our labours, the cessation of the symptoms, can only be expected when we have accomplished the complete analysis of every individual symptom; and indeed, if the individual symptoms are interconnected at numerous nodal points, we shall not even be encouraged during the work by partial successes. Thanks to the abundant causal connections, every pathogenic idea which has not yet been got rid of operates as a motive for the whole of the products of the neurosis, and it is only with the last word of the analysis that the whole clinical picture vanishes, just as happens with memories that are reproduced individually.

If a pathogenic memory or a pathogenic connection which had formerly been withdrawn from the ego-consciousness is uncovered by the work of the analysis and introduced into the ego, we find that the psychical personality which is thus enriched has various ways of expressing itself with regard to what it has acquired. It happens particularly often that, after we have laboriously forced some piece of knowledge on a patient, he will declare: 'I've always known that, I could have told you that before.' Those with some degree of insight recognize afterwards that this is a piece of self-deception and blame themselves for being ungrateful. Apart from this, the attitude adopted by the ego to its new acquisition depends in general on the stratum of analysis from which that acquisition originates. Things that belong to the external strata are recognized without difficulty; they had, indeed, always remained in the ego's possession, and the only novelty to the ego is their connection with the deeper strata of pathological material. Things that are brought to light from these deeper strata are also recognized and acknowledged, but often only after considerable hesitations and doubts. Visual memory-images are of course more difficult to disavow than the memory-traces of mere trains of thought. Not at all infrequently the patient begins by saying: 'It's possible that I thought this, but I can't remember having done so.' And it is not until he has been familiar with the hypothesis for some time that he comes to recognize it as well; he remembers—and confirms the fact, too, by subsidiary links—that he really did once have the thought. I make it a rule, however, during the analysis to keep my estimate of the reminiscence that comes up independent of the patient's acknowledgement of it. I shall never be tired of repeating that we are bound to accept whatever our procedure brings to light. If there is anything in it that is not genuine or correct, the context will later on tell us to reject it. But I may say in passing that I have scarcely ever had occasion to disavow subsequently a reminiscence that has been provisionally accepted. Whatever has emerged has, in spite of the most deceptive appearance of being a glaring contradiction, nevertheless turned out to be correct.

The ideas which are derived from the greatest depth and which form the nucleus of the pathogenic organization are also those which are acknowledged as memories by the patient with greatest difficulty. Even when everything is finished and the patients have been overborne by the force of logic and have been convinced by the therapeutic effect accompanying the emergence of precisely these ideas—when, I say, the patients themselves accept the fact that they thought this or that, they often add: 'But I can't *remember* having thought it.' It is easy to come to terms with them by telling them that the thoughts were *unconscious*. But how is this state of affairs to be fitted into our own psychological views? Are we to disregard this withholding of recognition on the part of patients, when, now that the work is finished, there is no longer any motive for their doing so? Or are we to suppose that we are really dealing with thoughts which never came about, which merely had a *possibility* of existing, so that the treatment would lie in the accomplishment of a psychical act which did not take place at the time? It is clearly impossible to say anything about this—that is, about the state which the pathogenic material was in before the analysis—until we have arrived at a thorough clarification of our basic psychological views, especially on the nature of consciousness. It remains, I think, a fact deserving serious consideration that in our analyses we can follow a train of thought from the conscious into the unconscious (i.e. into something that is absolutely not recognized as a memory), that we can trace it from there for some distance through consciousness once more and that we can see it terminate in the unconscious again, without this alternation of 'psychical illumination' making any change in the train of thought itself, in its logical consistency and in the interconnection between its various parts.

Once this train of thought was before me as a whole I should not be able to guess which part of it was recognized by the patient as a memory and which was not. I only, as it were, see the peaks of the train of thought dipping down into the unconscious—the reverse of what has been asserted of our normal psychical processes.

I have finally to discuss yet another topic, which plays an undesirably large part in the carrying out of cathartic analyses such as these. I have already [p. 281] admitted the possibility of the pressure technique failing, of its not eliciting any reminiscence in spite of every assurance and insistence. If this happens, I said, there are two possibilities: either, at the point at which we are investigating, there is really nothing more to be found —and this we can recognize from the complete calmness of the patient's facial expression; or we have come up against a resistance which can only be overcome later, we are faced by a new stratum into which we cannot yet penetrate—and this, once more, we can infer from the patient's facial expression, which is tense and gives evidence of mental effort [p. 294]. But there is yet a third possibility which bears witness equally to an obstacle, but an external obstacle, and not one inherent in the material. This happens when the patient's relation to the physician is disturbed, and it is the worst obstacle that we can come across. We can, however, reckon on meeting it in every comparatively serious analysis.

I have already [p. 266] indicated the important part played by the figure of the physician in creating motives to defeat the psychical force of resistance. In not a few cases, especially with women and where it is a question of elucidating erotic trains of thought, the patient's co-operation becomes a personal sacrifice, which must be compensated by some substitute for love. The trouble taken by the physician and his friendliness have to suffice for such a substitute. If, now, this relation of the patient to the physician is disturbed, her co-operativeness fails, too; when the physician tries to investigate the next pathological idea, the patient is held up by an intervening consciousness of the complaints against the physician that have been accumulating in her. In my experience this obstacle arises in three principal cases.

(1) If there is a personal estrangement—if, for instance, the

patient feels she has been neglected, has been too little appreciated or has been insulted, or if she has heard unfavourable comments on the physician or the method of treatment. This is the least serious case. The obstacle can easily be overcome by discussion and explanation, even though the sensitiveness and suspiciousness of hysterical patients may occasionally attain surprising dimensions.

(2) If the patient is seized by a dread of becoming too much accustomed to the physician personally, of losing her independence in relation to him, and even of perhaps becoming sexually dependent on him. This is a more important case, because its determinants are less individual. The cause of this obstacle lies in the special solicitude inherent in the treatment. The patient then has a new motive for resistance, which is manifested not only in relation to some particular reminiscence but at every attempt at treatment. It is quite common for the patient to complain of a headache when we start on the pressure procedure; for her new motive for resistance remains as a rule unconscious and is expressed by the production of a new hysterical symptom. The headache indicates her dislike of allowing herself to be influenced.

(3) If the patient is frightened at finding that she is transferring on to the figure of the physician the distressing ideas which arise from the content of the analysis. This is a frequent, and indeed in some analyses a regular, occurrence. Transference [1] on to the physician takes place through a *false connection*.[2] I must give an example of this. In one of my patients the origin of a particular hysterical symptom lay in a wish, which she had had many years earlier and had at once relegated to the unconscious, that the man she was talking to at the time

---

[1] [This is the first appearance of 'transference' (*Übertragung*) in the psycho-analytic sense, though it is being used much more narrowly here than in Freud's later writings. For a somewhat different use of the term see Chapter VII, Section C., of *The Interpretation of Dreams* (1900a), *Standard Ed.*, 5, 562 f. Freud next dealt with the subject of 'transferences' near the end of the last section of the case history of 'Dora' (1905e), *Standard Ed.*, 7, 116 ff.]

[2] [A long account of 'false connections' and the 'compulsion to associate' will be found above in a footnote on p. 67 f.—Freud had already discussed them in relation to obsessions at the beginning of Section II of his first paper on 'The Neuro-Psychoses of Defence' (1894a).]

might boldly take the initiative and give her a kiss. On one occasion, at the end of a session, a similar wish came up in her about me. She was horrified at it, spent a sleepless night, and at the next session, though she did not refuse to be treated, was quite useless for work. After I had discovered the obstacle and removed it, the work proceeded further; and lo and behold! the wish that had so much frightened the patient made its appearance as the next of her pathogenic recollections and the one which was demanded by the immediate logical context. What had happened therefore was this. The content of the wish had appeared first of all in the patient's consciousness without any memories of the surrounding circumstances which would have assigned it to a past time. The wish which was present was then, owing to the compulsion to associate which was dominant in her consciousness, linked to my person, with which the patient was legitimately concerned; and as the result of this *mésalliance*—which I describe as a 'false connection'— the same affect was provoked which had forced the patient long before to repudiate this forbidden wish. Since I have discovered this, I have been able, whenever I have been similarly involved personally, to presume that a transference and a false connection have once more taken place. Strangely enough, the patient is deceived afresh every time this is repeated.

It is impossible to carry any analysis to a conclusion unless we know how to meet the resistance arising in these three ways. But we can find a way of doing so if we make up our minds that this new symptom that has been produced on the old model must be treated in the same way as the old symptoms. Our first task is to make the 'obstacle' conscious to the patient. In one of my patients, for instance, the pressure procedure suddenly failed. I had reason to suppose that there was an unconscious idea of the kind mentioned under (2) above, and I dealt with it at the first attempt by taking her by surprise. I told her that some obstacle must have arisen to continuing the treatment, but that the pressure procedure had at least the power to show her what this obstacle was; I pressed on her head, and she said in astonishment: 'I see you sitting on the chair here; but that's nonsense. What can it mean?' I was then able to enlighten her. With another patient the 'obstacle' used not to appear directly as a result of my pressure, but I was always able to discover it if I took the patient back to the moment at which it had

originated. The pressure procedure never failed to bring this
moment back for us. When the obstacle had been discovered
and demonstrated the first difficulty was cleared out of the
way. But a greater one remained. It lay in inducing the patient
to produce information where apparently personal relations
were concerned and where the third person coincided with the
figure of the physician.

To begin with I was greatly annoyed at this increase in my
psychological work, till I came to see that the whole process
followed a law; and I then noticed, too, that transference of
this kind brought about no great addition to what I had to do.
For the patient the work remained the same: she had to overcome the distressing affect aroused by having been able to
entertain such a wish even for a moment; and it seemed to
make no difference to the success of the treatment whether she
made this psychical repudiation the theme of her work in the
historical instance or in the recent one connected with me.
The patients, too, gradually learnt to realize that in these
transferences on to the figure of the physician it was a question
of a compulsion and an illusion which melted away with the
conclusion of the analysis. I believe, however, that if I had
neglected to make the nature of the 'obstacle' clear to them I
should simply have given them a new hysterical symptom—
though, it is true, a milder one—in exchange for another which
had been generated spontaneously.

I have now given enough indications, I think, of the way in
which these analyses have been carried out and of the observations that I have made in the course of them. What I have said
may perhaps make some things seem more complicated than
they are. Many problems answer themselves when we find ourselves engaged in such work. I did not enumerate the difficulties
of the work in order to create an impression that, in view of
the demands a cathartic analysis makes on physician and
patient alike, it is only worth while undertaking one in the
rarest cases. I allow my medical activities to be governed by
the contrary assumption, though I cannot, it is true, lay down
the most definite indications for the application of the therapeutic method described in these pages without entering into
an examination of the more important and comprehensive

topic of the treatment of the neuroses in general. I have often in my own mind compared cathartic psychotherapy with surgical intervention. I have described my treatments as psychotherapeutic operations; and I have brought out their analogy with the opening up of a cavity filled with pus, the scraping out of a carious region, etc. An analogy of this kind finds its justification not so much in the removal of what is pathological as in the establishment of conditions that are more likely to lead the course of the process in the direction of recovery.

When I have promised my patients help or improvement by means of a cathartic treatment I have often been faced by this objection: 'Why, you tell me yourself that my illness is probably connected with my circumstances and the events of my life. You cannot alter these in any way. How do you propose to help me, then?' And I have been able to make this reply: 'No doubt fate would find it easier than I do to relieve you of your illness. But you will be able to convince yourself that much will be gained if we succeed in transforming your hysterical misery into common unhappiness. With a mental life [1] that has been restored to health you will be better armed against that unhappiness.'

[1] [The German editions previous to 1925 read 'nervous system'.]

APPENDIX A

THE CHRONOLOGY OF THE CASE OF FRAU EMMY VON N.

THERE are serious inconsistencies in the dating of the case history of Frau Emmy von N. as given in all the German editions of the work and as reproduced in the present translation. The beginning of Freud's first course of treatment of Frau Emmy is assigned to May 1889 twice on p. 48. The course lasted for about seven weeks (pp. 51 *n.* and 77). Her second course of treatment began exactly a year after the first (p. 78), i.e. in Máy 1890. This course lasted for about eight weeks (p. 51 *n.*). Freud visited Frau Emmy on her Baltic estate in the spring of the following year (p. 83), i.e. of 1891. A first contradiction of this chronology appears on p. 85, where the date of this visit is given as May 1890. This new system of dating is maintained at later points. On p., 91 Freud ascribes a symptom that appeared in the second course of treatment to the year 1889 and symptoms that appeared in the first course of treatment twice to the year 1888. He reverts, however, to his original system on p. 102, where he gives the date of his visit to the Baltic estate as 1891.

There is one piece of evidence which speaks in favour of the earlier chronology—that is, of assigning Freud's first treatment of Frau Emmy to the year 1888. On p. 101 he remarks that it was while he was studying this patient's abulias that he began for the first time to have grave doubts about the validity of Bernheim's assertion that 'suggestion is everything'. He expressed these same doubts very forcibly in his preface to his translation of Bernheim's book on suggestion (Freud, 1888–9), and we are told in a letter to Fliess of August 29, 1888 (1950a, Letter 5), that he had already completed the preface by that date. In this letter, too, he writes: 'I do not share Bernheim's views, which seem to me one-sided.' If Freud's doubts were first suggested by his treatment of Frau Emmy, that treatment must therefore have begun in the May of 1888, not 1889.

Incidentally, this correction would clear up an inconsistency in the accepted account of some of Freud's activities after his return from Paris in the spring of 1886. In his *Autobiographical Study* (1925*d*, Chapter II) he remarks that when using hypnotism he 'from the first' employed it not only for giving therapeutic suggestions but also for the purpose of tracing back the history of the symptom—from the first, that is, he made use of Breuer's cathartic method. We learn from a letter to Fliess of December 28, 1887 (1950*a*, Letter 2), that it was towards the end of that year that he first took up hypnotism; while on pp. 48 and 284 of the present volume he tells us that the case of Frau Emmy was the first in which he attempted to handle Breuer's technical procedure. If, therefore, that case dates from May 1889, there was an interval of at least sixteen months between the two events, and, as Dr. Ernest Jones remarks (in Vol. I of his biography, 1953, 263), Freud's memory was scarcely accurate when he used the phrase 'from the first'. If however the date of Frau Emmy's treatment were brought forward to May 1888, the gap would be reduced to only some four or five months.

It would have clinched the matter if it could have been shown that Freud was absent from Vienna for a period long enough to cover a visit to Livonia (or whatever country that may have represented) during the month of May either of 1890 or of 1891. But unfortunately his extant letters from those periods afford no evidence of any such absence.

The matter is made still more obscure by yet another inconsistency. In a footnote on p. 61 Freud comments on the over-efficiency of some of his suggestions made during the first period of treatment (actually on May 11, 1888 or 1889). The amnesia which he then produced was, he says, still operative 'eighteen months later'. This certainly refers to the time of his visit to Frau Emmy's country estate, for, in his account of that visit, he mentions the episode once more (p. 84). There, however, he speaks of the original suggestions as having been made 'two years previously'. If the visit to the estate was in May 1890 or 1891, the 'two years' must be correct and the 'eighteen months' must have been a slip.

But these repeated contradictions suggest a further possibility. There is reason to believe that Freud altered the *place* of Frau Emmy's residence. Can it be that, as an extra precaution against betraying his patient's identity, he altered the *time* of the treatment as well, but failed to carry the changes through consistently? [1] The whole problem must remain an open one.

[1] Cf. Freud's explanation in Chapter X of *The Psychopathology of Everyday Life* (1901*b*) of some of his own unnoticed slips in his *Interpretation of Dreams*. He accounted for these as unconscious retaliations for suppressions and distortions deliberately made by him in the material.

APPENDIX B

LIST OF WRITINGS BY FREUD DEALING PRINCIPALLY WITH CONVERSION HYSTERIA

[*In the following list, the date at the beginning of each entry is that of the year during which the work in question was probably written. The date at the end is that of publication; and under that date fuller particulars of the work will be found in the* Bibliography and Author Index. *The items in square brackets were published posthumously.*]

1886 'Observation of a Pronounced Hemi-Anaesthesia in a Hysterical Male.' (1886*d*)

1888 'Hysteria' in Villaret's *Handwörterbuch*. (1888*b*)

[1892 'A Letter to Josef Breuer.' (1941*a*)]

[1892 'On the Theory of Hysterical Attacks.' (With Breuer.) (1940*d*)]

[1892 'Memorandum "III".' (1941*b*)]

1892 'A Case of Successful Treatment by Hypnotism.' (1892–3*b*)

1892 'On the Psychical Mechanism of Hysterical Phenomena: A Preliminary Communication.' (With Breuer.) (1893*a*)

1893 Lecture 'On the Psychical Mechanism of Hysterical Phenomena.' (1893*h*)

1893 'Some Points for a Comparative Study of Organic and Hysterical Motor Paralyses.' (1893*c*)

1894 'The Neuro-Psychoses of Defence', Section I. (1894*a*)

1895 *Studies on Hysteria*. (With Breuer.) (1895*d*)

[1895 'Project for a Scientific Psychology', Part II. (1950*a*)]

[1896 'Draft K.', Last Section. (1950*a*)]

1896 'Further Remarks on the Neuro-Psychoses of Defence.' (1896*b*)

1896 'The Aetiology of Hysteria.' (1896*c*)

1901–5 'Fragment of an Analysis of a Case of Hysteria.' (1905*e*)

1908 'Hysterical Phantasies and their Relation to Bisexuality.' (1908*a*)

1909 'Some General Remarks on Hysterical Attacks.' (1909*a*)
1909 *Five Lectures on Psycho-Analysis*, Lectures I and II.
        (1910*a*)
1910 'The Psycho-Analytic View of Psychogenic Disturbance
        of Vision.' (1910*i*)

BIBLIOGRAPHY
AND AUTHOR INDEX

[Titles of books and periodicals are in italics; titles of papers are in inverted commas. Abbreviations are in accordance with the *World List of Scientific Periodicals* (London, 1952). Further abbreviations used in this volume will be found in the List at the end of this bibliography. Numerals in thick type refer to volumes; ordinary numerals refer to pages. The figures in round brackets at the end of each entry indicate the page or pages of this volume on which the work in question is mentioned. In the case of the Freud entries, the letters attached to the dates of publication are in accordance with the corresponding entries in the complete bibliography of Freud's writings to be included in the last volume of the *Standard Edition*.

For non-technical authors, and for technical authors where no specific work is mentioned, see the General Index.]

BENEDIKT, M. (1894) *Hypnotismus und Suggestion*, Vienna. (210)

BERGER, A. VON (1896) Review of Breuer and Freud's *Studien über Hysterie, Neue Freie Presse*, Feb. 2. (xv)

BERNHEIM, H. (1886) *De la suggestion et de ses applications à la thérapeutique*, Paris. (xi, 67, 77)

—— (1891) *Hypnotisme, suggestion et psychothérapie: études nouvelles*, Paris. (xi)

BINET, A. (1892) *Les altérations de la personnalité*, Paris. (7)

BREUER, J., and FREUD, S. (1893) See FREUD, S. (1893a)

—— (1895) See FREUD, S. (1895d)

—— (1940) See FREUD, S. (1940d)

CABANIS, P. J. G. (1824) *Rapports du physique et du moral de l'homme*, Œuvres complètes, Paris, **3**, 153. (195–6)

CHARCOT, J.-M. (1887) *Leçons sur les maladies du système nerveux, III*, Paris. (13, 15, 16)

—— (1888) *Leçons du mardi à la Salpetrière (1887–8)*, Paris. (134)

CLARKE, MICHELL (1894) Review of Breuer and Freud's 'Über den psychischen Mechanismus hysterischer Phänomene', *Brain*, **17**, 125. (xv)

—— (1896) Review of Breuer and Freud's *Studien über Hysterie, Brain*, **19**, 401. (xv)

DARWIN, C. (1872) *The Expression of the Emotions in Man and Animals*, London. (91, 181)

DELBŒF, J. R. L. (1889) *Le magnétisme animal*, Paris. (7)

EXNER, S. (1894) *Entwurf zu einer physiologischen Erklärung der psychischen Erscheinungen*, Vienna. (193, 195, 241)

FERENCZI, S. (1921) 'Psychoanalytische Betrachtungen über den Tic', *Int. Z. Psychoan.*, **7**, 33. (93)

[*Trans.:* 'Psycho-Analytical Observations on Tic', Chapter 12 of *Further Contributions to the Theory and Technique of Psycho-Analysis*, London, 1926.]

FISHER, J. (1955) *Bird Recognition III*, Penguin Books. (49)

FREUD, S. (1886*d*) 'Beobachtung einer hochgradigen Hemianästhesie bei einem hysterischen Manne (Beiträge zur Kasuistik der Hysterie I)', *Wien. med. Wschr.*, **36**, Nr. 49, 1633. (310)

(1887*b*) Review of S. Weir Mitchell's *Die Behandlung gewisser Formen von Neurasthenie und Hysterie*, Berlin 1887 (Translated G. Klemperer), *Wien. med. Wschr.*, **37**, Nr. 5, 138. (267)

(1888*b*) 'Hysterie' in Villaret's *Handwörterbuch der gesamten Medizin*, **1**, Stuttgart. (310)

(1888–9) Translation with Introduction and Notes of H. Bernheim's *De la suggestion et de ses applications à la thérapeutique*, Paris, 1886, under the title *Die Suggestion und ihre Heilwirkung*, Vienna. (xi, xxiii, 77, 228, 307)
[*Trans.:* Introduction to Bernheim's *Die Suggestion und ihre Heilwirkung*, C.P., **5**, 11; *Standard Ed.*, **1**.]

(1891*b*) *Zur Auffassung der Aphasien*, Vienna. (112, 212)
[*Trans.:* *On Aphasia*, London and New York, 1953.]

(1892*a*) Translation of H. Bernheim's *Hypnotisme, suggestion et psychothérapie: études nouvelles*, Paris, 1891, under the title *Neue Studien über Hypnotismus, Suggestion und Psychotherapie*, Vienna. (xi)

(1892–3*a*) Translation with Preface and Footnotes of J.-M. Charcot's *Leçons du mardi (1887–8)*, Paris, 1888, under the title *Poliklinische Vorträge*, **1**, Vienna. (xiii)
[*Trans.:* Preface and Footnotes to Charcot's *Poliklinische Vorträge*, **1**, *Standard Ed.*, **1**.]

(1892–3*b*) 'Ein Fall von hypnotischer Heilung nebst Bemerkungen über die Entstehung hysterischer Symptome durch den "Gegenwillen" ', *G.S.*, **1**, 258; *G.W.*, **1**, 3. (5, 91–2, 105, 310)
[*Trans.:* 'A Case of Successful Treatment by Hypnotism', C.P., **5**, 33; *Standard Ed.*, **1**.]

(1893*a*) With BREUER, J., 'Über den psychischen Mechanismus hysterischer Phänomene: Vorläufige Mitteilung', *G.S.*, **1**, 7; *G.W.*, **1**, 81.
[*Trans.:* 'On the Psychical Mechanism of Hysterical Phenomena: Preliminary Communication', C.P., **1**, 24; *Standard Ed.*, **2**, 3.]

(1893*c*) 'Quelques considérations pour une étude comparative des paralysies motrices organiques et hystériques' [in French], *G.S.*, **1**, 273; *G.W.*, **1**, 39. (xxiii, 45, 89, 213, 310)
[*Trans.:* 'Some Points for a Comparative Study of Organic and Hysterical Motor Paralyses', C.P., **1**, 42; *Standard Ed.*, **1**.]

(1893*h*) Vortrag 'Über den psychischen Mechanismus hysterischer Phänomene' [shorthand report revised by lecturer], *Wien. med. Pr.*, **34**, Nr. 4, 121 and 5, 165. (xiv, xix, xx, 197, 310)
[*Trans.:* Lecture 'On the Psychical Mechanism of Hysterical Phenomena', *Int. J. Psycho-Anal.*, **37**; *Standard Ed.*, **3**.]

(1894*a*) 'Die Abwehr-Neuropsychosen', *G.S.*, **1**, 290; *G.W.*, **1**, 59.

(xix, xxiii, xxiv, xxv, 10, 48, 69, 86, 90, 123, 147, 211, 214, 257, 269, 302, 310)
[*Trans.*: 'The Neuro-Psychoses of Defence', *C.P.*, **1**, 59; *Standard Ed.*, **3**.]

(1895*b*) 'Über die Berechtigung, von der Neurasthenie einen bestimmten Symptomenkomplex als "Angstneurose" abzutrennen', *G.S.*, **1**, 306; *G.W.*, **1**, 315. (xxiii, xxiv, 10, 88, 127, 210, 246, 257, 258)
[*Trans.*: 'On the Grounds for Detaching a Particular Syndrome from Neurasthenia under the Description "Anxiety Neurosis" ', *C.P.*, **1**, 76; *Standard Ed.*, **3**.]

(1895*c*) 'Obsessions et phobies' [in French], *G.S.*, **1**, 334; *G.W.*, **1**, 345. (69)
[*Trans.*: 'Obsessions and Phobias', *C.P.*, **1**, 128; *Standard Ed.*, **3**.]

(1895*d*) With BREUER, J., *Studien über Hysterie*, Vienna. *G.S.*, **1**; *G.W.*, **1**, 99. Omitting Breuer's contributions.
[*Trans.*: Studies on Hysteria, *Standard Ed.*, **2**.]

(1895*f*) 'Zur Kritik der "Angstneurose" ', *G.S.*, **1**, 343; *G.W.*, **1**, 357. (xxiv)
[*Trans.*: 'A Reply to Criticisms of my Paper on Anxiety Neurosis', *C.P.*, **1**, 107; *Standard Ed.*, **3**.]

(1896*a*) 'L'hérédité et l'étiologie des névroses' [in French], *G.S.*, **1**, 388; *G.W.*, **1**, 407. (48)
[*Trans.*: 'Heredity and the Aetiology of the Neuroses', *C.P.*, **1**, 138; *Standard Ed.*, **3**.]

(1896*b*) 'Weitere Bemerkungen über die Abwehr-Neuropsychosen', *G.S.*, **1**, 363; *G.W.*, **1**, 379. (xxiv, 10, 122, 133, 310)
[*Trans.*: 'Further Remarks on the Neuro-Psychoses of Defence', *C.P.*, **1**, 155; *Standard Ed.*, **3**.]

(1896*c*) 'Zur Ätiologie der Hysterie', *G.S.*, **1**, 404; *G.W.*, **1**, 425. (xxv, 310)
[*Trans.*: 'The Aetiology of Hysteria', *C.P.*, **1**, 183; *Standard Ed.*, **3**.]

(1898*a*) 'Die Sexualität in der Ätiologie der Neurosen', *G.S.*, **1**, 439; *G.W.*, **1**, 491. (88)
[*Trans.*: 'Sexuality in the Aetiology of the Neuroses', *C.P.*, **1**, 220; *Standard Ed.*, **3**.]

(1900*a*) *Die Traumdeutung*, Vienna. *G.S.*, **2-3**; *G.W.*, **2–3**. (xxvii, 70, 110, 175, 189, 194, 271, 302, 309)
[*Trans.*: *The Interpretation of Dreams*, London and New York, 1955; *Standard Ed.*, **4–5**.]

(1901*b*) *Zur Psychopathologie des Alltagslebens*, Berlin, 1904. *G.S.*, **4**; *G.W.*, **4**. (xxvii, 309)
[*Trans.*: *The Psychopathology of Everyday Life*, *Standard Ed.*, **6**.]

(1904*a*) 'Die Freud'sche psychoanalytische Methode', *G.S.*, **6**, 3; *G.W.*, **5**, 3. (110)
[*Trans.*: 'Freud's Psycho-Analytic Procedure', *C.P.*, **1**, 264; *Standard Ed.*, **7**, 249.]

(1905*a*) 'Über Psychotherapie', *G.S.*, **6**, 11; *G.W.*, **5**, 13. (111)

[*Trans.:* 'On Psychotherapy', *C.P.*, **1**, 249; *Standard Ed.*, **7**, 257.]

(1905*c*) *Der Witz und seine Beziehung zum Unbewussten*, Vienna. *G.S.*, **9**, 5; *G.W.*, **6**. (xxiv, xxvii)
[*Trans.: Jokes and their Relation to the Unconscious, Standard Ed.*, **8**.]

(1905*d*) *Drei Abhandlungen zur Sexualtheorie*, Vienna. *G.S.*, **5**, 3; *G.W.*, **5**, 29. (xxvii, 21, 133)
[*Trans.: Three Essays on the Theory of Sexuality*, London, 1949; *Standard Ed.*, **7**, 125.]

(1905*e*) 'Bruchstück einer Hysterie-Analyse', *G.S.*, **8**, 3; *G.W.*, **5**, 163. (xxv, 166, 247, 302, 310)
[*Trans.:* 'Fragment of an Analysis of a Case of Hysteria', *C.P.*, **3**, 13; *Standard Ed.*, **7**, 3.]

(1908*a*) 'Hysterische Phantasien und ihre Beziehung zur Bisexualität', *G.S.*, **5**, 246; *G.W.*, **7**, 191. (310)
[*Trans.:* 'Hysterical Phantasies and their Relation to Bisexuality', *C.P.*, **2**, 51; *Standard Ed.*, **9**.]

(1909*a*) 'Allgemeines über den hysterischen Anfall', *G.S.*, **5**, 255; *G.W.*, **7**, 235. (17, 311)
[*Trans.:* 'Some General Remarks on Hysterical Attacks', *C.P.*, **2**, 100; *Standard Ed.*, **9**.]

(1909*b*) 'Analyse der Phobie eines fünfjährigen Knaben', *G.S.*, **8**, 129; *G.W.*, **7**, 243. (257)
[*Trans.:* 'Analysis of a Phobia in a Five-Year-Old Boy', *C.P.*, **3**, 149; *Standard Ed.*, **10**, 3.]

(1910*a*) *Über Psychoanalyse*, Vienna. *G.S.*, **4**, 349; *G.W.*, **8**, 3. (xxvi, xxvii, 47, 90, 105, 181, 311)
[*Trans.: Five Lectures on Psycho-Analysis, Am. J. Psychol.*, **21** (1910), 181; *Standard Ed.*, **11**.]

(1910*i*) 'Die psychogene Sehstörung in psychoanalytischer Auffassung', *G.S.*, **5**, 301; *G.W.*, **8**, 94. (311)
[*Trans.:* 'The Psycho-Analytic View of Psychogenic Disturbance of Vision', *C.P.*, **2**, 105; *Standard Ed.*, **11**.]

(1910*k*) 'Über "wilde" Psychoanalyse', *G.S.*, **6**, 37; *G.W.*, **8**, 118. (257)
[*Trans.:* ' "Wild" Psycho-Analysis', *C.P.*, **2**, 297; *Standard Ed.*, **11**.]

(1912*f*) 'Zur Onanie-Diskussion', *G.S.*, **3**, 324; *G.W.*, **8**, 332. (258)
[*Trans.:* 'Contributions to a Discussion of Masturbation', *Standard Ed.*, **12**.]

(1913*h*) 'Erfahrungen und Beispiele aus der analytischen Praxis', *Int. Z. Psychoan.*, **1**, 377. Partly reprinted *G.S.*, **11**, 301; *G.W.*, **10**, 40. Partly included in *Die Traumdeutung*, *G.S.*, **3**, 41, 71f., 127 and 135; *G.W.*, **2–3**, 238, 359ff., 413f. and 433. (41)
[*Trans.:* 'Observations and Examples from Analytic Practice', *Standard Ed.*, **13**, 193 (in full); also partly incorporated in *The Interpretation of Dreams*, *Standard Ed.*, **4**, 232 and **5**, 409f.]

(1914*c*) 'Zur Einführung des Narzissmus', *G.S.*, **6**, 155; *G.W.*, **10**, 138. (258)

[*Trans.*: 'On Narcissism: an Introduction', *C.P.*, **4**, 30; *Standard Ed.*, **14**.]

(1914*d*) 'Zur Geschichte der psychoanalytischen Bewegung', *G.S.*, **4**, 411; *G.W.*, **10**, 44. (xxi, xxvii, 41, 206, 231)
[*Trans.*: 'On the History of the Psycho-Analytic Movement', *C.P.*, **1**, 287; *Standard Ed.*, **14**.]

(1915*c*) 'Triebe und Triebschicksale', *G.S.*, **5**, 443; *G.W.*, **10**, 210. (xix)
[*Trans.*: 'Instincts and their Vicissitudes', *C.P.*, **4**, 60; *Standard Ed.*, **14**.]

(1915*d*) 'Die Verdrängung', *G.S.*, **5**, 466; *G.W.*, **10**, 248. (135)
[*Trans.*: 'Repression', *C.P.*, **4**, 84; *Standard Ed.*, **14**.]

(1915*e*) 'Das Unbewusste', *G.S.*, **5**, 480; *G.W.*, **10**, 264. (xxvii, 45, 194, 212)
[*Trans.*: 'The Unconscious', *C.P.*, **4**, 98; *Standard Ed.*, **14**.]

(1916*e*) Footnote to Ernest Jones's 'Professor Janet über Psychoanalyse', *Int. Z. Psychoan.*, **4**, 42. (xiii)
[*Trans.*: *Standard Ed.*, **2**, xiii]

(1917*e*) 'Trauer und Melancholie', *G.S.*, **5**, 535; *G.W.*, **10**, 428. (162)
[*Trans.*: 'Mourning and Melancholia', *C.P.*, **4**, 152; *Standard Ed.*, **14**.]

(1920*g*) *Jenseits des Lustprinzips*, Vienna. *G.S.*, **6**, 191; *G.W.*, **13**, 3. (xix–xx, xxi, xxvii, 189, 194)
[*Trans.*: *Beyond the Pleasure Principle*, London, 1950; *Standard Ed.*, **18**, 7.]

(1921*c*) *Massenpsychologie und Ich-Analyse*, Vienna. *G.S.*, **6**, 261; *G.W.*, **13**, 73. (271)
[*Trans.*: *Group Psychology and the Analysis of the Ego*, London; 1922; New York, 1940; *Standard Ed.*, **18**, 69.]

(1923*a*) ' "Psychoanalyse" und "Libido Theorie" ', *G.S.*, **11**, 201; *G.S.*, **13**, 211. (xxvii)
[*Trans.*: 'Two Encyclopaedia Articles', *C.P.*, **5**, 107; *Standard Ed.*, **18**, 235.]

(1924*f*) 'A Short Account of Psycho-Analysis' [published as 'Psychoanalysis: Exploring the Hidden Recesses of the Mind'], Chap. 73, Vol. **2** of *These Eventful Years*, London and New York; *Standard Ed.*, **19**. (xxvii)
[*German Text*: 'Kurzer Abriss der Psychoanalyse', *G.S.*, **11**, 183; *G.W.*, **13**, 405. German original first appeared in 1928.]

(1925*a*) 'Notiz uber den "Wunderblock" ', *G.S.*, **6**, 415; *G.W.*, **14**, 3. (189)
[*Trans.*: 'A Note upon the "Mystic Writing-Pad" ', *C.P.*, **5**, 175; *Standard Ed.*, **19**.]

(1925*d*) *Selbstdarstellung*, Vienna. *G.S.*, **11**, 119; *G.W.*, **14**, 33. (xi, xxii, xxv, xxviii, 21, 41, 308)
[*Trans.*: *An Autobiographical Study*, London, 1935 (*Autobiography*, New York, 1935); *Standard Ed.*, **20**.]

(1925*g*) 'Josef Breuer', *G.S.*, **11**, 281; *G.W.*, **14**, 562. (xxviii)
[*Trans.*: *Int. J. Psycho-Anal.*, **6**, 459; *Standard Ed.*, **19**.]

(1925*h*) 'Die Verneinung', *G.S.*, **11**, 3; *G.W.*, **14**, 11. (76)
[*Trans.*: 'Negation', *C.P.*, **5**, 181; *Standard Ed.*, **19**.]

(1940*d*) With BREUER, J., 'Zur Theorie des hysterischen Anfalls', *G.W.*, **17**, 9. (xiii, xix, 10, 17, 45, 197, 310)
[*Trans.*: 'On the Theory of Hysterical Attacks', *C.P.*, **5**, 27; *Standard Ed.*, **1**.]

(1941*a*) Letter to Josef Breuer, *G.W.*, **17**, 5. (xiii, xix, xxiii, 197, 310)
[*Trans.*: *C.P.*, **5**, 25; *Standard Ed.*, **1**.]

(1941*b*) 'Notiz "III" ', *G.W.*, **17**, 17. (xiv, xxv, 13, 310)
[*Trans.*: 'Memorandum "III" ', *C.P.*, **5**, 31; *Standard Ed.*, **1**.]

(1950*a*) *Aus den Anfängen der Psychoanalyse*, London. Includes 'Entwurf einer Psychologie' (1895). (xi, xiii, xiv, xv, xix, xxiii, xxiv, xxvi, 8, 86, 110–11, 122, 127, 133, 189, 194, 197, 307, 308, 310)
[*Trans.*: *The Origins of Psycho-Analysis*, London and New York, 1954. (Partly, including 'A Project for a Scientific Psychology', in *Standard Ed.*, **1**.)]

HARTMANN, E. VON (1869) *Philosophie des Unbewussten*, Berlin. (45)

HECKER, E. (1893) 'Über larvirte und abortive Angstzustände bei Neurasthenie', *Zbl. Nervenheilk.*, **16**, 565. (258)

HERBART, J. F. (1824) *Psychologie als Wissenschaft*, Königsberg. (xxii)

JANET, PIERRE (1889) *L'automatisme psychologique*, Paris. (xiii, 7)
(1893) 'Quelques définitions récentes de l'hystérie', *Arch. neurol.*, **25**, No. 76, 417 and **26**, No. 77, 1. (xiv, 230)
(1894) *État mental des hystériques*, Paris. (xiv, 104, 196, 230)
(1913) 'Psycho-Analysis. Rapport par M. le Dr. Pierre Janet', *Int. Congr. Med.*, **17**, Section XII (Psychiatry) (1), 13. (xii)

JONES, ERNEST (1915) 'Professor Janet on Psycho-Analysis; a Rejoinder', *J. abnorm. (soc.) Psychol.*, **9**, 400. (xii)
[*German trans.*: 'Professor Janet über Psychoanalyse', *Int. Z. Psychoan.*, **4** (1916), 34.] (xii)
(1953) *Sigmund Freud: Life and Work*, Vol. 1, London and New York. (x, xxi, xxii, 41, 308)

LANGE, C. G. (1885) *Om Sindsbevaegelser, et Psyko-Fysiologisk Studie*, Copenhagen. (201)

MACH, E. (1875) *Grundlinien der Lehre von den Bewegungsempfindungen*, Leipzig. (210)

MOEBIUS, P. J. (1888) 'Über den Begriff der Hysterie', *Zbl. Nervenheilk.*, **11**, 66. (186)
(1894) 'Über Astasie-Abasie', in *Neurologische Beiträge I*, Leipzig. (215, 220)
(1895) 'Über die gegenwärtige Auffassung der Hysterie', *Mschr. Geburtsh. Gynäk.*, **1**, 12. (249)

MYERS, F. W. H. (1893) 'The Mechanism of Hysteria (The Subliminal Consciousness, VI)', *Proc. Soc. psych. Res., Lond.*, **9**, 3. (xv)
(1903) *Human Personality and its Survival of Bodily Death*, London and New York. (xv)

OPPENHEIM, H. (1890) 'Thatsächliches und Hypothetisches über das

Wesen der Hysterie', *Berl. klin. Wschr.*, **27**, 553. (191, 203, 242, 245)

PITRES, A. (1891) *Leçons cliniques sur l'hystérie et l'hypnotisme*, Paris. (177)

ROMBERG, M. H. (1840) *Lehrbuch der Nervenkrankheiten des Menschen*, Berlin. (220)

SCHOPENHAUER, A. (1844) *Die Welt als Wille und Vorstellung* (2nd ed.), Leipzig. (xxii)

STRÜMPELL, A. VON (1892) *Über die Entstehung und die Heilung von Krankheiten durch Vorstellungen*, Erlangen. (245)

(1896) Review of Breuer and Freud's *Studien über Hysterie*, *Dtsch. Z. Nervenheilk.*, **8**, 159. (xv)

WESTPHAL, C. F. O. (1877) 'Über Zwangsvorstellungen', *Berl. klin. Wschr.*, **14**, 669 and 687. (256)

LIST OF ABBREVIATIONS

G.S. = Freud, *Gesammelte Schriften* (12 vols.), Vienna, 1924–34
G.W. = Freud, *Gesammelte Werke* (18 vols.), London, from 1940
C.P. = Freud, *Collected Papers* (5 vols.), London, 1924–50
Standard Ed. = Freud, *Standard Edition* (24 vols.), London, from 1953
S.K.S.N. = Freud, *Sammlung kleiner Schriften zur Neurosenlehre* (5 vols.), Vienna, 1906–22
S.P.H. = *Selected Papers on Hysteria and Other Psychoneuroses*, New York, 1909–20

GENERAL INDEX

This index includes the names of non-technical authors. It also includes the names of technical authors where no reference is made in the text to specific works. For references to specific technical works, the Bibliography should be consulted.—The compilation of the index was undertaken by Mrs. R. S. Partridge.